ROBBING PETER TO PAY PAUL

SAMUEL EVAN MILNER

Robbing Peter to Pay Paul

POWER, PROFITS, AND PRODUCTIVITY IN MODERN AMERICA

Yale UNIVERSITY PRESS NEW HAVEN AND LONDON

Published with assistance from the income of the Frederick John Kingsbury Memorial Fund.

Published with assistance from the foundation established in memory of Calvin Chapin of the Class of 1788, Yale College.

Set in Scala and Scala Sans type by Integrated Publishing Solutions.
Printed in the United States of America.

Library of Congress Control Number: 2021935714
ISBN 978-0-300-25734-2 (hardcover : alk. paper)

A catalogue record for this book is available from the British Library.

This paper meets the requirements of ANSI/NISO Z39.48-1992 (Permanence of Paper).

10 9 8 7 6 5 4 3 2 1

For my parents
and for David M. Rubenstein, who enabled me to take the next step in my professional career

CONTENTS

ACKNOWLEDGMENTS

First place in this listing of acknowledgments belongs to Naomi Lamoreaux. Not only would she give detailed comments on my countless draft chapters and appropriate replies to my even more frequent lengthy emails, but she even took time away from visiting her family to provide feedback in person. In the many years that I worked on this project, she never faltered in her vision of what this book could ultimately become, and I appreciate just how central her guidance has been to this entire project. Further reflecting on my time at Yale, Jennifer Klein and Beverley Gage were more than the completion of my dissertation committee. They were, and still are, two independent foci in my understanding of American history. On top of their support, advice, and encouragement throughout my time in graduate school, their lessons and commentary have left an indelible impact on every chapter of this book.

My manuscript has also benefited from the commentary and feedback of numerous friends and colleagues, including those who have remained anonymous to me. I hope that, when they see their influence throughout this text, they can take satisfaction in knowing how much I truly valued their suggestions and ideas.

At Yale University Press, I was supported and encouraged whenever I interacted with my editors, Seth Ditchik and Margaret Otzel. Karen Olson proved quick to share her vast knowledge of how to transform a manuscript into a printed book. Andrew Katz meticulously copyedited the manuscript and provided a number of suggestions for clarifying my prose.

Funding for my research was provided by the Tobin Project, the Harry S. Truman Library Foundation, the Institute for Humane Studies, the Dwight D. Eisenhower Library Foundation, the Gerald Ford Library Foundation, and the Economic History Association. Special mention goes to Professor Tim Guinanne of the Yale University Program in Economic History, who provided the funding that catalyzed this program at its outset, and the Truman Library Foundation, whose generous Dissertation Year Fellowship made possible my final year at work on the dissertation.

I would also like to acknowledge the librarians, archivists, and research staff who helped me to locate and access the necessary collections. At the Western Reserve Historical Society, my original mentor, Sean Martin, proved an invaluable contact, alongside Margaret Burzynski-Bays, Vicki Catozza, and George Cooper III. At the Johnson Presidential Library, Allen Fisher's professional courtesy was matched by his earnest intellectual curiosity in my work. John Pollack of the University of Pennsylvania allowed me to access the Lemuel Boulware Papers on short notice and in the midst of renovations. At the Hagley Museum and Library, Lucas Clawson, Lynn Catanese, Andrew Engels, and Marsha Mills scrambled for containers and call slips to allow me to make the most of my visit. The Nixon Presidential Library's Jason Schultz reviewed a collection of over two thousand boxes in preparation for my visit, which was made even more productive thanks to the support of Carla Braswell, Juan Hernandez, Pam Eisenberg, and Ryan Pettigrew. On the other side of Los Angeles, Jennifer Mandel helped me to locate the relevant files at the Reagan Library. Mark Fisher of the Ford Presidential Library was an invaluable contact. At the Eisenhower Presidential Library, David Holbrook allowed me the run of the archives. Randy Sowell's knowledge of the Truman Library's holdings combined with Lisa Sullivan's financial expertise to make that trip possible. Rachael Dreyer and James P. Quigel Jr. at Penn State and Kristen Chinery at the Walter P. Reuther Library at Wayne State University expedited research trips into union papers.

Outside of library walls, I was fortunate to stay and visit with family around the country. The local community of Abilene, Kansas, provided superlative care during my visit to the Eisenhower Library. Adrian and Jay Potter of Abilene's Victorian Inn provided me with a home away from home, and Don and Mary Rickley and Dean and Bernie Nogel generously provided transportation. Closer to home, Peter Kelly generously gave of his time to discuss the inner workings of the steel industry, and Denise Jones helped to make my accommodations affordable.

Selections from my previous work, Samuel Milner, "The Problem of Productivity, Inflation and Collective Bargaining after World War II," *Business History Review* 92, no. 2 (Summer 2018): 227–250, and Samuel Milner, "Assuming Direct Control: The Beguiling Allure of Incomes Policies in Postwar America," *Journal of Policy History* 31, no. 1 (Winter 2019): 42–72, are reproduced with the permission courtesy of Cambridge University Press. I extend my sincerest appreciation to the United Steelworkers of America for permitting me to include its own historical perspective in this narrative. Finally, I would like to acknowledge the foresight of the corporations, unions, associations, and individuals that have enabled future historians to understand their worlds as they once were, including the United Auto Workers, the International Ladies Garment Workers' Union, the Ford Motor Company, Republic Steel, LTV Steel, the National Association of Manufacturers, the Chamber of Commerce of the United States, Lukens Steel, and DuPont.

Introduction

NO STATEMENT CAPTURES the pure essence of capitalism more aptly than the aphorism attributed to Alfred Sloan, the visionary executive who transformed General Motors into the model corporation of the mid-twentieth century: "General Motors is not in the business of making cars, it is in the business of making money." For all the wondrous pithiness of this famous statement, it is in fact a misquotation of how Sloan truly conceived of his corporation. In 1921, when Sloan proposed to GM's Board of Directors that it restructure a loose confederation of car brands into a unified whole, his point was not simply that General Motors existed to make money. Instead, Sloan argued that making money was merely a means to the specific ends of GM's corporate existence: "It is to be presumed that the first purpose in making a capital investment is the establishment of a business that will both pay satisfactory dividends and preserve and increase the capital value. The primary object of the General Motors Corporation, therefore, is to make *money*, not just to make motor cars."[1]

Nearly a century later, on August 19, 2019, General Motors CEO Mary Barra would join the chief executives of 180 of America's largest corporations in endorsing a very different set of priorities than Sloan's vision of a partnership between investors and their managerial agents. These corporate leaders, organized together as the Business Roundtable, thanked their investors for entrusting them with their capital, but they made it clear that shareholders would no longer hold a position of primacy within the corporation. Though promising investors that they would still receive "long-term value," the leaders of the Business Roundtable proclaimed that they would henceforth act in the balanced best interests of all of a corporation's stakeholders. To their customers, these executives promised higher value and lower prices. To their employees, they pledged fair compensation and respect. To their suppliers, there would develop a partnership of equals concerned with more than simply wringing out lower costs. And to the community at large, the Business Roundtable provided assurance that the corporation would play its part in creating a safer and healthier environment for all.[2]

There was a great irony that this vow to create "An Economy That Serves All Americans" emerged in the form of a unilateral declaration issued by an elite group of corporate executives. In describing how their newfound focus on stakeholders would result in outcomes fairer than that of a fixation with shareholders alone, these executives suggested, intentionally or otherwise, that a handful of individuals held the fate of the economy in their grasp. The distributive hubris of the Business Roundtable would have had little traction in the textbook model of a market economy. In that setting, impersonal competition between numerous buyers and sellers establishes the price at which supply meets demand, and management must obey the constraints set by the market. Yet ever since the second half of the nineteenth century, when new technologies united isolated communities and large-scale industry emerged to control the course of commerce on a continent-wide scale, these competitive markets have become increasingly rare. A decline in the overall number of firms in a given market did not inevitably result in a decrease in competition. Still, as sales became more concentrated, the market power of each firm over prices and profit margins grew, as did the ability to prevent the entry of new rivals that would otherwise compete for a share of profits. As the boundaries of these companies expanded, moreover, they internalized transactions that would once have occurred between independent firms. Management thus came to understand itself as the flesh-and-blood replacement for the invisible hand of the market in this modern economy, tasked not just with overseeing the allocation of labor and capital but also with determining the prices at which they would be bought and sold.[3]

Over the past several decades, changes in the structure of the economy have raised questions about whether management must accept a greater responsibility if it is to continue to exercise this great power. Since the 1970s, increased corporate concentration has coincided with reduced productivity growth, exacerbated income inequality, and a distribution of income that has shifted decisively away from labor and toward capital. Economists actively debate what, if any, degree of causation links these global trends with the embrace of shareholder primacy as the guiding concern of corporate governance, an orientation that was proposed in response to managerial autocracy in the 1960s and 1970s but that only became widely accepted as a result of the disappointing corporate performance and resulting takeover wave of the 1980s. Nevertheless, management today faces intensifying calls from both within and without to ensure that its actions are beneficial for all of the corporation's stakeholders, not simply the shareholders and owners of capital described by Sloan. Indeed, the Business Roundtable's present embrace of its stakeholders may best be described as a preemptive maneuver against those critics who have sought, to borrow their own words, to hold capitalism accountable to its stakeholders through means far less voluntary than the Roundtable's enlightened despotism.[4]

In concluding that increased awareness of stakeholders can reverse these contemporary economic trends, both the Roundtable and its critics have drawn on the collective memory of the unprecedented decades of prosperity and income equality that followed World War II, the so-called Golden Age of American Capitalism.[5] While these were decades in which strong growth freed management to operate with reduced scrutiny from shareholders and capital markets, they were also years in which other corporate stakeholders proved fully capable of demanding a share in the fruits of progress. Building on the social and political trends that had first coalesced during the New Deal, labor law and public approbation enabled workers to organize unions that leveraged their collective strength to bargain with management over the distribution of income. By the 1960s, moreover, a new wave of governmental regulations promised to safeguard consumers and citizens from the dangerous products and industrial pollution that management would abet if not forced to take the public interest into consideration.[6] Indeed, many historians have concluded that management felt so entrapped by these stakeholder demands that corporate leaders had no choice but to rely on a decades-long quest to engineer a more favorable business climate. In order to win flexibility to distribute income as they desired, corporate executives underwrote conservative media operations, think tanks, and even evangelical religious organizations that preached the importance of free-enterprise capitalism and the perniciousness of state-sanctioned unionism.[7]

Robbing Peter to Pay Paul: Power, Profits, and Productivity in Modern America provides a new and alternative interpretation of how the management of concentrated industry understood and exercised its ability to distribute income to its stakeholders during the Golden Age. Concerned by the immediate claims of stakeholders on profits, the management of these industries could not, as the common historical narrative suggests, simply afford to wait decades for the emergence of a friendlier political climate. Acquiescing to the demands of stakeholders would not only shrink capital's share of income. At a time in which management actively targeted returns on investment that would provide U.S. industry with the resources necessary to retain its edge in global markets, surrender to stakeholders would also jeopardize management's ability to invest in the long-run future of the enterprise.

In order for midcentury management to defend its own autonomous existence, it sought to define a role for itself as the arbiter between the corporation's stakeholders by implementing what was known as a "wage-price policy." Far more than a simple strategy of cost containment, wage-price policy provides a decades-long historical case study and cautionary tale of how corporate management attempted to balance the claims of its stakeholders during the Golden Age of American Capitalism. Wage-price policy emphasized that productivity should set the standard for determining rewards to stakeholders, akin to how that statistic determines the pace of real wage growth in textbook economic models. Just as would the vision of the Business Roundtable of 2019, the ideal wage-price policy promised higher compensation to labor, competitive prices for customers, and a steady stream of returns for shareholders. All the while, managerial discretion over the actual distribution of income would continue to supplant the automatic functioning of the invisible hand of the competitive marketplace.

Central to this book's analysis of wage-price policies are three of the leading industries of Golden Age America: motor vehicles, electrical equipment, and steel. Contemporaries not only considered these three to be pattern setters of industrial-labor relations, able to influence wages and benefits throughout the unionized sector of the economy if not the national economy as a whole. These were also the industries whose products and prices determined the ability of consumers to realize the American Dream in its postwar emphasis on consumption, with steel the key material in the construction of this abundance. At the same time, these vertically integrated heavy industries were unable to flee from their unionized workforces in the North as easily as would their contemporaries, the light manufacturers or high-tech defense contractors that relocated to the Sunbelt.[8] Only in the late twentieth century would the advent of global supply chains, trade reforms, and information technology allow some of these firms to outsource various functions and disperse employment across the United States and abroad. Even then, much of this industrial activity remains concentrated in unionized factories located across the Rust Belt.[9]

Implementing the distribution of income that wage-price policy prescribed for corporate stakeholders would not come easily for the management of these industries. As its name suggested, wage-price policy depended on management's ability to secure labor's support for a program that at best allowed compensation to rise no faster than productivity grew. Yet the purpose of collective bargaining was to force management to grant workers a larger share of corporate income, not freeze or even reduce it, as wage-price policy could well require in the name of balancing the claims of all stakeholders. As profits rose and inflation eroded nominal wages, the expected benefits that unions could gain by resisting management's wage-price policy also increased. Western Europe provided American managers with one possible set of institutional solutions to this challenge through what has been termed the "politics of productivity," in which cooperation over growth subsumed class conflict.[10] Workers agreed to show restraint in their wages so that management could invest these savings in generating a larger economy in which all shared in the future, but in return, European unions had gained the ability to monitor management's commitment to this bargain. In Germany, for instance, codetermination laws granted unions representation on corporate boards, while other nations published indicative plans detailing where the state expected resources to be invested or simply nationalized their core industries.[11] Such institutional solutions, of course, were too radical for the U.S. business community to consider, both then and now. As a result, the U.S. politics of productivity would be characterized by less cooperation and much more animosity than its European counterpart.

Yet even as corporate stakeholders resisted management's vision for wages at the bargaining table, management retained unilateral control over the key variable that influenced the distribution of income: prices. The core industries of Golden Age America were organized as oligopolies, markets in which only a limited number of firms dominated sales. Due to the paucity of their numbers, the management of each firm in the oligopoly learned over time to anticipate the behavior of its rivals. Were a single member of an oligopoly to cut its prices in an attempt to obtain a larger share of the market, it would expect its rivals to respond eventually with parallel reductions to defend their own sales. The resulting price war would leave each firm with the same share of the market as before but with lower revenues. Recognizing that this strategy would prove self-defeating, each firm's management could instead conclude that its own best interest was to avoid competing on prices, at least as long as any lower-cost sellers proved content with the higher profits yielded by this price umbrella. Conversely, if one company were to raise its prices or impose some extra charge in order to expand its profit margins, the other firms in the industry could find it in their own interests to follow its lead. Though they might tempt the entrance of new competitors or lose some customers to another market, each member of the oligopoly understood that all could obtain higher revenues for the time being without a loss of relative market share.

This unilateral pricing power ensured that management would retain its autonomy in its dealings with corporate stakeholders. The industrial managers of the Golden Age were aware of the market structure in which their firms operated, and they relied on this oligopoly pricing policy as the safety valve to dilute the excess claims of stakeholders on corporate incomes. Management's insistence on distributing income through a restrained wage-price policy risked jeopardizing its fragile peace with labor and other stakeholders. Price adjustments, in contrast, allowed management to meet the immediate demands of its most clamorous stakeholders while simultaneously preserving or even expanding returns on capital. In resorting to higher prices to paper over conflict about the distribution of income in the short run, however, management understood that it was weakening its long-run competitive position at home and abroad by unleashing a wage-price spiral, the outcome popularly known as "robbing Peter to pay Paul." The consequences of these managerial decisions would be felt across the entire economy, for as management and labor fought to enlarge their own shares of income, the exercise of private market power threatened to hold fiscal and monetary policies hostage. Faced with the possibility of rising unemployment and falling sales as wages and prices spiraled upward, federal policymakers could agree to provide the fiscal and monetary stimulus that would sustain overall demand. Yet doing so would validate the exercise of private market power and unleash "cost-push" inflation on the entire economy. Conversely, the government could engineer restrictive market conditions in order to encourage unions and firms to show restraint and prevent a run on the dollar, but in that case, society as a whole would suffer simply to prevent the misdeeds of the powerful few.[12]

As the origins of the wage-price spiral appeared rooted in the structure of modern industry, the most obvious solution to this challenge would have been to attack managerial discretion at its source. Closing the safety valve of prices would not only make the arbitrary allocation of income by management impossible. Restoring the distributive primacy of the invisible hand of the competitive marketplace would also eliminate the rationale for stakeholder governance by ensuring that no concentration of economic power could siphon off income for itself to the detriment of others. Antitrust policy of the Golden Age indeed proved zealous against corporate mergers, but the same theories of market structure that buttressed the fight against further concentration ironically created obstacles against the application of antitrust law to existing oligopolies. As parallel pricing came to be viewed as the rational consequence of industrial organization and not collusion or monopolization, courts concluded that this managerial behavior fell outside the scope of antitrust law. Despite repeated historical attempts to develop new legal theories or legislation that would permit an attack on this phenomenon, antitrust law continues to play little role in limiting the ability of existing oligopolies to exercise their power over the distribution of income.[13]

Unable to address the structural causes of corporate market power, postwar policymakers came to mirror the perspective that management had itself taken toward its stakeholders by insisting on confining the exercise of discretion to the bounds of wage-price policy. Historians have often claimed that the monetary and fiscal stimulus of World War II marked a transition from the structural reforms used to redistribute income during the New Deal to the focus of Keynesian economists on expanding all slices of a growing pie in the postwar years.[14] Departing from that macroeconomic perspective, this book emphasizes that government intervention in the distribution of income remained an indelible component of postwar policy making. Claiming to represent the stake of the public interest in corporate decision-making, the federal government would repeatedly demand that both big business and big labor show deference to the limits of productivity and exercise restraint in setting prices and wages. Historians are familiar with several conflicts over industrial pricing during the Golden Age, most notably Harry Truman's illegal seizure of the steel industry during the Korean War, John F. Kennedy's confrontation with the steel industry over its prices in 1962, and, most blatantly, Richard Nixon's wage and price controls.[15] This book emphasizes that these scattered confrontations were only the most visible engagements in a decades-long effort to discipline private discretion, a task based as much on the desire to protect the consuming public from higher prices as it was on the desire to liberate fiscal and monetary policies from the threat of cost-push inflation.

Past explorations of incomes policies have generally understood these tensions from the exclusive standpoint of the federal government, chiefly the White House, in large part due to a heavy reliance on presidential library records and former government staffers to reconstruct these efforts.[16] This book instead emphasizes management's stake in a federalized wage-price policy, investigating how incomes policies could both hinder and further corporate efforts to arbitrate among stakeholders. As the list of famous confrontations suggests, American management rarely viewed federal incomes policy to be identical to its own voluntary wage-price policy even when the two shared an emphasis on productivity and investment. Most importantly, whereas management selected its wage-price policy without any independent oversight of its pricing policies, federal incomes policies repeatedly insisted that management shoulder the burden of restraint by committing to competitive pricing.

Allowing the government such an expansive role in corporate decision-making was a steep price for American management to pay for wage restraint, but surprisingly, it was not always too steep. By the early 1970s, management had begun to deem the claims of labor against profits to be so intractable that it expressed a willingness to tolerate the frustrations of price controls in return for wage controls. Yet disappointing financial results, rising regulatory burdens, and a recurring political bias in favor of labor inevitably precipitated demands that the government return responsibility for wage and price determination back to the private sector. Only when market competition in the final decades of the millennium removed the power of these industries to choose how they would distribute income could the economic anxieties of the Golden Age finally be put to rest.

This book explores how top-level corporate managers, alongside economists, labor leaders, and government policymakers, devised, deployed, and ultimately discarded wage-price policy and its emphasis on stakeholder rewards across the span of the postwar Golden Age. Chapter 1 begins during the Great Depression, when policymakers first began to grapple seriously with the macroeconomic consequences of managerial market power. Concluding that managers had caused the Depression by holding real wages too low and keeping prices too high to sustain demand, federal policymakers who were unable to dissolve concentrations of power devised alternative means to protect society's purchasing power. Price controls during and after World War II represented the most direct approach, but management soon found itself trapped between controls designed to protect consumers and the higher wages demanded by labor unions. When controls collapsed at the end of 1946, economists interpreted the resulting wage-price spiral as evidence that labor and management were seeking to capture macroeconomic stimulus for themselves. These economists concluded that wages must be held to the limit of productivity so as to create the conditions for price stability, establishing the model for postwar wage-price policy.

Chapter 2 analyzes the challenges that corporate management faced in attempting to implement this wage-price policy in the decade following World War II. In 1948, General Motors became the first company to tie real wages to expectations of future productivity growth for the nation as a whole. GM expected that this wage formula would establish a long-run "peace treaty" that permitted management to distribute productivity according to its own noninflationary understanding. Instead, labor continued to view productivity as a floor for compensation gains, and GM chose to exceed its formula in order to maintain labor peace. Despite much resistance on the part of other industrial titans to the costs of this contractual formula, wage controls during the Korean War encouraged companies to match the length and costs of the GM contract without regard to productivity. Following the war, management continued to pay a premium for labor peace. Many paid lip service to the well-known proposal that wages should be held to the noninflationary standard of labor productivity, but the few that actually attempted to base bargaining on productivity statistics found their efforts frustrated.

Chapter 3 examines managerial pricing policy during this era of increasingly costly labor contracts. Midcentury executives explained that they determined prices to guarantee some target return on investment and to follow, not undercut, those of rivals. Such a definition would make little sense in a textbook world of pure competition, but these objectives appeared utterly rational in modern oligopoly, reinforcing the widespread concern that managerial self-interest generated macroeconomic instability. For a brief moment in the late 1940s, several landmark court rulings suggested that oligopoly price behavior fell afoul of the antitrust laws, but when subsequent decisions foreclosed this approach, policymakers switched their focus to the outcomes of market power. Arguments for increased regulation and intensified public scrutiny of corporate price policies ultimately failed to overcome the resistance of the Eisenhower White House, which together with the Federal Reserve instead engineered a series of recessions designed to force the private sector to recognize that restraint was in its own self-interest.

Chapter 4 traces how management fought for wage and price restraint in the late 1950s by taking a "New Look" at the importance of productivity. Central to these efforts was General Electric vice president Lemuel Boulware, who berated his fellows in the managerial community for relying on inflation to adjudicate between the various claimants on corporate income. Boulware and his emulators placed productivity at the center of collective bargaining negotiations by working closely with the economist John Kendrick, who had developed productivity measurements that related output to both labor and capital inputs. Transforming these economic arguments into concrete results required new strategies of industrial relations, and this chapter concludes by reexamining two of the most important efforts to implement the New Look: the victory of GE in its 1960 labor negotiations, and the protracted steel strike of 1959. At GE, Boulware and his successors proclaimed that their industrial-relations tactics adhered to the letter of labor law, but their insistence that workers should trust management to distribute income fairly arguably broke with its spirit. In the steel industry, management made a number of tactical errors throughout the strike, but all of its demands ultimately reflected its vision of wage-price policy: keeping compensation in line with productivity growth so that capital could enjoy adequate returns without higher prices.

Chapter 5 focuses on the transformation of wage-price policy from a voluntary initiative of the private sector into a governmental incomes policy during the 1960s. The "wage-price guideposts" unveiled by the Kennedy administration at the start of 1962 differed little from the approach previously adopted throughout corporate America, but when the steel industry sought to combine the federal support for wage restraint with a new round of price increases, the Kennedy administration responded by "jawboning" the private sector into compliance. Though Kennedy subsequently adopted a more conciliatory tone toward business, Lyndon Johnson embraced guideposts and jawboning as anti-inflationary alternatives to fiscal restraint. As excess demand pushed up the cost of living and rising profits provoked the ire of labor, however, not even the White House could secure restraint on wages. After the Johnson administration threw its support behind labor during several high-profile strikes, corporate management saw little reason to continue to hold out for restraint when it could pass these costs on to its customers.

Chapter 6 investigates how management sought to influence the Nixon administration's wage and price controls in order to enlist the government as an ally in reversing the trend of falling corporate profits. Despite Nixon's support for voluntary wage-price policy, management discovered that its methods no longer yielded the same success that they had in the late 1950s. Concluding that changes in labor laws, militant workers, and import penetration had rendered it impossible for management to restrain labor costs, the business community instead demanded that Washington intervene directly to achieve a balance between stakeholders. After Nixon imposed controls in 1971, management pressed the White House to place the brunt of restraint on wages while providing management with the flexibility to raise prices and expand profit margins. Instead, the government required profits to share in the costs of combating inflation. Even before the spike in the cost of oil spelled doom for Nixon's controls, the same businesses that had clamored for controls had denounced both the government's priorities and controls themselves as self-defeating for the economy.

Chapter 7 concludes this historical narrative by exploring how wage-price policy finally collapsed in both its voluntary and compulsory forms. The return of the wage-price spiral in the wake of the Nixon controls only reinforced the concern of Keynesian economists that big business and big labor could not be trusted to set prices and wages in the public interest. A new executive branch agency, the Council on Wage and Price Stability

(COWPS), promulgated yet more incomes policies in order to combat inflation, but as the costs of labor peace and regulatory compliance continued to cut into profits, these efforts once again proved unsuccessful. Instead, a decade and a half of inflation came to an end only after Federal Reserve chairman Paul Volcker demonstrated that blame for the wage-price spiral lay with Washington's macroeconomic mismanagement. In the face of serious recession, some industries took advantage of Ronald Reagan's permissive attitudes to seek restraint through hard-nosed bargaining tactics. But as competitive pressures from rivals at home and abroad broke apart familiar oligopoly arrangements, management learned that it could no longer rely on industry-wide adjustments when the future of the individual enterprise was at stake. Management had not only lost its ability to implement wage-price policy. As competition finally shut off the safety valve of pricing, the very rationale for wage-price policy had collapsed as well.

CHAPTER ONE

Monopoly and the Problem of the New Deal

WHEN THE GREAT DEPRESSION put an end to the economic prosperity of the 1920s, it had been almost two decades since the Supreme Court's landmark rulings that Standard Oil and American Tobacco must be dissolved for actively monopolizing markets and suppressing competition in order to expand their own profits. Yet as the nation struggled to recover from rampant unemployment and human misery, the challenge of corporate market power continued to loom large. Consolidation of industrial assets and corporate ownership had transformed the default model of industrial organization from competition into a variant of monopoly, in which the hand of management determined how much output would be made and at what price it would be sold. Even where competition seemingly existed in this modern economy, branding and advertising ensured that a Cadillac and a Chevrolet were viewed as distinctive goods serving individual markets, not as functionally equivalent substitutes.[1]

According to the influential theory that the economist Gardiner C. Means would famously describe as "administered pricing," it was this corporate power that had caused the Great Depression. When times had been good in the 1920s, management had seemingly captured the fruits of productivity for itself through rigid prices, not the higher wages expected in the textbook model of a competitive economy. As purchasing power fell behind rising corporate profits, consumption had inevitably collapsed, but management still chose to protect revenues in this downturn by cutting output instead of prices. This behavior may have been rational for the individual firm, but it suggested that society as a whole could not rely on private enterprise alone to restore prosperity.

Drawing on these economic models, New Deal Washington concluded that the government must force management to share its profits with the masses. Labor unions proved the most durable of the policy solutions to this challenge during the New Deal, yet the creation of powerful new interest groups provided an ironic solution to the problems linked to corporate market power. Economists and policymakers understood that the more direct answer would have been to restructure corporate pricing policies directly, but such an approach proved difficult to implement. New Deal investigations of corporate structure had pointed to the need for a renewed antitrust campaign; but legal doctrine remained in flux, and serious questions remained about potential losses of efficiency were this approach to succeed.[2]

The mobilization economy of World War II presented an opportunity to experiment with an alternative, regulatory means to force management to share the fruits of productivity with the public. During World War II, the aptly named Office of Price Administration (OPA) oversaw a series of price controls that, while justified primarily for the needs of the mobilization economy, also covered remaining civilian production. Following the end of the war, the staff of the OPA sought to continue its mission in order to engineer the transition to a peacetime economy marked by low prices and high wages. Instead, a wage-price spiral followed the collapse of OPA controls in late 1946, an outcome that historians have largely attributed to conservative business leaders who allegedly withheld their wares in order to sabotage the New Deal state.[3] Challenging that interpretation, this chapter draws on the wartime experience of civilian-goods producers to argue that the OPA did not eliminate managerial discretion so much as it merely displaced it from prices to other less desirable forms of adjustment when costs rose. As more and more industries converted back to civilian production after the war only to find themselves trapped in a profits squeeze, higher prices proved necessary to ensure that consumer tastes were fulfilled.

Traditionally, historians have argued that the government's focus on engineering prosperity through wage and price manipulation diminished after World War II. In a transition that has alternatively been labeled the

"Fiscal Revolution" or the "End of Reform," the stimulus of World War II had demonstrated that industrial structure need not prevent the government from using fiscal and monetary policy to engineer full employment.[4] Faced with the postwar wage-price spiral, however, the emerging "Keynesian Consensus" in political economy continued to express apprehension at the presence of powerful economic groups: not just businesses but also the labor unions created during the New Deal. Keynesian economists described how these groups possessed the market power to siphon off the macroeconomic stimulus intended to benefit society as a whole in the form of higher prices and wages for themselves, forcing the government to tolerate "cost-push" inflation in exchange for full employment. The Keynesians thus concluded that the only way for a free-market economy to achieve full employment without inflation would be for the private sector to accept the restraints of a wage-price policy voluntarily.

ADMINISTERED PRICES, MARKET STRUCTURE, AND CORPORATE POWER

It is an economic truism that labor productivity, the ratio of output to labor input conventionally measured in man-hours, provides a limit for how fast real wages can grow without changing the distribution of income.[5] Economists of the early twentieth century agreed that in a competitive economy, the surplus that resulted from higher productivity would be distributed in the form of lower prices, higher wages, and steady returns on increased amounts of investment capital. As George Soule explained in 1923, "The increase in productivity alone has been rapid enough to furnish substantial increases in income to every one, without robbing Peter to pay Paul."[6] Economists of that era were thus shocked to find that this relationship apparently failed to hold for the U.S. economy. Not only did early studies indicate that the real wages of factory workers had risen by far less than productivity had grown, by 5% compared to at least 30%, according to Soule's estimates for the period 1899–1920, but nominal wages had also failed to keep pace with the cost of living even before encountering the massive inflation of World War I. Instead of flowing to purchasing power as lower prices or higher wages, the fruits of increased productivity had seemingly accrued to profits.[7]

In truth, many of these early studies were based on poorly constructed data series. As economists came to develop more accurate indexes over the course of the twentieth century, they found that real wages had in fact kept pace with productivity over the long run of the previous century, as economic theory predicted.[8] After totaling all of the wages, salaries, proprietor income, and benefits awarded throughout the economy, the share of national income earned by labor hovered at a little short of two-thirds of gross domestic product. As the economy cycled from peak to trough and back again, the distribution of income never strayed far from the stylized fact of that constant ratio.[9] Why the distribution of income between capital and labor remained constant around this exact value, no one was quite sure. John Maynard Keynes, arguably the single most influential economist of the twentieth century, famously described this stability as "a bit of a miracle."[10]

Still, many of these updated studies also showed that wage growth tended to come in spurts over a lengthy period of time. In the decade preceding the start of the Depression, labor productivity for the nation as a whole had increased by about two-thirds, while real wages rose by only about half of that amount.[11] To explain this recurring lag, many economists of the 1920s and 1930s looked to the changing structure of the economy itself. As Edward Chamberlin observed in his landmark work *The Theory of Monopolistic Competition,* first published in 1933, there were few instances of pure monopoly in the modern economy in which a single seller dominated an entire market. At the same time, the discounts, advertisements, and marketing techniques that had arisen over the past decades were alien to the textbook conception of pure competition between homogeneous goods. These modern tactics enabled sellers to distinguish their goods from those of others, granting them a degree of monopoly control over their prices. Only if the number of sellers was large enough to make the effects of one negligible on all others would prices settle at what would be expected in the competitive textbook market. Otherwise, the prices established by a group of sellers, what Chamberlin termed an "oligopoly," would be able to approach the price set by a monopolist.[12] Expressed otherwise, the result of this phenomenon, which the Cambridge University economist Joan Robinson influentially described in 1933 as "imperfect competition," was that equilibrium output was lower and prices were higher than would be expected in a competitive market.[13]

It would be a fellow member of Chamberlin's graduate cohort at Harvard, Gardiner C. Means, who would draw the strongest connections between modern forms of industrial organization and empirical trends in wages, prices, and profits. Means had spent much of the 1920s running a textile business in Massachusetts concurrently with his formal economic studies, and he grew troubled that textbook models of competition and laissez-faire economics bore little resemblance to the modern business world with which he was familiar. Aware of this research interest, Means's former squad-mate from World War I, the Columbia University Law School professor Adolf Berle, invited Means to collaborate on a study of the relationship between the ownership and management of corporations.[14] The results of this investigation, published in 1932 as *The Modern Corporation and Private Property,* proved an instant classic by providing an institutional framework through which to understand real-life economic behavior. Berle and Means argued that the ownership of heavily capitalized modern industries had become too dispersed to exercise control over management. Instead, the locus of decision-making within the corporation had come to rest with salaried managers or, at best, a minority of owners able to coordinate among themselves more readily than the remaining majority. Though management was supposed to act in the best interest of the shareholders, Berle and Means described how these insiders took advantage of their de facto autonomy to maximize their own personal profits and stature, depriving the owners of the corporation of the property rights represented by their shares. Noting the increasing concentration of corporate activity within the largest and wealthiest corporations over the previous decades, Berle and Means concluded that a few hundred corporate directors and managers had replaced the impartial forces of marketplace competition in determining the distribution of income.[15]

Fresh on the heels of *The Modern Corporation,* the United States Department of Agriculture recruited Means to analyze the impact of industrial market power on farmers, one of the few sectors of the economy that could still be considered unambiguously competitive. The Great Depression had caused agricultural prices to plummet, and in response, Franklin D. Roosevelt had signed into law the Agricultural Adjustment Act of 1933 (AAA). The AAA established a system of subsidies to encourage farmers to leave their lands fallow, leading to a total reduction in agricultural supply and a higher price for the commodities sold by farmers. The Department of Agriculture, however, recognized that farmers would enjoy a higher purchasing power only if the price of agricultural goods increased relative to the industrial goods that farmers bought. Standing in the way of that objective was a second pillar of Roosevelt's New Deal, the National Industrial Recovery Act of 1933 (NIRA), which sought to reverse the deflation in industrial prices that had caused consumers to delay purchases and companies to slash output and employment. The NIRA established the National Recovery Administration (NRA), which in turn authorized "Codes of Competition" for individual industries. Essentially rulebooks for cartelization, some of these codes dictated prices outright, while others took a more roundabout approach to curbing "ruinous competition" by setting rules for markups and discounts or banning sales below costs. The codes also required businesses to recognize the right of labor to organize and bargain collectively, a provision intended as a way both to stop deflation in nominal wages and to limit competition between firms over labor costs. Although historians continue to debate whether the NRA succeeded in its objectives, contemporaries quickly soured on a program that appeared to raise prices at a time of mass unemployment and human misery.[16]

While the Department of Agriculture tasked Means with investigating the effect of the NRA on agricultural purchasing power, Means believed that managerial discretion over prices and output had become pervasive well before Roosevelt's sanctions for cartelization. Using data collected by the Bureau of Labor Statistics (BLS) on the wholesale prices of about 750 different commodities, Means discovered that most prices were either very flexible or very rigid. In the early years of the Depression, commodities with rigid prices had undergone much-larger cutbacks to production than those with flexible prices. From 1929 into the spring of 1933, the price of agricultural implements had fallen only 6% as production plummeted by 80%, whereas agricultural prices had fallen by 63% while output had declined only 6%.[17]

Means termed those prices that remained rigid despite changes in demand to be "administered prices." This phrase linked industrial pricing to the unchecked administration of corporate decisions by managerial insiders that he had previously described with Berle. Defining an administered price simply as one that "is set by administrative action and held constant for a period of time," Means emphasized that administered prices were not synonymous with monopoly prices and could occur in industries that would generally be considered competitive. Still, in an echo of Chamberlin, Means argued that the reduction in the number of firms competing over the production of a specific commodity served as a key determinant of the ability of individual business managers to displace the market, "even though there is no monopoly or collusion between the separate enterprises." When faced with a drop in demand, the manager with a choice between reducing prices and reducing output would generally prefer the latter strategy so as to avoid a ruinous race to the bottom. As more and more firms responded in a similar fashion, the economy would enter a downward spiral of increased unemployment, leading to less spending and even less demand than before. Had these managers instead acted against what they saw as their self-interest and lowered their prices, Means concluded, the severity of the Depression could at the very least have been greatly mitigated.[18]

Means, drawing on his work with Berle, reasoned that prices had failed to allocate resources properly across the economy because management had become isolated from market forces. Management no longer worked for the owners of securities, and consumers possessed insufficient economic power to challenge the firms that set administered prices. Without this external discipline, management could undertake actions that proved irresponsible for the economy as a whole. Asserting that modern technology made it infeasible to dissolve the administered sector into units small enough to interact through the impersonal forces of the marketplace, Means concluded that the only way to ensure that industrial price policy acted in the public interest would be to counterbalance management's interest with the interests of other corporate stakeholders. As the state encouraged labor, agriculture, and consumers to organize alongside the business interest, Means predicted the modern economy could restore the "balance which the policy of laissez faire was formerly expected to produce."[19]

Means's explanation for the Great Depression proved extremely influential in Washington as the Roosevelt administration looked to jettison the unpopular NRA even before it was held unconstitutional in 1935. According to the then-fashionable interpretation, the management of oligopoly industries had kept too much of the fruits of productivity for itself in the form of higher profits while suppressing wages, leading to the "underconsumption" of goods. Inadequate demand had in turn led to curtailed production, followed by mass unemployment and economic collapse.[20] Economists today are quick to dismiss this reasoning, attributing the coming of the Great Depression instead to Federal Reserve policy in an era in which the gold standard and not domestic concerns dictated monetary policy. Though the decline in consumption was more severe than in previous recessions, with the drop in durable-goods consumption especially acute, the ratio of consumption to total income only began to fall in 1930, whereas underconsumption theory would have expected a fall in this ratio to precipitate the crisis.[21]

Regardless of the economic merits of this model, the Roosevelt administration now reasoned that if management could not be trusted to share the fruits of productivity with society on its own volition, then workers would have to be empowered to dislodge their rightful purchasing power. The National Labor Relations Act of 1935, also known as the Wagner Act for its champion, Senator Robert Wagner of New York, thus granted labor the right to bargain collectively with management. To support these efforts, a new federal agency, the National Labor Relations Board, would serve as the guarantor of this right and prohibit management from engaging in unfair practices designed to weaken unions. The findings section of this law notably emphasized how "the inequality of bargaining power . . . tends to aggravate recurrent business depressions, by depressing wage rates." Individual workers could not make headway against an employer, but collectively, they could leverage their power to demand a greater share of income.[22] Industrial opposition to the Wagner Act was rife, but through a combination of union strike action, pressure from labor-friendly Democratic politicians, and shrewd calculations on the part of management, the new labor organizations embedded themselves in the nation's leading industries. Union membership had represented an estimated 8.5% of all employed workers in 1935, before increasing to 20% of all workers in 1941, or 28% when excluding agricultural workers.[23]

ANTITRUST AND THE STRUCTURAL SOURCES OF ADMINISTRATION

There was of course a great irony in the fact that the New Deal combated price administration by enabling unions to administer their own streams of income. If administered prices impeded the distribution of income expected in a more competitive economy, how could other concentrations of power acting in their own self-interest enhance the welfare of the public as a whole? The economics literature of the 1930s was replete with warnings about this parallel potential for administration, and this concern even proved a recurring theme for presidential addresses at the flagship American Economic Association. Already in December 1934, the labor economist

Harry Mills had used his address to caution against viewing unionization as a panacea for unemployment. Collective bargaining could help to overcome the frictions of the modern economy, but Mills also noted that "most unions, however, are not defending the wages they have had, but are on the offensive to get more; not infrequently, emphatically more."[24] In December 1938, Alvin Hansen of Harvard University, who had previously published revised statistics proving that wages indeed tracked productivity over the long run, similarly noted that while "totalitarian states have the great advantage that they can vigorously check the advance of costs, including wage rates," democracies could not "escape from the influence exerted by organized groups upon the operation of the price system."[25]

Rather than allowing those counterweights to claim a larger slice of income for their own members at the expense of the unorganized consumer and worker, many of these economists recommended that the real purchasing power of all social groups could be enhanced by containing administered prices and wages at their source.[26] Enhancing market competition also held clear political appeal for the Roosevelt administration. When the economy entered recession in 1937, unwarranted price increases again came in for condemnation, although economists today attribute this setback to the adoption of more restrictive fiscal and monetary policies.[27] On April 29, 1938, President Roosevelt responded to this crisis with a message to Congress on "curbing monopolies," in which he argued that "concentrated economic power" had caused "the disappearance of price competition in many industrial fields." Though Roosevelt used the phrase "managed industrial prices" instead of "administered prices," his causal chain was identical to that of Means. As companies cut production while maintaining high prices in a time of slackening demand, not even plummeting prices in the competitive sectors of the economy could sustain total output.[28]

Rather than establishing additional countervailing forces to challenge management, Roosevelt now requested a comprehensive study of concentration and competition in the U.S. economy. The White House initially offered Means the position of economic coordinator for this Temporary National Economic Committee (TNEC), but he declined out of concern that TNEC would recommend dissolution or other solutions that threatened the efficiency of modern industry. Means instead remained at the National Resources Planning Board, where he argued for greater stakeholder input and government planning as the proper counterweights to managerial power.[29]

In the place of Means, TNEC recruited as its executive secretary Leon Henderson. A notable advocate of the view that a rise of profits relative to wages had precipitated the Depression, Henderson had also been among the first to warn that rising prices in the first half of 1937 would lead to economic collapse.[30]

Over the span of two and a half years, TNEC held 193 days of hearings featuring 552 witnesses, investigated ninety-five industries, and produced over eighteen thousand pages of printed material in forty-three volumes.[31] TNEC's investigations typically began from the proposition that concentration and monopoly were always detrimental for the economy, although its own investigators ultimately undercut this emphasis in a report that concluded that "the degree of concentration in production is not a significant factor in determining price-quantity behavior of manufactured products with reference to the business cycle."[32] Despite this finding, the final report of TNEC insisted that industry had failed to pass on the gains of productivity to its various stakeholders and declared that intensified competition would reverse this damage. In recommending stricter limitations on corporate mergers and stronger antitrust laws, however, TNEC offered few concrete suggestions about how to address existing concentrations of economic power. Its final report did call for a ban on resale price maintenance, the abolition of basing-point systems, increased oversight of trade associations, and reforms to the patent laws, but none of these reforms addressed the fundamental issues of industrial structure that Roosevelt and TNEC claimed generated price administration.[33]

Could antitrust law even apply to the conditions associated with administered prices? The maintenance of high and rigid prices could result from overt collusion, cartelization, or conspiracy on the part of several producers banned under section 1 of the Sherman Act or the monopolizing banned by section 2. Yet as Means had recognized, firms in imperfectly competitive markets could also arrive at supracompetitive prices simply by acting out of awareness of what their competitors would do, a pattern of behavior known as "conscious parallelism." In contrast to the formal collusion clearly outlawed by the Sherman Act, courts had been reluctant to declare the conscious parallelism of oligopolies to be impermissible. Instead, jurists had largely adhered to the attitude summarized by Justice Edward T. Sanford in *United States v. International Harvester* (1927): "The fact that competitors may see proper, in the exercise of their own judgment, to follow the prices of another manufacturer does not establish any suppression of competition or show any sinister domination."[34]

Given the turmoil of the Depression that contemporaries linked to administered prices, the federal government had actively sought a way to circumvent this limitation on challenging parallel action. In the landmark case of *Interstate Circuit v. United States* (1939), the Supreme Court came its closest yet to interpreting parallel pricing through the lens of conspiracy, not inevitable market forces. In this case, Interstate Circuit, a first-run motion-picture exhibitor, had sent a letter to distributors of films requesting that they maintain specified prices and restrictions on showings of their movies at second-run theaters. Following the receipt of this letter, the distributors had adopted its terms. There was no direct proof that the distributors had explicitly reached an agreement with one another to abide by the terms of the letter. Instead, the Court had to infer from the conduct of the companies whether an agreement existed between them. Because the letter had been addressed to all of the distributors, each recipient knew that all of its competitors were considering this proposal simultaneously. Each was also aware that all stood to profit if all agreed to participate, whereas without unanimous action, those who participated would be at a competitive disadvantage. Given that the companies had all adopted the restrictive practices that none would have implemented on its own, the Court held that there were sufficient grounds to conclude than an unlawful agreement to restrain trade existed.[35]

As will be discussed in subsequent chapters, interpretations of *Interstate Circuit* after World War II would distinguish this case from a pure example of conscious parallelism on the basis of the existence of the letter as a coordination device. Still, many of the Roosevelt administration's antitrust authorities of the late 1930s celebrated the logic of this verdict as a means to impose discipline on industrial pricing. Corwin Edwards, chief economist of the Federal Trade Commission from 1937 to 1939 and subsequently an economic consultant to the Department of Justice, argued that the pricing policies of oligopoly industries displayed a unity of action indistinguishable from an old-fashioned collusive agreement or conspiracy. Practically, the government's best option would be to act proactively by preventing expansions of concentration and power, but Edwards suggested the government could prosecute existing concentrations for being a "group monopoly." A successful case would either force companies to set their prices in a more competitive manner or dissolve an industry into enough firms that "the market might provide less opportunity for tacitly concerted price fixing."[36]

Thurman Arnold, chief of the Department of Justice's Antitrust Division, doubted whether that latter course of action was feasible. In an economy in which monopoly had displaced competition as the default form of organization, Arnold agreed with Means that there was no hope of returning to an atomized economy of small producers lacking excessive market power. Arnold instead viewed antitrust law as a permanent referee on the side of the consumer. In 1940, the Antitrust Division opened ninety-two new cases, up from eleven in 1938, and its number of complaints more than tripled to 3,412. Unlike many others in the Roosevelt administration, moreover, Arnold recognized that administered prices were not the only potential threat to purchasing power. Any exercise of economic power that led to anticompetitive pricing would be considered a fair target, whether it arose from business practice, agricultural cooperatives, or even the restrictive practices of labor unions.[37]

Arnold's campaign to restore consumer purchasing power through antitrust enforcement soon ran up against insurmountable obstacles. As part of his flagship campaign to reduce construction costs, Arnold had challenged the restrictive practices of the United Brotherhood of Carpenters as a conspiracy that raised costs akin to administered prices. This attack on organized labor sapped much of Arnold's support within New Deal Washington even before the Supreme Court rejected this argument in *United States v. Hutcheson* (1941). In that case, the Court held that when a union acts in its self-interest and does not combine with nonlabor groups, the Clayton Antitrust Act rendered its peaceful activities immune from antitrust prosecution.[38] After this unfavorable ruling, Arnold refrained from launching subsequent industry-wide antitrust assaults. Soon after, the military intervened against Arnold's efforts to bring suit against defense contractors with the economy mobilizing for war. Arnold finally resigned in February 1943, postponing efforts to combat price administration through antitrust law until later in the decade.[39]

PRICE ADMINISTRATION GOES TO WAR

Ultimately, of course, the Great Depression came to an end not through the redistribution of purchasing power but due to the monetary expansion and fiscal stimulus of World War II. Between 1939 and 1944, real gross national product (GNP) rose by 55%, with overall civilian consumption steady as the share of military spending in the total product increased from 1.4% to 45%. While higher taxes covered about half of wartime spending and direct borrowing another quarter, monetary expansion funded 26% of the costs of the war. Under this stimulus, the labor force swelled by over seventeen million people, while another twelve million entered the armed services. Unemployment fell to a record low of 1% at the same time as the forty-eight-hour week became standard.[40]

During this wartime emergency, the federal government embraced a new understanding of wage and price administration to fulfill the needs of a mobilization economy. Wartime incomes grew faster than the available supply of civilian goods, but fiscal and monetary policy were unavailable to contain the inflation that resulted when aggregate demand exceeded aggregate supply.[41] Maintaining a free-price system in a period of wartime inflation would result in the misallocation of needed materiel to civilian users and encourage the withholding of supplies due to the expectation of higher future profits. Inflation could also foment consumer and labor unrest on the home front, and the memory of World War I, in which wartime inflation had been followed by a painful postwar deflation, also loomed large in the minds of policymakers.[42]

Faced with these conditions, the government chose to implement a series of wage and price controls over the economy. After a series of haphazard controls enforced through suasion, the passage of the Emergency Price Control Act on January 30, 1942, granted the Office of Price Administration (OPA) the authority to establish legally binding price controls and rationing requirements. Congress also established the War Production Board (WPB) to oversee materials allocation and the National War Labor Board (NWLB) to mediate disputes and avoid strikes.[43] Though military requirements justified the need for controls, the OPA, as befit its name, also represented an opportunity to open a new front in the long-standing assault on administered pricing. The initial director of the OPA was none other than Leon Henderson, and while Gardiner Means was unavailable to join the OPA, his former colleague from the Department of Agriculture John Kenneth Galbraith accepted the position of Henderson's chief economist and deputy director. Like Means, Galbraith perceived the U.S. economy as split between administered and competitive markets. In fact, Galbraith anticipated that the OPA would have an easier time implementing its controls in administered markets, as the OPA could take advantage of existing pricing machinery to implement price ceilings in line with the public interest. Industrial concentration would also assist the OPA, as having only a few units to monitor would make it much easier to enforce regulations.[44]

Henderson had also sought control over labor costs as an integral component of the fight against price inflation. The Roosevelt administration, however, feared that organized labor would not recognize the legitimacy of wage controls if the OPA used them as a way to limit incomes and aggregate demand. The administration was also concerned that declining real wages would result in strikes and disruptions to war production. When union members withdrew from the NWLB in late 1941 in support of the striking United Mine Workers, the Roosevelt administration expanded the scope of that agency to wage controls as well. In return for having a seat at this tripartite table alongside management and the "public," represented by industrial-relations academics, unions were expected to pledge not to strike for the duration of the war.[45] By the end of 1942, the NWLB had developed its own set of standards for wage adjustments known as the "Little Steel Formula," after the steelworker case in which it was first applied. This formula granted a cumulative cost-of-living adjustment of 15% over the wages paid as of January 1, 1941. The choice of this base period angered union leaders, as only about a third of wage earners in manufacturing were still entitled to any part of their Little Steel allowance by the time it was announced. Union representatives also criticized the official government cost-of-living index for disguising the extent of the wartime erosion of real wages. Nevertheless, average real earnings would rise during the war as hours of work increased and employers found ways to circumvent wage controls by offering fringe benefits.[46]

By using higher wages and benefits to secure organized labor's compliance with the wartime command economy at the same time that it demanded price restraint, the White House inadvertently set business, labor, and consumer interests at cross-purposes. Most industries focused on military production would not encounter the effects of rising labor costs on their margins until they lost the benefit of cost-plus government contracts. The New York dress industry, which uniquely retained an exclusive focus on civilian production throughout the entire war, provides a rare wartime example of the consequences of this inconsistency in the government's wage-price policy. Galbraith recognized that the apparel industry, which hewed closer to the model of a competitive market given its multiplicity of styles and easy entry of firms, presented serious challenges for price controllers. As long as an excess of demand for apparel products existed, Galbraith feared that manufacturers would respond to fixed ceilings by cutting back on the quality and quantity of staple goods to focus instead on higher-margin goods, contrary to the wartime ethos of universally distributed sacrifice.[47]

Galbraith believed that the best solution to the apparel situation would be to curb excess demand through rationing, but the Emergency Price Control Act permitted the OPA to implement rationing only when the WPB had first certified the need for this program. Although the WPB approved rationing for gasoline, shoes, food, and other goods, it refused to take this step for apparel. Frank Walton, the textile executive who served as chief of the WPB's Textile, Clothing, and Leather Division, informed the OPA that he would only implement rationing after having tried all other alternatives, including raising price ceilings so firms could afford the remaining supplies of fabric.[48] Unable to limit demand for apparel, Galbraith next sought to develop price regulations that would compel manufacturers to maintain their output of staple goods, lest dressmakers and other staple-good producers respond to a potential cost-price squeeze by dropping out of low-end production. The OPA's legal team soon put an end to this approach after it determined that legal responsibility for overseeing production rested with the WPB. That agency was no more willing to implement quotas on low-end production than it was rationing. A low-end order would not come into effect until 1945, well after shortages had developed.[49]

Galbraith and the OPA instead reluctantly placed the dress industry under what were known as formula regulations, which imposed ceiling prices as a function of costs. The most important of these regulations was Maximum Price Regulation (MPR) 287, which regulated women's outerwear from December 1942 to the end of controls in 1946. MPR 287 prohibited manufactures from exceeding the highest price-line that they had offered before controls. In order to sell a dress at one of their established price-lines, firms had to include at least the same dollar value of fabric, trim, and direct labor as that of a dress that they had sold at that price line in the prewar base period. While manufacturers could count higher textile costs toward this "minimum allowable cost," they could not include any increase in wages agreed on after July 1, 1942, a rule designed to stiffen the resolve of manufacturers against expanding the purchasing power of their workers at a time when demand was already excessive. In addition, manufacturers were required to reduce their peacetime margin over these costs by 10% due to the presumption that excess demand would permit dressmakers to produce larger runs of a fewer number of styles, reducing overhead costs. No gross margin would have to be reduced below 22% to shield the low-end segment of the market, known as the popular-priced street dress industry.[50]

The New York dress industry soon found itself caught between MPR 287 and wage controls when a series of wildcat strikes involving nearly half of the industry's eighty thousand workers led the NWLB to grant a Little Steel increase of 6% to the International Ladies' Garment Workers' Union (ILGWU) in March 1943; an additional 0.5% would later be added.[51] The NWLB decision represented a decrease in net margins of approximately 1.6 percentage points for all dressmakers. Because popular-priced producers operated on lower margins, the net margins on price-lines up to $3.75 were cut in half.[52] The industry insiders who staffed the OPA's Women's Outerwear Section declined to amend MPR 287 to address this squeeze, but they communicated to the industry that firms would not be "bothered" by the Price Department's enforcement staff were they to raise prices on the basis of their higher wage costs.[53] By early 1944, the OPA was aware that at least a quarter of New York's dress firms, most of them popular-priced producers, had taken advantage of the Price Staff's assurances and used these wage costs to qualify for higher price-lines.[54]

The OPA had hoped that this sanctioned evasion would secure the industry's goodwill enough that it would resume stable labor relations and not be tempted into more egregious violations of controls. This attitude changed in late 1943, when the OPA established a separate Enforcement Department that took a much less lenient view of such permissive actions that broke faith with consumers over price restraint.[55] Leading the new Apparel Enforcement Division was Joseph Forer, a lawyer who lacked the awareness of the industry possessed by the pricing staff. Forer gained a pretext to crack down on the wage-price pass-through in early 1944 when the existing collective bargaining agreement came up for renegotiation. For the sake of maintaining peaceful labor relations, the New York dress industry had circumvented the NWLB by agreeing to increase fringe benefits in lieu of a wage increase, but this peace came at a cost. Combined with the 1943 NWLB award, labor compensation in the New York dress industry had now increased by 10% since the start of controls, which if entirely absorbed would reduce net margins by about 2.5 percentage points.[56] Before manufacturers could raise prices further on the basis of this award, Forer issued an ultimatum to the leaders of the New York manufacturers' associations. Admitting that popular-priced firms had been forced down to a net margin of under 1%, Forer did not insist on collecting the traditional treble damages. Yet by requiring dressmakers to absorb the wage increase in future production, Forer had eliminated the possibility that dressmakers could respond to higher wage costs through price adjustments.[57]

Just as Galbraith had feared, dressmakers responded to the twin challenges of rising costs and fixed prices by adjusting their product mix to match the incentives inadvertently generated by the OPA. Contrary to calls for wartime sacrifice and the preferences of consumers for affordable, staple apparel, total production of street dresses held constant between 1943 and 1944 only because a sizeable expansion in the better-dress price brackets offset the decline in popular-priced production. The combination of fixed prices, rising costs, and Forer's enforcement continued to discourage popular-priced production into 1945. When popular-priced producers had been able to raise nominal prices on each style of dress before price controls were enacted, the total share of dresses wholesaling at or below the popular-priced demarcation of $5.50 had risen from 50% of the New York street dress market in 1939 to 55.8% in 1942. Under price controls, this fraction fell to 26.9% by 1945.[58]

OPA officers, most notably its penultimate director, Chester Bowles, described this shift to higher-priced lines as "uptrading," a strategy of wartime profiteering that they argued only a strong OPA could prevent from eroding consumers' purchasing power.[59] Yet because MPR 287 still forbade manufacturers from exceeding their highest prewar price-line, the shorthand of "uptrading" in fact masked two distinct pathways. The behavior of better street dress producers with higher price-lines and margins more closely hewed to Bowles's conception of uptrading as profiteering. With access to a broader spectrum of price-lines and facing a seller's market for apparel, these producers could engage in the process of "building-up," adding superfluous trimming to a garment to increase its cost and price-line without increasing quality. In contrast, popular-priced street dress producers were generally frozen at ceilings well below the price-lines where production was expanding. These producers responded to rising costs by cutting back on output and sacrificing quality.[60] Following Forer's intervention in the New York dress industry, the OPA discovered that low-priced rayon dressmakers had substituted poorer-quality textiles to reduce real costs while maintaining the same nominal minimum-allowable cost and hence the price-line.[61]

Contemporary surveys of clothing purchases reveal just how perversely price controls had failed to protect their ultimate consumer constituency, especially those lower-income women who were the most vulnerable to the disappearance of staple dresses. In 1944 and 1945, the WPB asked consumers to compare their purchases of seventy-five different articles of apparel with how much they had planned on purchasing and explain the reasons for any discrepancy. In the first quarter of 1944, consumers purchased twenty-eight million of the thirty million street dresses demanded. In the first quarter of 1945, they purchased only twenty-four million of the twenty-eight million demanded. When broken down by price-line, the effects of the cost-price squeeze were more varied. Of the demand for street dresses above a retail price of $6.00, corresponding to the $3.75 or $4.75 wholesale price-lines, 88% remained fulfilled. In contrast, only 72% of the dresses desired below this price were purchased in the first quarter of 1945, suggesting that popular-priced producers were indeed cutting back on production as better dressmakers expanded. The WPB survey also turned up evidence that popular-priced dressmakers were maintaining production by reducing quality to cut costs. Between 1944 and 1945, demand for popular-priced street dresses fell by 30%, compared to a drop of only 4% for better dresses. On the basis of interviews with consumers, the WPB concluded that "the upgrading of demand is not due to desire for higher priced merchandise, but to dissatisfaction with quality of the lower price lines."[62]

A WAGE-PRICE POLICY FOR PEACETIME

The experience of the wartime dress industry foreshadowed the difficulties that other producers would face in complying with the government's wage-price policy after the war's end. Despite organized labor's concerns that wage controls would not sustain the purchasing power of the working classes, the nominal hourly wage in manufacturing had managed to increase from $0.63 in 1939 to $1.01 in 1944, the final full year of war production, due to overtime premiums on a forty-eight-hour week and shifts to higher-paid war work. Nominal weekly earnings nearly doubled from $23.64 to $45.70. The consumer price index had risen by about 30% in that time, but average real earnings did rise over the course of the war by about 10%, as measured from the promulgation of Little Steel in July 1942, or 20% from January 1941, although higher taxes also took a bite out of paychecks.[63]

In the period of "reconversion" to follow the war, government planners feared the reversal of these trends as the decline in defense production threw millions of people out of work as enlistment simultaneously shrank. Official estimates of the post–World War II drop in private wages and salaries ran from $20 billion to $35 billion in the year following VE Day, at least one-quarter less than the level of the first quarter 1945. After factoring in postwar tax cuts, the Office of War Mobilization and Reconversion (OWMR) estimated that real disposable earnings for manufacturing workers in 1946 would fall 10% below the level of January 1941.[64] With organized labor calling for price controls as insurance against a return to underconsumption, the Truman administration's postwar wage-price policy accordingly sought to force corporate America to continue to distribute real purchasing power to workers and consumers.[65] Executive Order 9599 of August 18, 1945, lifted wage controls and permitted collective bargaining to proceed without government oversight. Wage increases approved by the NWLB could be used to apply for price relief, but price controls otherwise remained in effect.[66]

With this new policy in place, individual unions quickly served management with substantial wage demands based on their estimates of postwar cutbacks and downgrading. In the fall of 1945, the United Steelworkers demanded an increase of 25¢/hour, slightly over 20% of its then hourly earnings, and the United Auto Workers (UAW) presented General Motors with a demand for a 30% increase in hourly wage rates. Not content simply to win higher wages, these unions also demanded that management refrain from eroding real purchasing power by passing these costs to consumers in the form of higher prices. Most famously, UAW vice president Walter Reuther offered to reduce his demands only if GM could prove, after opening its financial records for public examination, that it could truly not afford this increase at its present prices.[67]

Business spokespeople usually accepted that some wages would have to rise in the reconversion period in order to correct wartime distortions in the labor market, such as the need to reallocate labor from durable to nondurable manufacturing in the postwar civilian market. However, they rejected the need for a policy of large universal wage adjustments to make up for any prospective reductions in earnings, arguing that this policy would spark expectations of inflation.[68] OPA administrator Bowles and labor spokespeople had insisted that higher productivity would allow businesses to absorb higher wages without raising prices, but labor costs had already more than exhausted this reservoir. With the Census of Manufactures discontinued until 1947, our best contemporary estimate of these wartime changes comes from a BLS study of cost and output for twenty-nine manufacturing industries. Although the report noted that unit labor costs in all sampled industries had fallen from 1944 to 1945, payrolls had far outpaced productivity since 1939. In all but two industries with available data, ice cream and rayon products, unit labor costs were above the level of 1939.[69] Subsequently compiled statistics suggest that real output per man-hour increased by about 30% for the entire private economy from 1939 to 1945, but unit labor costs, defined as employee compensation per unit of real gross value added for nonfinancial business, increased by about 35%.[70]

In addition to management's unease at having to bear even greater labor costs, it also found labor's insistence on bargaining over prices greatly disturbing. Not only did GM and other firms served with these demands decry an assault on managerial prerogatives and a backdoor attempt to replace free enterprise with communism. They also opposed the policy of both Reuther and Bowles that seemingly demanded that all of an individual firm's productivity be distributed to its employees in the form of wages, preventing management from rewarding owners and consumers at the same time. For instance, in response to the suggestion of DuPont vice president Buck Harrington that General Motors could afford a 10%–15% rise in wages without a change in prices due to the wartime "possible advance in technique," GM chairman Alfred Sloan refused to tie wages to GM's own ability to pay. As Sloan complained to the GM board member and DuPont president Walter Carpenter, "What's the use of trying to do a better job if the proceeds of same are to be immediately taken away from you by labor?"[71] According to the theme heavily discussed in the contemporary economics and business press, even if a highly productive company such as GM could afford to pay higher wages without raising its own prices, other firms and industries would face union pressures to match this pattern. Over the entire economy, unit labor costs would rise, resulting in the perpetuation of the wage-price spiral. Only if pattern-setting and highly visible employers such as GM held the pace of compensation to a level that the average-productivity firm could absorb would it be possible to prevent inflation.[72]

Bowles was willing to provide partial relief to industries that were operating at a loss under price ceilings, but he emphasized that the OPA would not grant price relief for higher wages until firms and unions completed their negotiations. In October 1945, Executive Order 9651 clarified that price relief could be granted for a voluntary wage settlement only after a six-month waiting period used to determine if a company was indeed unable to pay these wages.[73] Rather than wait, firms across the economy took a page out of the dress industry's playbook by changing production patterns, reducing quality, and refusing to bargain with the unions demanding even greater compensation.[74] The resistance of firms such as GM to the reconversion wage-price policy generated the United States' largest strike wave since 1919. During the war, labor had pledged not to strike in return for the NWLB recognizing the principle of the maintenance of union membership. Only 0.17% of available man-days had been lost to strikes from the start of 1945 to VJ Day, when the no-strike pledge expired. For the remainder of 1945, 1.07% of available man-days were lost, and according to the Department of Labor, 44% of man-days lost that year were due to disputes over wages and hours. The strike wave continued into 1946, with 1.43% of man-days lost to work stoppages for the year.[75]

Industrial-labor strife threatened to delay what had turned out to be a still-booming economy. Real consumption in 1946 was 12.6% higher than in 1945, supported by the liquidation of wartime savings, the abolition of rationing, and a reduction in corporate and personal income taxes.[76] Weekly nominal earnings in durable-goods manufacturing fell slightly with the end of war, but earnings in nondurable manufacturing rose, for an overall loss of only 2% in nominal terms. In real terms, hourly wages in manufacturing would not match their wartime peak until 1949, and the consumer price index rose more than 8% from 1945 to 1946 and wholesale prices by 14%.[77] Yet nonfarm employment bottomed out in September 1945 at 38.5 million employees, which was still 7 million above the corresponding month in 1939. Unemployment topped out at a little over 4% in early 1946, only a fraction of the 15% unemployment that had persisted into 1940.[78]

As this strike wave generated political controversy, Bowles's superiors in the White House began to reconsider the utility of a rigid wage-price policy. Bowles continued to urge Truman to support a fixed price-line, insisting that problems with production were only temporary hardships during reconversion or, more ominously, a conspiracy on the part of business leaders to destroy price controls and gouge the public.[79] Yet taking notice of Bowles's consumer outreach, outspoken defense of price controls, and frequent radio broadcasts to the nation, it seemed to some in the president's inner circle that Bowles was prioritizing his own future over Truman's. In the midst of this intense tug-of-war, the OPA director fell ill for several days in early February 1946. He returned to find that the OWMR had rewritten wage-price policy to be issued as Executive Order 9697 of February 14, 1946, which permitted instant price adjustment after the acceptance of a government wage recommendation.[80]

The OWMR's wage-price policy operated as the mirror image of that urged by labor groups. Whereas Bowles had sought to justify wages as high as management could afford to pay, the OPA now had to grant management prices sufficient to cover its labor costs in the name of expanding production. In the case of the steel industry, which more than any other was responsible for convincing the administration that it must shift its policy to bring an end to the strike wave, Bowles had previously been willing to offer price relief of $2.50/ton to account for the fact that the industry was producing many items at a loss, but the industry demanded more before it would resume collective bargaining negotiations. Under the new policy of EO 9697, the industry agreed to the 18.5¢/hour raise for the union proposed earlier in the year by Truman as a compromise sum in return for price relief of $5.30/ton of carbon steel.[81] Even though the 18.5¢/hour wage award had been crafted specifically for the steel industry, GM and others agreed to settle for this sum in order to receive immediate price relief from the OPA, preventing Reuther and other labor leaders from achieving their goal of making prices subject to bargaining alongside wages.[82]

The outmaneuvered Bowles resigned in protest over EO 9697. Although Bowles was quickly given a new appointment as director of the Office of Economic Stabilization, he had largely fallen out of favor with the White House. In a tense meeting in early June 1946 between the president and Bowles, Truman angrily informed Bowles that beyond rent, apparel, and food, price controls "could all go to hell." When Bowles suggested that price controls held down the cost of living, reducing wage demands and creating labor-management accord, Truman replied that "labor's promises were not worth the paper they were written on" and called Philip Murray, head of the United Steelworkers, a "son of a bitch" four times in the span of half an hour.[83]

In June 1946, Congress voted to extend the duration of price controls while imposing further restrictions on the OPA that would make it even easier for firms to raise prices in response to costs. Recognizing the widespread support that controls still enjoyed among a public fearful of inflation, Truman declared that no controls were preferable to bad controls and vetoed this bill, to the acclaim of consumer and labor groups. Without price controls to repress inflation, the consumer price index rose by nearly 6% over the span of three weeks, at which point Congress and the administration worked out a compromise that temporarily restored controls.[84] Soon after, a nationwide meat shortage developed, allegedly due to producers choosing to withhold their offerings in anticipation of the full end of controls. The administration could have made relative adjustments in the price of beef at slaughter relative to the price at feed lots to encourage marketings, but Truman rejected this course on the grounds that it would take an entire year for the supply of cattle to meet demand.[85] Truman preemptively lifted meat price controls on October 14, 1946, in a last-ditch effort to win votes in the midterm elections, but this action sealed the fate of controls. Following the Republican landslide in the November 1946 elections on the slogan "Had Enough?" the OPA and its price controls ended for good at the close of the year.[86]

Now that businesses had won the right to adjust prices freely, the wage-price spiral emerged on cue. The consumer price index increased by about a quarter from 1946 to 1948, and the wholesale price index for all commodities by about a third before the economy entered a recession in 1949.[87] From 1946 to 1948, prices in fact grew faster than the cumulative 13% increase in unit labor costs for corporate businesses, but considering that unit labor costs had increased by one-third since 1941 while prices could not adjust freely until after the end of price controls, the cumulative increase in prices hewed closely to the unit labor cost trend. Expressed differently, the share of income going to wages, having reached a twentieth-century peak during World War II, returned in 1946–1950 to the level at which it had hovered in the late 1930s. Consumers and workers did not suffer a serious loss of real purchasing power over this period, but neither had businesses gained a greater share of the distribution of income. As soon as the wage-price spiral had robbed Peter to pay Paul, it turned around and robbed Paul to repay Peter.[88]

Still, higher prices at least proved effective at restoring the production lost under controls, as the dress industry again illustrates. Following the end of controls, the price of unfinished cotton fabric nearly doubled between 1946 and 1948, and the ILGWU negotiated another 7% wage increase in early 1947.[89] Yet with OPA price ceilings removed, manufacturers were now able to pass on these costs in the form of higher prices rather than as changes in the quality and quantity of apparel. During the war, the nominal upper boundary of popular-priced producers had been frozen at $5.50, the level decided on by the Popular Priced Dress Manufacturers Association on the eve of price controls. Once price controls ended, the association now encouraged its members to price their existing styles into the new $5.75–$6.75 bracket. Production in what had been the wartime popular-priced dress brackets, $5.50 and below, had fallen to only 25.3% of total New York street dress output by 1948. However, as popular-priced dresses could now be purchased in the new $5.75–$6.75 nominal price bracket as well, the total share of popular-priced dresses reached 54.3%, a level not witnessed since 1942. Contemporary reports collected by the ILGWU suggest that the quality of these popular-price dresses matched consumer expectations, allowing them to win back the customers they had lost to better dresses under the OPA.[90]

FROM THE THEORY OF UNDERCONSUMPTION TO COST-PUSH INFLATION

The Great Depression had handed the helm of federal economic policy to those who insisted on combating price administration and maximizing purchasing power, but the stimulus of World War II demonstrated that this fixation on structure had been misplaced. Where Means and other economists of the New Deal looked to organized labor and state planning as counterweights to corporate management, the newly ascendant economists of the Keynesian Consensus were much more confident that the private sector was capable of maintaining full employment given the proper macroeconomic climate. Rather than promoting counterorganization and price controls to manipulate the distribution of income, the government's task would now be to engineer a growing pie for all claimants. The Employment Act of 1946 symbolized this shift in economic policy away from the microeconomic interventions of the New Deal toward the macroeconomic stabilization of the Keynesian Consensus. The act charged the government with the mandate to "promote maximum employment, production, and purchasing power." The act did not require any specific programs in pursuit of these objectives, and the legislative history of the act made it clear that the government was to rely primarily on countercyclical fiscal policy, not direct market interventions. To provide the government with the expertise necessary to govern the business cycle, the act established a Council of Economic Advisers (CEA) within the White House that would prepare an annual *Economic Report of the President* to be reviewed by the new congressional Joint Economic Committee.[91]

The emergence of the postwar wage-price spiral quickly imbued the Employment Act with a second significance that had been almost entirely overlooked during the legislative process.[92] The act implicitly promised that the government would provide enough economic stimulus to prevent the unemployment that the New Deal had attributed to private market power. If firms and unions interpreted the Employment Act to mean that the government would not allow them to feel the repercussions of their quest to claim a larger share of income, they could drop all inhibitions on price and wage administration. The microeconomic wage and price decisions of firms and unions could thus still hold the government's macroeconomic policy hostage, as private groups would determine how much inflation the government had to tolerate in order to avoid unemployment. Melvin W. Reder, the economist who received much of the credit from his contemporaries for incorporating the guarantees of the Employment Act into prewar models of administration, described the problem this way: "If the net result of Labor-Management bargaining is a trend in the level of wage rates that management will pay (and continue to offer a volume of employment sufficient to clear the labor markets) only if the price-level also has an upward trend, then the authorities' hands are tied. Either they acquiesce in the price-level trend and supply sufficient cash (or deficits), or they compel a reduction in employment."[93]

By the early 1950s, thanks largely to the influence of the Columbia University economist Albert Hart, this phenomenon had received its definitive name: cost-push inflation. In the traditional "demand-pull" inflation, monetary expansion is followed by an effort by consumers to spend that money. As the money supply has increased relative to money demand, the value of money declines, and prices become inflated. Cost-push inflation also describes a process whereby an increase in the money supply coincides with a higher price level, but in the reverse order as occurs in demand-pull inflation. In cost-push inflation, first comes a rise in prices or wages such as could occur through administration. In the prewar years, this action might have been feared to create underconsumption and unemployment, but now the government stood ready to use macroeconomic stimulus to accommodate the new wage-price level and prevent unemployment. In other words, too much money chasing too few goods was now seen as the symptom, not the cause, of inflation.[94]

In 1952, the British economist Peter Wiles described how the free nations of the West faced what he termed the "uneasy triangle" between price stability, full employment, and free collective bargaining. At best, only two of these three choices could coexist: Which would be sacrificed to obtain the others?[95] The most radical approach would have been to continue the model of the OPA: sacrificing free economic institutions to the twin goals of full employment and price stability. Truman's reelection campaign platform in 1948 tapped into the latent support for controls that still existed within the Democratic base by including a plank of selective price controls. As had Roosevelt in 1938, Truman repeatedly blamed macroeconomic dislocation on big business, its high profits, and its backers in the Republican Party. He also justified mandatory controls as necessary to prevent his proposals to expand foreign aid and military spending from creating an inflationary excess demand for domestic supplies. Truman won the election, but these proposals never managed to pass the Democratic Party–controlled Congress once the wage-price spiral had come to an end amid a mild economic downturn in 1949.[96]

A second, less drastic structural solution to cost-push inflation involved antitrust enforcement, but Keynesian economists largely rejected relying on this approach. Dissolving all monopolies or concentrations of power with the ability to administer prices seemed no more viable a solution than eliminating free collective bargaining or imposing mandatory price and wage controls would be.[97] A reliance on antitrust law would also leave untouched the ability of labor to administer wages, which postwar economists increasingly recognized as a threat to the public akin to price administration. Just as businesses could exercise their market power to select prices that were individually rational but socially harmful, so too could unions force wages beyond what productivity could absorb at the expense of higher prices, lower sales, and decreased employment.[98] Such an outcome appeared especially likely as economists came to understand that unions suffered from problems of governance reminiscent of the separation of ownership and control that Berle and Means had described for corporate business. Union leaders generally pursued a policy of holding wages rigid, even when the total income of workers would fall when these wage levels generated unemployment. Some postwar economists explained this "wage administration" by relating wages to the demand for labor, but others argued that just as management set prices in ways that reflected its isolation from market forces, so too could labor leaders act in ways that did not serve the interests of their individual members. Union leaders had a responsibility to maximize the economic welfare of their members, but the longevity of the union—and their own tenure at its helm—often took precedence.[99]

If a democratically accountable government wished to free itself from the inflationary constraints imposed by democratically unaccountable concentrations of power while maintaining a free-market economy, the consensus of the economics community was that management and labor would simply have to exercise their power over prices and wages responsibly. In the inaugural *Economic Report of the President* issued in January 1947, the CEA described how voluntary restraint would be necessary to realize the goals of the Employment Act: "labor should refrain from demands for excessive wage increases that would require price increases," and "management in turn should recognize that increased productivity permits wage increases in some cases as well as price reductions."[100] The CEA elaborated on its ideal wage-price policy in its *Midyear Economic Report* several months later by explaining that "prices, to support a prosperous economy, must be kept down to the lowest point compatible with costs and reasonable business incentives" and that "over the long run, trends in real wages should be based on general productivity trends."[101]

Students of postwar economists would have frequently encountered this appeal to private responsibility, including in the first (1948) edition of the most influential economics textbook of the century, Paul Samuelson's *Economics*. At the end of his chapter titled "Fiscal Policy and Full Employment without Inflation," Samuelson provided a brief overview of what he termed "a fundamental difficulty with full employment": "the fact that *wages and prices may begin to soar while there is still considerable unemployment and excess capacity.*" Samuelson attributed this inflation to the market power of "businessmen and trade-unions react[ing] perversely to an increased demand." Samuelson elsewhere warned that higher wages could result in unemployment, if borne as a cost, or inflation, as "corporations forced to pay higher money wages may pass on these increases to the consumer in the form of higher prices." Samuelson noted that the Employment Act affirmed joint public-private responsibility for economic stabilization, and he concluded that establishing a wage-price policy to reconcile microeconomic behavior with macroeconomic objectives remained "America's greatest problem and challenge."[102]

The most comprehensive of the early efforts to describe the mechanisms of this wage-price policy was provided by the economist Abba Lerner. Lerner was a leading advocate of the use of fiscal policy, or "functional finance," as he termed it, to maintain full employment. Lerner distinguished between two different conditions of full employment: "high full employment," the point beyond which only frictional unemployment existed and in which demand-pull inflation would proliferate; and "low full employment," the point at which prices began to rise. According to Lerner, inflation that occurred in between the low and high full employment conditions reflected the "excessive bargaining power of the workers" relative to management. Lerner argued that holding the economy to low full employment merely to prevent cost-push inflation could not be socially justified, but he also warned that cost-push inflation, if left unchecked, would slowly but inevitably accelerate into a hyperinflation. Adherence to a wage-price policy encouraged the low full employment condition to converge on the high full employment condition, permitting functional finance to move the economy to high full employment without inflation.[103]

Lerner's discussion of wage-price policy spanned fifty pages and four chapters of his influential 1951 interpretation of Keynesian economics, *The Economics of Employment.* Compared to Samuelson's rather brief description, Lerner laid out an intricately detailed approach to wage-price policy in which the above-average wages of growing industries were offset by frozen or shrinking payrolls in declining sectors. Yet by the time he wrote, there were few economists who seriously argued with his basic prescription. Wages should be tied to average labor productivity so that prices could fall when a firm with above-average productivity experienced declining unit labor costs.[104] Thus wage-price policy had emerged fully formed into the postwar period, but with a subtle twist. While the wage-price policy of the New Deal had argued that wages needed to be *raised* to match the growth of productivity, postwar policy held that wages needed to be *held down* to this trend to prevent the cost-push inflation that the Employment Act allowed private concentrations of power to unleash.

CONCLUSION

Administered prices were not synonymous with monopoly, but by the early twentieth century, so many industries had taken on aspects of monopoly power that the notion of competitive price-takers appeared to be the exception to the rule. Based on the knowledge available in the 1930s, the Roosevelt administration believed that the government must take steps to ensure that the distribution of income matched that of a more competitive economy. By creating new concentrations of economic power in the form of labor unions, the administration implicitly admitted that corporate pricing power, whatever its consequences for the nation as a whole, could not be avoided. Antitrust law had proven a tantalizing yet uncertain approach, with political realities dictating how far and how fast the Department of Justice or Federal Trade Commission could move against industry, let alone against other powerful interest groups. Relying on regulation to inject stakeholder oversight into management's pricing decisions also proved a difficult sell, for as the collapse of the OPA demonstrated, the government could not easily referee a balance between costs and prices on behalf of labor, management, and consumers simultaneously.

Following World War II, the Keynesian Consensus resolved many of these challenges by demonstrating that institutional reforms were not a prerequisite for full employment. Yet faced with an economy in which big labor now vied with big business for a share of productivity, the adherents of postwar Keynesian macroeconomics feared how price and wage administration would interact with the mandate of the Employment Act. The resolution of this tension relied on the same ideal of competitive wage and price behavior that had accompanied discussions of underconsumption during the Great Depression, but the rationale for this pattern had undergone a complete transformation to accompany the theory of cost-push inflation. Behind the commonly encountered proposal that wages should hold to productivity and prices fall where unit labor costs declined rested the same fundamental difficulty that had existed in the prewar period: How could oligopolistic firms and monopolistic unions actually be convinced to act responsibly in the public interest? Keynesian demand management may have resolved many of the economic challenges of the prewar era, but it remained to be seen whether powerful economic groups could voluntarily reconcile the national objective of economic stability with their own self-interest.

CHAPTER TWO

The Price of Peace

WAGE-PRICE POLICY IN THE 1940S AND 1950S

OVER THE COURSE of the 1940s and 1950s, business learned to live with organized labor by defining how the New Deal order would function amid the postwar prosperity. Assisted by the reforms to labor law embodied in the Taft-Hartley Act of 1947, management asserted its right to control the workplace, regularized the handling of grievances, and formalized seniority provisions. As a result, the adversarial nature of collective bargaining narrowed primarily to matters of wages and hours. Not all labor historians have interpreted this evolution in industrial-labor relations as a positive development, arguing that this emphasis on bread-and-butter issues allowed management to undermine labor as a political force and so weaken the New Deal order. These historians have in particular viewed the growth of fringe benefits and employer-sponsored pension and health-care plans as a means to diminish labor's advocacy for a comprehensive public welfare state. Still, many unions accepted these limitations at the time in return for a partial say in the distribution of corporate gains.[1]

This chapter provides an in-depth examination of the economic and financial principles that guided management as it bargained with labor over corporate income during this formative decade. The commonly accepted economic wisdom of the late 1940s dictated that the only way to reconcile full employment and price stability short of mandatory controls would be for firms and unions to show price and wage restraint in the national interest. In 1948, this proposal received an endorsement from the United States' largest corporation, General Motors. GM president Charles Wilson understood the economic rationale of placing productivity at the center of noninflationary wage-price policy, and he further believed that this approach could serve as the backbone of a multiyear "peace treaty" between capital and labor. Contemporary labor-relations experts described General Motors as one of a handful of firms that had the power to establish patterns for collective bargaining across the economy, which might suggest that the challenge of wage-price policy had been resolved by the decade's end.

Yet by the time that multiyear contracts had become standard in industry by the mid-1950s, the rationales of productivity and noninflationary compensation at best remained limited to the rhetoric of the bargaining table. When unions demanded compensation in excess of the levels widely agreed to be noninflationary, management generally found it easier to accede to these demands than to risk a protracted strike that would prevent the firm from taking advantage of the strong markets of the postwar Golden Age. The spread of fringe benefits further allowed companies to claim that wages remained noninflationary even as total compensation outpaced productivity. The few industries that attempted to force restraint onto labor, most notably the steel industry in 1956, ended up with little to show for their efforts except multiyear contracts in which total labor costs far exceeded estimates of national productivity growth. Instead of a balance between stakeholders, management had shown itself willing to risk inflation to safeguard its own distributive function.

LABOR LAW AND WAGE-PRICE POLICY

Labor's push for higher wages without higher prices had failed with the collapse of the OPA. Nevertheless, management remained on notice that it would continue to face a powerful rival over the distribution of income. To General Motors's Alfred Sloan and other executives who had been on the front line of the postwar strike wave, unions themselves did not appear to be the challenge so much as was the imbalance of power between the "union monopoly" and other claimants on corporate income. With the Democratic-controlled National Labor Relations Board (NLRB) expanding the definition of bargainable issues beyond wages and hours, Sloan and other leading managers perceived themselves to be in a lose-lose bargaining situation. The

National Labor Relations Act of 1935 (NLRA) imposed on management the fundamental duty to bargain with labor, but as management was quick to note, no parallel obligation bound labor itself. While unions could freely deliver their message to both workers and the public at large, managers feared they would be charged with unfair bargaining practices if they attempted to communicate their perspective directly to employees. The permissibility of the closed shop, in which the employer agreed to hire only union members, also led corporate spokespeople to complain of a "compulsory unionism" that enhanced the union's monopoly over the labor force. In an echo of Berle and Means's argument about corporate governance, management noted that closed shops diminished the responsiveness of union leadership to its captive stakeholders among the rank and file.[2]

There was little hope of targeting this "monopoly" through antitrust law, and not only because management was aware that any efforts would probably boomerang back into heightened scrutiny of industrial markets as well.[3] As Thurman Arnold had discovered in *United States v. Hutcheson* (1941), labor could not be held liable for restraining trade as long as it acted in its own self-interest, regardless of "the selfishness or unselfishness of the end of which the particular union activities are the means."[4] A second case, *Allen Bradley Co. v. Local Union No. 3 IBEW* (1945), demonstrated just how powerful unions could become under this sanction. Local 3 of the International Brotherhood of Electrical Workers (IBEW) operated a closed shop in New York City for both electrical contractors and manufacturers. By mutual agreement, only goods produced by Local 3 factories could be installed by Local 3 contractors anywhere in the city, resulting in an unambiguous monopoly. Local firms charged prices above the competitive level knowing that outsiders were excluded from this market, and union members shared in these monopoly profits in the form of higher wages. Several manufacturers based outside of New York City challenged this arrangement as a conspiracy in restraint of trade that violated the Sherman Act. Though the Supreme Court ultimately agreed with this interpretation, its ruling relied on the fact that Local 3 had acted in express combination with the contractors and manufacturers. Had such a monopoly situation arisen from the union acting independently, there would have been no violation. Writing for the Court, Justice Hugo Black admitted that this ruling "brings about a wholly undesirable result—one which leaves labor unions free to engage in conduct which restrains trade," but he indicated that it was up to Congress to draw the line as to what forms of monopolies were deemed undesirable for society.[5]

Management indeed turned to Congress to shift the pendulum of power away from labor. The postwar strike wave and the resulting wage-price spiral had dissipated much of the public's goodwill toward unions and suggested that the interests of labor and consumers were indeed in conflict. Dissatisfaction at the state of the economy allowed the Republican Party to retake Congress in 1946 for the first time since the Great Depression, opening a door for the business community to achieve its legislative goals.[6] In 1947, Congress passed over Truman's veto the Labor Management Relations Act, better known as the Taft-Hartley Act for its sponsors Senator Robert Taft and Representative Fred Hartley Jr., which amended the National Labor Relations Act. While retaining the original findings of the NLRA that inequality of bargaining power can depress wages and purchasing power and hence aggravate depression, Taft-Hartley also added the concern of management that "certain practices by some labor organizations, their officers, and members have the intent or necessary effect of burdening or obstructing commerce." In response, the government would now "prescribe the legitimate rights of both employees and employers" while also shielding the "rights of the individual employees in their relations with labor organizations." In particular, Taft-Hartley prohibited the closed shop, applied the obligation to bargain collectively to both the employer and the representatives of the employee, and enumerated certain labor practices as unfair, such as secondary boycotts. It also clarified that employers possessed the right to communicate freely with their employees as long as they made no threats of reprisal or promises of benefit.[7]

Taft-Hartley did not entirely free management from the New Deal vision of the representatives of labor and capital bargaining over the distribution of income. While this new law did cause the NLRB to reverse some of its previous rulings, the board continued to insist that the permissibility of employer practices depended on their context. For instance, although the NLRB no longer considered compulsory attendance at management-run information sessions to be an unfair labor practice, employers still had to take precautions against creating an atmosphere deemed to deprive employees of free choice. Likewise, the NLRB ruled that under Taft-Hartley, the obligation to bargain in good faith extended not just to wages, as management contended, but to all forms of remuneration and conditions of employment, such as pension funds. As a result, labor could continue to press management for a share of corporate gains across a wide spectrum.[8]

Still, Taft-Hartley did bolster management's ability to promote its own vision for the distribution of income, and few corporate leaders would take advantage of these permissions as did Lemuel Boulware, General Electric's vice president for employee and public relations. In 1946, GE had been caught off guard not only by the militancy of the striking United Electrical Workers (UE) but also by its public support. Noting that several affiliated plants managed by Boulware had avoided the strike, GE president Charles E. Wilson offered Boulware the chance to work his magic for GE as a whole. GE gave in to the pattern of the second postwar "round" of bargaining in 1947 without a fight, but Boulware planned an extensive course of preparation and educational outreach to prevent a third round of wage increases in 1948.[9]

Boulware's public outreach drew on contemporary discussions of wage-price policy to present management as the only force that could stop labor from capturing more than its fair share of productivity to the detriment of all other stakeholders. In a confidential memorandum prepared for the 1948 negotiations, Boulware noted how not just corporate economists but even "liberal" economists at the Brookings Institution and the White House Council of Economic Advisers (CEA) urged an end to the annual rounds of bargaining. Paraphrasing the argument that CEA chairman Edwin Nourse had long championed, Boulware described how another increase in wages would harm workers and the public by sustaining the wage-price spiral. Employee surveys suggested that union members believed that wage demands were set nationally as a pattern, and Boulware concluded that GE and other firms could combat the pattern by educating the public about the dangers of allowing this inflationary trend to perpetuate.[10]

Key to GE's gambit to stop the wage-price spiral was a preemptive declaration of price reductions contingent on the union forgoing a wage increase. As Wilson announced to his company's shareholders at the start of 1948, "any wage increase over and above that which represents economic gain is immediately reflected in higher prices." No single company could hold back the wage-price spiral on its own, but GE's average price reduction of 5% on selected lines would help reduce costs to customers and so enable subsequent price reductions down the value-added chain. The total worth of these cuts was estimated at $50 million, small compared to the company's $1.3 billion in revenue for 1947 but sizeable in relation to GE's $95 million in profit for that year and the $11.5 million in quarterly dividends that accompanied Wilson's announcement.[11] The UE decried these cuts as too little to make a dent in the higher cost of living; as UE chief negotiator James Matles charged, "People don't eat television receivers. They don't wear automatic dishwashers."[12] The public response to GE's actions was, however, widely laudatory, beginning with President Truman's call for other firms to join in this effort to create "a real bulwark against rising prices." CEA chairman Nourse also joined this praise, stating that GE was a "fine example of a company being ready to take leadership in a decisive way at a critical time."[13]

GE found a number of eager imitators to join its opposition to the third round. The consumer price index had risen by over 8% in the twelve months following the termination of price controls in November 1946. By early 1948, consumer resistance to higher prices had grown to the point that companies were beginning to explore the possibility of price cuts or at least a moderation in the rate of price increases. At the same time, companies also recognized that slowing the pace of prices would demonstrate to the public that it was corporate management, not organized labor, that was the true defender of the consumer's purchasing power. Although several industries, most notably meat packing, had already settled for higher wages at the start of 1948, the industries considered to be the major pattern setters, among them the electrical equipment, automobile, and steel industries, signaled agreement with GE in tying price reductions to the avoidance of wage increases.[14] For instance, U.S. Steel denied the United Steelworkers' request for a wage increase that April and cut prices by an average of $1.25/ton, equivalent to a reduction in revenue of slightly over 1%. U.S. Steel had only months before raised prices by $5/ton on select products constituting about 10% of total shipments, claiming that these products were sold at a loss. Still, as Nourse interpreted this apparent change of heart to Truman, U.S. Steel was now clearly indicating its interest to take part in a general effort to combat the wage-price spiral.[15]

Ford Motors also joined the no-third-round stance as a corollary to its efforts to regain the market share that it had lost decades before to General Motors and Chrysler. During the second wage round in 1947, John Bugas, right-hand man of Henry Ford II and director of the company's nascent industrial-labor effort, had declared that the union's insistence that "the pattern should be forthcoming solely and exclusively because a competitor has adopted it" was to his "way of thinking abominable." That year, Bugas had deflected the demands of the UAW's leadership for a pension and a wage increase by appealing to the rank and file with a choice between a pension with a 7% increase in wages or no pension with a 15% increase in wages. Given the high rate of inflation, workers chose the latter option, just as the company had hoped.[16]

As the third round approached in 1948, Ford now sought to further its objectives by joining in GE's wage-price initiative. Ford's economic consultants, Sumner Slichter of Harvard University and Theodore Yntema of the University of Chicago, advised Bugas and his staff of the growing consumer resistance to inflation with the warning that "price decreases by major companies are expected in the not too distant future." If the durable-goods industries did not achieve a moderation in the third round of wages, these economists concluded that inflation would continue to spiral until the postwar boom collapsed into a bust. Bugas was unwilling to commit the company to decreasing prices in return for a straight wage freeze out of concerns about low profit margins on older models and the uncertain costs of the new models to be unveiled later in the year. When it came to wages, however, Ford would go farther than GE and U.S. Steel in its opposition to the third round by demanding that the UAW cut wages as much as 10¢/hour, or 6.5%, to remove the wage differential that placed Ford at a labor-cost disadvantage to General Motors. Despite the specific differences between Bugas's program and Boulware's, Bugas spoke favorably of the steel industry's resistance to wage increases that would inevitably result in higher prices, demonstrating that he considered Ford to be taking part in this cross-industry effort to avoid wage patterns.[17]

WHAT'S GOOD FOR GENERAL MOTORS . . .

As the industrial giants of the postwar United States applied their new public- and employee-relations techniques toward breaking the national wage pattern, they found their stance undercut by the largest and most powerful corporation in the United States, General Motors. GM wished to break from the prevailing pattern of annual wage contracts in favor of a multiyear agreement. This "labor peace," as the concept came to be known, would smooth the long-run production schedule while avoiding the strain on executive man-hours created by annual negotiations.[18] As GM chairman Alfred Sloan would later reflect to Harry Anderson, GM's labor-relations chief in the 1950s, the company was seeking "to get away from the eternal conflict with labor and put it on a business-like basis."[19]

Unlike GM's counterparts at GE, U.S. Steel, and Ford, the top management of General Motors possessed a different outlook on the economic responsibility of management to its workers. As the third round loomed, GM president and CEO Charles E. Wilson, nicknamed "Engine Charlie" to distinguish him from GE's "Electric Charlie," doubted that the wage-price spiral could actually be halted when food prices were pushing up the cost of living. Boulware, in contrast, felt it was unfair to shield workers from inflation if customers and the public did not receive the same guarantee.[20] GM's official mythology suggests that Engine Charlie had this epiphany about the cost of living and take-home pay when, laid up in the hospital with a broken hip in 1941, his thoughts had turned to the unfortunate plight of the workingman. In fact, Wilson's concern about the cost of living stretched back decades. During World War I, when Wilson had worked as an engineer for Remy Electric, workers striking over falling real wages had prevented him from entering the factory—and as Wilson realized at the time, his own salary also felt the bite of inflation. From this experience, Wilson developed a strong conviction that management could only win the trust of workers once they were shielded from the cost of living. GM management had explored tying wages to the cost-of-living index as early as 1935 but had given up upon discovering that the available statistics failed to account for the regional variations in the location of GM plants.[21]

Sloan had also been interested in establishing a wage formula that would relate wages to the cost of living as well as productivity as early as 1941, but his staff had recommended against this approach at that time. One rationale explained that higher productivity should be passed to society as a whole through lower prices or better-quality products rather than as a wage premium to a select group of workers. Sloan himself seems to have been most persuaded by the argument that union leaders would never accept such a passive role in wage determination: "The 'scientific' approach, however desirable it might be from the standpoint of an intelligent contribution to the course of a higher standard of living of the worker, is 'out' at the moment because of the fact that it is politics and unintelligence rather than economics and intelligence, which are the governing factors."[22]

By the late 1940s, GM's executives felt that the labor-relations climate had shifted such that it would be possible to take a fresh look at implementing this wage formula. GM knew Walter Reuther, now UAW president, was facing pressure from his rank and file to do something about the cost of living, and they correctly gambled that Reuther would not risk a strike that could expose his incomplete grasp on power.[23] On the morning of May 21, 1948, GM negotiator Louis Seaton presented the union with a prepared statement on wage policy, made all the more stunning by the fact that other major blue-chip industrials were at that time adamantly refusing to discuss wage increases. GM's statement noted that the easy thing for it to do would have been to side with other companies and hope for a favorable harvest that would reduce food prices and alleviate pressure on the cost of living. Instead, GM accepted that it shared a responsibility with labor for protecting purchasing power from inflation and promised that "the buying power of [an] hour of work will increase as the nation's industrial efficiency improves." In return, the company asked that the union recognize its responsibility to stabilize labor relations for a lengthy period of time, creating a model of productive industrial statesmanship.[24]

The first two components of GM's offer, a one-time boost in wages to offset wartime inflation and a pledge to make regular cost-of-living adjustments (COLA) in the future, conceded the UAW's argument that the real purchasing power of workers should be defended from inflation. Contract clauses calling for an adjustment of wages in the event of inflation had cropped up from time to time in previous decades but had fallen out of favor by the time that GM offered to include a COLA escalator. The U.S. Bureau of Labor Statistics estimated that only a quarter of a million manufacturing workers possessed this clause at the start of 1948, making GM a pioneer in reintroducing this contract form (see table 1).[25] Using 1935–1939 as the reference point, GM calculated that workers had gained 60% in wages against a 69% change in the cost of living, and it offered 8¢/hour to make up for that difference. Going forward, the company would key wages to the Bureau of Labor Statistics' national cost-of-living index. At the time of negotiations, the index was at 169.3, and average straight-time earnings at GM including all fringe adjustments except for shift premiums and overtime were $1.49/hour. Dividing these two yielded a ratio of 1.14 points increase in the cost-of-living index for a 1¢ increase in wages, and so henceforth, GM would agree to pay an additional 1¢/hour each quarter for every 1.14 points increase in the index.[26]

Because the COLA would merely freeze real wages in the face of inflation, the company offered to couple this clause with a truly unique proposal: to share the gains of national productivity growth with the union through an "automatic" or "annual improvement factor" (AIF). The AIF was a landmark innovation in the postwar evolution of industrial-labor relations. The U.S. Bureau of Labor Statistics (BLS) had on file only one other contract to make such a guarantee of increasing real wages, and that was from 1942.[27] GM estimated that nationwide, labor productivity had grown by 2% annually over the long run. Whether this figure was more than a rule of thumb is unclear. Sloan commented in his memoirs only, "Over the years, it had been estimated, productivity in the United States had been rising about 2 per cent a year. How good that estimate was, I do not know."[28] Most likely, GM obtained this statistic from the work of the New York University economist Solomon Fabricant, whose studies of productivity would later be cited by other firms as they considered their own deferred increase plans.[29] GM thus offered the UAW 2% of the present $1.49 wage, 3¢/hour, as the AIF to be paid every year. GM had not actually calculated its own productivity trend, but it safely assumed that it was well above the national average. On this point, GM labor executive Harry Anderson would several years later assure Sloan, then busy on his memoirs and concerned that perhaps workers had ended up taking all of the productivity gains for themselves, "our improvement factor is greater than the productivity allowance in the contract, 'a way more.'"[30]

According to the reminiscences of GM executives, Wilson had explicitly constructed this proposal in light of contemporary discussions of inflation and wage-price policy. The idea of the AIF had been Wilson's, although perhaps only as an "afterthought" to his overall goal of obtaining a long-run contact. It had been Wilson who insisted that the AIF be based on the national average, brushing aside suggestions to base it on the productivity of individual plants as the kind of bonus incentive or piece-rate plan that he felt would be unacceptable to the union. Moreover, Wilson seems to have understood the noninflationary rationale of using the national productivity rate as opposed to allowing GM's own trend to set a costly pattern. Questioned by other executives about whether the union would break with this formula as soon as it could, Wilson replied with a defense right out of the prevailing economic discussions of the time: "They mustn't do that.... That's all there is to wack up. Anything beyond would be inflationary.... This isn't just expediency, it's a fundamentally sound document." Wilson in fact hoped that GM could leverage its clout and visibility to encourage other companies to embrace this noninflationary wage policy as the path to labor peace, but GM's Finance Committee, which had to sign off on this proposal, held mixed feelings on the AIF and would go no farther than allowing GM to advocate this approach for itself.[31]

The UAW was unwilling to accept the formula as the basis of a five-year contract as GM had suggested, but it agreed to a two-year contract in which most strike action would be prohibited.[32] There was only one problem with this formula as the basis for labor peace: Chrysler had already offered 6¢/hour to the UAW if it would call off its ongoing strike of that company, but GM guaranteed the UAW only the 3¢ of the AIF. No problem, replied Seaton: 3¢ of the COLA would be made permanent, meaning that the most workers could lose during a deflation was 5¢ of the initial 8¢ COLA. Seaton understood that this compromise destroyed the concept of total indexation and hence could raise costs more than originally anticipated, but this extra premium proved acceptable to Wilson as the price to pay for his multiyear contract. Four days after GM made the offer, an exhausted Wilson announced that the agreement had been completed.[33]

When it came to a wage-*price* policy, GM executives feared that this new wage formula might be misconstrued as dictating pricing, which they understood to be the exclusive domain of management. This was not an idle concern, given that the UAW had linked its wage demands to pricing in 1945 and 1946 and that, upon signing the 1948 contract, the UAW issued a press release claiming GM could cut retail prices by $230 and still earn an after-tax return of 6% on shareholder investment.[34] GM had in fact considered holding its prices steady on the 1949 models, but as board member Walter Carpenter suggested to Engine Charlie Wilson, "If you were to announce that the effect of this adjustment alone would not result in an adjustment of prices, the union would promptly respond that that is what they have been saying all along."[35] Earlier in the year, an internal review of GM's pricing policy had recommended that "if costs are increased, move prices up immediately." In addition to the need to demonstrate that pricing was independent of political and union pressures, the review provided several economic rationales for its conclusion. Given postwar inflation, nominal auto prices were too low to clear the market and so had generated excess demand and speculation. Through an analysis of newspaper advertisements for car sales, the review suggested that the "free market" price of GM cars was 36% higher than the manufacturer's suggested retail price, allowing dealers to make "unwarranted gains" at the expense of the manufacturer. The report further explained that GM faced its own cost-of-living challenge. Inflation had eroded the value of dividends such that $6.09 in February 1948 dollars were needed to equal the $3.67 average dividend of 1939–1941, and the company required higher revenues to meet this amount in tandem with its inflated postwar capital requirements.[36]

Given these concerns, GM merely pledged at the time of the labor settlement not to raise prices until it unveiled its 1949 models, at which point it hiked its list prices from 3.2% to 7.5% depending on the line. Still, GM defended its pricing strategy as being entirely in the public interest, and not only because higher prices signaled the inherent value of products and smoothed over relationships with distributors. By calculating costs at a "standard volume," GM only changed its prices to reflect variable material and labor costs, not fixed overhead charges. Sloan and other executives rationalized this "administered pricing" as being in the public interest. When demand was high, price administration prevented the company from gouging the public. When demand was low, administered prices kept margins high enough to ensure that production would be available once conditions improved.[37]

GM's explicit recognition of the productivity principle furthermore helped to ensure that the company would not pass on all increases in labor compensation to consumers. As Wilson would later explain, the AIF would not raise GM's unit labor costs: "Productivity is assumed to increase at least as fast as hourly wages. Therefore, no price increase should result from such wage increases." Nominal unit labor costs could still increase due to the COLA payments, but Wilson noted that the COLA depended on factors largely outside the control of GM or the UAW, such as fiscal and monetary policy and harvests. Wilson thus implied that when the company passed on these nominal costs, it was merely adjusting its prices to the existing inflation rate and was not raising the real cost burden.[38] Indeed, when a fall in the cost of living reduced the COLA payment by 2¢ in each of the first two quarters of 1949, General Motors passed on these savings to consumers by reducing car prices by $10–$40 at each adjustment. At only about 1% of list prices per quarter, these cuts did not fully offset the previous increases. Yet the second time that GM cut prices coincided with the payment of the 3¢ AIF, and GM had not raised prices in response to this new productivity-linked payment. Wage cuts under the COLA occasioned much grumbling among the UAW. Over the life of the contract, the net increase in wages rose only from the initial 11¢/hour in May 1948 to a total of 12¢/hour in March 1950, even after factoring in the second AIF payment.[39] Still, Reuther quelled dissention in the ranks by defending the contract as recognition of what his union had long sought: a progressive policy of sharing productivity gains with workers as real purchasing power. GM for its part was thrilled the contract had held down wage inflation while maintaining the cooperation of the union in preventing work stoppages.[40]

RESISTANCE TO THE GM PATTERN

As the largest and richest corporation in the country, General Motors exerted heavy influence over what businesspeople considered the strategy for success. But when it came to wage-price policy, what was good for General Motors did not appear good for anyone else. GM's decision to break ranks with the business community did not win the corporation any friends, as GE, U.S. Steel, and other firms that had rejected paying any wage increase expressed extreme disappointment that GM had set a new pattern for higher wages. In a letter to shareholders, GE president Charles Wilson was frank in blaming the auto industry for the $50 million in costs added by his company's new settlement—a sum that just happened to match the price reductions made earlier that year. After contrasting the company's opposition to patterns with the "air of expectancy among [its] own employees" that any settlement in one industry must be followed by others, Wilson concluded his letter with the notice that prices would have to rise in order to balance the needs of customers, workers, and investors.[41]

Apart from concerns about the costs of the GM's pattern, many of the leading economist advocates of wage-price policy, including Melvin Reder and Solomon Fabricant, argued that the GM formula was a fundamentally flawed approach to noninflationary labor peace. These economists cautioned that even if the national productivity trend could be measured accurately, which they warned had not yet been done, unions had come to identify the growth of the national productivity trend as the absolute minimum standard for a one-year deal. Inducing unions to give up the right to strike for multiple years at a time would require that a company pay compensation above this trend, and firms with above-average productivity would probably be more willing to pay this premium. As a result, these economists suggested that high-productivity firms would continue to pay compensation above the national productivity rate and so perpetuate the wage patterns that lay behind the fear of cost-push inflation.[42]

In hindsight, skeptics of the GM wage-price policy proved prescient. When GM was compelled to decide between its goals of multiyear labor peace and a noninflationary compensation pattern, it chose the former. In 1950, GM and the UAW agreed to maintain the AIF and COLA as the basis for an unheard-of five-year contract, which became known as the "Treaty of Detroit." Under the Treaty of Detroit, the AIF increased from 2%, or 3¢/hour, to 2.5%, or 4¢/hour, a decision made after Wilson inadvertently stated that the national productivity trend could range from 2% to 2.5% a year.[43] While the new AIF still fell within the commonly accepted estimates of national productivity growth, albeit at the upper end, GM also added to its total compensation bill in 1950 by establishing a new pension plan and increasing insurance benefits, fringes that the 1948 contract had explicitly prohibited the UAW from demanding until the next contract negotiations. These additional payments were not counted against the AIF and thus pushed real labor compensation over the national productivity trend. GM expanded fringe benefits further in 1953 and again in 1955. Only in the 1958 negotiations would GM show enough concern about paying more than what it had considered to be noninflationary that it was willing to risk a company-wide strike to slow this pace. As Seaton explained management's preferred balance to Reuther that year, "There's two things. The worker's entitled to an equitable wage. . . . We've also got an obligation to our stockholders. These benefit plans are costly and they help increase cost." Nevertheless, labor peace still took priority, and GM ultimately agreed to liberalize fringe payments further above the formula without a strike.[44]

How much had GM paid in addition to its formula by the time of its stillborn attempt to return this strategy to its noninflationary principles? Average straight-time hourly wages at GM were $1.50/hour in 1948 and $2.47/hour in 1958. Including wage premiums and vacation pay gives average hourly earnings of $1.65/hour in 1948 and $2.82/hour in 1958, and accounting for all fringe benefits increases total compensation to $1.70/

hour in 1948 and $3.11/hour in 1958, the real equivalent of about $2.60/hour in 1948 dollars. During this decade, the AIF paid out 52.5¢/hour and the COLA a cumulative 47¢/hour including the 3¢ excluded from deescalation by Seaton. Accepting GM's understanding of the AIF as the "real" portion of the wage formula leaves 37.5¢/hour of the approximate 90¢/hour real increase in total compensation to be explained by sources other than the formula.[45]

Putting to rest the most direct cost-push concern, GM generally absorbed this compensation into its above-average productivity growth. The quality-adjusted new car price index increased by 24.5% over this ten-year period, but over half of that increase had occurred during the initial two-year contract, when fringe benefits were at their smallest. Although nominal auto prices continued to increase into the late 1950s, quality-adjusted automotive prices held steady for nearly two decades after 1951.[46] Nevertheless, noninflationary wage-price policy relied on firms with above-average productivity such as GM to hold their labor compensation to the growth of the national productivity trend while lowering prices to reflect falling unit labor costs. When GM set compensation above the national productivity average and introduced new fringe benefits, other companies faced upward cost and price pressures. Labor productivity for the nonfarm business sector as a whole grew at an annual rate of about 2.8% over this ten-year span, compared to about 4.3% for GM's real compensation.[47]

Even before the true costs of the GM formula had become apparent, GM's blue-chip compatriots resisted adopting the innovations of its wage formula. The GM formula for labor peace proved slow to spread in the wake of the collapse of the no-third-round movement. The BLS counted only 700 of 11,700 contracts in effect at the end of 1949 as two years in length, and of 4,700 contracts signed between November 1949 and April 1950, only about 200 ran for three or more years.[48] By September 1950, the BLS estimated that there had been a net gain in COLA coverage of only 550,000 manufacturing workers since the start of 1948, and GM alone accounted for over half of this increase (see table 1).[49]

Not even GM's closest competitor and the UAW's second-largest employer, Ford Motors, adopted GM's wage-price policy, despite its active emulation of GM's organizational structure.[50] Henry Ford II feared that GM's commitment to pay the AIF and COLA in the contract's second year meant that additional wage increases at Ford were "probably inevitable" in 1949.

Still, hoping that his company could negotiate a better deal in the future, Ford agreed only to a one-year, 13¢/hour deal for 1948, as did Chrysler.[51] When that one-year deal expired, the executives who composed Ford's Industrial Relations Committee mused about a contract in which wages and "all economic matters will be closed for 2 years" for the sake of labor peace, but the minutes of their deliberations give no indication that they ever considered adopting GM's automatic formula. They instead apparently focused on freezing wages over the life of the contract. Recognizing that uncertainty over the future economic climate presented too many risks for both the union and the company to commit to this path, the committee resigned itself to offering the union a chance to renegotiate the matter of wages in the second year of the contract.[52]

It would only be after the outbreak of the Korean War on June 25, 1950, that the components of the GM contract spread to the rest of the auto industry. The outbreak of war brought back fears of shortages, rationing, and direct controls that unleashed panic buying and touched off a self-fulfilling prophecy of price increases. The Truman administration requested authorization to implement wage and price controls to stop this spiral, but by the time that Congress passed the Defense Production Act of 1950, the North Korean invasion had been repulsed and fears of inflation had calmed to the point where controls no longer appear needed. That outlook changed after China entered the war and made it clear that U.S. troops would not be home by Christmas after all. When the White House finally imposed wage and price controls in January 1951, the consumer price index had already risen by about 7% over the second half of 1950 and the wholesale price index by about 15%. Inflation then subsided for the remainder of the war period as independent monetary policy checked monetary expansion and higher taxes limited the recourse to deficit funding.[53]

Reuther remembered how hard the UAW had fought during and after World War II simply to maintain real wages, let alone increase them. Given the upswing in the price indexes in the summer of 1950 and the uncertainty about how long and how hot the Cold War would be, Reuther embraced the GM formula as the best way for workers to make real gains in purchasing power. In late August 1950, Reuther asked Ford to replace its 1949 contract with a five-year program that matched GM's contract.[54] In a quick reversal of the position taken the year before, Bugas now noted that there was no chance that the UAW would agree to a long-run contract without the use of the GM formula. Ford's Industrial Relations Committee discussed whether Ford could reduce the frequency of the COLA, develop its own AIF expressed as a percentage instead of cents, or decrease the AIF if the COLA fell below its base, but it recognized that Ford was trapped by the Treaty of Detroit. Noting that Ford would have to copy every AIF adjustment paid by GM in any case and realizing that the price of a settlement would increase the longer Ford delayed, Bugas suggested that the company should switch tactics from 1948 and no longer consider wages to be "a legitimate field of competition." After internally agreeing to the rationale of basing the AIF on the productivity of the economy as a whole rather than that of a specific industry, Ford signed on to GM's Treaty of Detroit.[55]

Concerned that wartime controls could rupture the wage formula that now served as the basis of the auto industry's labor peace, both the UAW and the auto industry urged the government to craft its wage-stabilization program around the AIF and COLA. After Ford and GM raised prices on the grounds of higher variable costs, the government issued Ceiling Price Regulation (CPR) 1, freezing new car prices as of December 1, 1950. The Defense Production Act required that wage controls be imposed when an industry fell under price control, and a panicked Reuther flew to Washington and warned of the unrest that could develop from interference with the COLA and AIF. As a result, Wage Stabilization Regulation 1 only imposed a temporary freeze until March 1, 1951, buying time to decide on how to treat deferred compensation before the next scheduled COLA payment.[56]

To save the auto industry from the difficulties of having its wage formula disrupted, Engine Charlie urged the government to enshrine the COLA and AIF as the basis of the national wage-stabilization pattern. According to his "Plan for Industrial Mobilization," the industry's five-year agreement should become the standard throughout the economy, albeit with wage boosts paid in the form of savings bonds rather than cash so as to avoid creating excess demand pressures. Wilson seemingly departed from the standards of wage-price policy when he suggested that manufacturers be allowed to pass on half the costs of the AIF as prices, but he justified this request on the basis of the expectation that productivity growth would slow as it had during World War II. If there was no war load on industry, then "producers on the average" could still absorb the entire AIF without raising prices.[57]

Yet beyond the UAW and its employers, few firms and unions had embraced the GM formula, and most wanted that state of affairs to continue. A gradual lengthening of contract durations had occurred by the end of 1950 not through formulae but by permitting the renegotiation or "reopening" of wages at a future date in response to ex post changes in the cost of living or similar exigencies. Only about eight hundred thousand workers in major contracts possessed a COLA clause as of September 1950, according to the BLS, and a survey of contracts collected by the National Industrial Conference Board in the second half of 1950 suggested that only 5% of contracts signed after the outbreak of the Korean War contained an AIF.[58] General Electric, for instance, refused to meet the demands of the International Union of Electrical Workers, which had largely supplanted the Communist-linked UE, for a COLA clause and productivity-linked increase on the lines of the GM pattern. GE instead provided only a reopening clause based on the cost of living and the differential between wages at GM and GE.[59] The United Steelworkers (USWA), moreover, stuck to the traditional approach in December 1950 when it negotiated a one-year contract that raised wages without any provision for future adjustment. USWA president Philip Murray remained skeptical of the COLA, and he also hoped that he could create his own pattern to prove he was the true leader of the CIO, not Reuther.[60]

The business community pushed back vigorously against Engine Charlie's plan. Wage stabilization during World War II had encouraged the spread of fringe benefits, which persisted well after the end of that conflict, and few wished for a repeat based on the Treaty of Detroit. Hiram Hall, one of the management representatives on the Wage Stabilization Board (WSB) tasked with formulating wage-control policy, acknowledged at an American Management Association panel the concern of the WSB that even tacit approval for the AIF would create a postwar pattern "whether or not the company can afford it, whether or not it is physically possible, whether or not it is even desirable from the standpoint of the union."[61] The National Association of Manufacturers (NAM) similarly argued against allowing the WSB to implement this sweeping change to labor relations. Among the NAM representatives sent to the WSB in early 1951 was Boulware, who made a presentation in which he rejected COLA clauses as self-defeating. When the WSB labor member Emil Rieve of the Textile Workers Union inquired if Boulware's attack on the COLA implied that wage increases should be granted on the basis of higher productivity, Boulware replied in the negative. Once all wages had caught up to the inflation that had occurred before the imposition of controls, Boulware stated, "we ought to say that no more new influences come in that community of a national movement type."[62]

The WSB walked a thin line between establishing a postwar pattern and disrupting industrial-labor relations in the auto industry. Initially, the WSB sided with opponents of the formula by permitting workers only a 10% "catch-up" in wages over the level of January 1950, similar to the Little Steel standard used during World War II. Once this cap was reached, no further compensation could be paid, even if the contract specified additional deferred payments. Far from being a workable compromise, this decision incensed the labor members into staging a total walkout from the mobilization program until their demands were met.[63] With the UAW threatening a strike if the March 1951 COLA payment failed to be paid on schedule, the government issued a clarifying directive that permitted existing COLA and AIF provisions to operate through the end of June 1951. On March 8, 1951, the WSB permitted existing escalator clauses to continue to operate beyond the 10% limit. Recognizing that this exception granted preferential treatment to the UAW, the WSB later revised this rule to allow contracts without a preexisting COLA to still pay a semiannual cost-of-living adjustment above the 10% with WSB approval. Subsequent rulings also held that fringe benefits would not count against the 10% cap, enough to induce labor to rejoin the WSB.[64]

The result of the WSB's policies was to permit companies to match the costs of the GM formula without mandating the adoption of a productivity-based AIF. By the time that the reconstituted WSB began work on a productivity rule, Congress had deprived it of the ability to issue further regulations. Wage stabilization instead developed along the grounds that Professor Herbert Northrup of the Wharton School of Business aptly described as "leapfrogging," in which "special cases" repeatedly shattered the ceiling set by the general wage regulations and so permitted the spread of the wage pattern. Leapfrogging avoided setting an institutional precedent for the postwar period even as compensation packages could end up costing firms more than the AIF would have by itself.[65]

Although corporate managers were angered that they still had to follow GM in practice, they largely welcomed the fact that the WSB spread this pattern on grounds other than productivity. The National Industrial Conference Board, the nation's preeminent provider of business economics research, noted in 1951 that it had received reports of many different approaches to granting wage requests, but apart from GM, companies professed that their interest was in following the pattern and not tracking productivity.[66] This distinction was on full display when the WSB permitted GE to make payments matching GM on the grounds of interplant inequities and a traditional tandem relationship. Boulware reminded the unions at GE that any similarity between this payment and that being paid by GM was purely coincidental and did not constitute an AIF. Behind the scenes, Boulware thanked Hall and the other industry members of the WSB for having avoided committing the country to productivity-based wages and their support against the "foolish misrepresentation" that any payment of 2.5% was an AIF.[67]

Leapfrogging wages unbalanced by a productivity standard nevertheless generated cost pressures at a time when prices fell under wartime controls, and in the steel industry, these tensions erupted into one of the greatest constitutional crises in U.S. history. When the USWA's existing, prewar contract expired, the union demanded a straight increase of 15¢/hour as a cost-of-living adjustment plus an additional deferred payment equal to 4% of wages for two years. The USWA did not describe this payment as an AIF, but it did argue that the recent increase in the industry's productivity growth meant that this payment could be absorbed into the present price structure. The industry, however, was in no mood to absorb these costs, for, as Benjamin Fairless, the president and chairman of U.S. Steel, explained, post-tax earnings had fallen 17% since 1950, and paying these wages would further "rob Peter to pay Phil [Murray]."[68]

Before Murray could call out his men on strike, Truman certified this dispute to the WSB. There, the public members attempted in vain to secure Fairless's agreement to a one-year, 13¢/hour settlement, but the U.S. Steel leader believed he had more to win from the government by having his arm twisted. Afraid of a three-way split on the tripartite board, the public members sided with the labor representatives to grant the USWA a wage package that matched the GM pattern in all but name: an eighteen-month contract lasting to June 30, 1953, with a 12.5¢/hour raise followed by two 2.5¢/hour increases every six months. The board also recommended increased fringe benefits and, in a ruling that especially angered the steel industry, the adoption of a form of the union shop. Overall, the settlement was estimated to cost about 26¢/hour.[69]

This amount far exceeded what the WSB's standard rules would have allowed, but the hand of the GM pattern was clear. In a memo in which USWA counsel Arthur Goldberg evaluated this ruling, WSB chairman Nathan Feinsinger was quoted as noting that "the Steelworkers are 'catching up' to patterns already established, rather than blazing a new trail." Feinsinger was also noted as suggesting that this settlement took into account "the cost of living, productivity, the maintenance of a balanced wage structure, comparative wage movements in other industries, and the recommendation that there be no further wage reopening in 1952."[70] Harold Enarson, a veteran of World War II wage stabilization who served as a White House special assistant during the Korean War, likewise recognized the unmistakable contours of the GM pattern in his evaluation of the WSB award: "The magic of the GM contract is so great that it was recommended even though the union didn't ask for it and didn't apparently know what was good for it."[71]

For the steel industry, the WSB's ruling at the least carried a silver lining in that it did not explicitly endorse GM's AIF. According to minutes of a meeting held between Fairless and Murray under White House auspices in early May 1952, Fairless opposed the two proposed 2.5¢/hour step-ups on the grounds that "the industry felt that this represented a recognition of an [annual] improvement factor of 5 cents per year." On this principle, the USWA president was more than happy to agree: "The Union did not regard this step up as an improvement factor since it had not asked the Board for one as such but that rather the Union looked upon it as a deferred wage increase." Asked by Murray if he could think of an alternative to the step-up that would give the union the same money package, Fairless had suggested a one-year contract of 15¢/hour, eliminating the second deferred payment entirely.[72]

Regardless of the semantics of the step-up, the overall costs of the award once more had set wage and price controls at cross-purposes in the steel industry. Conscious of the dislocations that had accompanied the OPA, the government had taken steps to allow for a limited degree of cost pass-through as part of its Korean War price controls. On April 25, 1951, the Office of Price Stabilization (OPS) issued CPR 22, the Manufacturers' General Ceiling Price Regulation. CPR 22 required manufacturers to select a base price from before the period when inflation had begun to drive cost-price relations awry, any calendar quarter between September 30, 1949, and June 24, 1950, and then add increases in wage and fringe benefits made up to

March 15, 1951, and in material costs up to December 31, 1950.[73] Congress soon after permitted manufacturers to adjust their ceiling prices to reflect all costs, including materials, labor, and overhead, incurred up to July 26, 1951. The complexities of this calculation and the possibility that expanded volumes could actually necessitate price reductions resulted in few companies availing themselves of this "Capehart Adjustment," with one notable exception: by March 1952, the auto industry had claimed $279 million of the $800 million total in adjustments granted under this rule.[74]

Under standard OPS rules, none of the steel industry's most recent labor-costs changes could be considered for price adjustment. Still, in a repeat of 1946, the steel industry refused to make its new compensation payments until its price ceilings increased by $12/ton, of which half represented its new labor costs and the remainder other charges incurred since the start of the control period. The OPS considered the industry's requested adjustment to be much too high, reasoning that, on a pretax position, the industry could absorb $13.60/ton in costs and still have a greater return than in 1947–1949. OPS director Ellis Arnall also noted that if "steel is required to absorb nothing, steel users cannot fairly be required to absorb higher steel prices."[75] Despite several clandestine offers of a price adjustment of a smaller degree, the industry held firm, while the USWA indicated it would not continue working without its wage adjustment. On the day before the announced start of the strike, April 9, 1952, President Truman attempted to preempt this crisis by ordering the federal government to seize the nation's steel mills. The Department of Commerce designated the existing management of the mills as its operating agents and requested the delay of the strike, but the companies challenged the ability of the White House to order the wage increase in court. Two months later, on June 2, 1952, the Supreme Court ruled in a 6–3 decision that Truman had overstepped his authority in seizing private property. With the mills returned to owners no more willing to grant higher wages than before, the USWA went out on strike, creating the crisis that Fairless had sought. Eventually, just as had occurred in 1946, the White House ordered the OPS to grant the steel industry an increase of 4.7%, or $5.20/ton.[76]

Unlike in the aftermath of World War II, the stringent fiscal and monetary policies adopted earlier in the war ensured that this denting of controls did not translate into the resumption of the wage-price spiral. A decontrol committee appointed in February 1952 had already recommended suspending controls on products for which prices remained stubbornly under ceilings, which by the end of Arnall's tenure included such consumer goods as wool yarn, televisions, and leather.[77] The election of Dwight Eisenhower foreclosed the possibility of extending controls further into peacetime, but Eisenhower still prioritized combating inflation through other means, going so far as to request an extension of the wartime excess-profits tax through the end of 1953 to reduce a forecasted deficit. The Federal Reserve also continued to hold to its restrictive course. After the inauguration, the OPS safely decontrolled the rest of the economy in seven waves, ending with steel on March 17, 1953.[78]

THE AGE OF ESCALATION

Following the end of the Korean War and its controls, business and labor continued to move in the direction set by the WSB in favor of multiyear contracts, a development that the University of California, Berkeley, labor-relations professor Joseph Garbarino deemed the "Age of Escalation."[79] According to the labor-relations advisory firm the Bureau of National Affairs (BNA), between 1950 and 1952, the frequency of one-year contracts in manufacturing fell from 45% to 29%. Two-year contracts, which had constituted half of all manufacturing contracts in 1950, fell in popularity to 41% as contracts of over two years in length grew from 5% to 30% of all manufacturing contracts; the trend to longer durations was present but less pronounced in the nonmanufacturing sector as well. The BNA noted in its analysis that the 1950 GM-UAW contract could be held responsible for inspiring the multiyear trend, especially as 87% of contracts in the transportation-equipment industry were of three years or more in length by 1952. This lengthening continued after the war, such that by 1960, 43% of all contracts lasted eighteen to twenty-four months and 39% lasted thirty to thirty-six months.[80]

As part of this trend to long-run labor peace, COLA clauses and deferred payments became an increasingly common component of the post-Korea industrial landscape. According to the BLS, only 800,000 manufacturing workers possessed an escalation clause in September 1950, compared to 3 million covered by September 1951 and 3.5 million by January 1, 1952, roughly equivalent to half of all workers in major contracts of 1,000 or more workers. Once the wartime inflation of about 6% a year in 1950–1951 turned into price stability in 1952–1953 and a 0.5% deflation in 1954, unions temporarily abandoned COLA clauses fearing a deescalation of wages. At the start of 1955, 1.7 million manufacturing workers, or 23% of those in major contracts, still possessed a COLA. When inflation again began to creep upward, the COLA clause became more common, and by the late 1950s, fully half of workers in major contracts were again covered (see table 1). Deferred payment clauses also expanded as a necessary component of a long-term contract. Beginning in 1955, contractually stipulated deferred wage increases began to replace wage reopening clauses. The Bureau of Labor Statistics noted that about 5 million workers would benefit from a deferred increase in 1957, including 3 million who had signed contracts in 1956 and another 2 million in years before that.[81]

Yet these deferred payments did not adhere to the anti-inflationary productivity logic embedded in the form of GM's AIF. In fact, only a handful of labor-relations departments actually made use of productivity statistics during the 1955–1956 bargaining round that had signaled the start of the Age of Escalation. According to a National Industrial Conference Board survey of 213 firms and 39 unions with 8 million members, three-quarters of unions with 7.3 million members utilized productivity statistics during bargaining as compared to only a quarter of firms. The report noted that unions emphasized labor productivity to call attention to the distribution of income necessary to expand the economy to full employment, with some unions still referring to the 1920s and underconsumption to justify higher wages. In contrast, when management cited productivity statistics, it did so primarily to stress that capital and not labor was responsible for generating most of the gains of productivity. The survey found that larger firms were actually less likely to use productivity than smaller firms were, and comments made in response to this inquiry suggested that the firms that prepared productivity data did so defensively in order to refute union claims rather than proactively as part of a wage-price policy. Some respondents did cite the influence of the GM formula and its emphasis on national trends, but others in the sample indicated that they resisted the use of national data, leading the authors of this study to conclude that productivity remained a slogan more than a real issue.[82]

The spread of fringe benefits not counted as part of deferred compensation further ensured that labor compensation would exceed the long-run productivity average embodied by the auto industry's AIF. Despite being a phrase only coined in 1943, fringe benefits expanded rapidly following the end of World War II, such that by 1954, eleven million workers outside the public sector and railroads possessed at least one common form of benefit, including health insurance or a pension plan. During the 1950s, fringe benefits grew at a faster rate than did wage compensation alone, expanding as a share of total compensation for the entire workforce from 5% in 1950 to 7.8% in 1960.[83] The U.S. Chamber of Commerce's survey of this "hidden payroll" at 1,020 companies in 1957 suggested an even larger increase, partially because it oversampled large firms but also because it used a broader definition of fringe benefits that included such benefits as paid rest periods, payments for time not worked, and profit-sharing plans. The Chamber found that fringes in 1957 had reached 21.8% of payroll costs for the overall economy. For the 102 companies that had been included in the Chamber's biennial survey since 1947, fringes had grown from 15% to 23.7% of payrolls.[84]

To union spokespeople as well as many labor-relations academics, fringe benefits appeared less inflationary than did other forms of compensation. Fringes such as pensions would not be converted into consumption for decades, health-care benefits could be spent only on a narrow range of services, and supplementary unemployment benefits replaced some of the purchasing power lost to layoffs when demand would otherwise contract.[85] A second line of reasoning developed by the Fact Finding Board appointed by President Truman to oversee steel-industry negotiations in 1949 described fringe benefits as a depreciation allowance for the "human machine." Even as the Fact Finding Board rejected union demands to raise wages on the basis of the industry's own productivity and accepted the industry's argument that wages must track the productivity of the nation as a whole, the board ruled that the steel industry bore a social responsibility to supply these benefits beyond any productivity-determined ceiling.[86]

The companies that granted higher fringe benefits nevertheless bore these costs up front even if workers would not receive their full compensation for decades, a realization made clear in Ford Motors' internal preparation for negotiations in 1955. According to this analysis, 14.1% of Ford's hourly labor costs accrued from fringe benefits. Fringe benefits at Ford granted since 1947 totaled 17.2¢/hour. Combined with increases in skill premiums adding to 3.9¢/hour, nonwage compensation had increased at a rate equivalent to 1.7% of the base wage rate per year. As Ford's analysis thus noted, "If we add the 1.7% per year for fringes and skilled workers to the recent 2-1/2% improvement factor, we have actually been granting improvements to our employees at the rate of 4.2% per year [exclusive of the COLA]." The report recommended that "if the GM formula is accepted as a basis for negotiations in 1955, the positions be established that fringe benefits and all other wage increases must be included in base rates when considering the percentage increase in real earnings of workers from year to year." But instead of counting all fringe benefits against the AIF in that year's negotiations, Ford agreed to provide additional fringe benefits in the form of "Supplementary Unemployment Benefits." Ford apparently feared that a strike would not only cause it to lose market share but also jeopardize the Ford Foundation's plan to raise funds by selling its majority stake in Ford to the public, and so it chose to ignore its own advice to reduce the premium for labor peace.[87]

Facing expectations of strong sales and future growth, most firms in the mid-1950s reasoned similarly to Ford that they should pay for improved labor relations while turning a blind eye to the inflationary consequences of their actions. In 1955, the head office at General Electric foresaw ten years of uninterrupted growth and directed Boulware's labor-relations staff to do as GM had and secure five years of labor peace. Boulware warned that a contract of this length would come at a heavy price. International Union of Electrical Workers (IUE) president James Carey had already threatened to strike as soon as he could, and Boulware feared that GE faced a choice between investing in a strike to stick to what was economically valid or giving in to Carey's demands to avoid a showdown. In return for five years of labor peace, GE offered deferred payments starting at 3% year and later rising to 3.5%, a quarterly COLA, and new fringe benefits. As Boulware would later reflect, this increase was clearly in excess of the national productivity growth trend and hence inflationary, but like the company's grudging concession to the GM pattern in 1948, GE made this offer "in fairness to [its] employees" and in recognition of the "fashion of inflation which was being spread more or less irregularly across the economy."[88]

The attempt on the part of the steel industry to implement a noninflationary wage-price policy in 1956 served as the exception that proved this rule that companies prioritized labor peace over wage-price policy during the Age of Escalation. After having completed three contract negotiations in the course of four years, the latter two raising annual compensation by at least 8% a year and the 1955 payment coming after a costly one-day shut-down, the steel industry had decided that it would prefer to place relations on a longer-run basis, preferably a five-year deal as in the electrical industry (see table 2). Yet despite being among the final industries to negotiate during the 1955–1956 bargaining round, the steel industry believed that it could take part in the movement toward long-run labor stability while bucking the concurrent trend of expensive settlements.[89] The three leading firms in the industry, U.S. Steel, Bethlehem, and Republic, agreed to cooperate by establishing a Coordinating Committee, ensuring that each made the same offer to the union. This way, the union could not "whipsaw" or single out a single firm for a strike in order to pressure it into agreeing to a settlement the union would then demand from the rest of the industry. While new to the steel industry, multiemployer bargaining was a long-recognized institution in atomized industries with high labor mobility, such as apparel, laundries, and construction. Considered a constructive practice exempt from antitrust law, multiemployer bargaining had survived an attempted prohibition during the debates surrounding Taft-Hartley on the grounds that it enabled employers to match the strength of their organized employees.[90]

With the steel industry looking forward to its first multiyear contract agreed on without federal intervention, U.S. Steel's Executive Policy Committee directed Executive Vice President for Administrative Planning R. Conrad Cooper to devise an acceptable productivity index for use in bargaining. Cooper had explored productivity statistics since at least the 1949 bargaining round. Cooper feared that output per man-hour statistics failed to account for the capital investment and tools that management provided to workers, but he had continued to rely on that conventional measure in order to refute the USWA's claim that the industry's own productivity had increased such that it could afford much-higher wages.[91] Seven years later, Cooper renewed his attempts to calculate a measure of productivity that incorporated all inputs, but he and his staff encountered insurmountable difficulties in measuring capital inputs. Cooper optimistically reported that he would have this metric finalized within the year, but the earliest evidence of a total-factor productivity (TFP) index at U.S. Steel does not appear in the archival records until 1967.[92]

Although unsuccessful in calculating TFP, Cooper drew on wage-price theory to advocate for the importance of productivity in bargaining negotiations. Cooper contrasted the annual growth in output per man-hour in the steel industry, 2.8%, with an annual rise in employment cost per man-hour since 1940 of 7.6%–8%, equivalent to 3%–3.5% in real terms. Cooper's best guess for the industry's annual TFP trend was about 2%. As a result, Cooper argued that "labor realized a real gain in excess of the increased product per man-hour, leaving no benefit for the shareholder and less than no benefit for the consumers," who faced higher prices as a result of passing on nominal unit labor costs. Cooper concluded that the industry's long-term objective in bargaining negotiations should be to close that gap between labor compensation and productivity. For the 1956 negotiations, the industry thus established a goal "to cut the 8% in half on the basis of five years of labor peace."[93]

The problem with the steel industry's approach was that the steel negotiations occurred at the end of the 1955–1956 bargaining round, and new United Steelworkers president David McDonald was intent on ensuring that his workers did as well as or better than Reuther's. Like his deceased predecessor Philip Murray, McDonald hoped to set a pattern for the newly combined AFL-CIO that would show the USWA to be the dominant force in the industrial labor market. The union interpreted the industry's argument for a five-year contract with a slower rate of compensation growth from previous contracts as evidence that "the Industry seeks to provide its workers with an even smaller portion of their share of increased output per man-hour." While the USWA did accept that real wages could only increase at the rate of productivity growth in the long run, it also argued that compensation had to increase by more than this amount when necessary to change the distribution of income, and it warned that "there is no such equitable sharing [of income] in the steel industry today." The USWA's statistics further suggested that real straight-time earnings had lagged productivity growth in the steel industry since 1939. While this calculation apparently did not include fringe benefits, the USWA elsewhere argued that because fringe benefits had not been liberalized in the steel industry since 1952, steelworkers were entitled to have their fringes increased so as to match those since received by other workers.[94]

After the previous rounds of bargaining, the leaders of the USWA were surprised at the industry's newfound insistence on holding compensation to a productivity trend. The industry argued that industrial-labor relations had matured to the point that five years of labor peace were feasible. McDonald countered by expressing the puzzlement of the union negotiators at "why the industry suddenly, and without provocation, demands an end to [their] hitherto peaceful and constructive relationship of the past several years," based on annual contracts.[95] The industry permitted a strike to occur, but it lost its resolve after twenty-seven days and an uncharacteristic threat from President Eisenhower to appoint a fact-finding board if the strike could not be resolved quickly. The final settlement ran for three years but was estimated to cost the industry 6% a year before factoring in a COLA, essentially continuing the nominal pattern of 8% settlements.[96]

Overall, the companies that took part in the Age of Escalation paid for the labor peace that would allow them to take advantage of the strong markets of the 1950s. Real compensation in the nonfarm business sector rose by 10% from the end of 1954 through the end of 1957, the first three-year contract period of the Age of Escalation. That was the statistic of most relevance to labor, as it reflected gains in real purchasing power, but the theory of cost-push inflation required a comparison between nominal prices, compensation, and unit labor costs. Whereas adherence to a noninflationary wage-price policy was supposed to stabilize unit labor costs and prices, unit labor costs grew by almost 12% in this period, as total labor compensation per hour increased by 16%.[97] Contemporary economists soon noted how the prices of capital goods were leading an inflation of about 3% as measured by the entire GNP deflator. Durable-goods producers seemingly possessed little concern about holding labor compensation to the productivity average when they could instead pass on their premium for labor peace to customers in the form of higher prices.[98]

CONCLUSION

In the aftermath of World War II, business leaders had attempted to position themselves as guardians of the public interest against the inflation believed to result from wage administration. Companies such as General Electric argued that the solution to the wage-price spiral was to ensure that productivity growth would not be absorbed entirely by workers but shared more broadly in the form of lower prices and adequate returns on investment. Taking advantage of the more permissive labor-law climate enacted by the Taft-Hartley Act, they attempted to convince their employees and the public to trust management's judgment. This unilateral approach faltered as General Motors conceived of a less confrontational approach to wage-price policy. By raising real wages in line with national productivity growth,

Engine Charlie Wilson believed that the private sector could safeguard the public interest in price stability while convincing labor that it could trust management to ensure a fair deal for all.

By the mid-1950s, GM's strategy of deferred payments and COLA clauses had taken hold across much of the industrial economy, but not for the reasons that Wilson had enunciated. During the Korean War, the Wage Stabilization Board had encouraged firms to match the costs of the GM pattern while distancing these payments from the rationale of productivity growth. Then, as employers envied GM's ability to secure labor peace amid the strong markets of the mid-1950s, they proved willing to pay substantial premiums above the productivity average to shield production from strikes. In particular, the spread of fringe benefits allowed labor to share in corporate earnings while claiming that hourly wages remained within the noninflationary bounds of productivity. GM paid an increasingly steep premium for its labor peace, but at least that firm was productive enough to afford these higher payments. For many others, the costs of the GM formula resulted in higher unit labor costs that would eat into profits unless passed on to the consumer. As Justice Black had warned in *Allen Bradley*, unions acting independently in their own self-interest had obtained higher compensation, while industries acting in their own self-interest had likewise raised prices. The Taft-Hartley Act had preserved the New Deal's vision of big business and big labor contending over the distribution of income, and thanks to management's quest for labor peace, parallel conduct had seemingly pushed the distribution of income even farther from the ideals of competition.

CHAPTER THREE

Corporate Pricing and the Public Interest

LOOKING BACKWARD, it is difficult to appreciate the deep puzzlement that surrounded the mild "creeping inflation" of the mid-1950s. Modern economic theory recognizes that unemployment was far below the rate at which inflation would begin to accelerate, and monetary policy had restored price stability by the decade's end.[1] At the time, however, it did not escape the notice of contemporaries that the unionized oligopoly industries in which labor compensation had risen the fastest during the mid-1950s also tended to have prices advancing ahead of the national average. By corporate America's own admission, industrial price policies reflected not just unit labor costs but also the profit targets determined by management. As those industries raised their prices even as demand and sales tapered off into recession, the Keynesian warnings that the Employment Act would beget cost-push inflation had never seemed more prescient.[2]

These conditions inspired a renewed search for a means through which public policy could compel concentrations of economic power to act responsibly in society's best interest. Antitrust law could block mergers that lessened competition and prevent firms from fixing prices through explicit collusion, but neither of these approaches readily applied to existing oligopolies. Firms might not need to rely on formal collusion to maintain higher prices when, with so few sellers in their markets, they could each arrive at that outcome simply by recognizing how one's actions impacted the rest.

This conscious parallelism had already come under scrutiny in *Interstate Circuit* (1939), and after World War II, several landmark cases suggested that evidence of price leadership or the persistence of market shares might suffice to prove the existence of an illegal conspiracy to monopolize. Rather than draw on these precedents to combat creeping inflation, however, the antitrust authorities ultimately demanded some additional proof that could differentiate self-rational actions from illegal collusion.

With existing antitrust law struggling to treat the problem of price administration, policymakers identified a more practical solution in the form of price regulation. During the late 1950s, congressional Democrats and many Keynesian economists advocated for some new authority that would directly subjugate corporate pricing to the public oversight of an incomes policy. The Eisenhower administration agreed that private market power lay behind creeping inflation, but it envisioned a more indirect model of regulation that relied on the government's existing fiscal and monetary levers. By exercising its own responsibility to combat inflation, the government would engineer a macroeconomic climate in which private actors deemed restraint to be in their self-interest. As recession led to higher unemployment, however, this apparent retreat from the Employment Act only intensified controversy about how to shield society from the irresponsible actions of the powerful few.[3]

THE MAKING OF INDUSTRIAL PRICES

When Gardiner Means updated his statistics on administered prices for the 1950s, the macroeconomic conditions of the postwar Golden Age could not have been more different from the context of his original study during the Great Depression. Means had originally defined administered prices by their rigidity in the face of declining demand, but he now discovered that administered prices had become quite flexible, at least in the upward direction. In the two years ending in June 1957, administered prices, which Means defined as those that had changed fewer than eight times in the past eight years, had risen by 10.2%, compared to only 1.4% for prices that had changed more than seventy-seven times in the previous eight years.[4]

This increase in prices should not have come as such a surprise given the strong demand for capital goods during the 1950s and the tight industrial labor markets that had encouraged industrial unions to raise their own wage demands.[5] Still, several unusual features of this inflation raised doubts in the minds of many contemporary economists about the explanatory power of supply and demand alone. As the economist Charles Schultze noted in an influential report written for the congressional Joint Economic Committee (JEC) in 1959, prices had risen faster than did output in 1955–1957, at 3.5% a year compared to 1.5%, which was contrary to expectations of recovery from the post–Korean War recession. Labor productivity had grown slowly despite heavy investment, while prices had risen fastest where output increased the most. Although prices had outpaced unit wage costs, profit margins had declined for manufacturers as a whole even as they increased for capital-goods producers.[6]

To Schultze and many of his contemporaries, these trends suggested that at least some of the inflation of the 1950s resulted from cost-push pressures in the industrial sector. According to the theory of the "demand shift," the capital-goods boom had bid up prices and wages in expanding industries, which would normally be offset by falling wages and prices where demand declined. Instead, those firms attempted to protect their margins in the face of increased overhead costs while their unions shielded their members from losses, preventing prices and wages from declining. In particular, firms making heavy investments had attempted to recapture these outlays through increased margins. When higher prices lessened demand and output while raising unit costs, firms responded with a self-defeating spiral of additional price rises. It also was not inconceivable that oligopoly industries simply preferred to share their supracompetitive profits with labor than to compete on the basis of lower costs and prices.[7]

No industry exemplified midcentury concern about the inflationary dangers of price administration more than did steel. From 1947 to 1953, the price of finished steel had risen by 54%, compared to about 20% for all industrial commodities. Although not an insignificant difference, this spread had widened substantially following the end of the Korean War. By 1958, the price of steel had risen a cumulative 107%, compared to a rise of 33% in all industrial commodities.[8] Grilled by Congress on these trends in 1957, Roger Blough, the chairman and CEO of U.S. Steel, pleaded that the industry's behavior was not proactive but reactive: "Rising prices do not cause inflation; they are the result of inflation."[9] Blough and his fellow executives argued that steel pricing could be understood entirely as the result of rising costs, namely, those of labor. Referring specifically to the industry's 4% price increase in 1956, Robert Tyson, the chair of U.S. Steel's Finance Committee, noted that employment represented the company's largest cost, equal to 39.7% of sales in 1956 exclusive of the labor built into the costs of the company's materials. U.S. Steel had agreed to a contract with the United Steelworkers that year that increased wages by about 6% a year, compared to the industry's own productivity growth trend of about 2%. Had the company not raised prices to close this gap, Tyson claimed that U.S. Steel would have lost $330 million in revenues, which would have reduced the after-tax funds available for reinvestment and dividends from 8.2% of sales to 4.9%, a difference of $158 million. At this pace, Tyson concluded, it would have taken only a little over a year to eliminate profits entirely, starving workers of their pay, suppliers of their reimbursement, and the government of tax revenue and ultimately costing the public even more in prices to resume production.[10]

Labor costs had indeed outpaced the steel industry's productivity trend since the 1940s. According to Bureau of Labor Statistics figures, total compensation per man-hour had risen by 118% between 1947 and 1958. Output per man-hour tended to fluctuate year to year, but it had risen by no more than a quarter over this period, with the result that steel's unit labor costs had increased by anywhere from 70% to 100%.[11] Up through the end of the Korean War, steel prices had risen at about the same pace as unit labor costs, indicating that management was exercising its pricing power to preserve the distribution of corporate income. Beginning around 1954, however, the price of steel had started to grow faster than did unit labor costs, suggesting that the industry had chosen to use its pricing policy to expand its profit margins. Between 1940 and June 1959, steel prices rose 178%, whereas unit labor costs for wage employees had risen only 131% and for all employees by 153%.[12]

The steel industry, to its credit, was forthright in admitting that it had sought to increase profits over this period. Forecasting expanded demand in the future, the industry's executives recognized that they would have to invest in additional capacity while modernizing their existing plant. Yet as the industry's spokespeople emphasized at every opportunity, obtaining the funds to support that program would be a challenge.[13] The government had provided an accelerated depreciation schedule to encourage investment during the Korean War, but depreciation charges based on the original costs of equipment failed to account for the effects of inflation on replacement prices. In 1956, Benjamin Fairless, who had retired as CEO and chairman of U.S. Steel to become president of the American Iron and Steel Institute, estimated that depreciation allowances would have to equal 2.15 times the original investment cost simply to maintain existing plant without dipping further into cash flows.[14] The industry had run a surplus of cash flow over capital expenditures in the decade after the end of World War II, but as it expanded its capital spending in the mid-1950s, it accumulated a cumulative deficit of over $200 million from 1946 to 1958. Over that span of a dozen years, the industry had also paid out $4.4 billion in dividends, compared to $4.8 billion in retained earnings, but Tyson defended these payments to shareholders as necessary to entice investors, given that steel's return on net assets tended to rest below the average for all manufacturing.[15]

Management's ability to raise prices annually, at discrete and announced times, and in order to widen profit margins further suggested that the industry had not relied entirely on conventional market forces in enhancing its economic fortunes. In what amounted to an annual ritual, individual steel companies made public statements about the need for higher prices to cover costs and investment. A few might test the water with price increases, but once U.S. Steel published its price list, the rest of the industry would fall into line. The higher that prices rose, of course, the more likely would steel users be to seek out substitute products or imports. U.S. Steel did not know where the loss of sales revenue outweighed the gain from higher prices, but by making annual price adjustments, the company could gradually probe for this level.[16] In 1954, return on equity in the steel industry was 12.4%, which placed it in the bottom quartile of manufacturing industries as ranked by the First National City Bank of New York. In 1955, after it had expanded its margins, it achieved an absolute return of 15%. While this value then slipped over the next several years, in relative terms the industry remained in the top 40% of manufacturing industries.[17]

When Blough declared before Congress, "my concept [of competition] is that a price that matches another price is a competitive price," he probably did not mean to acknowledge the oligopoly nature of the steel industry. After all, in a perfectly competitive market, all firms would also obey a single price at which they chose how much output to produce. Still, common sense would dictate that the process of competition entailed firms jockeying to undercut each other's prices, and Blough's thinking seemed to foreclose this possibility.[18] Arthur Homer, the president of Bethlehem Steel, second only to U.S. Steel in overall size, was more forthright in acknowledging to the Senate the realities of price leadership in the industry. Like Blough, Homer described a competitive price as one equal to that of competitors, but he explained this definition through a classic application of oligopoly. According to Homer, industry executives viewed the demand for steel as being very insensitive to price, with the result that lower prices would not call forth greater demand. If one company were to drop its price, it would only expand its share of the market at the expense of other firms, and when those companies responded by matching the lower price, profits would fall for everyone. It was better to achieve greater efficiencies and so widen the gap between a firm's own costs and the industry's prices than to allow such a price war to lower return on investment for the industry as a whole.[19]

A textbook model of perfect competition the steel industry was not, especially in the minds of its own executives. But then again, neither were most of the industries that dominated the midcentury U.S. economy and that led the price parade of the mid-1950s. And perhaps surprisingly, it did not take a public grilling before Congress for management to admit it. In the middle of the 1950s, a team of economists from the Brookings Institution investigated corporate pricing behavior through an approach so crazy that it just might work: ask those who were responsible for setting prices how they did so. Alcoa, General Motors, and U.S. Steel were just three of the twenty blue-chip firms to agree to take part in this investigation. With the exception of A&P, Kroger, and Sears Roebuck, all of the companies were manufacturers or processors.[20]

Most of the interviewed managers signaled a belief in their power to adjust prices in pursuit of corporate goals. By far, the most common objective that they described for price policy was, as in the steel industry, to achieve a target return on investment. The average target return of the twenty surveyed firms was about 14% after tax, but there was a wide degree of variation. U.S. Steel targeted an after-tax return of 8% on invested capital, whereas General Electric and General Motors both sought 20% returns after tax.[21] Firms that adopted this target tended to calculate their prices in accordance with the standard-volume methods pioneered at DuPont and General Motors in the 1920s. In this approach, as noted in chapter 2, a company calculated its costs on the assumption of some standard volume of output and then added a margin. No matter the short-run conditions of demand, the standard-volume method kept prices rigidly focused on the long-run objective. The GM executives interviewed by the Brookings team in fact referred the Brookings team to an article written by its former treasurer and current board member Donaldson Brown in 1924 as an accurate model of the company's pricing strategy three decades later.[22]

Many of the managers in the Brookings survey moreover explicitly described price stability as a service provided by their firm to its customers. By making changes to prices only as direct costs such as wages rose, and by doing so at well-publicized times, the entire industry could move prices in lockstep while minimizing the number of price revisions to which customers would have to adapt. Price stability also meant prices would remain relatively low in times of expanding demand and relatively high in times of falling demand, contrary to the textbook economic assumption that firms are profit maximizers. One contemporary explanation for the apparent willingness of management to leave profits on the table harked back to Berle and Means. As long as returns sufficed to keep stockholders placated, management could operate without serious challenges to its autonomy while obtaining the resources needed to secure the future viability of the operation. It was also not implausible that management selected profit targets below the profit-maximizing level in order to burnish their public image and avoid scrutiny over potentially anticompetitive oligopoly practices.[23]

The sophistication and precision of these price calculations varied greatly. At GM, model changeovers dictated an extremely detailed approach to pricing that began thirty months before the new car was introduced. First, the company forecasted what consumers would want in a car using the current models as a base for costs. Once the new car was designed and the new jigs had been ordered, the policy group at the top level of management would draw on the data supplied by its divisions to calculate the standard unit cost of the car at 80% capacity and then add a profit margin based on its target returns.[24] In the case of U.S. Steel, where products did not change so frequently, the company could afford to take more shortcuts. In 1956, the company's executive management had instructed its Price Division to recommend a new price schedule. After computing standard costs on the assumption of 80% capacity usage, U.S. Steel then adjusted this value to account for changes in capital and labor costs on the basis of the rule of thumb that each cent in hourly labor costs would add another cent in all other costs as well. The Price Division provided figures on profits as a percentage of sales for different products in its recommendations, but the Brookings study noted that the company's top executives focused on returns on investment when selecting the price.[25] The other steelmaker in the Brookings study, National Steel, relied on even simpler calculations. As National traditionally followed the prices chosen by U.S. Steel, there was no need for it to develop a target independent of the price leader's.[26]

Closer inspection of the empirical data on industrial prices, however, suggested that management may not have always acted quite as autonomously as it believed. That profit targets fluctuated so widely across industries indicated that managers did consider the distinct market conditions that they faced when selecting this objective. In the period studied by Brookings, 1947–1955, moreover, average posttax rates of return on investment had exceeded the specified targets for nearly all of its investigated industries. Those who had fallen below their target had presumably attempted to achieve all that they could. Those who had exceeded the target had made no modifications to their pricing formula to fall in closer line with the publicly announced targets that, as U.S. Steel declared, were "just, fair, and economic."[27]

Even if an industry's posted prices followed the leader's, moreover, it was possible that individual firms secretly offered concessions or discounts off that price to attract more business. This price shading would permit companies to pursue the price that maximized profits for their own firm even as they claimed to adhere to the list prices calculated to target a return for the entire industry. The likelihood of such behavior would increase as executives at one firm had reason to believe that their competitors were already undermining the cartel-like lockstep of the industry through this approach, such as when a recession led to slackening sales across all sellers. When such discounts became known, every seller would have to match that price, bringing prices closer to the level expected in a competitive market.[28] By interviewing buyers of products and investigating government bids, economists of the midcentury discovered that the prices paid by companies did change more often and with wider amplitudes than suggested by the government statistics on list prices that Means and others had used to calculate price rigidity. Many of the commodities commonly assumed to be administered in the late 1950s and 1960s, including nonferrous metals, chemicals, fuel, electrical machinery, and rubber tires, exhibited transaction prices that rose in times of high demand and fell during slack. Yet even in these studies, one class of commodity stood out for having quoted prices that rarely if ever deviated from list prices: finished steel products. In periods of economic expansion, steel transaction prices had tended to decline alongside list prices, whereas they had actually increased during periods of contraction.[29]

ANTITRUST AND ADMINISTERED PRICES

Although some critics of the administered price thesis urged that these competitive indications should be generalized across the industrial economy, the overwhelming scholarly and political consensus of the mid-twentieth century viewed the pricing behavior of steel and key industrial commodities as a clear departure from the patterns expected in competitive markets. From 1957 to 1963, Senator Estes Kefauver, chairman of the Senate Subcommittee on Antitrust and Monopoly, conducted hearings into administered prices in which he forced executives from such leading industries as steel, automobiles, and electrical equipment, as well as more obscure targets including bread and asphalt, to explain their pricing policies publicly. Kefauver and his staff grilled management about how it established margins and corporate salaries, questioned whether price reductions would not allow industries to expand markets, and demanded cost justification for recent price increases.[30]

Kefauver's preferred solution to administered prices, as he had explained at the start of his hearings, was antitrust law: a method to subjugate private power to the market and "recreate the conditions under which prices would automatically be determined by competitive forces."[31] Senator Kefauver admitted that existing antitrust law, while the "approach most in keeping with our American traditions," might not be suitable to combat existing concentrations of economic power without additional legislation.[32] Still, he urged that the government not wait to press this assault. Kefauver's own legislative record supported his zeal. In 1950, he had cosponsored one of the most important modifications to antitrust law in the postwar period, the Celler-Kefauver Act. Previously, section 7 of the Clayton Antitrust Act had prohibited the substantial lessening of competition through stock acquisitions, but that language did not prohibit one firm from simply buying the assets of another. The Cellar-Kefauver Act closed this loophole, extending section 7 to all corporate mergers and ushering in a new era for antitrust vigilance that significantly discouraged horizontal mergers between firms operating within a single industry.[33]

As Kefauver was well aware during his hearings, this new authority had greatly aided the government in preventing greater concentration in those industries already suspected of price administration. In one of the most important antitrust suits brought by the Eisenhower administration, the government had challenged the proposed merger of Bethlehem Steel with Youngstown Sheet and Tube. These two companies justified their merger as the most efficient way to expand and modernize production in the growing Chicago market. Bethlehem possessed the experience and know-how to enter into the production of structural shape and plate, but it contended that constructing a new facility in Chicago would be uneconomical compared to the acquisition of Youngstown's existing plants. Youngstown meanwhile lacked the ability to produce those products without the support of its larger partner.[34]

In ruling against this merger, Judge Edward Weinfeld of the Southern District of New York concluded that these alleged benefits would come at the expense of steel consumers. A merged corporation would not only possess 20% of the industry's overall capacity and even higher amounts in certain product lines. It would also eliminate the possibility of Bethlehem entering into the Chicago market as a competitor. Judge Weinfeld notably indicated that the industry's pricing strategy also recommended against the merger. U.S. Steel was at present the industry's undisputed price leader, and Bethlehem and Youngstown were followers. An increase in concentration in the Big Two of the industry to over 50% of ingot capacity through this merger would only intensify this existing oligopoly situation, with the result that it would "make even more remote than at present the possibility of any real competition from the smaller members of the industry who follow the leadership of United States Steel." One goal of the Cellar-Kefauver Act had been to prevent the formation of oligopolies that avoided competing on prices, and although it was too late to prevent this effect entirely, Judge Weinfeld reasoned that Congress had clearly intended to prevent conditions from deteriorating further.[35]

The primary goal of Kefauver's administered price hearings, however, was not to discourage further concentration but to police the behavior of existing industrial concentrations. On this subject, Kefauver's hearings would help to uncover one of the most celebrated antitrust conspiracies of the mid-twentieth century. In 1959, newspapers began reporting on identical bids on equipment for the Tennessee Valley Authority. Kefauver launched hearings into the electrical-equipment industry's pricing in his home state, but he put his investigation on hold and turned over his findings after the Department of Justice impaneled a grand jury. Representatives of General Electric, Westinghouse, and other companies had met in hotels, dining rooms, and conventions to compare costs and price lists while arranging who would submit the lowest bids on government contracts. Sometimes the low bidder was chosen by drawing a name out of a hat, while other times the winner was assigned according to a cycle akin to the phases of the moon. The government ultimately fined twenty-nine companies nearly $2 million in total and secured criminal charges against fifty-two individual defendants. Because all of the defendants had pleaded nolo contendere or guilty, there was no public trial, and an incensed Kefauver reopened his hearings to expose these details to the public.[36]

Kefauver's investigation of the electrical price conspiracy exposed salacious wrongdoing in corporate America, but it did not fundamentally advance his overall objective of combating administered prices. Executives at GE and its fellow defendants had been caught red-handed coordinating with one another to fix prices. This explicit collusion was radically different from the administered pricing that Kefauver railed against in steel and automobiles. These were the industries that had generated such concerns about the threat of cost-push inflation in the wake of the Employment Act, as their oligopoly structure suggested that they could arrive at outcomes contrary to competitive expectations without the formal communication and agreement banned by the Sherman Act.[37]

Could antitrust law apply to the consciously parallel behavior of firms within an oligopoly? Kefauver was not alone in believing that the Sherman Act's prohibition on monopolizing provided a solution for oligopoly pricing patterns as well. One leading authority for this hope lay in *United States v. Aluminum Co. of America* (1945), better known as *Alcoa*. Thurman Arnold had originally brought this case in the late 1930s seeking to dissolve Alcoa on charges of monopolizing the market in virgin aluminum. Although Alcoa held over 90% of this market, the trial court had found Alcoa not guilty due to a lack of proof that the company had intended to monopolize this market. It instead attributed Alcoa's dominance of the market to legitimate business practices. The government appealed, but because conflicts of interest prevented the Supreme Court from hearing this case, Congress allowed the Second Circuit Court of Appeals to issue a final ruling. Writing for that court, Judge Learned Hand reasoned that if monopoly had been unavoidably "thrust upon" a company "by force of accident," the Sherman Act would not be violated. Alcoa, however, had consistently held onto over 90% of the ingot market for decades while expanding its capacity eightfold to forestall new competitors, enough to demonstrate that it had "meant to keep, and did keep" its monopoly, "for no monopolist monopolizes unconscious of what he is doing."[38] Fortunately for Alcoa, the sale of surplus aluminum plants built by the federal government during World War II spared Alcoa from dissolution, as new rivals purchased these facilities and permanently diluted its market share. Ironically, while Alcoa had previously avoided charging monopoly prices, it became the price leader of the new aluminum oligopoly, which adopted the profit targets and price rigidity that proved so bothersome in steel and autos.[39]

Alcoa established the important principle that the persistence of market control could support a finding that a company had violated the Sherman Act's ban on monopolizing. Judge Hand declined to indicate a specific threshold for what constituted monopoly, but he suggested that it would come at a high bar: "It is doubtful whether sixty or sixty-four percent would be enough; and certainly thirty-three per cent is not."[40] This level seemingly disqualified *Alcoa* from applying directly to many of the oligopolies in which no single firm rose to this level of concentration, but a second landmark case decided in 1946, *American Tobacco Co. v. United States,* suggested that several firms that displayed consciously parallel behavior could jointly be considered a monopoly. In this case, a jury had convicted the three major cigarette makers, American Tobacco, Liggett & Myers, and R. J. Reynolds, on four counts: conspiracy in restraint of trade, monopolization, attempt to monopolize, and conspiracy to monopolize. The government did not present any evidence of a formal agreement between these three cigarette firms to prove monopolization. Instead, as in *Alcoa,* the government relied on the circumstantial evidence of the industry's own behavior and conduct during the 1930s to argue that these three firms had sought to exclude competitors. At the start of this period, these three firms had held over 90% of the domestic cigarette market, and at no point in the decade did they fall below 68%. When purchasing tobacco leaf at auction, each of the three cigarette makers refused to bid unless the other two were present, purchased specific grades of tobacco distinct from the others, and continued to bid up the price until a certain level in order that all would pay the same price. Although there was no evidence that these companies coordinated their bidding practices, their purchases had the effect of raising the cost of cheaper grades of tobacco leaf beyond where their rivals, lower-priced cigarette manufacturers, could compete on prices effectively.[41]

The industry's parallel pricing provided further circumstantial evidence of a conspiracy to exclude competition and thereby monopolize the market. In June 1931, Reynolds had raised the list price of Camel cigarettes from $6.40 to $6.85 per thousand, even though costs and demand had both fallen during the Depression. The same day, the other two producers matched Reynolds's price. None offered an economic justification, and Liggett's executives even claimed that the increase was a mistake but had to be matched in order to keep pace with rivals' advertising spending. When cheaper 10¢ brands then made inroads into the Big Three's market share, the latter cut list prices and pressured distributors to limit the price differential between theirs and the 10¢ brands to no more than 3¢. The Big Three individually rewarded those who met this standard and withdrew sales and subsidies from those who did not. Once sales of 10¢ brands fell, the Big Three again raised their list prices.[42]

The industry's behavior could have represented the rational self-interest of firms operating in an oligopoly. Without another firm of sufficient size to make a dent in the leaf market, each member of the Big Three understood that there was no point raising its own costs by bidding against each other past a certain point where they could otherwise divide the leaf market among them. In the cigarette market, Reynolds would not have raised its prices during the Depression unless it believed that American and Liggett would recognize that all stood to benefit from higher margins and all stood to lose by competing on prices. Reynolds may have miscalculated the elasticity of demand facing the companies' brands, with all three losing market share as a result, but consciously parallel pricing does not require successful outcomes.[43]

Despite this self-rational explanation for the industry's behavior, the Supreme Court concluded that the evidence presented to the lower court had sufficed to conclude that the members of this oligopoly had conspired to establish a joint monopoly. In the Court's opinion, Justice Harold Burton emphasized that the prohibition on conspiracy applied not to the means but to the ends of corporate activity. "Wholly innocent acts" could effectuate an illegal conspiracy when their result had been to exclude competitors. No formal agreement was necessary, nor was actual exclusion necessary to prove illicit monopolization. Although each cigarette firm had developed its bidding practices and predatory retail pricing on its own, the industry's actions as a whole displayed the "unity of purpose" or "meeting of minds in an unlawful arrangement" that justified the finding of a conspiracy to monopolize. Endorsing Judge Hand's holding in *Alcoa,* Justice Burton concluded that the maintenance of the tobacco industry's market concentration over time had required firms to conspire to maintain that monopoly, rendering them in violation of the Sherman Act.[44]

American Tobacco contained the landmark suggestion that consciously parallel pricing behavior could suffice to prove an oligopoly had violated the Sherman Act, but it did not establish what legal remedies existed for this conduct. As a criminal case, *American Tobacco* resulted in fines of $255,000 for the defendants, but it did not enjoin the industry's behavior or order the divestitures or dissolutions that would have weakened market concentration and prevented the continuation of these practices.[45] In subsequent cases, the Supreme Court would uphold the ability of the Federal Trade Commission to order changes to industrial practice on the basis of parallel pricing behavior. In *FTC v. Cement Institute* (1948), the government charged that the cement industry had violated section 5 of the Federal Trade Commission Act, which prohibits unfair methods of commerce, by adhering to a basing-point system. Under this system, cement producers calculated shipping costs on the basis of the distance from a single city, regardless of where the producer was actually located. The FTC had argued that the resulting uniformity of prices proved the existence of an unlawful agreement between the industry's trade association and its individual members. Pleading self-interest, the cement industry contended that such a pricing system would inevitably develop in a market characterized by a standardized product and high transportation costs. In the Court's opinion, Justice Hugo Black expressed skepticism that cement firms could have arrived at identical pricing without any explicit understanding. Such a system of pricing "runs counter to what many people have believed—namely, that, without agreement, prices will vary—that the desire to sell will sometimes be so strong that a seller will be willing to lower his prices and take his chances." Yet even were the industry's economic arguments accurate, Justice Black concluded that the FTC had properly derived the existence of an unlawful agreement. The Cement Institute had worked to maintain this system, the pricing system did produce uniform prices, and the industry conformed to this pattern, enough to meet the standard established in *Interstate Circuit*.[46]

These precedents provided Kefauver with a model through which to challenge oligopoly pricing. During his hearings on the steel industry, Kefauver affirmed that parallel pricing behavior could serve as admissible circumstantial evidence of a conspiracy by referencing how *American Tobacco* had established the existence of a conspiracy without direct evidence. Given that one of the most convincing pieces of evidence in that case had been the parallel increases in cigarette prices in 1929 and 1931 in the face of already-high profits, declining costs, and falling demand, Kefauver suggested that the analogous behavior of the steel industry could also be held as evidence of a conspiracy to monopolize.[47] Kefauver's subcommittee further noted in its final report on steel prices that the testimony of Blough, Homer, and other industry leaders made it extremely likely that the steel industry engaged in some form of price leadership without formal combination. If it were too difficult to find the industry in violation of the Sherman Act, the report suggested that *Cement Institute* provided an alternative strategy to address this behavior. In 1951, the steel industry had entered into a consent decree with the FTC that banned its own use of the basing-point system, but prices had nevertheless remained uniform. If it could be shown that a common course of action continued to determine prices, Kefauver's report suggested that the industry could be held in violation of section 5 of the FTC Act.[48]

The report of Kefauver's subcommittee on the auto industry also proposed a path for antitrust action. The report emphasized that the auto industry exhibited factors identical to those that had "laid the background" in *American Tobacco:* "giant power, financial might, large expenditures in advertising, and dominance by three leading manufacturers." General Motors, the undisputed price leader of the auto industry, held about half the market and was nearing the threshold that *Alcoa* had suggested would prove monopoly in itself. Even if GM remained below that level, the report suggested that the 89% cumulative share of the Big Three automakers should at least establish the grounds for a more thorough investigation of the industry's pricing.[49]

Yet by the time that Kefauver expressed this enthusiasm, courts had already shown their reluctance to continue the trend of *Interstate Circuit* and

American Tobacco toward allowing equivocal pricing evidence to serve as a means to regulate corporate behavior. For instance, in *Milgram v. Loew's* (1951), the Third Circuit Court of Appeals emphasized that conscious parallelism could not by itself enable the inference of a conspiracy. This case centered around the unanimous refusal of movie distributors to license films to a drive-in theater on a first-run basis. The facts of this case supported the "inference of joint action," but the court cautioned that "this does not mean . . . that in every case mere consciously parallel business practices are sufficient evidence." In *Milgram,* each firm had "acted in apparent contradiction to its own self-interest" in rejecting higher fees from the drive-in. Of course, as the Third Circuit acknowledged, "businessmen are not guilty of conspiracy because a court finds their business reasons poor ones," but in this case, the distributors' executives had failed to offer any convincing explanation for how their behavior could have been arrived at independently. Since "the competitive forces of our economy" would have led to a different outcome, the reasons cited by the industry failed to absolve their guilt.[50]

The Eighth Circuit Court of Appeals similarly warned against drawing inferences of conspiracy purely from circumstantial behavior in *Pevely Dairy Co. v. United States* (1949). This case involved two milk companies convicted of a conspiracy to fix prices in St. Louis, where they held 63% of the combined market for fluid milk. Once again, the government had offered only circumstantial evidence of a conspiracy in the form of identical prices and the close proximity of price changes to one another. Reversing the lower court's finding of conspiracy, the Eighth Circuit explained that the companies had determined prices based on a system laid out by the International Association of Milk Dealers and that they only changed prices after a "complete evaluation of the economic considerations and factors going into the cost of production." The evidence suggested that no other factors influenced prices. Citing Chamberlin's *Theory of Monopolistic Competition* but not *Interstate Circuit,* the Eighth Circuit concluded that because both firms felt economic changes equally, such changes could be explained as rational business decisions without having to resort to understanding or agreement. Without additional evidence of a conspiracy, "mere uniformity of prices in the sale of a standardized commodity" could not establish a violation of the Sherman Act.[51]

In 1954, the Supreme Court definitively declared that conscious parallelism alone could not prove the existence of a conspiracy. In yet another case involving the motion-picture industry, *Theatre Enterprises v. Paramount Distributing*, a suburban movie theater had applied to several distributors for a license to show first-run movies, only to be turned down due to the distributors' policy of granting first runs only to downtown theaters. Justice Tom Clark wrote for the Court that there were insufficient grounds to find that an illegal conspiracy existed. *Interstate Circuit* and *American Tobacco* had allowed business behavior to be admissible as circumstantial evidence of an agreement, formal or otherwise. Still, in contrast to the treatment of innocent acts in *American Tobacco*, Justice Clark noted that parallel behavior could also stem from independent decisions that did not rise to the level of an illicit agreement. Additional evidence would be required to make this distinction for, as Justice Clark famously concluded, "'conscious parallelism' has not yet read conspiracy out of the Sherman Act entirely." No such additional factors were present here. Unlike in *Milgram v. Loew's*, each distributor had submitted copious evidence that "attributed uniform action to individual business judgment motivated by the desire for maximum revenue." No tacit agreement had been necessary to arrive at parallel action.[52]

In the wake of *Theatre Enterprises*, legal scholars largely agreed that it would be much more difficult to combat oligopoly price behavior through the antitrust laws. Without additional evidence of a conspiracy, such as the letter in *Interstate Circuit* or the exclusionary intent shown in *American Tobacco*, it would be impossible to establish the existence of an illegal conspiracy simply because firms were acting in the self-interest dictated by their industrial structure.[53] According to one of the most influential efforts to square the antitrust laws with oligopoly behavior during this period, Carl Kaysen and Donald Turner's landmark text *Antitrust Policy: An Economic and Legal Analysis* (1959), it would be difficult to uncover additional evidence of conspiracy even in those situations where firms were engaged in more than tacit collusion. To circumvent this challenge, Kaysen and Turner argued for new legislation that would establish the possession of undue market power as a crime in itself. That way, no proof of conspiracy would be necessary in those industries where firms jointly possessed market power. As an additional benefit, this new legislation would provide a solution for the structural conditions that caused supracompetitive oligopoly pricing. Transforming a tight oligopoly into a loose oligopoly would reduce the market power of individual firms and make parallel action more difficult due to the larger number of players. In contrast, for the courts to enjoin certain pricing behavior or for the FTC to impose cease-and-desist orders would compel firms to behave irrationally given the logic of oligopoly structure.[54]

Thus, by the time that Kefauver had begun his hearings, the antitrust authorities had settled on their traditional understanding of oligopoly pricing. Following *Cement Institute,* the FTC had announced its intention to continue to challenge conscious parallelism in the same manner as it would overt collusion, arguing that an agreement existed when firms took parallel action expecting others to act similarly. After *Theatre Enterprises* foreclosed the FTC's ability to prove conspiracy solely from the identical conduct of firms, this approach came to a premature end. Likewise, in 1955, the Eisenhower administration's landmark National Committee to Study the Antitrust Laws had embraced the conclusion of *Theatre Enterprises* that "'conscious parallelism' is not a blanket equivalent of conspiracy." A number of different considerations would instead have to be weighed to determine when parallel behavior rose to the level of agreement necessary to prove conspiracy, including the existence of independent business justifications for parallel action and the uniformity of leadership and following.[55]

Kefauver's proposals for combating price administration thus found little traction with the antitrust authorities. When the senator presented his views on steel prices to Victor Hansen, the assistant attorney general in charge of the Antitrust Division, the latter expressed doubts about the ability to control prices through antitrust laws. Hansen explained that the government would not be able to prove that the steel industry was conspiring under the Sherman Act without some other evidence than prices alone. U.S. Steel could also not be charged for monopolizing due simply to its role as price leader without full consideration of the size and power of the other players in the industry. Hansen did suggest that steel firms might utilize press releases about prospective increases as a form of tacit agreement to a price-fixing conspiracy, but without more information on the economic justifications for price increases, he was not willing impanel a grand jury on such equivocal evidence.[56]

REGULATION AND ADMINISTERED PRICES

In addition to the difficulties of securing the evidence required to charge that oligopoly members violated antitrust law though their pricing policies, many economists of the late 1950s questioned whether antitrust law could supply the appropriate remedies to the challenge of price administration. Appearing before Kefauver's subcommittee, Gardiner Means had warned that because modern industry would inevitably take a concentrated form, the only way to restore pricing to the conditions that Kefauver had in mind would be "to pulverize industry." That assault would in turn entail a significant loss of economic efficiency.[57] John Kenneth Galbraith similarly described at Kefauver's hearings how he felt "appalled by the amount of reconstruction" required to eliminate pricing power in concentrated industries through the use of antitrust law.[58] A survey of academic economists at 150 institutions conducted by the JEC in October 1958 found that 60% of the 615 respondents agreed that "the strengthening of competition (through vigorous antitrust and related policies)" would reduce the need for direct price controls. However, an even greater percentage, 65%, indicated that this need could not be eliminated entirely through antitrust action.[59]

Kefauver had declared at the start of his hearings that if private industry continued to abuse its power, the only alternative to destroying this power through antitrust law would be to control it through some form of regulation. Although expressing his preference for the former option, Kefauver had also dedicated a significant part of his hearings to examining what forms of regulation would prove feasible. Kefauver himself had introduced a bill to create a federal Department of Consumers as a formal counterweight to private market power, but he considered a bill from Senator Joseph O'Mahoney of Wyoming, a member of the Subcommittee on Antitrust and Monopoly and the former chair of the Temporary National Economic Committee (TNEC), to fit more naturally into the existing institutional order.[60] O'Mahoney's bill would have required any industry in which eight firms constituted at least half of the industry's sales and had capital of at least $10 million to notify the Department of Justice, FTC, Speaker of the House, and president of the Senate before altering prices. The FTC would then hold public hearings on the "reasons for and the justifiability of the proposed increase" as well as its impact on competition and the national economy. As the FTC already enjoyed the discretion to investigate pricing, Kefauver emphasized that all that would change under this legislation would be the requirement that hearings occurred automatically.[61]

The authorities named by O'Mahoney's bill disagreed with this regulatory approach as much as they had Kefauver's calls to target conscious parallelism through antitrust law. FTC chairman John W. Gwynne spoke on the unanimous behalf of the commissioners in noting that the FTC's ability to combat restraints of trade stemmed from its ability to "stop monopoly in its incipiency and thus fight inflation by maintaining healthy, free, and active competition." Using the FTC to shine a spotlight on price decisions would not provide a fundamental answer for price administration but only lead to finger-pointing between management and labor, with the end result that "there would be no unanimity of thought . . . which would result in driving down prices." From a practical standpoint, moreover, Gwynne suggested that prices would probably become rigid if firms feared having to go through this process, and they would probably not cut prices if they could not raise them again in the future.[62] Similarly, Robert Bicks, the acting assistant attorney general for antitrust, emphasized that the goal of antitrust law was to ensure that competitive forces determined prices, not to substitute government inquiries for free-market forces. Simply because antitrust laws were incapable of challenging every exercise of market power did not mean that the government should abandon those efforts for this new approach.[63]

Neither the bill for prenotification nor that for the Department of Consumers made it out of committee. The only successful piece of legislation to pass from Kefauver's investigation concerned pharmacological safety, and that was primarily due to the fact that the senator had happened to be interrogating Big Pharma over its pricing practices at the time of the thalidomide scandal. Facing an uphill battle in Congress, Kefauver instead turned to the White House to make some contribution to the industrial pricing situation. In 1958, Kefauver asked President Eisenhower to take up the initiative from Congress in making the steel industry aware of its responsibilities to the public. Anticipating that the industry would raise prices that July alongside its deferred wage payments, Kefauver asked Eisenhower to hold informal conferences with the industry and union and release a public analysis of any justifications for higher prices.[64] In back-and-forth missives that summer, however, Eisenhower repeatedly declined to adopt this approach.[65]

Eisenhower did not disagree with Kefauver about the dangers that concentrations of private power presented to the public. Throughout the Age of Escalation, Eisenhower expressed concerns about the actions of private firms and unions. Writing in his diary on January 16, 1956, Eisenhower recorded a meeting with Secretary of the Treasury George Humphrey and CEA chairman Arthur Burns in which they discussed how the economy seemed to be teetering between recession and inflation. Although both of his advisers thought that a recession would be more likely, Eisenhower's diary entry noted that wage increases and the upcoming steel negotiations pointed to inflation.[66] Similarly, in a conversation with economic aide Gabriel Hague in February 1956, Eisenhower described the threat of inflation using language that would not have been out of place in the work of Berle and Means: "Great inflation could result from the decision of a Board such as U.S. Steel, a board perhaps representing only 2 per cent of the total stockholders of such a corporation. . . . 'There is something to be said for the tycoon age as against the directorship age.'"[67]

Unlike Kefauver, however, Eisenhower preferred to limit his intervention to generalized exhortations to the private community. As he had warned Bernard Baruch, the financier who had overseen price controls during World War I, when rejecting an extension of Korean War wage and price controls, to do more than encourage private statesmanship would "change in revolutionary fashion the kind of government in which we live" and hence be unacceptable except in times of extreme national crisis.[68] Beginning with his 1957 State of the Union Address, Eisenhower made this appeal for voluntary restraint a recurring theme of his second term. Eisenhower endorsed the cost-push theory of inflation by declaring that business and labor had the power to "help counteract or accentuate such [inflationary] tendencies by their wage and price policies." He called on businesses to "avoid unnecessary price increases" and for total labor compensation, both wages and benefits, to be "reasonably related to improvements in productivity," lest political pressures build to substitute control for private decision-making.[69] An extended discussion of the wage-productivity linkage also appeared in that year's *Economic Report,* which explained that wages and benefits "should be consistent with productivity prospects." Otherwise, the government would have to rely on fiscal and monetary restraint to combat inflation, stifling growth and trading higher unemployment for stable prices.[70]

To encourage the private sector to embrace microeconomic restraint, Eisenhower emphasized the federal government's responsibility to stabilize the macroeconomic climate. In addition to aiming for federal budget surpluses, Eisenhower supported the efforts of Federal Reserve chairman William Martin to act against inflation. Martin believed that once expectations of inflation had become ingrained, it would require resolute action by the Fed to prevent inflation from spiraling out of control. As he explained to Eisenhower's new CEA chairman Raymond Saulnier during a meeting in April 1957, "[Credit ease] would convey to the business community the impression that the Board's policy is to validate price levels inflated by a cost push and that this would induce an inflation-minded psychology and have very damaging long-run consequences."[71] By the time of that meeting, the Federal Reserve had been steadily raising the discount rate for three years, from 1.5% in April 1954 to 3.5% in August 1957, the highest rate since the Great Depression. Continued concern about inflation resulted in a discount rate of 4% by September 1959.[72] Martin's efforts, although crude in comparison to the economic theory of the later twentieth century, successfully combated inflation at the cost of higher unemployment, which rose from under 4% in 1957 to over 7% in 1958 and again in early 1961. Eisenhower accepted this trade-off in the expectation of noninflationary growth in the future, but economists of a more liberal persuasion critiqued the apparent decision to hold the economy to what Abba Lerner had in 1951 termed "low full employment."[73]

CONCLUSION

As the 1950s ended, there was a broad consensus that controlling inflation required some form of private-sector restraint. In both the hearings of Senator Kefauver and surveys of corporate executives, it appeared that industrial wage and price policies diverged from those of a competitive economy. The business community charged that labor compensation had run ahead of productivity, with the result that unit labor costs would eat into profits unless passed on to the customer in the form of prices. That claim was broadly correct, but it elided the fact that industries seeking to obtain a larger share of income in the form of profits had also exercised their market power to obtain higher prices and margins.

Identifying the means through which wage and price behavior could be made to act in a more competitive manner proved more contentious. *Alcoa* and *American Tobacco* fostered the belief that the antitrust laws could be used to combat concentration and conscious parallelism, but after *Theatre Enterprises,* the government would find it much harder to build a case of conspiracy on these facts alone. Kefauver's faith in the antitrust remedy never faltered, but the legal and economics communities increasingly came to echo the argument of Kaysen and Turner that oligopoly remained outside the present scope of the antitrust law. With antitrust ruled out, it remained possible to subject price and wage movements to some form of public scrutiny, ranging from the formal mechanisms of the O'Mahoney bill to the crucible of the Kefauver hearings. Yet as long as this scrutiny uncovered no blatant wrongdoing as in the electrical-equipment industry, the steel or automobile industries had little to fear. None of the legislative proposals advanced to combat cost-push inflation presented a real threat of passing Congress, and hearings could also provide corporate America with a free opportunity to pontificate against the inflationary effects of union wage policy.

President Eisenhower agreed with Kefauver, Means, and Kaysen and Turner about the power of modern industry, but he doubted that the structure of oligopoly markets inevitably led to supracompetitive outcomes. Instead, Eisenhower's discussions of inflation suggested that the strong markets of the Age of Escalation had given the private sector an incentive to use the wage-price spiral to plaster over industrial-labor disputes. By reshaping this business climate through monetary and fiscal restraint, Eisenhower and Martin hoped to make firms and unions face the consequences of wage and price irresponsibility. Faced with these conditions, management would soon be forced to take a new look at the wage-price policy promoted by Keynesian economists, Engine Charlie Wilson, and Dwight D. Eisenhower alike.

CHAPTER FOUR

Management's New Look, 1955–1960

DURING THE AGE OF ESCALATION, organized labor had sold employers long-run peace at a steep premium, well above those productivity figures that were everywhere discussed but rarely heeded. Those costs had not been such a concern to management when strong markets had enabled firms to raise list prices, not infrequently enlarging profit margins at the same time. By the late 1950s, however, the wage-price spiral had fallen out of vogue. Public scrutiny of corporate pricing policies had intensified, while anti-inflationary fiscal and monetary policies had cooled off demand. Domestic producers were also beginning to learn that they could only push prices so far without inviting European and Japanese industry into the U.S. market.

Facing these new facts of life, corporate America recognized that it was time to adopt an alternative strategy to the Age of Escalation, one that the Wharton professor and General Electric consultant Herbert Northrup would term "Management's 'New Look.'"[1] Leading executives, especially those who formed a community around GE's vice president for employee and public relations, Lemuel Boulware, had come to regret having paid so dearly for labor peace during the Age of Escalation. Even before the advent of recession, they had begun to search for a means of shielding profits from labor without having to raise prices. These executives were especially intrigued by the new metric of total-factor productivity (TFP), which accounted for the role of capital in economic growth and so held out a greater possibility for preserving returns on investment than did the conventional labor-productivity statistics. By collaborating with one another to calculate and introduce productivity statistics into collective bargaining, this corporate community developed a new approach to wage-price policy in which it would be possible to achieve labor peace without having to rob Peter to pay Paul.

The challenge for U.S. industry would be to implement its new vision for the distribution of income within the institutional framework of labor law. The New Deal had empowered labor in its fight for a larger claim on the fruits of productivity, precisely the outcome that management now sought to foreclose. Faced with this social reality, Boulware and his followers recognized that they would have to find a way to adapt, and not simply to reject, the New Deal order in order to implement wage-price policy. Fortunately, the Eisenhower administration not only proved receptive to privative initiatives to combat inflation but also appointed the first-ever Republican majority on the National Labor Relations Board. This political climate would encourage Boulware and other managers to claim that they were operating within the boundaries of labor law even as they sought to transform collective bargaining from a method designed to enhance labor's strength into a tool to marginalize unions' claims on productivity.

Alongside General Electric's resounding victory for wage-price policy in its 1960 bargaining round, there was no conflict over the distribution of income as integral to the New Look as that of the steel industry. In one of the greatest labor upheavals of the postwar period, the industry faced a strike lasting 116 days and involving half a million steelworkers in order to implement its wage-price policy. Past historical accounts reliant on union records have placed the blame for this crisis on a management rudely awakened by recession to the futilities of sourcing investment funds through higher prices, with some historians incredulously claiming that management had failed to share those monopoly rents with labor.[2] Other accounts have focused on management's demands to make unilateral changes to work rules in an effort to cut costs, concluding that the failure to win this concession marked the point of no return in the industry's long decline.[3]

Even if recession had been necessary to spur the steel industry's resolve, that factor alone is insufficient to explain how its management had designed its wage-price policy. This chapter provides a novel reconstruction of the industry's bargaining strategy, based on the internal deliberations of its Coordinating Committee, through which the industry's dozen largest firms planned and implemented their bargaining strategy. Representatives from Republic Steel sent detailed records of these proceedings back to corporate headquarters, where they were dutifully marked as confidential and filed away. These records would probably have never seen the light of day had a bankrupt Republic not been bought by LTV Steel in 1984. When LTV went through its second bankruptcy in the early 2000s, it donated the papers to the Western Reserve Historical Society in Cleveland, preserving this unique record of how the industry's leaders understood the relationship between wages, prices, and productivity. These records situate both the recession and work-rules controversy within the broader efforts of corporate America to take a New Look at its interaction with its stakeholders. Recognizing that a changing competitive landscape would make the old strategy of annual price hikes difficult, the managers of the steel industry came to believe that they could afford investment and price stability only if labor also showed restraint. Labor's compensation had exceeded the industry's productivity trends for decades; it was only fair, the industry argued, that the United Steelworkers of America now recognize the rightful claims of capital. Although the industry admittedly made many missteps during these negotiations, it ultimately achieved a hard-fought victory to bring labor costs and prices in line with productivity.

THE CORPORATE REDISCOVERY OF PRODUCTIVITY

Where the framers of the National Labor Relations Act of 1935 had perceived conflict over the distribution of income, Lemuel Boulware saw harmony. In his voluminous writings, Boulware argued that corporations had no identity distinct from their "contributor-claimants": investors, customers, employees, suppliers, and community neighbors. Above these stakeholders sat corporate management, entrusted with the sacred duty to distribute the corporation's funds according to each group's contribution. Although Boulware allowed that "the manager technically works for the share owners," he cautioned that "he cannot work successfully for them, and will be fired by them, unless he achieves a balanced and acceptable return for all the contributor-claimants." Unfortunately, according to Boulware, public policy had disrupted management's ability to balance the needs of its stakeholders by confusing the interests of employees with those of unions, an organized interest group that claimed to represent its members. With the support of the government and public opinion, unions had garnered so much political and bargaining power that they could shift the distribution of income beyond what management deemed proper. When unions demanded wages higher than productivity justified, management then had to raise prices to make up for the difference, or else "the business will be choked to death." However, Boulware fretted that management, by using inflation to solve its labor-relation problems, had failed its duty to all of its contributor-claimants and instead became "a party to cheapening all the dollars just as much as the force of the unions."[4]

The 1955–1956 bargaining round that marked the start of the Age of Escalation convinced Boulware that management had lost sight of its economic role, a charge that began with GE itself. In the 1955 negotiations, Boulware and his staff had received orders from their superiors to pursue peace at any price so that GE could take advantage of a favorable climate for growth. Boulware had warned that labor peace could only be had at a high price. After the company offered to pay deferred wages of at least 3%, additional health insurance, a COLA, and other benefits, Boulware quickly came to regret having weakened the credibility of his earlier anti-inflation outreach through such a costly package. Soon after the ink had dried on this five-year agreement, Boulware complained to GE chairman Ralph Cordiner, "[The steel industry is] interpreting this year's events [at GE] as reflecting a complete rejection of our old theory and practice (as well as of me personally) and the adoption of a new soft appeasement approach more like their own 'Fairlessness.'"[5]

Boulware viewed the repeated failures to make a dent in inflation during the Age of Escalation as evidence that management did not take the wage-price spiral seriously. As he wrote to Allan B. Kline of the American Farm Bureau Federation shortly after the end of the 1956 steel strike, he had become discouraged that businesspeople—his own industry included—had become lulled to the "short-term 'good business'" despite the long-run trend toward union domination and inflation: "If [labor compensation] isn't gotten down to the 3% a year increase in productivity (of our machines and methods—not just of men—across the whole economy), then all the other contracts which try to keep prices from rising will simply choke the economy to a standstill."[6]

In December 1956, Boulware personally delivered a call to arms before a meeting of the National Association of Manufacturers (NAM) in a speech titled "Wages and Economic Growth." Boulware opened with a prediction of future economic growth before noting that the rise in real hourly wages since 1919 had closely paralleled the increase in output per man-hour, which he estimated as something like 3% a year for manufacturing and 2% for the economy as a whole. The relationship between real income and productivity was unmistakable, but nominal wages and prices had nonetheless risen much faster than this guidepost. Boulware surprisingly refused to blame unions for this pressure, insisting that it was management that paid higher wages and benefits. Boulware criticized the largest employers with the fastest productivity growth for establishing compensation patterns that pushed up unit labor costs and prices across the economy. He also noted that businesspeople had distributed the cost savings yielded by higher productivity too strongly in the form of "immediate pay raises" as opposed to "price reduction, research expansion, and capital formation for faster progress." In order to stop the resulting inflation, Boulware called on businesspeople to recognize their responsibility to educate the public and accept a leading role in "[contributing] to a sound solution that will bring all along together to fair and rewarding shares of an ever larger pie."[7]

Boulware's renewed call to treat wage-price policy seriously was well received among his emulators in the business sector. As Boulware noted to a colleague at the Automotive Parts Manufacturers' Association, he had never been as gratified at a response to any of his many speeches as he had by this address on wage inflation. Some of Boulware's correspondents in fact attributed the now-pervasive argument that wages that outpaced productivity growth were inflationary to the GE vice president himself. Boulware was much more modest in attributing this interest to a general zeitgeist surrounding inflation, including the messages delivered by the Eisenhower White House.[8] Until his full retirement from GE in 1960, Boulware nevertheless relentlessly expounded on what he deemed "the 2-1/2 to 3% gospel." Writing to his counterpart at Bethlehem Steel that year, Boulware described this message on productivity and inflation as "one of the most tedious subjects we have ever had to deal with here" but one that was absolutely necessary to spread to both businesses and the public as a whole.[9] Boulware even wrote to the White House that year to urge the administration to "speak up more aggressively on this inflation problem," moving beyond Eisenhower's well-minded appeals in order to get to the root cause of inflation: the public's willingness to fool itself into believing the "rather disgraceful robbing-Peter-to-pay-Paul ideas" that he attributed to labor unions and New Deal liberalism in general.[10]

NAM and other business groups issued many statements about productivity and inflation during the 1950s, but the leading forum for top-level managers to discuss these issues among themselves was the Employers' Labor Relations Information Committee (ELRIC). Established in 1953, ELRIC was the brainchild of GE president Ralph Cordiner and Champion Paper and Fiber Company president Reuben Robertson Jr. The latter's experience as an industry member of the Wage Stabilization Board during the Korean War had convinced him that the "wage problem" would only be solved when management figured out a way to distribute productivity fairly without adopting the one-size-fits-all approach of the GM formula. To accomplish this, Robertson believed the rest of the business community would have to create greater understanding of a fair and equitable distribution of income in its community, personnel, and political relations.[11] As Robertson pitched this new group to ELRIC founding member Crawford Greenewalt of DuPont, his goal was to promote "wide-spread public understanding of the necessity for having a balanced labor-management relations program." The group soon attracted members from a number of leading companies, including U.S. Steel and Goodrich Tires.[12]

Most of ELRIC's early programs concerned employee and community opinion programs, labor-law lobbying activities, and the dissemination of communications programs through several pamphlets and a magazine, the *Communicator*. Boulware took great interest in this new group for its obvious parallels to his efforts at GE, although he stepped back from the operations of ELRIC lest his involvement attract negative publicity.[13] By the end of the 1950s, ELRIC had also become the leading clearinghouse for corporate studies of productivity. ELRIC's fifth annual report in 1958 described how the organization had shifted its efforts to the wage-inflation problem in light of the recession, noting that "the question of wage increases not fully earned by increased productivity has disturbing implications for future management planning." Echoing Boulware's 1956 speech before the NAM, this report concluded that the fundamental problem was not labor power but the inability of management to communicate its own perspective to the public and build support for corrective action. Over the next two years, ELRIC would increasingly dedicate its energies to developing a rigorous theory of wages and prices that businesses could publicize.

At its meetings, executives debated whether wages and prices should be determined by free-market forces or by some productivity trend. If the latter, what measure of productivity should be used: the national pattern, industry-specific trends, or something else?[14]

TOTAL-FACTOR PRODUCTIVITY

Among the most important questions raised at ELRIC and other corporate meetings concerned the place of capital investment in productivity metrics. The traditional labor-productivity figures related outcome only to labor inputs, but corporate managers insisted that this measure failed to recognize the increasing capital-labor ratio and so enabled labor to deprive the owners of capital of their share of economic growth.[15] Boulware had long argued that the phrase "labor productivity" itself played into the arguments of union leaders such as Walter Reuther to claim an enlarged share of national income for workers, as "it is other factors of input which are the *dynamic determinants* of productivity growth." Although Boulware acknowledged that real wages had tracked labor productivity over the long run, he expressed doubts that this trend was inevitable given the importance of inputs other than labor, and he was concerned that simply maintaining the growth of productivity at its present rate would require management to invest ever-greater amounts of capital from savers.[16] Similarly, as the manager of DuPont's Industrial Relations Division suggested in 1959, President Eisenhower's exhortations to follow a noninflationary wage-price policy may have in fact been doing the business community more harm than good by promoting the use of labor productivity: "The labor unions and many others will interpret his use of the term 'Productivity' to mean 'output per man hour' without any recognition of the contribution of capital and material resources to the increase in productivity."[17]

The search for a wage-price policy that would aid capital-deepening investment took on special meaning as forward-looking businesspeople began to consider the threat of import competition. For the most part, imports had not yet taken serious market share away from U.S. firms and hovered at about only 4% of gross domestic product for the entire decade.[18] Still, competition in low-value-added products such as flatware and barbed wire had placed industry on notice that the wage-price spiral could not proceed indefinitely. In Boulware's newsletters and the speeches of leading executives, the business community voiced its concerns that deferred increases and

COLA clauses would raise labor costs in the United States far above those of foreigners and deprive management of the investment capital necessary to keep U.S. technology ahead of the competition in a post-Sputnik age.[19]

The new science of growth accounting provided an empirical understanding of this threat. Economic interest in national planning during the Great Depression, the need to manage the mobilization economy of World War II, and Cold War geopolitics had catalyzed the development of statistics on gross national product and the interdependence of sectors across the economy. Through these statistics, American economists, policymakers, and business executives sought an explanation for this apparent shift in international competitiveness. Was it the result of technological leapfrogging, with foreign governments diverting resources and technological know-how toward high-value sectors? Or was it extensive growth, with increased investment driving convergence to the U.S. capital-labor ratio?[20] And in either case, how could U.S. free enterprise keep pace not only with the Soviet system but with what the British economist Andrew Shonfield termed the "modern capitalism" of western Europe, in which such neocorporatist approaches as French governmental planning, British nationalization, and German codetermination ensured that a society prioritized long-run growth over a short-run scramble to redistribute income?[21]

Fortunately for those American businesspeople reconsidering the use of labor productivity as the basis of wage-price policy, these global concerns had propelled the search for a measure of productivity that could distinguish growth based on factor investment from that owing to technological development. Ironically, corporate management had discovered this literature thanks to none other than the CIO. Following the end of the Korean War, the CIO had begun to justify its bargaining demands by citing the work of John Kendrick, an economist who had spent the Korean War at the Office of Business Economics within the Department of Commerce.[22] There, Kendrick had decomposed total output into its various inputs: man-hours of labor, the cost of capital net of depreciation, and the rent of land. In 1951, Kendrick first presented his estimates of the increase in output per man-hour in the U.S. economy for the period 1909–1950.[23] Discussions of Kendrick's work and the CIO's interpretation of Kendrick quickly appeared in the publications of groups such as the National Association of Manufacturers and the internal planning of companies such as Ford Motors. These analyses generally noted that the CIO had appended its own figures for

1951–1953 to Kendrick's data in order to claim a 3.2% annual rate of productivity growth since 1933, whereas Kendrick's own conclusion emphasized a 2.1% annual growth rate for 1909–1950.[24]

Kendrick's subsequent efforts to distinguish between output per man-hour, capital returns, and total-factor productivity quickly raised him into the ranks of the business community's favorite economists. After Kendrick became affiliated with the National Bureau of Economic Research in 1953, he received support for his growth accounting project from Alfred Sloan's eponymous foundation as the GM chairman sought to address his lingering concerns about the effects of the GM formula, and the AIF specifically, on the economy.[25] Kendrick went on to become a frequent guest speaker at trade-group meetings, a correspondent with corporate economists, and an essayist for managerial periodicals.[26] Kendrick even coauthored a handbook for corporate economists on how to calculate their own TFP trends in 1961, an offshoot of the National Industrial Conference Board's "Economics for Executives" program. According to the 1965 edition of this handbook, the rationale for the corporate use of productivity statistics was no longer limited to cost control or market projections, as it had been in the early 1950s: "National productivity trends have also been recognized as a major factor determining increases in real wages as well as the extent of average money-wage advances consistent with a stable general price level, or conversely the extent of a decrease in the general price level consistent with a stable money-wage level."[27]

In Kendrick's 1961 masterpiece *Productivity Trends in the United States,* he calculated that TFP had risen by 1.7% a year for the private economy since 1889, compared to a 2% increase in output per weighted labor input, 2.4% per unweighted man-hour, and 1% per unit capital. Kendrick noted that there appeared to a be a break in this trend around 1919, with TFP rising 1.3% a year in the thirty years before this break and 2.1% a year after it. In the long run, 1919–1957, the average annual rate of change in the real income per unit capital was about constant at 0.3%, while real income per unit labor had risen by 2.7% a year, about parallel to the increase in labor productivity. Just as the textbook economic models predicted, more capital had been invested at a fixed return, and labor had received higher wages, preserving an approximately constant distribution of total income. But for the post–World War II period, 1948 to 1957, real income per unit labor had risen at 3.9% a year, while real income per unit capital had actually fallen at an average of 3% per annum. Kendrick did not take an alarmist view of this short-run trend, attributing it to diminishing marginal returns, growing productivity in capital-goods production, and relative factor demands. He also noted that over this period "the expected marginal rate of return [on capital] was still sufficient to induce a volume of new investment consistent with relatively full employment." Still, Kendrick acknowledged that this decline in the return on capital could not continue forever without dampening new investment. To induce further investment would eventually require inflation, higher productivity, or, in a suggestion with appeal to Kendrick's corporate readers, that "the increase in wage rates relative to the price of capital slows."[28]

Kendrick's investigations led him to recommend a somewhat different approach to wage-price policy than the classic description of limiting compensation to national labor productivity. In an overview of his productivity research penned for industrial-relations professionals, Kendrick doubted that efforts to tie wages to either TFP or labor productivity through a formula such as the GM annual improvement factor would prove effective. The AIF had become "merely part of a larger package" possessed by the UAW and was unable to hold the entire compensation package, fringe benefits and all, to a noninflationary ceiling. Rather than "throw productivity out the window as a practical guide," as Kendrick acknowledged that the somewhat pessimistic tone of his article might be interpreted as recommending, he urged his readers to recognize that productivity still limited the extent that real wages could grow without inflation. Productivity in both its labor and total-factor definitions remained "an important background factor in labor negotiations" with the potential to minimize creeping inflation. While TFP by definition set the limit for how much the combined income of labor and capital could rise without inflation, determining the precise amount that labor compensation could grow without inflation required knowledge of the capital side of the equation as well. Only when the output per unit capital remained constant could firms hold to the "usual over-simplified proposition" that wages must track output per man-hour in order to maintain price stability and preserve a constant return on capital. If output per unit capital increased faster than the return on capital, real labor compensation could in fact rise by more than the increase in output per man-hour without inflation. Likewise, if real capital input rose faster than did output—which Kendrick found had been the case between 1953 and 1957—then labor compensation would have to rise by less than output per man-hour in order to compensate the extra capital inputs. Otherwise, profits would be squeezed if final prices were not raised.[29]

Union economists who engaged with Kendrick's work found much to be appreciated from this flexible wage-price policy, especially in his comments that wages could rise faster than labor productivity without inflation as long as the return on capital did not rise as fast as capital productivity. Still, the growing affinity between businesspeople and Kendrick did not escape the notice of organized labor. In July 1960, AFL-CIO research director Stanley Ruttenberg sent a missive to the research directors at all of its affiliated unions warning that "there has been a trend on the part of some large companies to claim that the appropriate productivity measure for collective bargaining is a new productivity index called 'total factor productivity.'" Ruttenberg noted that Kendrick himself had discouraged the use of TFP as the single yardstick for collective bargaining before listing two reasons of his own for why unions could not allow "this measure [to] become a recognized factor in collective bargaining." The more obvious of the two was the fact that TFP generally rose slower than labor productivity and so would result in a lower ceiling for labor compensation gains. More ominously, Ruttenberg noted that discarding labor productivity in favor of TFP would reduce the employee share of income in favor of capital.[30] If wages rose in proportion to TFP and not labor productivity, the return per unit of labor and the return per unit of capital would grow at the same rate. Since it could be assumed that the quantity of capital investment grows faster than labor inputs, capital's share of total income would rise relative to labor's share. According to union economists, this redistribution of income would encourage underconsumption by lowering the relative purchasing power of wage earners. Moreover, by preventing the return on labor from increasing relative to the return on capital, businesses would also face fewer incentives to invest in labor-saving equipment, slowing the pace of technological adoption and economic growth.[31]

Labor's rejoinder that the widespread adoption of TFP would generate a shortfall in investment overlooked the fact that corporate management's interest in introducing TFP to wage determination had arisen explicitly because of its desire to expand investment. Kendrick's work on TFP went straight to the core of business concerns that workers had claimed such a large share of income that there were insufficient resources available for investment in new machines and technologies, at least not without relying on higher prices to shield returns. Over the course of the late 1950s, business economists collaborated with each other in resolving the technical difficulties and unlocking the potential of TFP, using Kendrick's figures as a basis to develop a new wage-price policy that they believed would acknowledge the importance of capital and the managers who oversaw investment. Managers such as Boulware who had rejected the wage-price policy of the "General Motors Era," as Northrup termed the period 1948–1957, did not suddenly propose that wages be tied to the annual TFP trend akin to the AIF of the GM formula. Instead, they hoped to educate the public and employees on the importance of keeping wages within the bounds of this productivity measure, reversing Kendrick's postwar capital-rents squeeze through collective bargaining while emphasizing the importance of capital investment to maintaining the United States' competitive edge.[32]

TFP would have been the most meaningful for corporate efforts to boost investment when analyzed at the company or industry level, but corporate discussions during this period continued to emphasize national TFP, just as wage-price policy traditionally focused on national labor productivity. Kendrick suggested one potential reason for retaining this familiar perspective: relating labor compensation to national productivity trends prevented disruptions to the national wage structure, such as if high- and low-productivity firms within a single industry attempted to set different wage rates.[33] A less charitable and more likely explanation for the continued focus on national measurements was that even large corporations with dedicated economics staff were never able to master the statistical complexity of TFP calculations, as suggested by several case studies in the 1965 edition of Kendrick's handbook. In one case study of the "Mideast Manufacturing Company" heavily implied to be GE, an explicit effort by the industrial-relations department to introduce TFP into bargaining ended up severely understating total-factor productivity by using gross inputs and outputs rather than value-added figures, resulting in an estimate of 39% TFP growth for 1947–1957 compared to Kendrick's revised calculation of 84%. In another case study of Johnson & Johnson, the company's economists omitted structures and purchases from other companies in calculating total inputs, and when it came time to summate the total-input denominator, they converted the value of machinery not into dollars but into the more familiar denominator of man-hours.[34]

Despite these difficulties in calculating TFP, this new statistic generated a burst of collaborative effort among the blue-chip firms that composed ELRIC. In early 1958, DuPont president Crawford Greenewalt announced to other ELRIC members, as U.S. Steel president Cliff Hood recalled when writing Greenewalt for more information, that his staff had a "handle" on productivity, "which may prove effective in definitizing [*sic*] production [productivity] measurement." Greenewalt invited other corporations to send representatives to DuPont to learn about this new measure of "Total Factor Productivity." Other companies had been working on calculating this metric on their own, and they eagerly took up Greenewalt on his offer. By the end of 1960, a total of fifty-nine groups, including U.S. Steel, General Electric, and the NAM, had viewed DuPont's slide presentation. Importantly, testimonials by those who viewed this presentation suggest that DuPont's effort developed along the same lines of the economic analysis under way at their own firms, yielding increased flows of information among the ELRIC community.[35]

The findings of DuPont, and by implication those of other firms, built on Kendrick's work to argue for using TFP as a guide for collective bargaining and a replacement for the rigidity of GM's AIF. DuPont's thirty-minute slide narration, "The Measure of Productivity—A Challenge to Management," began by noting how wage-price policy had become a subject of public controversy without properly defining "productivity." Echoing Boulware's contentions, management now had to ensure that the public properly understood the meaning of this concept. DuPont's economists cited Kendrick to argue that labor productivity omitted changes in the amount of nonlabor inputs. While the presentation accepted that the growth of real labor compensation would approximate productivity for the economy over the long run, it nonetheless concluded that "this over-all concept of economists is not valid if applied as a wage determinant to all collective bargaining situations." Each industry and market faced its own unique circumstances, and to subjugate a firm's best interests entirely to the nation's noninflationary aims would not always prove successful. Just as Kendrick had noted the discrepancy between long-run wage patterns and short-run changes in capital intensity and profitability, the DuPont report cautioned, "If an employer bases his wage increase decisions upon estimates of long term productivity trends, he may price himself out of business before the [business] cycle is completed." Thus, like Kendrick, the report concluded that employers should not adopt a rigid AIF even as they continued their engagement with productivity, especially its total-factor variety, so that "intelligent decisions can be made" in bargaining.[36]

GE president Ralph Cordiner presented a similar analysis of productivity to the ELRIC board, titled "Observations on the Usefulness of Productivity in Establishing Compensation Levels." Cordiner urged against using output per man-hour statistics as the basis for setting labor compensation, and like Boulware, he stressed that management generated productivity, whereas employees were merely provided with new tools. Cordiner then quoted the results of Kendrick's study to demonstrate that TFP increased slower than did labor productivity. Nevertheless, Cordiner also recommended against relating compensation to changes in any productivity index on the grounds that productivity was difficult to measure, unsteady from year to year, and varying across industries and firms. Rather than having businesses educate the public on the need to relate wages to productivity, specifically the national TFP, Cordiner urged a different program of public education: "It is essential that industry take a public stand to dispel the current erroneous notions that wage increases should be related to changes in productivity indexes and that all the benefits of improved productivity should be passed on to employees."[37]

Although Cordiner's report was seemingly a repudiation of the efforts that Boulware had long promoted, Cordiner was in fact not beating a complete retreat from wage-price policy. Rather, his report to ELRIC echoed Kendrick in suggesting that businesses take a more flexible approach to wage-price policy than the AIF devised by Engine Charlie Wilson. Boulware's staff economist, Francis Highton, revealed this meaning of Cordiner's stance in the course of his regular correspondence to his counterpart at General Motors, the director of labor economics Arthur Thornbury. According to Highton, GE's official position was that productivity served as a means to a financial end, rather than the end itself, as in the GM AIF: "A key point, we believe, in the use of the rate of change of productivity, is the distinction between productivity increases as a specific *measure* for the precise amount of annual, uniform compensation adjustments, and a general guidepost and *educational tool*." According to Highton, GE did endorse the use of TFP because it demonstrated the importance of capital and investment better than did labor productivity. Yet while national productivity growth served as the public's primary guidepost to gauge the potential for inflation and,

Highton believed, a potential counterweight to union political power, this concern had to be weighed against other corporate priorities at the bargaining table and so could not be applied uniformly in every circumstance.[38]

Under Highton's guidance, GE's Employee and Public Relations Division continued to release statements stressing the need for "competitive guideposts" of productivity for more than a decade after Boulware retired in 1960. This approach emphasized that U.S. companies such as GE faced growing competition from foreign producers with lower labor costs and faster productivity growth thanks to increasing scale and mechanization. Ensuring that prices remained stable on average was thus no longer enough for U.S. firms. Instead, GE and other firms would have to increase their capital-labor ratio further to be able to compete in this newly globalized arena, which in turn required that investors receive a greater reward than was assigned under the traditional labor-productivity guidepost. While real wages had risen in parallel to productivity over the long run, this pattern did not necessarily hold over the short run, given swings in capital investment such as Kendrick had identified following World War II. Information on output and man-hours alone was thus insufficient to calculate the wage trend compatible with stable prices because it failed to take into account the returns necessary to compensate investors for these increased amounts of capital. By promoting TFP as a component of any wage or price guidepost, GE and other companies could hold compensation growth below the standard output per man-hour figures and so boost the return to capital, at least in the short run, without having to commit to an annual deferred wage formula as GM had a decade before.[39]

PRODUCTIVITY IN PRACTICE, PART I: GENERAL ELECTRIC

By the end of the 1950s, management had developed a coherent vision for the distribution of income. By linking compensation with productivity, preferably its total-factor variety, labor would still enjoy higher real incomes, but consumers would also be able to purchase better goods at stable or falling prices, shareholders would receive adequate returns, and, perhaps most importantly, management would have the capital funds to invest in remaining competitive without having to raise prices or turning to outside capital. Transforming that guidepost of productivity into actual results at the collective bargaining table, of course, would be another task entirely. Rising unemployment might cause workers to prioritize job security over higher wages, but convincing union leadership to accede to management's positions entirely would be a tall order in any macroeconomic climate. After all, the New Deal had laid out its own model for how the gains of productivity—namely, in its traditional labor variety—should be bargained out between workers and employers, and the Taft-Hartley Act had not freed management from this legal framework.

How could management retake the initiative in distributing the fruits of productivity? To Boulware, the answer seemed simple enough: eliminate a union's monopoly over the labor force, as well as the compulsory dues payments that allowed union leadership to act independently of its members, and both its economic and political power would collapse. In practice, these goals could be accomplished most directly by granting individual workers the right to work without joining or paying fees to the union.[40] The Taft-Hartley Act of 1947 had allowed states to pass right-to-work laws, but they had initially failed to take hold outside the South. The creeping inflation of the 1950s and high-profile charges of corruption and racketeering within union ranks encouraged management to believe that the public would now prove responsive to these policies. In 1957, Indiana adopted a right-to-work measure with the support of the National Right to Work Committee (NRTWC), a business-backed outreach organization. Buoyed by its success in Indiana, the NRTWC and its local affiliates pushed forward to secure right-to-work legislation in several other states, but a union movement that perceived itself to be fighting for its very existence put up much-stiffer opposition than anticipated. Through public outreach and intense voter registration, the AFL-CIO and its local affiliates managed to defeat five out of the six right-to-work proposals on the ballot in 1958. In California, the bid failed by a 60%–40% margin, and in Ohio, by nearly a 2-to-1 ratio.[41]

The collapse of the right-to-work movement reinforced the sense among management that it could yet not escape the New Deal order. Still, a National Labor Relations Board operating under its first-ever Republican majority was willing to grant Boulware and other labor-relations officials more leeway in their interactions with employees under the framework of the National Labor Relations Act. In the past, the Democratic-dominated NLRB had generally operated on the belief that because employees were economically dependent on their employer, communications from the employer were inherently coercive. Now, employer speech that was not blatantly threatening or coercive would be tolerated as permissible free speech. For instance, the NLRB had previously mandated that management must allow unions equal time to offer rebuttals whenever it held a captive-audience meeting. Under the Eisenhower NLRB, management would be allowed to make a speech on company time and company property while denying the union the opportunity of replying as long as some access to employees existed.[42]

This permissive legal attitude toward communications enhanced Boulware's ability to promote management's role as chief arbiter of prosperity. His strategy, coined "Boulwarism" by its detractors, sought to establish management's credibility in doing right for all of a corporation's contributor-claimants. Months before the start of negotiations, Boulware's staff sounded out what employees desired so that the company would be ready with a "fair" offer to the union when the negotiations began. This "job marketing" allowed the company to craft what critics derided as a single take-it-or-leave-it offer when it came time to negotiate the collective bargaining contract. Boulware's staff also prepared regular briefing material for line management to use when communicating to employees, most notably the weekly *Employee Relations News Letter* that provided over twenty thousand managers and nonsupervisory personnel with information that would have been impossible to disseminate in a timely manner down the command chain through word of mouth.[43] These managers also played the company's different unions against each other to ensure that none was powerful enough to shut down the entire company. If all went according to plan, employees themselves would pressure union leaders to accept GE's proposal, minimizing dispute over what GE management claimed was right for its employees.[44]

In preparing for negotiations in 1960 with GE's primary union, the IUE, productivity, costs, and wage-price policy served as the key messages of this communications program. Though the company publicly committed itself to the argument that labor compensation could not rise faster than productivity grew on an economy-wide basis if inflation were to be avoided, it also realized that securing the loyalty of the employees required making a fair offer that accounted for short-run market trends. Reflecting on the attempt to defeat inflation by "going it alone" in 1948, Highton's office concluded that the company must make an offer priced to meet the market rate of labor, in relation to both other firms and existing public expectations. The company's overall goals for bargaining still included curbing inflation and improving the company's competitive position, but its immediate objective would be to craft an agreement that proved both economically rational and competitive in a labor market still beset by patterns. The long-run trend in TFP of approximately 2% a year would serve as a means to win public support for the company's eventual offer, but it was unrealistic as a practical target for negotiators in a time of general inflation. As GE's employee-relations staff evaluated the company's position in a report to the executive office, "We would be asking our employees to offer themselves in a lonely sacrifice to the cause. . . . Especially in a year of rising profits, we might find the employees eager to sacrifice the Company instead."[45]

Although Boulware himself had entered phased retirement and would not participate in negotiations directly, his handpicked successors implemented his trademark approach to bargaining over the course of 1960. GE did not decline to discuss the IUE's general demands, but it also did not make any counterproposals of its own. Instead, GE asked the union to explain the factual bases for these arguments so that management would be able to adjust its own eventual offer. At the same time, GE provided its interpretation of the IUE's demands in its employee newsletters, arguing that they would drastically expand employment costs and cause the destruction of thousands of jobs. Stressing the threat from foreign competition, GE explained that profits must be high enough to obtain the investment capital that would make workers more productive—and employable. In keeping with Boulware's model of contributor-claimants, GE notably emphasized the need for higher profits to attract external capital from investors, not simply to provide internal funds for management to invest on its own. In its communications, GE also called into the question the sincerity of IUE leader James Carey, reprinting his comment from the earlier year, "I owe GE a strike," to show he acted out of personal animosities, not the interests of his members, whereas management stressed that it remained committed to providing its workers with everything that they were rightfully due.[46]

On August 29, 1960, GE gave the IUE a preview of the offer that it formally introduced the next day: a three-year contract including a 3% wage increase that year and a 4% increase eighteen months later. No COLA was offered. The IUE representatives immediately rejected the offer as unresponsive to the union's own positions, which had included a 3.5% AIF.[47] GE in turn stated that its offer represented the best way to balance the interests of all concerned and was one that the union could "sell" to its members. GE did agree to modify its wage schedule by substituting the ability to reopen the matter of wages in lieu of the deferred increase, but it refused the IUE's request for an AIF on the grounds that "there is no direct relationship of productivity to wages." When pressed by the IUE about the factors that had gone into the wage offer or the costs of the package, the company refused to provide specifics. Of course, GE possessed the answers to these questions from its own comprehensive preparations, but it did not want these figures to become a floor to negotiations that would allow the IUE to "ask and bid" for higher wages.[48]

Carey asked the company to delay the public release of this offer, but GE's representatives insisted that employees had a right to know. Plant officials had already received a slide presentation and script to explain the company's offer. The script included the argument that employees would realize real gains without putting the "Company in an impossible competitive position" and concluded by asking employees to tell their union representatives whether they approved of the company's proposal. Beyond this presentation, plant management also held roundtable discussions to explain the offer and the company's economic justifications, all the while attempting to convince workers that the offer should be accepted.[49]

By appealing directly to employees while stonewalling their union representatives, Boulwarism directly challenged the power balance established in the National Labor Relations Act. Section 8(a)(5) of the NLRA established that it was an unfair labor practice for an employer to refuse to bargain collectively with the representatives of the employees, and even the Eisenhower NLRB agreed that management could not refuse to disclose substantiation for its economic arguments.[50] Nevertheless, Boulware, as well as GE's lawyers, insisted that the company's bargaining tactics remained safely within the letter, if not necessarily the spirit, of the NLRA. Section 8(c) of the act clarified that the expressing of views without any threat of reprisal or promise of benefit did not constitute an unfair labor practice, and GE interpreted this clause as validating its ability to communicate to workers directly. Otherwise, management would be at a strong disadvantage: the union could explain its stance to its members, but the employer could not advance its own argument to those selfsame employees. In any case, section 8(d) stated explicitly that the obligation to bargain collectively "does not compel either party to agree to a proposal or require the making of a concession." GE ultimately did not make any substantial changes to its offer, but it attributed this persistence to the obstinacy of union leadership, not the managerial close-mindedness that would constitute bad-faith bargaining. Instead, GE insisted that it was still desirous of reaching an agreement and willing to modify its proposals on the basis of convincing union evidence.[51]

Carey found GE unresponsive to his demands and rejected the company's offer. It was at this point that GE's communication strategy began to show its value, as only thirty thousand of the IUE's sixty-five thousand members at GE voted to strike. Among the locals rejecting the strike was that at GE's largest facility in Schenectady, New York, which at first refused to take part in the strike. Pressured to join the walkout, the local's leadership authorized the workers to return to work after only a few days.[52] Smaller unions at GE also agreed to its contract offer and returned to work. In a last-ditch effort, the IUE proposed on October 19 an eighteen-month contract with a 3.5% wage increase, but GE rejected the notion that "shake down bargaining" could force it to purchase "peace" above what the company had decided was fair. Within a week, the IUE called off its strike, but a victorious GE then declined to take advantage of its broken foe to squeeze out any additional concessions.[53]

Looking back on the success of these negotiations, Boulware prepared to ride off into the sunset having assuaged any remaining guilt over his role in the Age of Escalation. In a lengthy memo to Cordiner, Boulware reflected on the lessons of his career and the future of industrial-labor relations. Noting the downward trend in major bargaining settlements over the past several years, Boulware expressed his relief that industry was finally on its way to "achieving a belief by all concerned that managers are capable, fair and warmly human." Boulware noted that union officials at GE had put up less resistance than even he had expected. This was partly due to the macroeconomic conditions that had flattened inflation over the past years, but more importantly, Boulware explained this submission as a recognition on the part of labor that management would not budge from the wage-price policy it considered economically correct. As a retiring Boulware prepared to turn over the reins to his successors, he hoped that the industrial-labor profession that he had fostered would carry this trend to its ultimate end: fully eliminating the use of COLAs and the "prior 2-1/2% 'improvement' percentages . . . to make room for the appropriately lower settlements in auto and steel before we [GE] come up again."[54]

PRODUCTIVITY IN PRACTICE, PART II: STEEL

Boulware's victory at GE indeed represented part of a larger trend. Median hourly wage increases negotiated in a given year had fallen from 10.7¢ in 1956 to 8.7¢ in 1960 and 7¢ in 1961. Expressed as percentages, 64% of employees party to a collective bargaining agreement with at least one thousand workers had negotiated a wage increase of 3.5% or more in 1959. Only 39% did in 1960, the year of the GE settlement, and only 35% in 1961. The percentage receiving less than 2.5%, the value of the GM AIF and the high estimate for long-run labor productivity according to many businesspeople, had risen from 8% to 30% of employees in these contracts.[55] The Age of Escalation had been premised on corporations paying a premium for labor peace, but just as Boulware had hoped his outreach and communication efforts would ensure, work stoppages and the amount of man-days lost to strikes actually declined even further in the period of the New Look. From 1957 to 1961, a total of 112.5 million man-days were lost to strikes involving one thousand workers or more, compared with 131.5 million in 1952–1956 and 140.7 million in 1947–1951. This decreasing trend is clear despite the outlier of 1959, whose 60 million man-days lost holds the post-1947 record in both absolute and percentage terms (see table 3).

The reason for this anomalous spike was the great Steel Strike of 1959, in which half a million steelworkers struck for nearly four months in response to an attempt led by ELRIC member U.S. Steel to implement a noninflationary wage-price policy. After years of annual price hikes, the steel industry had discovered limits to this strategy. The increased scrutiny of Senator Kefauver was certainly irksome, but given the political coverage offered by the Eisenhower White House, the industry surely found market conditions to be the more existential of its concerns. Recession had strongly cooled the demand for steel, and production had fallen from 113 million tons in 1957 to 85 million in 1958, pushing capacity utilization down to 55%. Despite the implementation of higher prices in 1958, a move led by U.S. Steel and timed to coincide with the final scheduled wage increase of the 1956 contract, profits as a return on sales fell from 7.3% to 6.3% over those two years.[56]

The steel industry also recognized that imports, while small overall and concentrated in low-value products, had risen from 1.2% of domestic consumption in 1955 to 2.9% in 1958 and would inevitably continue to rise unless something was done to enhance the competitiveness of U.S. steel.[57]

This competition spelled disaster for the industry's traditional pricing policy. The members of an oligopoly industry acting through conscious parallelism would, in order to maximize profits, seek the price at which increased revenues just covered the loss of sales. Unsure precisely where this point was, U.S. Steel led the industry in its annual ritual of price hikes to see how far prices could go before this strategy proved counterproductive. Because imported steel served as a substitute for domestic steel, the demand for the industry's production would now become much more sensitive to changes in prices. For a time, the domestic industry might tolerate the loss of some of its market share to imports while keeping its own prices high, but if foreigners took too large of a share of the market, individual firms would eventually face pressure to shade their prices to compete. Unless the industry was willing to risk falling afoul of the Sherman Act through explicitly collusive maneuvers, the lack of mutual trust would soon shatter the discipline of price leadership and the ability to administer steel prices.[58]

Although a few smaller steelmakers operating in those geographic markets with the most direct exposure to import competition called for tariffs, the industry's leaders refused to resort to protectionism at this point. Instead, they argued that the industry would have to find a way to meet this competition head-on by adopting new technologies, boosting productivity, and lowering costs.[59] Investing in the technologies needed to remain competitive with imports would require additional capital funds, but the industry had long complained that its subaverage returns prevented it from attracting such resources from outside investors. Since market conditions no longer allowed the industry to rely on price hikes to increase its return on investment, the industry would have to gather these funds the old-fashioned way by cutting costs. But if it did not have enough resources to invest in new technologies as it was, how could it cut costs? By holding labor compensation in line with productivity or, even better, below productivity, the industry could stabilize unit labor costs and free up resources for investment without raising prices.[60]

Given the steel industry's past difficulties in implementing wage-price policy, it recognized that it needed to develop a new approach to collective bargaining, one that applied the personnel tactics of Boulwarism to the economic arguments of Kendrick. For the 1959 negotiations, the Coordinating Committee planned on sending a four-man Negotiating Team to the bargaining table, composed of a chief negotiator and one representative each from U.S. Steel, Bethlehem, and Republic. The fourth- through twelfth-largest steelmakers would regularly meet with the Negotiating Team to ensure agreement on the industry-wide stance.[61] The chief negotiator for this round would be U.S. Steel's R. Conrad Cooper, well known to be an emulator of Boulware's methods. A member of Boulware's staff noted shortly after the steel industry's 1956 negotiations that Cooper, then already the presumptive choice, was a "strong believer in 'Boulwarism.'"[62] The chief counsel of the United Steelworkers of America (USWA), Arthur Goldberg, also labeled Cooper an emulator of Boulware, which he certainly did not mean as a compliment.[63] While it is unclear if Boulware ever communicated with Cooper directly, the GE luminary did praise Cooper's leadership to another of his contacts at U.S. Steel: "Even though excitedly occupying a seat in the stands—as both a U.S. Steel stockholder and long-time sufferer in the field of your present activity—I couldn't be more enthusiastic about how you and your associates are conducting this contest on your own without any gratuitous coaching from the sidelines."[64]

The structural factors that supported Boulware's hard-nosed tactics were largely absent at U.S. Steel. GE was a single firm able to play its many unions off each other and prevent any one from shutting down the entire company, whereas the entire steel industry faced a monolithic partner in the USWA. When it came to economic philosophy, however, there was little distance between Cooper and Boulware. Recall that in 1956, Cooper had described the industry's long-term objective as restraining the annualized pace of employment costs that had prevailed since 1940, which he gave in nominal terms as 7.6%–8%, to the industry's own annual productivity growth, which he estimated at about 2.8% in terms of output per man-hour. Of course, nearly every discussion of wage-price policy emphasized tying labor compensation to *national* productivity trends, but the steel industry's emphasis on its own productivity reflected its objective to improve its own profitability while stabilizing the price of steel, not to raise prices by however much unit labor costs rose or by however much the industry's own productivity growth fell short of the national trend.[65]

Under Cooper's guidance, the Coordinating Committee expected that the "key criterion" of negotiations in 1959 would be productivity, and it acknowledged, "we should be much better prepared in this area than we have been in the past." Similar to the discussions then being hashed out at ELRIC, the Coordinating Committee's report noted "the prominence recently given to the relationship between wages and productivity and the confusion which has resulted from a welter of productivity and wage measurements." The industry would have to "convince both the general public and the [Eisenhower] administration that [the industry's] standards are correct and [its] resistance [to union demands] is in the public interest."[66] The Coordinating Committee approached none other than John Kendrick to provide a discussion of this topic for public consumption. According to "very confidential" information shared by Republic Steel's representative on the Coordinating Committee to his headquarters, one of the companies on the committee was already engaged on an elaborate study of productivity; this most likely referred to U.S. Steel, given that it was an active participant in the ELRIC investigation of TFP. To assist this effort, the Coordinating Committee had reached out to Kendrick on the grounds that he was a "very outstanding public proponent of productivity increases as the only fair basis for cost increases."[67]

Kendrick's productivity discussion was included in a "fact book" designed as part of a Boulwarist campaign of public outreach, although it is unclear how much of this publication Kendrick actually authored. The fact book presented an analysis of productivity alongside discussions of other important claims advanced by the industry, including the growing threat of foreign competition and the need to source investment capital. After a brief discussion on the need to use TFP under the heading "The Irrelevance of Output per Man-Hour to Wages," the fact book argued that employment costs per man-hour in the steel industry had increased by 7.8% a year between 1940 and 1958, much higher than Kendrick's 2.3% annualized figure for TFP nationwide in this period or the 1.5% growth per year in steel shipments per man-hour worked. The discussion cited Kendrick's shrinking postwar returns to capital as further evidence that inflationary pressure had emerged on the cost side. The fact book elsewhere calculated that the industry would have suffered a cumulative loss of $35 billion had it absorbed all costs at their nominal value from 1946 to 1957 without raising prices. Thus, until the labor-cost trend could be contained by bringing labor compensation in line with the steel industry's own productivity growth, the industry would be left with no choice but to continue to raise prices.[68]

On the basis of these preparations, Cooper and the Negotiating Team set out an objective of ending the wage-price spiral and stopping the upward creep in unit labor costs. On March 20, 1959, the Coordinating Committee decided that the basis of its offer to the union would be an extension of the existing contract minus the COLA clause, essentially freezing wages in return for price stability. However, on April 8, 1959, the Negotiating Team began to have second thoughts. Although still maintaining the objective of avoiding an increase in labor costs, the team feared that there was no reasonable chance that it could achieve this freeze without a strike. As a contingency, the Negotiating Team had devised a program of "affirmative action" to win governmental and public support for its anti-inflationary efforts. Since the previous year, the industry had investigated the potential cost savings attainable by ending restrictive union work practices then protected by section 2-B of the contract. If the "safe platform" of the freeze did not prove successful, the industry would offer an affirmative Plan B: negotiating changes to contractual language that would remove barriers to higher productivity and so justify an offer of somewhat-higher wages.[69]

When negotiations began in earnest on April 10, 1959, the industry explained the objective of the freeze to the union in the language of wage-price policy: "to avoid further employment cost increases, and thus restrain inflation and encourage continued progress essential to increasing employment opportunities." As steelworker compensation had long outrun productivity gains no matter the basis of measurement, the industry declared that it was time for labor to give back to the other claimants on income. Under the wage freeze, steelworkers would still be able to maintain what amounted to some of the highest hourly pay and benefits of any group of workers, at $3.60/hour when including benefits and pay for time not worked, or a $3.03/hour straight-time wage, compared to the average of $2.19/hour for all workers. In return, the industry pledged to keep its prices stable, allowing the industry to better deal with foreign competitors and assure customers a steady supply of output.[70] During negotiations, Cooper repeatedly justified the wage-price freeze by reference to costs and productivity. Making use of the fact book, Cooper argued that shareholders had not received a greater return through price increases, whereas customers were beginning to show resistance to continually rising prices. Other members of the negotiating team seconded these contentions. Of special note was the reaction of Republic Steel's John Morse to the union estimate of a 4% annual growth trend in postwar labor productivity: the knee-jerk declaration that output per man-hour was not the same as "productivity."[71]

Unfortunately for Cooper and the other industry negotiators, the leadership of the USWA did not share these attitudes. The USWA hoped to use this round of negotiations to build on the gains won in 1956 by shortening hours, providing for better unemployment compensation, and sharing the industry's productivity growth with its remaining employees through higher wages. The USWA also sought to keep up with gains achieved by other unions and called for liberalizations in fringe benefits to match what it described as the new pattern of four-week vacations, double time for holiday work, and higher shift premiums.[72] As in 1956, the union contended that the industry's plan to freeze wages would allow management to capture a higher share of productivity in the form of record profits—not far off from what the industry in fact sought to do. The USWA rejected the industry's comparison of nominal labor costs with productivity as meaningless from the perspective of real purchasing power, and it warned that the union would have to demand nominal wages that exceeded productivity growth if the industry continued to raise prices. The USWA further argued that the steel industry had already captured more than its fair share of productivity, charging that real productivity in the steel industry from 1939 to 1956 had outpaced real straight-time hourly earnings by 68.8% to 47.1%. Despite its questionable choice of base period and apparent omission of fringe benefits, the USWA presented this calculation as evidence that the industry could again afford to pay higher wages without increased prices.[73]

These two rival interpretations of the wage-price spiral collided at the bargaining table. Goldberg alleged that the industry's figures would never pass an independent review and stated that the union could not trust statistics prepared by an outsider such as Kendrick. Goldberg insisted that only government statistics were trustworthy, especially when he could read from the government's tables that output per man-hour had increased nationwide by 3.2% a year since 1939. It is unclear to which statistics Goldberg was referring, but if he was making use of Bureau of Labor Statistics data, then he was ironically rejecting the industry's use of Kendrick by citing government figures based on the man-hour calculations of none other than Kendrick himself.[74] Goldberg also read back the testimony offered by the steel industry at the Kefauver hearings that steel prices were not *that* inflationary to paint the industry's newfound concern about inflation as a ruse designed to turn the public against the union. Cooper and the other members of the Negotiating Team in turn interpreted the USWA's rebuttals as evidence that the union continued to turn a blind eye to the wage-price spiral and sought to win higher wages based on the industry's own profits, summarizing the position of USWA president McDonald this way: "We should still consider ourselves free to make price increases and give the Union what it wants."[75]

Cooper, finding the union to be unresponsive to his proposal for a wage and price freeze, now raised the possibility of moving on to the "affirmative" Plan B. As Cooper wrote to the Coordinating Committee on May 27, 1959, management could no longer continue to offer the initial proposal for a wage and price freeze and ignore the union's counterdemands in good faith. Faced with an impasse, he suggested that it was time for the industry to move from a stance of "no increase in wages or benefit" to "no employment cost increase per unit product." Although the industry would now be willing to explore some contractual areas as long as there was no resulting increase in unit labor costs, Cooper understood this new approach as another route to the same noninflationary outcome. The industry could still absorb some wages and benefits into its subaverage productivity growth, while higher wages would also allow the industry to buy out contract clauses believed to impede productivity. Cooper indicated that no price tag would be attached to this offer so as not to upset the public into siding with the union over work rules.[76]

The industry's sudden shift in priorities appeared surprising to many observers at the time, as well as to later historians without access to the industry's own records. That the industry only raised this issue when the USWA appeared on the verge of submitting to the company's economic demands led the USWA to conclude that the industry's goal all along had been to back McDonald into a corner that he could escape only by exchanging higher wages for modifications to work rules. An irate McDonald rejected this proposal out of hand and, in a charge reminiscent of the language surrounding Boulwarism, attacked the Negotiating Team for "[appearing] willing to permit the Union to continue to exist, but only at the price of converting it into a Company union."[77]

Despite this change in tactics, Cooper's approach continued to emphasize the same need to correct the cost-productivity imbalance, and he viewed the work-rules issue as yet another method to achieve a noninflationary wage-price policy. Cooper explained his perspective to a confused Robert H. Moore of the Federal Mediation and Conciliation Service, who inquired of Cooper in July whether he had been willing to retain 2-B in the initial offer.

Cooper replied in the affirmative: if the union had agreed to a one-year wage freeze, then the companies would have been fine keeping 2-B in the contract. When the union had not shown interest in this proposal, Cooper went on, the Negotiating Team countered by offering to provide some economic gains as long as employment costs per unit would not increase. Moore then asked what benefit 2-B's repeal would yield for the industry, implying that any productivity gains provided by its repeal would be a one-time gain. The industry's Negotiating Team agreed that these gains would be the grounds for a unique wage boost and did not posit them as the basis for an annual wage increase such as an AIF: "[Moore] said he simply wanted to know whether we had in mind some concept such as a 3% rise in productivity per year, and we [the Negotiating Team] disabused him of entertaining any such idea."[78] Like the negotiating team at GE, Cooper did refuse to place the company's own economic offer or estimate of noninflationary growth on the table, even though the steel industry obviously possessed estimates of national and its own productivity. Cooper justified his hesitance to make a quantifiable offer out of the concern that any suggestion would become a floor rather than a ceiling for bargaining. The USWA clearly did not believe this argument, but Cooper's explanation echoed the corporate concerns about the risk of placing a floor under wage growth that had accompanied the GM formula of 1948.[79]

Still, raising the work-rules issue proved to be what Northrup deemed an "inept handling" of what otherwise could have been a textbook engagement with the New Look. Cooper's demands to make unilateral changes to work rules provided McDonald with an issue around which to rally his economically apathetic workers.[80] McDonald threatened a strike unless the industry granted higher wages without work-rule modifications. Red in the face, according to the minutes of negotiations, McDonald declared, "all [I] wanted was [my] fair share of productivity."[81] The union's demands included an annual wage increase of about 7¢/hour, equivalent to the AIF enjoyed by the autoworkers. Factoring in fringe benefits and the costs of the COLA demanded in addition to this deferred wage, the total package was much too large for the industry to consider. The Coordinating Committee evaluated the costs at 22¢/hour a year or about 6% in annual costs, and the union's own estimate of 15¢/hour or 4% was also considered by the industry as too high to permit the stabilization of unit labor costs.[82]

President Eisenhower appealed for a delay of the strike once the contract formally expired, but two weeks later, on July 15, half a million steelworkers stopped work. In an effort to provide a peaceful resolution, in August 1959 the Bureau of Labor Statistics released an official report on economic trends in the steel industry, known as the Mitchell Report after Secretary of Labor James Mitchell. Without touching on the work-rules issue, the conclusions of the Mitchell Report tended to support the industry's contentions about unit labor costs. The report found that output per man-hour in the steel industry had increased by 74% from 1940 to June 1959 for wage employees and 58% when accounting for the growing share of white-collar or overhead workers. In the postwar years, 1947–1957, steel's output per total employee man-hour had risen by 2.6% a year, compared to 3.7% for the economy as a whole and 3.1% for the manufacturing sector. As labor compensation had risen faster than productivity, employment costs per unit output had increased by 131% for wage employees and 153% for all employees in the steel industry from 1940 to June 1959, although steel prices, up 178% since 1940, had outpaced both unit employment costs and the commodity wholesale price index, which grew by 134% in that time.[83]

Both the industry and union found statistics in the Mitchell Report that backed their positions on wage-price policy. The steel industry welcomed this report for supporting its arguments about wages, prices, and competition, especially by showing that total employment costs in the steel industry had exceeded productivity growth for the industry as well as for the economy as a whole.[84] In response to these figures, Cooper, who had been reluctant to name a specific figure for what the companies felt they could absorb lest it become the union's minimum target, identified 2% and then finally the industry's own postwar labor-productivity growth of 2.6% a year as the maximum amount the industry considered absorbable without price adjustment.[85] USWA president McDonald also cited the Mitchell Report to reject Cooper's 2% offer on the grounds that the industry "should at least agree to an economic package which will keep [its] unit labor costs at the same level, rather than decrease them." The USWA further noted that the Mitchell Report showed a fall in unit labor costs since 1957, a trend that "demonstrates that hourly wages and benefits can be increased without requiring a price increase." The USWA estimated that the real costs of its current compensation demands fell within the 3.7% annual increase in output per man-hour for the postwar economy as a whole cited by the Mitchell Report. According to orthodox wage-price policy, an industry with a subaverage productivity would be allowed to raise prices if it paid compensation at the national average rate, but given steel's objective of price stability, Cooper rejected any nominal settlement that exceeded the idiosyncratic productivity rate.[86]

With the two sides unable to compromise over productivity and work rules, Eisenhower reluctantly decided to invoke the Taft-Hartley Act. Under that law, the president could enjoin a strike for eighty days, followed by a vote on the company's final offer. But as that deadline neared, McDonald steered the USWA to wage packages in the can and aluminum industries estimated at 52¢/hour over thirty months. McDonald had also convinced Kaiser Steel, one of the smaller and more maverick firms in the steel industry, to accept a similar settlement rather than try the route of a Taft-Hartley injunction. McDonald felt no reason to settle for any less from the rest of the steel industry, suggesting that the strike would resume after the injunction ended. Fearing what the Democratic Congress, already antsy about inflation, might do in response to this election-year turmoil, Vice President Richard Nixon and Secretary of Labor Mitchell made a backroom intervention: a compromise package that they valued at 41¢/hour over thirty months, with a joint study commission to examine the work-rules issue.[87]

Traditionally, this outcome has been seen as at best a stalemate and at worst, as Jack Metzgar concludes in his history-cum-memoir of the 1959 strike, "a sweeping victory for the union, a humiliating defeat for the companies."[88] The USWA emerged from the strike with higher wages and section 2-B still intact, but to treat the steel industry as the unambiguous loser of this dispute ignores that Cooper's goal for the better part of a decade had been to stabilize the industry's unit labor costs. In 1959–1960, Cooper accomplished the objective he had set out in 1956: cutting the long-run labor-cost trend in half. Cooper estimated that this settlement would raise labor compensation for the industry by 3.5%–3.75% a year. Though more than the industry's own 2.6% productivity growth trend identified in the Mitchell Report, Cooper and U.S. Steel chairman and CEO Roger Blough both appreciated that a sharp break had been made with the 8% annual increases in labor compensation that had prevailed since 1940. For the first time in a decade, the steel industry had gone a whole year without paying a wage increase, and the new contract limited the costs of the COLA such that the clause was virtually inoperable. Had the industry not held out for this deal, it most likely would have had to settle for the contract that the

United Steelworkers had wrung out of Kaiser Steel, which cost about 30% more. The new Human Relations Research Committee, moreover, offered the possibility of modifying work practices as well as of reaching some sort of mutual understanding about the relationship between labor costs and productivity moving forward. Viewing all of these results optimistically, the industry declared that it would not raise the price of steel—for the time being, at least—and so maintained the price stability that had prevailed throughout 1959.[89]

The Human Relations Research Committee would indeed go a long way toward restoring some of the trust between management and labor that had been lost over the issue of work rules. The fundamental premise of this new organization was that management should be able to harness technology to create benefits for capital without adversely impacting labor. Operating on a standing basis without the pressure of an impending contract deadline or media scrutiny, the committee replaced posturing with problem solving in its many fact-finding subcommittees. When it came to seniority, for instance, the two sides recognized common objectives in creating a broad-based labor pool and dealing with the challenges of technological unemployment. On grievances, both parties recognized a need to simplify and speed up their resolution.[90]

On one key issue, however, the animosities of 1959 remained implacable: wages. The USWA intended to use the Economic Guides Subcommittee to reach agreement with management on a more favorable set of standards for wage and benefit determination, such as the cost of living or productivity. Instead, the industry's representatives refused to discuss anything resembling an annual wage formula and held fast to its previous arguments that steelworker compensation had run ahead of productivity over the long run. USWA research director Otis Brubaker wrote after the fifth meeting that the industry apparently saw no use for the subcommittee other than to "brainwash the Union representatives," and he feared that the industry's demand for the union to acknowledge this "debt" heralded a future collision. Brubaker acknowledged that although there may be a "highly questionable justification" for making this argument as part of a public-relations campaign, the industry's insistence on pushing this approach at a private meeting signaled a "declaration of war." The industry continually refused to provide the union with cost data to justify its emphasis on "competitiveness" as a guide for bargaining, apparently fearing that data disclosures would become fodder for a union "fishing expedition." Still, its projection of productivity growth at 2% a year left the USWA with the unmistakable impression that the industry intended to hold the union to this amount or less when the contract was up for negotiation in 1962.[91]

Compared to this continued conflict over the distribution of income, the experience of Kaiser Steel demonstrated that a more amicable attitude toward wages and productivity was possible in the steel industry. After settling the strike, Kaiser and the USWA had formed an independent long-range committee of their own to consider issues of productivity, technology, and employment. Compared to the "guides" that the Coordinating Committee offered to the USWA, Brubaker expressed his satisfaction that Kaiser was much more willing to discuss how it would share the "fruits" of productivity with its workers.[92] After three years of friendly discussions, in 1963, the committee introduced a Long Range Sharing Plan in which employees who gave up their individual incentives would be entitled to 32.5% of all cost savings that resulted from greater efficiency. Some of the savings were paid out as a monthly bonus, with the rest placed in reserve to match the costs of wages and benefits elsewhere in the industry. The plan also promised that any employees who were displaced from their job through technology or changed work practices would be entitled to continued employment elsewhere with the company.[93]

Although ostensibly a landmark in managerial-stakeholder relations, Kaiser's bilateral approach did not entirely address the concerns that had led the Coordinating Committee to tolerate the animosities of the New Look. Just as Boulwarism had developed in the unique context of GE, so too did this plan reflect the idiosyncrasies of Kaiser. The company operated from a single plant in Southern California, a fast-growing market where it would not be hard for workers to find another job. Of its seven thousand employees, less than 40% had operated on the individual incentive system, compared to the industry average of over 75%. The rest of the industry could also question the appropriateness of profit sharing as a strategy to restrain costs and boost returns. When employees began to grumble about declining bonus payments after several years, Kaiser committed in 1967 to pay out all cost savings as a bonus, even though this meant it would have to match the industry's compensation entirely out of the share of income earmarked for investment and investors.[94] Kaiser continued to avoid crisis bargaining and was able to introduce new technology and reduce work crews with less resistance than other firms, but it did so at the cost of having the highest-paid employees in the industry even as it operated on the front lines of the import invasion on the West Coast. To the remainder of a steel industry so concerned about the danger of higher costs to profits and competitiveness, the uncertain costs of Kaiser's gamble rendered this strategy too risky to emulate.[95]

CONCLUSION

When inflation subsided in the late 1950s, contemporaries steeped in cost-push theory attributed this outcome to more than fiscal and monetary policy alone. Eisenhower's final *Economic Report of the President* noted in January 1961 that price stability had been achieved through governmental fiscal and monetary policies acting jointly with "the control of unit production costs—a responsibility that in our free society rests primarily with private individuals and groups."[96] Of course, wage-price policy was theorized to remove the need to trade higher unemployment for reduced inflation, whereas management's New Look developed against the backdrop of high unemployment. The White House had also played a much more hands-on role in the steel settlement than its calls for voluntary behavior would suggest.

Nevertheless, recession, imports, and the Eisenhower administration ultimately provided the push that enabled industry to achieve the goal that it had already adopted for itself. The industrial leaders who came together in groups such as ELRIC, concerned about their ability to fund capital investment in an increasingly competitive environment, recognized that productivity offered the solution to their problems. The executives who spearheaded the New Look, most notably Boulware, had been among the most outspoken opponents of the GM formula during the 1940s. In the place of this rigid approach to wage-price policy, Boulware and his emulators developed a more flexible strategy in which productivity served as a guide rather than a rule for negotiations. Firms worked to understand the new concept of total-factor productivity and consulted with its leading advocate, John Kendrick, about the implications for returns on capital if they substituted this metric for the traditional labor productivity.

Translating these theories into an actual wage-price policy would prove more difficult. Management argued that wage restraint was in the best interests not simply of capital but of labor and the public as well, as it would enable price stability and the increased investment necessary to maintain industrial employment in the United States. When unions, accustomed to sharing the rents of oligopoly pricing and concerned about technological unemployment, disagreed with this argument, management could have reached a compromise, as demonstrated by Kaiser. Yet by and large, corporate American management chose to work not with organized labor but around it. Buoyed by the Eisenhower NLRB, Boulware and his staff at General Electric pushed the boundaries of what constituted good-faith bargaining by directly communicating their best offer to their employees. In the steel industry, management adopted an unyielding position in collective bargaining to achieve its cost objectives. These New Look tactics fulfilled their intended goals, producing multiyear contracts at much less cost than those of the previous decade. The frictions, animosities, and resentments that they left in their wake, however, suggested that management had not yet found a permanent replacement to prices as the means to control the distribution of corporate income.

CHAPTER FIVE

Assuming Direct Control

WAGE-PRICE POLICY BECOMES INCOMES POLICY, 1960–1968

DURING THE NEW LOOK of the 1950s, corporate America had come its closest yet to the ideal distribution of a noninflationary wage-price policy. To the economists of the Keynesian Consensus, this performance left much to be desired. It was not only that management was pushing the boundaries of what could be considered free collective bargaining, seen by the Keynesians as one of the institutional pillars of democracy that wage-price policy was supposed to preserve. More importantly, restraint had only occurred once recession temporarily shifted the balance of power to management. When the economy moved back into expansion, what force could prevent firms and unions from attempting to hijack this macroeconomic stimulus into their own coffers?

This chapter explores how wage-price policy transformed from a private and voluntary initiative into a governmental, quasi-mandatory incomes policy during the 1960s. That decade witnessed the culmination of the "Fiscal Revolution" in postwar U.S. political economy, in which policymakers embraced a commitment to growth through the "commercial Keynesian" tax cuts contained in the Revenue Act of 1964.[1] Before taking these steps, the Keynesians of the White House Council of Economic Advisers (CEA) had insisted that the government stand ready to enforce wage-price policy. John F. Kennedy's famous showdown with the steel industry over its pricing in April 1962 represented more than a one-time assertion of presidential power over private business.[2] Rather, the steel dispute marked the starting point for Keynesian efforts to force the private sector to distribute income in accordance with wage-price policy. Kennedy subsequently adopted a more conciliatory tone toward business, but the CEA's "guideposts" received a second wind under Lyndon Johnson as an alternative to anti-inflationary fiscal restraint.[3]

Past accounts of the guideposts have focused on how a host of colorful White House policymakers applied suasion and jawboning to industries ranging from such familiar concerns as steel and autos to more exotic markets such as shoe leather, molybdenum, and New York City subways.[4] Rather than repeat this encyclopedic approach, this chapter asks why steel and the other industries that had previously committed themselves to restraint during the New Look needed to be jawboned into compliance only a few years later. After all, the guideposts were in essence little different from the distributive arguments about productivity that ELRIC and its members had previously popularized, and management achieved its objective of stabilizing unit labor costs during the recovery from recession in the early 1960s. Although the steel industry persisted in its efforts to widen margins, industrial costs and prices remained remarkably stable in the first half of the decade. Economists have reached differing conclusions about the causal role of the guideposts in shifting managerial attitudes toward pricing, but it is notable that prices remained stable despite the failure of Kennedy and Johnson to follow through on threats to apply antitrust law or to expand imports in order to weaken the power of industrial oligopolies.[5]

As this chapter argues, the true conflict between the managerial and federal understandings of wage-price policy and stakeholder value emerged on the side not of prices but of wages. The Fiscal Revolution expanded demand and output, allowing profits to reach postwar highs even as the prices of commodities that were long considered to be administered remained relatively stable. But the economy soon expanded too far, past the point of full employment, and as Lyndon Johnson pressured the Federal Reserve to keep monetary policy relaxed, demand-pull inflation emerged.[6] Given these conditions, it was labor, not management, that realized that it had more to gain by opposing the distribution of income prescribed by the guideposts. As excess demand pulled up competitive market prices and cut into real wages, union members voted out their old leaders and demanded a larger slice of economic growth. Once the Democratic White House had sided with its key political supporters and begun to encourage firms to pay for labor peace, corporate management saw little reason to continue to hold out for restraint, whether in the form of the government's guideposts or its own voluntary efforts, until economic conditions changed.

THE PHILLIPS CURVE IN CAMELOT

The trade-off between inflation and unemployment was not a novel theory when the Eisenhower recessions of the late 1950s rekindled interest in finding a way out of this dilemma. Melvin Reder had described an economy operating under a full-employment guarantee in 1948, and Abba Lerner had discussed the need for wage-price policy to combat cost-push inflation in 1951; but the trade-off between inflation and unemployment had not become known as the Reder Relation or the Lerner Line. Instead, this relationship only received its definitive name in the late 1950s in response to an influential paper that in fact had nothing to do with the United States at all: "The Relation between Unemployment and the Rate of Change of Money Wage Rates in the United Kingdom, 1861–1957," by A. W. Phillips of the London School of Economics. Phillips's conclusion was not simply that a trade-off existed but that it had remained stable since the second half of the nineteenth century, suggesting that institutional change and unionization had not replaced the laws of supply and demand in the United Kingdom.[7] To economists on both sides of the Atlantic seeking alternatives to fiscal and monetary austerity, Phillips's paper appeared in the right place at the right time to become the foundational text for a much more ambitious approach to policymaking. As Abba Lerner later commented, the "Phillips Curve" revolutionized the literature by showing that there existed a continuous set of trade-offs from which could be selected the optimal point where harm from added inflation equated the benefits of reduced unemployment.[8]

Phillips of course had not named this set of trade-offs after himself. That honor would be bestowed in 1960, when two of the leading American economists of the twentieth century, Paul Samuelson and Robert Solow of the Massachusetts Institute of Technology, applied Phillips's analysis to the United States in an attempt to distinguish movements *along* the curve from movements *of* the curve itself.[9] Samuelson and Solow described movements along the curve as the "menu of choice" available to policymakers in selecting different trade-offs between inflation and unemployment. Samuelson and Solow made a rough estimate of these two conditions by fitting a curve through the U.S. data for 1933–1958. They found that what Lerner had termed "high full employment," the point where cyclical unemployment was eliminated and beyond which demand-pull pressures would emerge, involved a trade-off between 3% unemployment and an annual inflation rate of 4.5%. But these data also suggested that the U.S. curve had shifted over time, an effect that "might represent the institutional changes on which cost-push theories rest," such as the development of union market power or postwar expectations of full employment. Before the Great Depression, U.S. manufacturing wages had risen at the same rate as productivity grew and hence were consistent with price stability at 3% unemployment; in the period since 1946, Samuelson and Solow suggested that it could take as much as 5%–6% unemployment to obtain price stability.[10]

Samuelson and Solow closed their paper with the suggestion that policymakers should not only choose what point along the curve the economy would function but also attempt to shift the curve to obtain better trade-offs. An entirely more favorable menu of choices would be obtained through the use of "feasible institutional reforms . . . designed to move the American Phillips' curves downward and to the left."[11] Wage-price policy, although not cited in the paper directly, was one such method. As Samuelson later elaborated, incomes policy shifted the entire curve by causing a less-than-competitive economy to better approximate the set of trade-offs that would exist in a more competitive and less sticky economy.[12] Samuelson served as economic adviser to the presidential campaign of John F. Kennedy, and following the election, he urged the president-elect to apply "government influence . . . without invoking direct controls on wages and prices" to combat inflation without placing the economy in recession.[13] Solow, meanwhile, would bring this perspective directly to the Kennedy CEA, where he served as its chief staff economist. Given Solow's work with Samuelson, it was fitting that the first memo that Kennedy's new CEA chairman, the University of Minnesota economist Walter Heller, sent to Solow included a request for an early meeting on the wage-price issue.[14]

Initially, the White House had hoped that the private sector could, under proper supervision, arrive at this conclusion on its own. Kennedy's inaugural secretary of labor was Arthur Goldberg, who in his previous capacity as counsel to the United Steelworkers had been a proponent of the 8%-a-year settlements of the mid-1950s. Goldberg interpreted the hard-line bargaining such as he had experienced in 1959 not as part of an effort to engineer a more competitive relationship between costs, prices, and productivity but as part of a wider corporate project to undermine the fabric of the New Deal order. To forestall this outcome, Goldberg created the President's Advisory Committee on Labor-Management Policy. At best, Goldberg anticipated that this committee would form the basis of a broad social compact that would reaffirm the New Deal order and convince management to grant labor a larger share of income with a smile on its face. Even if the committee did not rise to that lofty goal, bringing corporate and labor leaders together might provide a more peaceful way to resolve the pressing industrial-labor relations issues of his day: automation, work rules, strikes and compulsory dispute settlement, and international competitiveness.[15]

Goldberg's tripartite commission quickly ran into difficulties. The labor side attracted top names, including Walter Reuther and David McDonald, and the public membership also drew from the leading ranks of industrial-labor relations experts and economists. But the management side was second rate, as Goldberg intentionally sought out executives whom he perceived as receptive to the New Deal order. The committee included Ford but not GM, Inland Steel instead of U.S. Steel, and Reynolds in the place of Alcoa. Most egregiously, there was no representative from the leading firm in the realm of industrial-labor relations, GE.[16] A second problem quickly encountered by the committee was that almost every discussion led back to the problem of wages and prices. The subcommittee tasked with discussing improvements to collective bargaining stumbled over incorporating wage-price policy, "statesmanlike conduct," and the public interest. The task force on international competition faced concerns from management representatives about inflationary cost and pricing trends.[17]

Subcommittee Number 5, where matters of wage-price policy were to be hammered out definitively, never even made it past the working-paper stage.[18] Although the labor members of the subcommittee included some proponents of a national incomes policy, the majority of its members could not be considered advocates. It certainly did not help that the executives and economists most responsible for developing voluntary wage-price policy in the 1940s and 1950s, including R. Conrad Cooper of U.S. Steel and Lemuel Boulware of GE, were missing from the subcommittee and its cohort of economic consultants. Instead, the chief economic consultant to the subcommittee was the conservative industrial economist George Shultz. A former staff economist at the Eisenhower CEA, Shultz had gone on to join the

University of Chicago, where he had been strongly influenced by Milton Friedman on the importance of the free market.[19]

Shultz and most of the subcommittee expressed deep skepticism about the feasibility of a national wage-price policy. In Shultz's first draft of the subcommittee's report, he was willing to commit the subcommittee to a guidepost of productivity only to the extent that ELRIC had in the previous decade: "We cannot endorse proposals . . . that the national rate of productivity change sets an appropriate standard for particular wage changes and that efforts to make all wage changes conform to this standard are the way to achieve non-inflationary wage bargaining." Exhortations from the government to enforce this standard would not make it any easier to fit square industries into a round wage-price peg, a criticism similar to that offered against GM's AIF over the previous decade.[20] The business representatives to the subcommittee protested that Shultz's report did not accept the existence of pattern bargaining in labor markets, and the labor consultants filed a long dissent in favor of a wage-price review board. Yet every member of the subcommittee agreed that a single productivity guide should not be adopted for individual wage-price decisions, stressing that other factors had to be considered in actual practice.[21] When Shultz revised his draft, he expressed fewer qualms about using productivity as a guide "on the average," but just as had John Kendrick and the members of ELRIC, he clarified that "'on the average' does not provide an adequate guide for individual cases."[22]

The failure of Subcommittee Number 5 to produce anything more than a vague assertion of the importance of productivity came as no surprise to CEA chairman Heller, who had given Kennedy less than fifty-fifty odds that the Advisory Committee would solve the wage-price problem on its own.[23] Kennedy had ordered his CEA "to try hard to bring the wage-price problem under control" that June after Federal Reserve Chairman William Martin had informed the president that the Fed would be more willing to take an aggressive stance on monetary policy if the wage-price situation were resolved. Yet as the CEA worked to develop standards independently of Goldberg's subcommittee, it found that Keynesian economists also disagreed over the same practical issues that had rendered Goldberg's committee so unproductive. As CEA member Kermit Gordon was the first to admit at a meeting with outside economic consultants the day after Kennedy had charged them to resolve the wage-price issue, the council was groping for a wage-price strategy. Lloyd Ulman, the CEA's chief labor economist, argued that accepting a cost-push creep was the lesser of evils: "An overall wage policy is dangerous. We should not insist on price stability growth, etc., and then not be able to deliver." Other CEA consultants suggested pursuing full employment, inflation be damned, and hoping that higher productivity would offset any wage-push pressures. The middle-ground position was to develop a wage-price policy that would permit the attainment of full employment with price stability, but these economists, including Paul Samuelson, still lacked a consensus on how to enforce such a theory on the private sector if necessary.[24]

With recovery from recession under way in the summer of 1961, the economy appeared to be moving toward the danger zone where firms and unions would become bolder in experimenting with cost-push inflation. To the CEA, the most immediate threat to the three-year record of price stability emanated from the steel industry.[25] Although the steel industry remained committed to its New Look understanding of productivity, it was beginning to question whether wage restraint was a sufficient precondition of financial success. Profitability in the steel industry had continued to fall, from 7.3% as a percentage of sales in 1957 to 5.7% in 1960, while shipments slipped by about 10%. As spending on modernization and expansion continued, the industry's capital spending exceeded its cash flow by a cumulative $870 million between 1958 and 1961. Capacity usage had recovered from its 1958 low, but it remained below the rates of the mid-1950s. When it came to foreign competition, a second motivation for wage-price restraint, imports also remained higher than they had been before the period of restraint, at 4.7% of domestic consumption in 1960 and 1961. The recession surely lay behind many of these poor outcomes, but the industry concluded that its decision to absorb wages into frozen prices was responsible for these disappointing financial trends.[26]

Considering it likely that the industry would try to expand its profit margins at the same time that it paid the final deferred increase of the 1960 contract, Kennedy himself directed his administration to implement a noninflationary wage-price policy for the steel industry. In the summer of 1961, Kennedy and Heller worked out a plan of action in which Democratic senators would launch a preemptive assault on the industry's claims to a price increase through a series of speeches written by the CEA.[27] Kennedy then wrote to the industry to emphasize that statesmanship in absorbing wage increases would place the burden on the union to restrain wages when the contract expired in 1962.[28] Roger Blough, chairman and CEO of U.S. Steel, acknowledged Kennedy's between-the-lines offer to pressure the USWA, and on September 21, 1961, Blough informed Kennedy that there would be no price increase that year.[29]

This encounter with the steel industry suggested to Heller that the private sector could not be counted on to hold to wage-price policy voluntarily. At the same time, the White House's success in preventing a steel-price increase also indicated a viable strategy to combat cost-push pressures. In several speeches that October, Heller introduced a new component to the formerly voluntary approach to basing wages and prices around productivity, an innovation that he described to the president as "[not] very sexy, but it may still be seminal." The federal government's role in wage-price policy was no longer simply to prevent excess demand from emerging but to persuade and to induce management and labor to negotiate in the public interest. Where the Eisenhower administration had refused to make more than general exhortations, Heller argued that a "reasoned and persuasive appeal for specific actions" such as had been made in steel was a constructive tool to ensure adherence to wage-price policy.[30]

The administration's new approach would be formally unveiled in the 1962 *Economic Report of the President* in a discussion apparently written largely by Solow.[31] In industries where firms and unions held discretion over prices and wages, the CEA welcomed bargaining over the distribution of income as long as the two sides did not try to paper over this dispute and "bargain implicitly about the general price level." To avoid rent-seeking and close the safety valve of prices, the report provided "guideposts" of how prices and wages should behave in a "smoothly functioning competitive economy operating near full employment." The key principle of the guideposts was, as always, the algebraic relationship that labor compensation can rise in percentage terms as fast as output per man-hour does without generating inflation or causing a shift in the distribution of income. An industry's prices should then rise or fall based on the difference between the national trend rate of productivity and its own idiosyncratic rate. If an industry's own rate of productivity growth exceeded the national average, then by relating wages to the national average, unit labor costs would fall and the industry could afford to lower its prices. Conversely, for those industries whose productivity grew slower than the national rate, prices would be allowed to rise to offset the excess cost absorption. Unlike the members of

ELRIC, the CEA emphasized that basing compensation on the standard of labor productivity would not deprive capital of its fair returns, given the textbook expectations of economic growth. However, the CEA implicitly backed management's position on costs when it linked national productivity to changes in *nominal* rather than *real* labor compensation. In other words, the CEA did not contemplate a COLA adjustment on top of the national productivity factor.[32]

THE SHOWDOWN IN STEEL AND ITS AFTERMATH

The *Economic Report* on its face contained one of the most detailed discussions of wage-price policy to date, but there was little new in its policy prescriptions. During a roundtable discussion on the guideposts sponsored by the National Industrial Conference Board, Solow later expressed his surprise "that so much originality and special character have been imputed to the guideposts" when the Eisenhower CEA had included a similar discussion in its own *Economic Report.*[33] Even the nomenclature was not that novel. Lemuel Boulware and Francis Highton of GE had used "guidepost" to describe the relationship of wage growth to the national productivity trend during the company's 1960 labor negotiations. While it is unclear if Heller and Solow were aware of this earlier usage, the coincidence did not escape the notice of the unions that bargained with GE, which criticized Kennedy for having endorsed a wage policy utilized by their employer.[34]

Nevertheless, the 1962 *Economic Report* represented a major shift in federal economic policy. Behind these discussions of productivity and performance on the average was the implicit threat that the government would take actions to ensure that firms and unions followed these microeconomic rules. The section of the report above the president's signature never actually used the word "guidepost," distancing the president from what was sure to be a controversial tactic. The CEA's section described only the benefit of "an informed public . . . equipped [with the guideposts] to judge for itself their compatibility with the national interest." But as Heller explained to Kennedy in comparing the guideposts to the British government's recent demands for labor's compliance with wage restraint, the CEA's euphemism of public opinion was a "cautious subterfuge" intended to achieve the same result as a European incomes policy.[35]

With guideposts in hand, the administration prepared its intervention in the next steel bargaining round. Heller calculated that steel's output per man-hour had risen by 2.4% a year since 1947, although adjusting for different rates of capacity produced a trend of 3.4%, about equal to his estimate of the national postwar productivity rate. Given these trends, Heller concluded that a wage settlement of 2.5%–3% a year would be in line with the industry's productivity, preventing the rise in unit labor costs that would legitimize higher prices under the guideposts.[36]

In a White House meeting on January 23, 1962, Kennedy urged David McDonald of the USWA and Roger Blough of U.S. Steel to expedite their negotiations and arrive at a noninflationary settlement, stating that the key to price stability would be to keep wages within the bounds of overall productivity. Where the conversation then turned is less clear. Secretary of Labor Goldberg states in his recollection of this meeting that he called for "a modest settlement within the range of productivity and consistent with price stability," but he also claims to have indicated that it was not proper to bargain terms with the president. Blough's memoirs also deny any specifics being mentioned. But according to McDonald's account of this meeting, Kennedy asked him to accept a 3% productivity factor as a limit. McDonald recognized the concept from the *Economic Report,* and he reluctantly accepted the president's request. McDonald also relates that Blough argued at this meeting that the productivity factor should be considered closer to 2% than 3%, similar to the position taken in 1959 and on the Human Relations Committee. All three accounts agree that Blough refused to make any commitment on prices. When negotiations hit an impasse a month later, Goldberg ultimately brokered a compromise settlement of about 10¢/hour, or 2.5%.[37]

Blough later claimed that the industry and the USWA would have agreed on a low compromise without White House involvement, noting that it was hard to square Kennedy's supposed wage ceiling of 3% with McDonald's ultimate capitulation to 2.5%.[38] The union's focus in 1962 centered on matters of job security rather than wage scales, and the joint industry-union Human Relations Committee aided in settling these noneconomic issues three months ahead of the contract's expiration date.[39] As wage rates remained constant in the contract, the CEA estimated that the total costs of this settlement represented a 2.6%, or 10.9¢/hour, annual increase. In hindsight, it could actually have cost even less, at 2.2%, well below the 3.6% annual costs of the thirty-month contract signed in 1960 (see table 2).[40]

Despite having finally brought labor costs in line with its productivity trend, the goal that R. Conrad Cooper had established in the previous decade, the steel industry refused to abandon its drive for higher prices. Its unease with even a low 2% settlement was apparent to Kennedy when he called Cooper to congratulate him on reaching a noninflationary settlement. Kennedy later asked Treasury Secretary C. Douglas Dillon to sound out Blough about why Cooper had seemed rather unhappy. Blough struggled to come up with an explanation, but a comment that Blough made to Dillon suggests the likely reason: the cost of the settlement left U.S. Steel "with a four year old problem [of inadequate financing]," even though, as Blough separately explained, "the settlement may be the best in 20 years."[41] As Blough explained to the press shortly thereafter, competing with foreign producers required investment in modern technologies. In order to attract the capital needed to compete in the long run, the steel industry would have to raise prices at the risk of damaging its short-run competitive position.[42]

The guideposts of the 1962 *Economic Report* indeed contained an escape clause permitting higher prices where necessary to permit capital investment. From this perspective, an upward adjustment in steel prices might be interpreted as guidepost compliant. Of course, the guideposts had also stated that prices should fall or at least rise slowly in an industry that had previously used its market power to push up its profits compared to investments of comparable risk. To the steel industry, however, this caveat applied to the mid-1950s, not the disappointing experience of voluntary restraint.[43] Heller subsequently admitted that he was receptive to the industry's argument about the need for capital investment, but he stressed that economic recovery would increase capacity utilization and reduce unit labor costs if prices did not rise. In any case, Heller also noted that the industry had not cut dividends to increase retained earnings.[44]

Concerned that steel had again begun to make public statements about its finances, Heller urged Kennedy to dispute the industry's arguments that "would make steel eligible for a price increase under that section of the wage-price guidelines which allows price increases to industries with below-average productivity trends." Unfortunately for Heller, this memo arrived on the president's desk five hours too late to be anything but "an ironic note, now mainly of historical interest."[45] At 5:30 that evening, April 10, 1962, Blough entered Kennedy's office. At 6:00, Kennedy called in Goldberg and handed him the same statement that Blough had just read: U.S. Steel would raise its prices by 3.5%, or an average of $6/ton across the line in order to "catch up" with the long-run excess of labor compensation above productivity.[46] The CEA estimated that this increase would add a total of $290 million to the industry's profits at a 75% utilization rate, as opposed to $500 million if utilization rose to 90% in the absence of a price increase.[47]

Blough later claimed that the decision to inform Kennedy in person was a courtesy and better than the president reading about the increase in the morning paper.[48] But Blough revealed a more convincing explanation over a decade later in a chance conversation with Walt Rostow, the economist who had served as Kennedy's deputy national security adviser. Blough had by then retired from U.S. Steel and was attending, irony of ironies, a conference on wage-price policy sponsored by the Kennedy Presidential Library. Rostow and Blough were on friendly terms by then, as Walt's brother, Eugene, was the dean of Blough's alma mater, Yale Law School. Rostow decided to ask Blough about the 1962 incident. As Rostow recalls the conversation, Blough explained that the increasing government interest in his industry's behavior represented "a violation of the right of private enterprise to set prices freely; and he and his colleagues had to react."[49]

After all the administration had done to achieve a clearly noninflationary settlement, Kennedy took Blough's action as a personal insult, telling McDonald over the phone that evening, "You've been screwed and I've been screwed."[50] The White House now undertook its first coordinated effort at enforcing its model for the distribution of corporate income. When Robert Tyson, chairman of the U.S. Steel Finance Committee, asked Goldberg what could make this animosity all go away, the secretary of labor was blunt: if the industry rescinded the price increase, Goldberg would recommend a governmental review board to determine what amount of price increase was permissible. U.S. Steel rejected Goldberg's offer out of hand as yet another government intrusion into private business. Even had it been receptive, others within the White House warned against a board, fearing that it could rule in favor of the industry's pricing.[51]

The Kennedy administration also flirted with an antitrust case that would destroy the steel industry's pricing power. The administration had previously floated the possibility of impaneling a grand jury to hear evidence on monopolistic behavior and price leadership in the steel industry, but as recently as September 1961, Lee Loevinger, Kennedy's antitrust chief, doubted that any indictable offense would be uncovered and warned of negative perceptions of government impropriety and harassment.[52] The events of April 1962 threw that caution to the wind. The Department of Justice had been about to charge the industry with fixing the price of extras and standards for carbon steel sheet, but that case involved an explicit case of conspiracy under section 1 of the Sherman Act, not oligopoly behavior, and it actually postponed this filing so as not to confuse that issue with the present crisis.[53] A grand jury was impaneled, and investigators quickly uncovered textbook evidence of conscious parallelism. Officials from each individual company claimed that they had reached their own conclusion on prices without any formal collusion, but with the exception of price leader U.S. Steel, these meetings were "remarkably brief and casual," with no written material prepared. The degree of price leadership in the industry was also suggested by the quick reversal of opinions held by Bethlehem Steel's Edmund Martin, who, the FBI would verify, had only hours before the announcement of the price increase stated that the industry should continue to hold the line and even cut prices in the face of competition.[54]

Still, an antitrust case was not a quick fix to the administration's immediate problem, nor was it a foolproof one on the basis of this circumstantial evidence alone. When a few of the smaller steel companies hesitated to follow U.S. Steel's lead, the CEA advocated for a different competitive strategy to combat price leadership. Break off enough capacity from the overall price pattern and market forces would do the rest in bringing prices back down. Behind the scenes, Undersecretary of Commerce Edward Gudeman contacted Joseph Block, the chairman of Inland Steel, to urge him not to follow U.S. Steel. Block was a member of the president's Labor-Management Advisory Committee, which raised the hopes of the administration that he would recognize the importance of the public interest in managerial calculations. It also did not hurt that Inland Steel, which focused on high-value thin, flat-rolled products, was in the best financial health of any major steel company, with 1961 earnings at 7.5% of sales and a 1960 operating rate of 78.6%. U.S. Steel, in contrast, focused on the production of heavy steel and had a net income of 5.8% of sales in 1961 and a 65.1% operating rate in 1960.[55] Which of these factors weighed more heavily on Block's mind is unknown, but on April 13, 1962, Inland's board rejected following U.S. Steel. When Armco and perpetual maverick Kaiser Steel likewise decided not to follow, the others capitulated. Seventy-two hours after first announcing the increase, U.S. Steel rescinded its price increase.[56]

Exhortation, backed up by the threats of jawboning, had scored a stunning success for both the wage and price guideposts, but there was a problem with this approach: the private sector could fight back. Unease about Kennedy's intent to intervene in other markets and a gloomy outlook for profitability if forced to absorb labor settlements compounded business pessimism about an economic recovery that had already begun to slow.[57] When on May 28, 1962, the Dow-Jones Industrial Average suffered its largest one-day decline since the Great Depression, Kennedy and many financial commentators believed that the steel dispute had precipitated this drop by eroding business confidence. As much as Heller attempted to attribute these market fluctuations to the draining of inflationary expectations for capital gains, uncertainty had real consequences. Business planned investment declined by 12% in the second quarter of 1962 from the preceding quarter, with steel's plans down by 56%.[58]

Concerned that the guideposts had become an economic liability, Kennedy quickly backed away from his antagonistic efforts to shift the Phillips Curve. By July 1962, at a farewell reception for CEA member James Tobin, it was clear to the guest of honor that the president "was obviously having second thoughts about [the steel crisis] and the whole matter of wage-price guideposts": "With a knowing look at me, he said we may have bit off more than we can chew."[59] When Secretary of Labor Goldberg resigned in September 1962, the appointment of longtime mediator W. Willard Wirtz as his replacement also signaled to the business community that the Department of Labor would take a less interventionist approach to wage and price policy.[60] The guideposts reappeared in the 1963 *Economic Report,* but the CEA downplayed the risks of cost-push inflation in the coming year, stating that jawboning steel had removed the "principle threat to the continuation of price stability."[61] When in April 1963 the steel industry raised prices on selected products facing strong domestic demand and favorable export trends, the same Kennedy who had been apoplectic the previous year now demonstrated a reluctance to take action, commenting, "there shouldn't be a collision, but there ought to be at least our concern about the effect."[62]

The administration also sought to calm business nerves by backing off from its antitrust strategy. In the immediate aftermath of April 1962, a number of legal commentators had interpreted the impaneling of the grand jury as a sign that the government would soon launch a new assault on oligopoly pricing practices.[63] When the White House assembled a team of academic experts including Carl Kaysen to consider the longer-range problem of market power in the steel industry later that April, they had expressed a consensus that the Justice Department should attempt to dissolve U.S. Steel and perhaps Bethlehem into several smaller companies.[64] The problem with this suggestion, of course, was that the prevailing legal doctrine held that consciously parallel pricing alone could not prove collusion under the antitrust laws. The Kennedy administration had previously supported several bills intended, in the vein of Carl Kaysen and Donald Turner's 1959 text, to allow the courts to use concentration as evidence of monopolization, but it backed down from that stance as part of its damage-control efforts with the business community. A month and a half after impaneling the grand jury, Loevinger thus concluded that insufficient evidence existed to justify bringing an antitrust suit against the steel industry and closed the case.[65]

Nevertheless, the CEA continued to investigate ways to influence private price decisions through its "Cost-Push Group." Led by new CEA member John Lewis, the Cost-Push Group noted that business spokespeople who had emphasized the relationship between compensation and TFP in the 1950s had recently critiqued the CEA for potentially awarding too much of the benefits of productivity to labor. Lewis even circulated to his Cost-Push Group "the ambitious study of the guideposts that GE just has done—of all places in the '*Relations* News Letter.'" Had the White House possessed a better appreciation of the corporate New Look, Lewis would not have been nearly so surprised at the economic sophistication of GE's labor-relations staff. This essay had been written by Francis Highton for use in GE's 1963 collective bargaining negotiations. The essay largely repeated the company's arguments of the previous decade. Productivity guideposts should be based on the principle not of price stability but of international competitiveness, that is, on the principle that the share of income going to capital must increase in order to provide for the investment necessary to compete with foreign rivals. TFP served as the proper measure of productivity in this setting, at least over the short run, because it took into account changing levels of capital inputs and permitted management to compensate investors properly for this increase.[66] The Cost-Push Group commissioned several studies of the long-run impact of the guideposts on the economy from top economists, including the future Nobel laureate Kenneth Arrow, and ultimately dismissed this criticism as unfounded. Still, that the CEA had even undertaken this study in response to management's concerns illustrates how seriously Heller, Lewis, and other Keynesians viewed an incomes policy as an indispensable component of modern economic growth.[67]

By late 1963, Heller had decided that the inflation situation was threatening enough that the CEA had to reemphasize the guideposts. The minutes of a confidential CEA staff meeting that September reveal that Heller sought "implicit or explicit support from the President," and Heller's instructions for the drafting of the 1964 *Economic Report* were unambiguous: "Include both a clearer definition of the guideposts and an exploration of ways and means of bringing public opinion to focus more sharply on major wage and price decisions."[68] When the steel industry again raised prices in October, Heller urged Kennedy to act before the Federal Reserve interpreted a creep in the industrial price level as a new investment boom and a threat to the balance of payments that would necessitate a return to the high interest rates of the late 1950s. "Jawbone control," Heller wrote to Kennedy, was unpleasant, but it "may be a reasonable cost to incur" to preserve macroeconomic expansion alongside price stability.[69]

A NEW PRESIDENT AND THE USUAL WAGE-PRICE SUSPECTS

Kennedy's assassination on November 22, 1963, provided an unhappy opportunity to reinvigorate the activist approach to resolving the Phillips Curve dilemma. Lyndon Johnson was widely seen as less economically sophisticated than his predecessor, and in private, it was rumored that he would on occasion believe rising prices and growing unemployment to be positive developments because they trended upward. Outside of a steel industry briefing in April 1962, Johnson had largely avoided the wage-price debates.[70] But Johnson was also known well known for his willingness to twist arms in order to get his policies enacted, and as Lewis wrote to Heller, this "new President with a different style" also offered the CEA an opportunity to carry out "selective personal presidential non-publicized jawbone control."[71]

The CEA would make two major changes to guidepost policy in the 1964 *Economic Report* to reflect Johnson's strengths. For the first time, the president's ghostwritten section explicitly called for compliance with the guideposts; Kennedy's *Economic Reports* had only used the "g-word" in the discussions written in the name of the CEA. In a second shift, the 1964 *Economic Report* repeated one estimate of productivity in several tables: the five-year moving average of the change in output per man-hour, 3.2%. The repetition of this figure in the report was apparently unintentional, but during the press conference held to announce the *Economic Report,* Heller was asked if 3.2% was intended to be the official value of the guidepost. Heller was unwilling to rule it out entirely, and the press soon reported that 3.2% was the official guidepost, an impression that the CEA did little to correct.[72]

As Heller explained to Johnson, if the "good unions" bargaining in 1964, such as the UAW, would take it easy for another year and set a responsible wage pattern, by the time the next bargaining cycle began, tax cuts would have had the time to move the economy back to full employment without cost-push inflation.[73] Such an outcome did not appear likely to develop on its own. Walter Reuther had incorporated the guidepost discussions of the *Economic Report* into the UAW's platform for 1964 contract negotiations, but he insisted that output per man-hour both for the private economy and for production workers in the automotive industry had risen by 4.9% a year in the postwar period, not 3.2%. Reuther demanded that the auto industry increase the AIF to 4.9% a year, charging that the 2.5% AIF had fallen short of productivity growth in the postwar years while again overlooking the costs of fringes in calculating the gains of labor. The UAW Research Department also criticized the CEA for setting the 3.2% guidepost on the basis of nominal rather than real wages, noting that the government had provided no machinery to assure that industries such as motor vehicles actually lowered prices to offset price increases in industries with subaverage productivity.[74] Heller hoped that President Johnson could pressure the auto industry to cut prices up front in return for a pledge to hold Reuther to 3.2%, but Johnson was unwilling to wade into this controversy during an election year. As early as April 1964, the Democratic National Committee had reached out to Johnson to understand how much he prioritized a guidepost-complaint outcome if it involved the possibility of an election-time strike. Asked if he desired to meet with Ford about prices, Johnson replied tersely, "Hell no."[75]

Whether or not presidential intervention could have convinced the auto industry to reduce its prices, Johnson's hands-off approach all but guaranteed that the auto industry would again pay for labor peace. The final settlement between the UAW and the auto industry that October was valued at about 55¢/hour over three years, or a 4.5% a year increase, maintaining the AIF at 2.5% while again expanding fringe benefits. After factoring in cost-of-living adjustments, the nominal costs of the contract would rise to 5%–6%

a year. If there was a silver lining to this violation of the wage guidepost, it was that negotiations had dragged on until after the industry had unveiled its new 1965 models, preventing a price increase.[76] Heller portrayed this outcome as an exceptional occurrence in which labor had been tempted to seek above-average wages from an industry that had not passed on productivity gains in the form of reduced prices. Looking forward to 1965, the bargaining calendar would be dominated by steel, an industry in weaker financial health and with a less powerful union than the auto industry.[77]

Gardner Ackley, who succeeded Heller as CEA chairman following the 1964 election, was not willing to take any chances. There were few Americans more familiar with price controls than Ackley. During World War II, Ackley had served as the assistant director of the Consumer Goods Price Division of the Office of Price Administration, where his duties had included regulating dress prices. He had then returned to Washington during the Korean War as the assistant director of the Office of Price Stabilization. Having urged the government to stand firm during the steel seizure of 1952, Ackley now proclaimed that the steel industry's negotiations in 1965 would serve as "the key test of the guideposts—both for wages and prices." Beyond the steel industry's economic importance, it had become "the symbol of the Government's determination to hold the price-cost line." Ackley warned Johnson that unless a guidepost settlement in steel preserved price stability, spiraling inflation would jeopardize the relaxed fiscal and monetary stances that supported economic expansion and enabled the Great Society: "If prices start to rise, it will be hard to hold [Federal Reserve Chairman] Bill Martin in check."[78]

Ensuring that the USWA would not violate the wage guideposts would prove a taller order than in the past. In the previous two contract negotiations in 1962 and 1963, USWA president David McDonald had accepted that the union could no longer contribute to the industry's pricing itself out of markets. The settlements achieved those years were, at close to 2%, arguably affordable within the industry's own labor-productivity trend (see table 2). Yet while McDonald's industrial statesmanship won praise from Washington, his rank and file had greeted it with confusion, as they fell behind the gains won by the UAW. Fringe benefits had risen slightly since 1962, but wage rates had not. The cap on COLA payments in 1960 and the removal of the COLA clause in 1962 were especially vexing to the union, which estimated that increases in the consumer price index since 1959 had caused steelworkers to suffer a loss in real wages of 23.5¢/hour, equivalent to about 5% of hourly earnings.[79] In elections for a new set of union officers, the steelworkers sought a "new President with a different style" by voting out McDonald in favor of his erstwhile lieutenant, I. W. Abel. The new USWA president quickly demanded from the industry a settlement costing an estimated 8% a year over three years, equivalent to the settlements in the mid-1950s that had occasioned the New Look.[80]

Despite this change in the USWA's bargaining posture, the steel industry remained committed to wage restraint, even at the risk of a strike and increased import penetration. The industry's initial compensation offers ranged from 2% to 2.6% a year, continuing the familiar approach of basing compensation on the industry's long-run labor-productivity growth trend as the grounds for cost and price stability. Yet as the USWA had already broken the 3.2% guidepost that summer with a 3.5%-per-year settlement in the can industry and 4.1%-per-year contract in aluminum industry, there was little reason for it now to settle for less. The USWA argued that the real costs of its demands fell within the guideposts and could be absorbed by the industry's productivity growth, but both the steel industry and the CEA had always insisted on tying nominal compensation growth to productivity. If nominal compensation exceeded productivity growth, then even the CEA's guideposts acknowledged that management would be justified in raising prices.[81]

Behind the scenes, the White House worked to prevent Abel from exceeding the wage guidepost, lest the industry feel justified in undertaking its customary price response. The CEA released a report that summer estimating that labor productivity in the steel industry had outpaced labor costs since 1961, but it allowed that much of the apparent 4.9% annual increase in output per man-hour reflected increased capacity utilization. Adjusting for this factor, the CEA concluded that the industry could maintain price stability "so long as wage increases in steel approximate the economy-wide productivity trend (that is, are in accord with the 'guideposts.')"[82] This suasion failed to broker a settlement before the strike deadline arrived on September 1, 1965, forcing Johnson to intervene directly. After meeting with representatives of the industry and union, Johnson essentially locked negotiators from both sides into the Executive Office Building and refused to let them out until they agreed to abide by the guideposts. In the early hours of September 3, the two sides finally agreed on a settlement brokered by Wirtz and Secretary of Commerce John Connor. Ackley conveniently evaluated the contract as 48¢ over thirty-nine months, or 3.2% a year.[83]

Though the White House had assisted the steel industry in bringing the USWA down to the wage guidepost, management was furious that the White House had pressed it into granting compensation that exceeded its own estimates of its productivity. Throughout the dispute, the industry had argued that since its productivity was lower than the White House calculated, it would have no choice but to hike prices in the event of a 3.2% settlement. Ackley had suggested to Johnson that a settlement costing less than 3.2% would indeed be preferable from the standpoint of price stability, but it was also unrealistic. As the administration had inserted itself into this negotiation in order to defend both the wage and price guideposts, Ackley stressed that the administration must not trade permission for higher prices in return for the industry agreeing to move its offer up to 3.2%.[84]

Following the signing of this contract, Cooper and other industry spokespeople again criticized the costs of this settlement and the government's role in establishing it, but the price front remained quiet until December 31, 1965, when Bethlehem Steel announced an increase in the price of structural steel of 4%, about $5/ton.[85] If management had hoped to catch the government off guard at New Year's, it was in for a surprise. Johnson replicated Kennedy's fury and announced to the steel industry that it could no longer "consider the interests of [its] country and [its] company with complete freedom." Secretary of Defense Robert McNamara followed this exhortation by banning companies that raised the price of structural steel from receiving defense contracts, while the Department of Justice again impaneled a grand jury and opened an investigation into a possible conspiracy over prices. The concern that steel prices would set off another round of inflation proved so threatening that the administration even placed a reduction in trade barriers on the table, potentially sacrificing the balance of payments to preserve price stability.[86]

As in 1962, however, the administration was more interested in a quick fix than using this crisis as justification for structural reform. The industry's traditional price leader, U.S. Steel, had internally expressed its disapproval of Bethlehem's unilateral action, but Blough did not wish to break the industry's price discipline by undercutting a competitor. In talks with McNamara, he instead worked out a compromise that entailed adjusting some prices up and others down. This compromise solution proved roughly guidepost compliant, and the 1966 *Economic Report* even mentioned specific firms for the first time to condemn Bethlehem and praise U.S. Steel.[87]

THE COLLAPSE OF THE GUIDEPOSTS

Up through 1965, the Kennedy and Johnson administrations had presided over an economic expansion accompanied by virtual price stability. Unemployment fell in response to the tax cuts of the Revenue Act of 1964, and when the civilian unemployment rate finally hit its full-employment target of 4% in January 1966, the consumer price index was only 6.7% higher than when Kennedy had taken office five years before, and the wholesale price index only 3.5% more. Unit labor costs for the manufacturing sector had actually fallen since 1961, while real wages had increased (see table 4). Over the course of this macroeconomic expansion, moreover, management had accomplished one of the key objectives of its New Look: boosting profits. Total pretax corporate profits had risen from $59.3 billion at the end of 1961 to $88.3 billion in 1965, and after-tax profits increased from $36.4 billion to $60.9 billion. Not only did total profits rise and real rates of return reach postwar highs, but capital's share of income also reached its highest level since the Great Depression.[88]

As management's share of income had risen, labor's had fallen, provoking intense resentment on the part of unions against the Johnson administration's incomes policy. Industrial prices may have remained remarkably stable during the mid-1960s, but prices determined in competitive markets remained flexible, with food, apparel, and footwear driving a 1.7% increase in the consumer price index in 1965. Because the CEA had insisted on establishing the guidepost at a nominal figure of 3.2%, the cost of living prevented labor from fully sharing in the real fruits of productivity as intended by the wage guidepost. During congressional hearings on the 1966 *Economic Report,* AFL-CIO research director Nathaniel Goldfinger argued that adherence to the guideposts threatened to bring a premature end to economic expansion by depriving workers and consumers of the purchasing power needed to sustain total demand, a process that the labor movement of the 1920s had termed "underconsumption."[89]

Despite the growing hostility of labor to the guideposts, Ackley insisted on maintaining a nominal wage target. Bolstered by the administration's recent success in the steel industry, the CEA formally declared the wage guidepost to be 3.2% in the 1966 edition of the *Economic Report,* with no

COLA adjustments permitted. There was one large problem with this choice of guidepost. Past *Economic Reports* had arrived at 3.2% by calculating the five-year arithmetic moving average of labor productivity, but for 1966, that average now equaled 3.6%. In truth, this higher figure was somewhat misleading, for as the economy had reached what was considered to be a point of full employment, labor productivity had risen by only 2.8% in 1965. A higher wage guidepost would thus inadvertently sanction an inflationary increase in unit labor costs as actual productivity trailed behind compensation gains. To avoid this outcome, Ackley instructed the CEA to experiment with alternative measures, as long as the final result would "yield the same value as the present method would yield." The 1966 *Economic Report* apparently switched to the five-year *geometric* average, with years weighted equally to preserve 3.2%.[90]

Only with hindsight would Ackley recognize how much of a mistake it had been to insist on holding wages to 3.2%. As Ackley colorfully described the situation the next year, asking labor to hold to 3.2% had provoked an adverse response akin to "telling children not to put beans up their noses."[91] The perception that the CEA had changed the rules in the middle of the game provoked an especially antagonistic reaction from labor groups that had never accepted the guideposts, or indeed the wage-price restraint of the New Look. As UAW research economist Carrol Cobrun had previously cautioned, "If the Council started this kind of gimmickry, the guideposts would have no pretext of economic validity, but would simply represent what some bureaucrat in Washington thought was a proper limit on wage increases."[92]

In the face of this open hostility from labor, what sensible industry would even bother attempting to maintain voluntary restraint now? Ackley informed Johnson that there was one remaining hope: "GE and Westinghouse are *out on a limb in support of the Government's wage policy*. Sawing it off would damage for a long time the credibility of any wage policy."[93] As GE prepared for negotiations with the International Union of Electrical Workers (IUE) in 1966, it continued to call attention to both the administration's noninflationary guideposts and the firm's own "competitive guide post." Under the latter strategy, the firm would hold compensation below the national productivity average in order to increase returns on capital and so promote the investment required to keep an edge over foreigners converging to the U.S. capital-labor ratio.[94]

In practice, of course, GE continued to recognize that productivity was a guide, rather than a rule, for bargaining. For the company to insist on adhering to a competitive guidepost of around 2% at a time when few companies seemed to be holding to even a noninflationary guidepost of 3.2% would prevent GE from claiming that its offer was "fair." And if GE made an unfair offer, it would undercut the claim that had proven so successful in 1960, that management was acting in the best interests of all of the corporation's stakeholders. Given the fact that General Electric remained the sole industrial advocate for the lower guidepost figure, and given that prices in the electrical-machinery industry had risen by 2.1% in the first half of 1966 after falling by about 10% from 1960 to 1965, Highton advised his superiors that the company could not credibly commit to a guidepost position closer to 2% only to exceed it later.[95] Although during bargaining Highton still cited a productivity trend of 2.6% a year as economically rational, GE's actual offer was much higher, at about 5% a year for three years by its own estimation or about 4.5% according to the CEA, although it continued to reject the inclusion of a COLA clause.[96]

This time, however, GE would not be able to marginalize the IUE so easily. The IUE had a new president in Paul Jennings, elected as part of the same wave of dissatisfaction at meager gains that had carried Abel to the leadership of the USWA. In the past, GE management had reached quick settlements with several of its smaller unions and then forced the IUE to accept these settlements as the pattern for its national settlement. To prevent GE from picking them off one by one during the 1966 collective bargaining round, Jennings formed a coalition with many of these rival unions.[97] After the Democratic-controlled National Labor Relations Board forced GE to bargain with this coalition, GE doubled down on a second component of Boulwarism: the refusal to allow a strike to sway management from its initial offer. With a strike all but certain, the Justice Department began preparations for the Taft-Hartley injunction that the Labor Department warned would probably cause the unions to lose. Concerned about the political repercussions of this action, Johnson again called on management and labor to continue negotiations under the auspices of the White House, but he tellingly justified his request in terms of the Vietnam War and not inflation. In Washington, the administration strong-armed GE into accepting an offer officially valued at about 5% a year in order to allow defense production to proceed unimpeded. Not only had Johnson's intervention forced GE to budge from its initial offer, but GE also acquiesced to the restoration of the COLA.[98]

The administration's interventions at GE led other businesses to conclude that the CEA's wage guideposts were no longer in effect. Ackley noted that within the Business Council's Liaison Committee, "the passing of 3.2% was mourned by many who opposed it when alive." These business leaders described excessive wage settlements as the most serious problem facing the economy, and they complained that the White House was "not sufficiently outspoken in condemning excessive wage increases."[99] Likewise, within Johnson's Labor-Management Advisory Committee, Ackley detected bitterness on the part of labor leaders who had shown restraint in previous years, especially USWA president Abel, toward those who had recently gotten away with more. Henry Ford II did not help this situation when he remarked at one of these meetings that "of course, he did not expect to pay any attention to the guideposts when he bargained with Reuther next year." As Ackley noted, Abel disliked this comment as much as did Ford's fellow industry representatives.[100]

Both business groups and Johnson's Keynesian advisers agreed that a wage-price policy designed to combat cost-push inflation would have little effect in the face of the excess demand from which the economy now suffered. In an echo of the late 1950s, the Federal Reserve had also begun to raise interest rates in an effort to arrest demand-pull inflation, with Federal Reserve Chairman Martin warning Johnson that "[wage-price] persuasion can be helpful, but it has limitations." Yet as all sides urged Johnson to consider fiscal restraint, Johnson refused to contemplate any cuts to spending on the Great Society and the war in Vietnam.[101] Instead, Johnson instructed his administration to double down on the use of jawboning wherever prices rose. Unable to keep up with this workload at the CEA, Ackley turned to Johnson's domestic adviser Joseph Califano to appoint an administration "price czar." Califano in turn hired his old classmate John Robson and then, when Robson resigned, Califano's legal colleague Stanford Ross.[102] Nominally employed at the Bureau of the Budget, Robson and Ross served as liaisons to the business community, discussing pricing concerns and warning industry representatives of potential consequences. Steel, motor vehicles, and other manufacturing giants remained their most visible targets, but Robson and Ross monitored such a range of industries that Robson could warn Ackley in late 1966 that “the situation in men’s underwear is tight.”[103]

For every fight the administration picked and won in newsprint, gasoline, or x-ray film, it was inescapable that the firms that had once fought to restrain wages to productivity now acquiesced to the inevitability of higher costs and prices. In no industry was this reversal more pronounced than steel. In 1959, 1962, and 1965, R. Conrad Cooper had led the Coordinating Committee to implement an anti-inflationary and Boulwarist program of restraint. Moreover, in 1967, Cooper announced to the Coordinating Committee that his team had finally succeeded in calculating the industry’s total-factor productivity. Omitting the wartime slump of 1942–1945, TFP had risen by only 0.6% a year from 1940 to 1965, a total increase of 18%, compared to a 66% rise in output per man-hour. After inflating net capital inputs to reflect the cheapening of the dollar over this period, the cumulative increase in TFP shrank to only 8%, “next to nothing.”[104]

As the 1968 negotiations approached, however, Cooper recognized that the shape of things to come would be inflationary, “pre-ordained by a combination of major factors beyond the control of the companies or the union.” Unlike in the past, when the White House had pulled out all stops to ensure what was at least in its own mind a noninflationary wage outcome, Johnson would be expected to prioritize ensuring a steady supply of steel for Vietnam. The resulting labor peace would come at high cost for management, as GE had learned the hard way. Moreover, the USWA had received total nominal increases in compensation of about 3% per year over the past eight years, whereas the cost of living had risen by about 2% a year in that time. Given that the IUE had ridden dissatisfaction with real compensation to a costly settlement at GE, a pattern that had continued into 1967 in such industries as trucking and motor vehicles, Cooper warned that there was little to no chance that the steel industry could achieve “a modest, voluntary settlement, even on the verge of a strike deadline.”[105]

Doubtful that a hard-nosed stance could now prove effective, Cooper proposed renouncing the use of strikes in favor of binding arbitration. As long as the arbitration deadline was set well before the contract expired, steel users would be confident that they could obtain an uninterrupted flow of steel. This would discourage them from turning to the imports that continued to serve as the industry’s nightmare, and it would permit the industry to reach a settlement without government involvement. Cooper was in fact so desperate to avoid these adverse outcomes that he was even willing to waive the industry's ability to request arbitration on matters involving section 2-B of the contract.[106]

"Operation Heresy," as the Coordinating Committee termed this approach, initially struck Abel as career suicide, but he quickly came around in order to forestall unwelcome government intervention such as a Taft-Hartley injunction. Yet Abel had been elected president of the USWA on a pledge to give more voice to union members, and most remained skeptical of arbitration even when Abel, with Cooper's blessing, portrayed this as his own idea and not that of management. When the union's Executive Board voted down Operation Heresy, both Abel and Cooper realized that the only way for Abel to maintain control of the union would be to return to the classic strategy of brinksmanship and power plays.[107] According to the union's economists, real wages had fallen over the life of the expiring contract due to the lack of COLA protection. Even were fringes to be included in a total calculation, the union charged that "there has *not* been appropriate Steelworker *sharing* in productivity gains in recent years." As a result, the USWA sought both a wage increase larger than "normal" and protection against future unanticipated increases in the cost of living.[108]

Cooper and the Coordinating Committee still rehashed such tropes as that the industry's productivity defined its ability to absorb costs and that if one party exceeded this trend, then another must receive less. Cooper even reflected on insisting to the USWA that TFP served as the real measure of productivity and one that trailed the labor productivity emphasized by the government.[109] Yet when Abel rejected the Coordinating Committee's first offer, which at 4.5% already exceeded the cost the industry would have liked to pay, Cooper realized that there was no chance of achieving an offer "that might have made economic sense." The options that Cooper now faced were not much of a choice at all. He could hold out for a strike, risking higher import penetration and Johnson's intervention on the side of the USWA, or he could take the union's offer as it stood. After offering a "few pounds of flesh" in additional benefits to win over union hardliners, the industry and USWA agreed on a three-year contract that entailed the largest increase in nominal costs since 1956 (see table 2).[110]

The steel industry now saw little reason to restrain itself on prices. While profits over the life of the expiring contract had experienced their best run since the mid-1950s, capital expenditures had exceeded cash flow for the third straight year in 1966, by almost $200 million against $2 billion in expenditures that year alone. In an ominous specter of things to come, 1966 was also the first year since 1961 that the industry's unit labor costs had increased, a trend that the new contract perpetuated. Thus, scarcely had the ink dried on the industry's latest agreement when Bethlehem Steel announced a 5% general price increase, the first across-the-board attempt since U.S. Steel's in April 1962.[111]

Unfortunately for Bethlehem, this price increase came within months of the passage of the Revenue and Expenditure Control Act of 1968. The culmination of two years of struggles between the White House and Congress over how to restrain the burgeoning demand-pull inflation without relying on excessive monetary stringency, the act imposed a 10% surcharge on all income taxes and required the president to reduce fiscal expenditures by $6 billion in the next fiscal year. The Johnson administration proclaimed that it had now accepted fiscal discipline and immediately called on firms and unions to restrain themselves in setting prices and wages.[112] Of course, the administration had made no effort to intervene in the name of the wage guidepost during the negotiations, but it foresaw that Bethlehem's action would discourage other businesses from showing price restraint. As in 1962 and 1966, Johnson denounced the steel industry and issued a directive that the government would not purchase steel from those who followed Bethlehem. The administration again positioned U.S. Steel to allow the industry an out, and Blough complied by undercutting Bethlehem with a price increase of 2.5%, an amount that the CEA deemed justifiable.[113]

As the Johnson administration sought to discipline prices, it was ironically depriving itself of a lever capable of influencing steel's behavior: trade policy. The market share of imported steel had continued to rise into the double digits, peaking at over 16% in 1968, and the USWA by now shared the industry's recognition of the threat that this competition presented. As economists had predicted, this foreign competition produced a remarkable change of attitudes in the industry's oligopoly pricing strategy. Traditional price leader U.S. Steel had begun to shade its prices, secretly offering customers prices under list prices to defend its market share from foreigners. If carried on long enough, price shading would undercut the discipline of the industry to move together on prices. To prevent this total collapse, Bethlehem responded by openly cutting its list prices for rolled steel products in September by 18%–22% to match foreign prices.[114]

The CEA recognized that this competition could provide a structural solution to cost-push inflation and had suggested that the White House leverage this threat to jawbone the industry. Labor and management were then jointly lobbying Congress for formal quotas and tariff competition, and the White House was seeking to preempt this effort through a voluntary system of quotas negotiated with Japan and the European Coal and Steel Community (ECSC).[115] The CEA suggested that the administration could condition these talks on Bethlehem rescinding its price increases, but the Commerce Department intervened with the reminder that walking away from this deal would penalize even those steelmakers attempting to show restraint.[116] Four months later, the administration secured the agreement of Japan and the ECSC to limit exports to fourteen million tons in 1969 and limit the growth of their sales to 5% a year. Within a few months, Bethlehem and the others had rescinded their price reductions, secure that they would no longer lose market share to foreign producers when they raised prices in pursuit of higher returns.[117]

Antitrust policy also remained off the table as a means for price restraint. In 1965, Johnson had raised the possibility of an antitrust investigation of steel and other metal prices with Attorney General Nicholas Katzenbach, but the latter made it clear that he considered this behavior to be that of a normal oligopoly and hence beyond the reach of the antitrust laws.[118] This reluctance was reinforced later that year when Johnson named Donald Turner as the assistant attorney general for antitrust. By this time, Turner had begun to rethink his earlier argument with Kaysen that oligopoly pricing lay outside the realm of existing antitrust law. Building on *Alcoa,* Turner now felt that a firm or industry could be found guilty of monopolizing under the Sherman Act simply if it had managed to maintain its market power over a period of time. Although the consciously parallel workings of an oligopoly industry meant that no finding of conspiracy was automatically warranted, the persistence of wide margins or extensive concentration could be enough to recommend divestiture or dissolution as a structural resolution.[119]

While at the Justice Department itself, however, Turner did not test whether the courts would prove receptive to this interpretation. Instead of targeting existing oligopolies, Turner prioritized the traditional prophylactic strategy of combating concentrations of economic power before they emerged. These efforts culminated with the release of "Merger Guidelines" in 1968 that designated the levels of market share at which the government would intervene against proposed mergers.[120] Simultaneously, Johnson's White House Task Force on Antitrust Policy concluded that no existing legal remedy could discipline the parallel behavior of existing oligopolies. Although reasoning that industrial concentration inevitably led to high corporate profits and detrimental outcomes for society, the task force also found that such anticompetitive behavior appeared to be the natural result of entirely rational conscious parallelism. Without a new law that would deem existing oligopolies illegal once their market concentration crossed a certain threshold, the task force concluded that antitrust authorities could do little to target this oligopoly pricing.[121]

Johnson's final hurrah on steel prices thus could not disguise the fact that his administration had developed no durable solution for the wage-price spiral. As the final report of the President's Advisory Committee on Labor-Management Policy made clear in December 1968, both business and labor believed that there was a pressing need to align wages and prices with productivity across the entire economy. At the same time, they emphasized that this responsibility no longer rested primarily with the private sector. While modifications to the structure of collective bargaining and industrial-labor relations might provide some assistance, the chief source of inflationary pressure had become the federal spending that fueled excess demand.[122] Thus, by the year's end, the Business Council demanded fiscal restraint as the solution for inflation. Although concerned about the political feasibility of slamming on the brakes, the leaders of the United States' blue-chip industries insisted that they would accept whatever it cost in terms of lost output and unemployment to "break the back of inflationary expectations."[123]

CONCLUSION

Paul Samuelson, Robert Solow, Walter Heller, and Gardner Ackley all agreed that a democratic government, or at least the Democratic Party, could not sacrifice full employment to escape the inflationary consequences of private self-interest. Through the use of an incomes policy, the economy could attain an entirely more favorable Phillips Curve trade-off in which unemployment and inflation were both lower than would have otherwise been the case. The Keynesian CEA rejected the use of TFP in favor of the traditional labor-productivity metric for its guideposts, but otherwise, its strategy was nearly identical to management's vision for wage-price policy, down to its very terminology. Without structural market reforms in the form of trade or antitrust policy, the success of the guideposts would require firms and unions to continue to view restraint as being in their own best interests, just as management had insisted when developing the wage-price policy of its New Look.

Unfortunately for management's traditional understanding of wage-price policy, federal incomes policy introduced a political asymmetry into the balance of interests between capital and labor. As markets recovered, the White House required industries like steel to rely on economic recovery to expand profits, resulting in the great collision of April 1962. When profits rose and excess demand pulled up the price of the commodities produced in competitive markets, labor was also expected to shoulder the burden of anti-inflationary restraint. Modifying the nominal 3.2% standard could have assuaged labor by keeping real wages in line with productivity growth, but in such a case, management would also have been entitled to relief for rising costs. Instead, Johnson forced profits and prices to absorb the costs of labor peace while failing to curb the fiscal and monetary stimulus that was the true impetus for higher wage and price demands. The White House still scored some jawbone victories, but as Kennedy had learned, there were limits to how far private enterprise would tolerate such interventions. Yet, remarkably, the failures of incomes policy had not dimmed the confidence of the business community that a private wage-price policy could still restrain labor's claims once the government put its fiscal house in order. It would take the reintroduction of macroeconomic austerity for them to determine whether the experience of the guideposts had rendered voluntary restraint a more difficult task than in the past.

CHAPTER SIX

If at First You Don't Succeed

THE BUSINESS COMMUNITY AND NIXON'S WAGE AND PRICE CONTROLS

HAVING OPPOSED THE COMPULSION of the Kennedy-Johnson guideposts, management recognized an opportunity to retake the initiative on wage-price policy from the federal government in the late 1960s. The election of Richard Nixon suggested that the White House would once more support management in relying on macroeconomic tools, rather than incomes policy, to fight inflation. Yet only a few years later, Nixon's ultimate solution for the problem of inflation would be to impose mandatory wage and price controls, which lasted in various forms from August 15, 1971, to April 30, 1974.[1] Traditionally, historians have explained Nixon's abrupt shift in political terms. Constrained by a weak electoral mandate and challenged by a Democratic Congress, Nixon believed that he could win reelection only by taking bold action to boost the economy and combat inflation. Labor historians in particular have portrayed Nixon as a master manipulator who exploited social upheaval and the Vietnam War to divert the working class from its economic concerns. After all, Nixon managed to win a slim majority of the union vote in 1972 despite having imposed controls on union members' earnings.[2]

Nixon may have acted out of political calculations, but this chapter spotlights a more unexpected show of support for mandatory controls: that of the business community. Scholars have struggled to provide an analysis for what the historian Benjamin Waterhouse has termed the "cognitive dissonance" of free-market advocates backing controls beyond the familiar narrative of the long-run assault on the New Deal order. According to this interpretation, controls allowed organized business groups to paint labor as a structural source of inflation. Once the red tape of controls generated headaches for firms, corporate lobbyists mobilized to terminate them. The importance of controls thus rests not in their economic effects but in their role as a trial run for the strategies used over the subsequent decades to weaken the power of unions and combat threats to business autonomy.[3]

This chapter provides a different perspective on management's affinity for controls by focusing not on lobbyists but on the individual firms that Nixon expected would prefer voluntary restraint to federal compulsion. Returns on capital had begun to fall under the guideposts, and when the economy entered recession, management once more demanded that labor assist capital by shouldering the real costs of combating inflation. As in the late 1950s, General Electric and others risked lengthy strikes in the hopes of bringing the costs of collective bargaining in line with their overall financial objectives. Yet a decade after the New Look had succeeded against the backdrop of a similar macroeconomic climate, management discovered that its voluntary methods no longer yielded the same success in linking compensation with productivity. Changes to labor law and a growing militancy on the part of a new generation of workers prevented recourse to the strategies employed during the New Look, while rising import penetration decreased the tolerance of the steel industry for a work stoppage of any length. With the managers of these industrial firms unable to implement a wage-price policy on their own terms, they demanded that Washington intervene on their behalf. Seen in this context, corporate support for controls developed not as part of an uphill political struggle against the New Deal but out of the ongoing efforts to engineer management's preferred balance between corporate stakeholders from within the confines of the existing social order.

By contrasting the corporate support for controls with labor's bombastic denunciations, historians have generally concluded that Nixon's controls displayed what Waterhouse deems an "institutional favoritism toward business."[4] As this chapter reveals, management may have played a decisive role in convincing Nixon to adopt controls, but corporate America was far from pleased with how his program distributed income to stakeholders. Business leaders asserted that the administration must hold nominal compensation to less than the sum of national productivity and the cost of living in order to preserve incentives for investment. Price controls meanwhile should afford flexibility to management to capture the larger profits needed to fund investment internally. Yet in practice, controls perpetuated the tendency of the guideposts to shoulder prices and profits with the burden of restraint, souring management on the ability of the state to enforce a favorable wage-price policy. Frustrated by these economic outcomes, the business community quickly recanted its support for incomes policy and demanded a return to flexible wages and, even more so, prices.

JAWBONING AND BACKBONING

By the late 1960s, management believed that it was living out the nightmare that it had discovered in the writings of John Kendrick in the 1950s: labor was gaining at capital's expense. Management had enjoyed good years in the first half of the 1960s as the share of income going to corporate profits rose, but after 1966, unexpectedly large increases in wage payments, sagging productivity, and shrinking markups had resulted in a fall in the profits share.[5] Despite the long-standing concerns about oligopoly market power and price administration, corporate America as a whole had been unable to reverse this fall in the returns to capital. Some drop in aggregate profits was to be expected given the state of the business cycle, but according to at least one contemporary estimate, which appeared in the leading managerial periodical *The Conference Board Record,* half of the total dollar decrease in profits, $16.5 billion between 1966 and 1969, could be explained by an increase in labor's share of income.[6] When Campbell Soup CEO W. B. Murphy made a presentation on this challenge to his fellow blue-chip executives at the May 1972 meeting of the Business Council, he notably singled out August 18, 1966, as the date on which this shift in fortunes had occurred. That was when Johnson's Labor-Management Advisory Committee had recommended, over the objections of the management members, according to Murphy's recollection, the abandonment of the wage guidepost, allowing wage settlements to grow much faster than the pace of productivity advances.[7]

The election of Richard Nixon presented management with an opportunity to assert once again a wage-price policy of its own design, freed of Washington's meddling. As was well known to his contemporaries, Nixon had briefly worked in the OPA's tire-rationing section in 1942. This experience had left him with the lasting impression that price controls not only produced inequities and shortages but also empowered bureaucrats who were "obsessed with their own power and [who] seemed to delight in kicking people around, particularly those in the private sector."[8] Nixon's stint at the OPA lasted only several months, but his fear that government regulation would stifle the private sector remained an entrenched conviction. According to the Nixon speechwriter William Safire, Nixon directed that his presidential speeches contain a "boilerplate paragraph on the horrors of wage and price controls, how they would lead to rationing and black markets and a stultifying government domination of the economy."[9]

Nixon instead embraced what his speechwriters described as "backboning." Whereas jawboning amounted to the "government wagging a finger at business and labor to act with restraint while government acts without restraint," backboning required the government to put its money, quite literally, where its mouth was: "Government setting an example of restraint by its own, admittedly unpopular, belt-tightening actions, thereby earning the right to call for others to follow that example." Once the government implemented fiscal and monetary restraint, it could backbone the private sector by warning that those who failed to adjust risked pricing themselves out of markets.[10]

Unemployment surged from 3.4% at the start of Nixon's term to 6.1% by the end of 1970 as the Federal Reserve committed itself to a course of monetary restraint that was much more stringent than the gradual path Nixon had in mind.[11] Yet, in contrast to the similar macroeconomic climate that had buttressed the New Look, the growth of nominal compensation barely slowed, from an annual rate of 7.3% in the first quarter of 1970 to only 6.4% a year later for the nonfarm business sector. The median annual increase in wages in major collective bargaining situations of one thousand or more workers during 1970 was 8.9% over the life of the contract, up from 7.4% in 1969 and 6% the year before, exclusive of COLA clauses.[12]

The experience of the Business Council's leader, GE chairman Fred Borch, captures many of the difficulties that management now faced in implementing its traditional wage-price policy. Approaching negotiations in 1969, GE's largest union, the IUE, charged that the 12.4%, three-year package it had won with Johnson's help in 1966 had been all but wiped out in real terms due to inflation, and it again demanded that GE negotiate with a coalition of unions to prevent the divide-and-conquer tactics that had proven so successful in 1960. Internally, GE admitted that the company was in a "vulnerable" position due to the cost of living.[13] Borch explained to Nixon that "the realities of the bargaining table and a sensitivity to the needs of our employees" required that the company make an immediate wage offer that would continue to perpetuate inflation and force the company to raise prices to cover costs. Still, he signaled approval of Nixon's backboning, and he noted that GE desired to avoid a settlement that incorporated "unrealistic" expectations of continuing inflation into second-year and third-year compensation.[14]

As in 1966, GE's offer denied the union coalition its desired COLA clause, instead offering an immediate raise in wages of about 6%, with two later opportunities to renegotiate pay in 1970 and 1971, "when it will be possible to negotiate with full knowledge of the economic situation at that time." Behind the scenes, Francis Highton, the economist who had remained with GE after Lemuel Boulware's retirement in 1960, explained that workers should agree to shoulder some of the risks of unanticipated inflation. By using scheduled wage reopening clauses in the place of an automatic COLA clause, the company could delay decisions on wages until a future date when it would be known whether the economic climate was as sour as management expected it to be.[15]

A decade before, GE had taken advantage of a permissive National Labor Relations Board to win a quick victory for its contract through the Boulwarist strategies of communication and outreach to individual employees. Over the course of the 1960s, however, the labor-law pendulum had swung back toward favoring unions. Whereas the NLRB had taken an expansive view toward employer free speech under Eisenhower, the restoration of Democratic control under Kennedy and Johnson signaled that the board would again consider the wider economic context of employee-employer relations when evaluating when speech became coercive.[16] Following GE's victory in 1960, the IUE had challenged the company's tactics before the NLRB, and in 1964, the NLRB had ruled that GE's totality of conduct indicated a failure to bargain in good faith. The NLRB concluded that GE had attempted to establish that "the employer rather than the union is the true protector of the employees' interests," an attitude entirely contrary to the company's legal duty to bargain with employees through their union. GE's insistence on holding to its initial fair offer had left no room for management to maneuver in negotiations, and management's refusal to disclose the information that supported its economic claims demonstrated that the company sought to bargain around the union, not with it. The board ordered management to avoid withholding relevant economic information from union officials and forbade the use of tactics that prevented workers from bargaining collectively through their chosen representatives.[17]

GE had appealed this ruling, rendering it largely moot during the 1966 negotiations that were overshadowed by Johnson's intervention. Only in 1969, nine years after the events in question had occurred, did the Second Circuit Court of Appeals uphold the NLRB's decision. Whereas the NLRB had labeled only certain communications as part of the company's take-it-or-leave-it bargaining strategy, the ruling of the Second Circuit went further by applying this designation to GE's entire approach to communications.[18] As the IUE's general counsel succinctly summarized this ruling for the press, "Boulwarism is dead." This new labor-law climate could not have come at a worse time for GE, as only the day before, the IUE-led coalition of thirteen unions comprising nearly 150,000 workers had gone on strike. As was widely understood, not just wages but GE's entire labor-relations machinery hung in the balance.[19]

Assisted by the Federal Mediation and Conciliation Service, the two sides reached a shaky compromise after 122 days of work stoppage. Labor notched a further victory against Boulwarism by setting all of its individual contracts to expire on the same date, which institutionalized coalition bargaining. On the other hand, the coalition did not obtain its desired union-shop clause or the arbitration mechanisms that would have further weakened GE's personnel tactics. On economic issues, GE prevailed with its initial first-year wage offer of 6%, but it had to accept a COLA clause and higher deferred increases that, when including fringe benefits, raised compensation by about 30% over forty months. Borch pleaded with Nixon not to label this settlement anti-inflationary lest workers remain on strike for an even larger settlement, but the White House assured the public that this settlement "doesn't look alarming from an inflationary standpoint."[20] That statement was quickly proven to be meaningless when GE raised personal-appliance prices by an average of 3% on the grounds of costs. As the general manager of GE's appliance and television sales division explained to the press, the timing was intentional: "Of course, as a result of the new union contracts we will also have substantial increases in wages."[21]

By foreclosing the ability of firms such as General Electric to apply

Boulwarist tactics, the NLRB had deprived management of one of its primary tools for instituting wage-price policy. The auto industry had long taken an alternative approach of relying on its formula for labor peace to collaborate with union leaders while avoiding the frictions of Boulwarism, but this strategy had also recently begun to prove unreliable. After two decades of COLA payments and generous fringe benefits, GM no longer enjoyed the stability in operations that Engine Charlie Wilson had envisioned for his multiyear contracts. The Treaty of Detroit committed the UAW to cooperation with GM management in increasing productivity; but 13.3 million man hours had been lost to strikes in 1969, and the absenteeism rate had risen from 2.5% of working hours in the 1950s to 5% in 1970. The company blamed this newfound militancy on a younger and more diverse generation of workers lacking the discipline of their fathers.[22] Compounding these shop-floor difficulties, the auto industry was also beginning to show concerns about import competition, which had reached 15% of the domestic market despite quality-adjusted auto prices remaining constant for most of the 1960s. Given these trends, auto executives concluded that modifications to the Treaty of Detroit were necessary to remain competitive. Summarizing a telephone call from Chrysler president Lynn Townsend, CEA chairman Paul McCracken warned Nixon that "the companies are not apt to accept readily a further major increase in costs. Thus the work stoppage, if it occurs, could be a long one."[23]

The willingness of General Motors to endure a labor stoppage in order to hold down its labor costs was matched by the resolve of the United Auto Workers to shield its members from inflation. During the previous bargaining round in 1967, Walter Reuther had overestimated Johnson's ability to combat inflation and agreed to place a cap on the COLA clause in return for higher benefits and skill premiums. By July 1969, the COLA cap had cost workers at General Motors at least 7¢ an hour, and factoring in the 1968 income surtax, the UAW estimated that real disposable weekly earnings of autoworkers had only risen from $101.33 in 1965 to $103.61 in the first half of 1969. The UAW had afforded slightly better protection to its members than manufacturing workers in general, but on net, autoworkers had hardly shared in the real pace of productivity over this period.[24] Reuther pledged to inflation-proof paychecks in the 1970 negotiations, but his death in a plane crash on May 9, 1970, left the leadership of the UAW to its GM

Department head, Leonard Woodcock, who viewed a large settlement at GM as his best chance of cementing his hold on an increasingly militant union. Under Woodcock, the UAW prepared for negotiations much as Reuther would have: by focusing on the futility of winning higher nominal wages that simply covered the cost of living; weighing the immediate benefit of wage gains against the expansion of fringes; and debating how the union could justify demands for wages that exceeded the national productivity rate.[25]

GM refused to tolerate the uncertainty of future liabilities that would result from an uncapped COLA, and when the UAW struck that October, GM shut down entirely for the first time since 1946.[26] As its inventories ran low and bad publicity mounted, after sixty-seven days, GM predictably lost its resolve and agreed to continue its traditional formula: an AIF of 3%, an unlimited COLA, and expanded fringe benefits, including offering a full pension at the age of fifty-six with thirty years of service. Of the estimated 51¢/hour cost of this package, over half represented catch-up to the inflation level since 1967.[27] The Nixon administration once again proved sanguine about the outcome of the GM strike, for as Secretary of Labor George Shultz noted, "the cost of the settlement [i.e., the COLA] will vary directly with our success in controlling inflation."[28] Still, the fact that GM publicly described the settlement as noninflationary did not prevent car prices from going up by $24 on average in the wake of the settlement, in addition to a $208/car increase enacted three months before. Between 1970 and 1971, quality-adjusted new car prices rose by 7%, as much as they had from 1960 to 1970.[29]

First GE's Boulwarism had been declared illegal, and now GM's Treaty of Detroit had failed to prevail over the militant worker movements of the early 1970s. There was little reason to think that any other company contemplating a voluntary return to wage-price policy could succeed in the face of union pressures. The unwillingness of the steel industry to resurrect its New Look strategy was perhaps the most glaring example of the business community's surrender to the inevitability of cost-push inflation. With the collective bargaining contract up for negotiation in 1971, I. W. Abel set his union's key demand as an uncapped COLA and compensation matching the UAW's. At the negotiating table, the union promised a strike if the industry returned to the hard-nosed "no money" stance of previous negotiations. Abel's team also reminded the members of the Coordinating Committee that they had almost been voted out of their offices over Operation Heresy several years before, and so arbitration remained off the table.[30]

Believing that the steel industry would interpret GM's contract as a total capitulation to cost-push inflation, the Nixon administration tepidly employed the jawboning tools at its disposal. The administration was at the time renegotiating the voluntary agreement established in January 1969 that required European and Japanese steelmakers to limit their exports to the United States in order to avoid legislated trade barriers. When Bethlehem Steel raised the price of certain products in early 1971, the White House vetoed this increase by alluding to its detrimental effects on trade negotiations, suggesting that the industry would have to hold out for wage restraint.[31] Nixon later uncharacteristically invited representatives of the industry and union to a friendly chat in which he reminded them that he had spent his Christmas vacation of 1959 arbitrating a settlement. Referencing his administration's involvement in negotiating quota extensions and the effect of rising costs on pricing the domestic industry out of global markets, Nixon made no suggestion of a guidepost figure and indicated that there would be no federal involvement in the event of a strike. Instead, he offered broad hopes about the need to avoid both a strike and inflation while permitting real gains for workers and shareholders alike.[32]

Negotiations went down to the wire that summer, yet unlike 1956 and 1959, when the industry refused to budge at the risk of a strike, and 1965, when the White House intervened on behalf of the guideposts, the Coordinating Committee blinked. As management knew, even the mere possibility of a strike could encourage a permanent increase in import penetration. A strike had been avoided in 1968, but imports had still shot up from 12.2% of domestic consumption in 1967 to 16.7% in 1968 before settling at a level higher than before, 13.7%–13.8%, in 1969–1970.[33] At the strike deadline, the industry thus capitulated to a three-year contract including an uncapped COLA that the union declared "the best ever." R. Heath Larry, Cooper's replacement as lead negotiator for the committee, minced no words by labeling the settlement, estimated to raise labor compensation by at least 30% over the next three years, as "certainly inflationary," and he acknowledged that the industry's primary rationale in agreeing to this deal had been to avoid a strike.[34] Less than twenty-four hours later, the steel industry ignored

Nixon's threats by raising the price of steel by another 8% on average, bringing the total increase in steel prices for 1971 to 15%.[35]

DRASTIC TIMES AND DRASTIC MEASURES

In the 1940s and 1950s, GE, GM, and U.S. Steel had led the search for a noninflationary wage-price strategy that would stabilize labor relations without having to rewrite the contours of labor law in its entirety. By the early 1970s, the voluntary tactics that had proven successful during the New Look and the Eisenhower recessions no longer appeared feasible. At GE, the collapse of Boulwarist tactics in the face of a union coalition and unfavorable legal rulings prevented the company from driving a hard bargain against the use of the COLA. For General Motors, the recognition that its wage formula was more inflationary than Wilson had proclaimed came too late for the company to craft a replacement peace treaty with a new generation of militant workers. In the steel industry, the threat of foreign competition trumped any recourse to the use of a strike to hold costs in line with productivity. As Republic Steel noted in an internal review of the labor situation as it stood in November 1972, the industry now recognized that the days of the New Look were no more: "There was a time when we had hopes of dividing productivity gains between employees, stockholders and customers. That ball game has been lost in recent years and the only question is how much *more* than the productivity increase labor will receive."[36]

Even before these setbacks, a significant minority of the business community had begun to express doubts about management's ability to combat cost-push inflation voluntarily even in a recession. These executives described how seniority and supplementary unemployment benefits rendered union members impervious to fears of unemployment. With management unable to restrain labor costs, prices would have to follow wages upward to avoid a profits squeeze.[37] Secretary of Commerce Maurice Stans summarized this attitude based on his interactions at the October 1969 meeting of the Business Council. Companies still accepted the necessity of macroeconomic tightening to combat inflation, even as soft markets squeezed profits. They also understood that translating this macroeconomic restraint into microeconomic behavior would probably entail strikes. Yet without some direct assistance by the administration in holding down wage settlements, firms feared they would be forced to give in to unions seeking to win compensation in excess of the productivity level, rendering sacrifice meaningless.[38]

Looking beyond voluntary efforts, the National Association of Manufacturers, the U.S. Chamber of Commerce, and other business organizations had established working groups to study an option that would have been unthinkable were a Democrat in the White House: incomes policy. Officially, major business groups were unwilling to endorse mandatory controls, preferring instead the traditional educational efforts on the relationship between wages, prices, productivity, and profits. Internally, however, a substantial number of business leaders had reached the conclusion that the administration must couple macroeconomic restraint with labor-law reforms and incomes policy if inflation were to be stopped short of a major depression.[39] Some backed a presidential board to review major wage and price decisions, while others insisted that nothing short of comprehensive controls would prove effective at bringing wages in line with productivity and permitting profits to claim a greater share of income.[40]

These business leaders' search for some form of compulsory guideposts or controls to achieve their financial objectives found an ally in Arthur Burns, Nixon's handpicked choice to succeed William Martin as Federal Reserve chairman. Burns did not doubt that monetary restraint would eventually stop inflation, especially by moderating union wages. Still, cognizant that the American public barely tolerated even a 4% rate of unemployment, Burns foresaw that a reliance on macroeconomic restraint alone would lead to a political reaction so intense as to spell the end of independent central banking in the United States.[41] Burns was especially disturbed by the week-long illegal strike by postal workers in March 1970. Nixon had declared a national emergency and placed the military in charge of the post office, only to capitulate to the union's demands shortly thereafter.[42] Burns interpreted this surrender as evidence that "the Government might be leading the wage parade" and "had lost its strong moral position in the effort to keep wages under restraint." Burns described how the inflation that the economy now faced "was of the cost-push variety" and "could not be dealt with successfully from the monetary side" without risking additional congressional meddling.[43] Although much of what Burns considered an "incomes policy" were structural reforms such as antitrust enforcement or a rebalancing of labor law, in a widely publicized speech in December 1970, Burns also endorsed "a high-level price and wage review board which, while lacking enforcement power, would have broad authority to investigate, advise, and recommend on price and wage changes."[44]

Nixon was aware of backboning's dwindling support among those whom he had expected would be its strongest backers. As Nixon's Treasury secretary John Connally summarized the situation in late June 1971, "businessmen think that we've given up on inflation, because we're not putting in controls, wage controls." Following a briefing of congressional leadership on July 15, 1971, Connally presented Nixon with a stark choice: "If we don't propose a responsible new program, Congress will have an irresponsible one on your desk within a month."[45] Already in December 1969, Congress had given the president the power to direct the Federal Reserve to implement credit controls, and the next year, it had passed the Economic Stabilization Act, which provided the president with a standby ability to freeze and control prices, wages, rents, and salaries. Nixon signed the act lest a veto disrupt critical defense programs contained elsewhere in its text, but he had dared Congress to impose controls itself if it felt so strongly that incomes policy and not macroeconomic restraint was the solution to inflation and unemployment.[46]

A year later, with even Nixon's business supporters demanding drastic action on inflation, the president's appraisal of the Economic Stabilization Act had shifted. The golden opportunity to jettison backboning arose in August 1971, when the deficit in the balance of payments had reached $30 billion and the annualized current account fell into the red for the first time in the twentieth century.[47] Following the announcement of this trade deficit, speculators had begun to dump dollars, and Connally warned Nixon that they were in danger of losing the initiative the longer they delayed. Together with Shultz, by then promoted to director of the Office of Management and Budget, Nixon and Connally decided to move forward with a drastic shift in policy agreed on several days before: ending the ability of foreign governments to convert dollars into gold, allowing the dollar to float, imposing a 10% import tax, and instituting a wage and price freeze.[48]

Why did a solution to an international payments crisis require domestic wage and price controls? When the administration's economic team assembled at Camp David on August 13 to discuss their next steps, Connally noted that imposing an import tax to force realignment in currency values would raise the price of imports and hence be inflationary. Yet the administration had until now largely treated the balance-of-payments program separately from the domestic inflation-unemployment problem, and two days later, Nixon downplayed the inflationary effects of devaluation in announcing this program to the public.[49] Nixon's choice to renege on years of personal opposition to incomes policy can be explained better through his personal political calculus. As he noted to Connally as they prepared to depart for Camp David, "The great advantage of your program [is] in the way we put it of one, big, bold, play, that you do the whole damn thing at one time."[50] Still, Nixon recognized that the freeze, however popular it would be at first, could not last more than a brief period, three months at most. The administration would have to follow the freeze with some form of incomes policy, but Nixon still stressed that the economy could not be straitjacketed by another OPA.[51]

THE CORPORATE MODEL OF CONTROLS

The freeze announced on August 15, 1971, later to be known as Phase I of the Nixon controls, proved immensely popular. Consumer surveys referenced by the White House staff reported that three-quarters of the public believed the freeze was a positive development, and there was little evidence of panic buying in anticipation of an inflationary shock after the freeze ended.[52] The only major stakeholder to oppose the freeze openly was organized labor, which complained that the exemption of farm prices, dividends, and interest rates from the freeze, as well as the failure to invoke credit controls, would place the burden of controlling inflation on wages. Still, during the freeze, only 6% of all violations occurred on the wage side, suggesting that labor's vociferous denouncements did not noticeably impact its behavior.[53]

In contrast to labor's vocal rejection of controls, business groups poured in their congratulations at the fact that Nixon had finally taken firm action against cost-push inflation. Less than two weeks before the freeze began, the administration had sounded out the feelings of a number of blue-chip industrials on the state of the economy. Most felt that the economy was improving, but they expressed concerns at the lack of solutions for cost-push inflation. Referring to the recent negotiations in steel, GM president and chairman James Roche even suggested that with the major bargaining contracts out of the way, it was time for Nixon to pinpoint for the benefit of the general public the cause of the economy's ills: "The wage-cost push, with labor costs increasing far beyond productivity gains." Following the freeze, these firms now praised the administration for finally having taken action, and they described controls as a positive step toward resolving the cost-push problem over the next round of bargaining.[54] In private, of course, many expressed serious reservations about the freeze. Nixon would undoubtedly replace the freeze with a series of comprehensive controls lasting for an indeterminate amount of time, and history suggested that incomes policy could easily encourage complacence when it came to fiscal or monetary stimulus. Still, even those who had hesitant outlooks expressed appreciation at this opportunity to educate the public on the need to balance wage and productivity growth.[55]

Though Nixon basked in the glow of praise for his decisive economic management, he wanted little to do with the operation of his new controls. Arnold Weber, the executive director of the new Cost of Living Council (CLC) created to formulate control policy, relates that a week after the freeze started, Nixon asked why the CLC had placed professional football contracts under the wage freeze. Informed that football players had high visibility, Nixon replied, "I guess you're right. But whatever you decide leave me out of it."[56] At first, the CLC could spend its time on such trivial matters as how to set the price of Halloween candy or whether the Denver Broncos could price regular season tickets at the same price as pre-freeze preseason games. (No, they could not.) By the second month of the freeze, however, more substantive policy issues had emerged. Deferred payments could not be indefinitely denied to workers, while businesses caught between fixed prices and rising costs were beginning to feel the squeeze.[57]

Planning soon began on Phase II of controls, which would correct these inequities while draining expectations of inflation from the economy. To management, Phase II provided an opportunity to reestablish the competitive guideposts of the New Look through federal compulsion. Management would have a direct say in the formulation of Phase II wage controls through membership in the tripartite Pay Board. As initially designed, representatives of the public, organized labor, and business each received five seats apiece on the board. The unofficial spokesman of the five business representatives, and the only one to dedicate himself nearly full-time to wage control, was Virgil Day, the General Electric vice president who had succeeded Boulware as head of GE's labor relations. Supplementing Day's unofficial leadership, GE lent staff to the other business members to assist in the formulation of wage controls.[58] To reverse the decline in profits while also combating cost-push pressures, Day and the other managerial representatives called for holding labor's total real compensation to no more than the trend in productivity, and preferably less. Expressed as a nominal pay standard, labor could not be allowed to obtain more than the sum of productivity and the cost of living. Drawing on GE's long tradition of wage-price policy, the business members proposed a flat cap of 5% for total annual compensation, including deferred payments in existing contracts. After labor countered with a 6% general standard with many exceptions, the business and public members unveiled a compromise of 5.5%. Of this sum, 3% represented the real gains of productivity and 2.5% a cost-of-living adjustment. Deferred payments in existing contracts would be allowed to operate subject to review by the board, but payments scheduled for the freeze could only be made with board approval.[59]

The labor representatives interpreted the lopsided 10–5 vote in favor of this wage guide as proof that management had won the battle to institute its competitive guidepost, and four of the five labor representatives resigned in March 1972. The administration had prepared for this contingency and reconstituted the board as an entirely public body composed of the five public members, the business member Rocco Siciliano, and Teamsters president Frank Fitzsimmons, the leader of a conservative union whose loyalty Nixon had secured by pardoning Jimmy Hoffa the previous year.[60] Under the supervision of this all-public Pay Board, labor compensation indeed decelerated. Average hourly nonfarm earnings had increased by 6.9% a year in the two years prior to controls. From February 1972 to the end of 1972, this pace fell to a rate of 5.6%.[61] In major bargaining contracts, first-year payments, which generally contained a one-time boost to account for past inflation, slowed from a pace of 11.6% in 1971 to 7.4% in 1972. The board's economists attributed about a fifth of that drop to their own direct interventions and the remainder to the overall macroeconomic climate and declining expectations of inflation.[62]

At the same time that management successfully argued that labor must bear the real costs of disinflation, the Pay Board's counterpart over pricing policy, the all-public Price Commission, insisted that management too must share the gains of productivity with the public. For manufacturers and service providers, the commission permitted prices to rise to reflect "allowable cost increases" that had occurred since the firm's most recent price increase or January 1, 1971, whichever was later. However, while the Pay Board in special cases granted exceptions above its pay standard, the

Price Commission refused to recognize any compensation above the pay standard as the basis for price adjustment. Though the commission intended that this policy would ensure that the government did not abet cost-push inflation, companies were quick to complain that the commission was purchasing price stability at the expense of profits.[63]

The Price Commission initially made a major concession to management by allowing individual companies to supply their own measure of productivity growth when calculating the changes in unit labor costs that could justify higher prices.[64] Very quickly, the commission discovered that it had inadvertently created an incentive for firms to report the lowest possible productivity statistic in order to overstate unit labor costs and so receive higher prices. Even worse, over a decade after Kendrick had first engaged with ELRIC over improving productivity measurements, few companies kept records sophisticated enough to pass the commission's muster. To close this loophole, in May 1972 the commission required firms to determine the allowable amount of price relief by applying the industry-level figures compiled by the BLS to their individual costs. Using an industry-wide adjustment would also reward those firms whose productivity exceeded that of their industry: if prices were adjusted by the same measure of productivity for all firms, those with above-average productivity would have below-average unit labor costs and so be able to retain more of the gains of productivity than their less productive rivals.[65]

As a second line of defense against excessive prices, the Price Commission complemented its controls with a restriction on profit margins. Companies that raised prices faced a ceiling on profit margins equal to the best two out of the three fiscal years prior to the start of controls. Commission chairman C. Jackson Grayson agreed with management's contention that profits had indeed fallen to too low a level, especially given the need to increase productivity through investment in new technology. Nevertheless, he distinguished margin controls that merely buttressed price controls from regulations on profits per se. The commission did establish a minimum margin of 10% return on investment for which all companies were eligible, but many industries predictably complained that this limit was arbitrary and too low to support the capital investment needed to improve productivity.[66]

The business community quickly proposed its own alternative to the rules created by the Price Commission. In December 1971, a representative of Dow Chemical contacted the Price Commission with a unique offer. Given the number of chemical products that Dow produced, it was infeasible for the company to submit applications for cost-based adjustment on each and every line. Dow claimed that it could justify a 3.9% total increase, but in return for the flexibility to adjust individual prices at will, the company offered the commission a guarantee that its total weighted average price increase would not exceed the administration's overall 2.5% inflation target.[67] DuPont and other chemical firms soon followed with requests of their own, and within two months, 81 firms had entered into term limit pricing (TLP) agreements. The Price Commission believed that use of the TLP would not expand far beyond these early adopters, but by the end of Phase II, 187 firms representing about a fifth of all sales operated under TLP.[68]

Freed from the need to justify individual price adjustments on the basis of costs, companies could take advantage of TLP to raise prices on those products for which market demand allowed them to exceed the ceilings of the commission. Inadvertently, TLP also provided a government sanction for the exercise of market power over prices that the commission's rules on profits and margins were supposed to prevent.[69] Public criticism over firms unduly expanding their share of income at the expense of the public quickly led the Price Commission to constrain the flexibility afforded by TLP. In a justification familiar to past incomes policies, the commission sought to ensure that high-productivity industries cut their prices by more than the average in order to offset prices in low-productivity ones. In addition, because items such as food were not under direct control, the TLP limit on industrial firms had to be held to less than the overall inflation target to offset the effect of these headline items. Whereas Dow had initially proposed a 2.5% TLP, the commission insisted on a 2% cap. As public commentary remained skeptical of the ability of the TLP to combat inflation, in March 1972, the commission unilaterally reduced the overall limit to 1.8%, and it also forbade any individual price from being increased by more than 8%. Over the course of Phase II, the average price adjustment for firms with TLP was 1.92%, compared to 5.44% for firms of comparable size not using TLP, although as the commission admitted, a firm probably would not have opted into this program if it thought that it could otherwise justify more through individual adjustments than this TLP limit.[70]

PHASE III, FREEZE II, PHASE IV, AND DECONTROL

As Phase II neared the end of its first year, the business community recognized that its influence over incomes policies had been more limited than expected. The Price Commission's rules on margins and profits had forced management to share in the attack on cost-push inflation at a time when the business community prioritized an expansion in capital's share of income. After-tax profits as a fraction of income had risen from the nadir of 1970 but remained well below their post–World War II peak, let alone the higher levels of the early 1960s, and management remained unconvinced that the Nixon administration was serious about backing its objectives through controls.[71] Reinforcing these concerns, management's initial success in shaping the pay standard had not lent itself to further reductions in the nominal standard that would force compensation to conform more closely to the limit of productivity. Instead, Congress had pressed the Pay Board to liberalize several provisions of the standard, including by permitting an additional 0.7% allowance for fringe benefits. Just as businesses had charged in response to GM's wage formula two decades before, the failure of the pay standard to count fringes against productivity raised the nominal standard from 5.5% to 6.2% and so contributed to the perpetuation of cost pressures.[72]

Nevertheless, management accepted that controls remained necessary for the time being, especially as the prospect for voluntary restraint appeared dim in the absence of any notable changes to labor law.[73] Business groups continued to press for controls that would extinguish the premium for inflation built into the pay standard and shift more of the costs of disinflation onto labor. Even as they anticipated that the uncontrolled prices of food would probably present challenges during wage negotiations in the coming year, business spokespeople insisted that labor should have to absorb more of the overall rise in the cost of living than it did at present so as to bring compensation closer in line with productivity. As to the Price Commission, they argued that only through a greater tolerance for higher profit margins would it be possible to increase investment and productivity and so bring an end to inflation. Looking forward, business leaders urged the administration to liberalize TLP, including by lifting the 8% cap on individual adjustments, and to permit the greater pass-through of Pay Board settlements as prices.[74]

Businesses believed that they could exert more influence over the shape of the control program with the transition to Phase III, an orderly return to the free market unveiled on January 11, 1973. The Pay Board and Price Commission were abolished, with the administration intending to use the specter of renewed enforcement to promote voluntary compliance. Otherwise, most Phase II policies continued in self-administered form. Prices still had to be cost based, and wage contracts were to maintain the general Phase II standard of 5.5% plus the fringe allowance.[75] Not only had the CLC declined to tighten the pay standard to the level sought by management, but it had also explored ways to curtail the flexibility granted under the TLP. In addition to requiring more reporting to determine if firms used this authorization to implement undue price increases, the CLC seriously considered lowering the TLP standard to 1.5%. This change would have forced firms to shoulder even more of the responsibilities of disinflation than they had under Phase II, although the CLC ultimately stuck with the 1.8% standard.[76]

Inflation performed much worse during Phase III than it had during Phase II, owing not to administered industrial prices but to uncontrolled food prices. The consumer price index (CPI) overall rose at an annualized rate of 8.3%, compared to a 3.3% rate under Phases I and II, in the first half of 1973, with the price of food up 20.3%. A series of adverse supply shocks had hit agricultural markets that winter, ranging from bad weather and poor harvests to a collapse in the Peruvian anchovy harvest that pushed up the prices of animal feed and meat. The most famous of these shocks was the "Great Grain Robbery." In the spirit of détente, Nixon permitted the Soviet Union to purchase U.S. grain. When the Russians unexpectedly exercised their entire purchasing option at once, they took a full quarter of the 1972 wheat crop with them.[77]

As prices rose, the White House faced a critical decision about the future of its controls. Just as unions had torpedoed the 3.2% guidepost in 1966, labor placed Nixon on notice that it would abandon any pretense of compliance with the wage standard if he did not take action to shield real earnings. During hearings on a one-year extension of the Economic Stabilization Act in March 1973, AFL-CIO president George Meany issued a clear warning about the future of wage restraint: "If food prices aren't brought down there is no way union members are going to let their unions settle for a wage increase that won't even pay for their increased food bill.

That's not a threat. That's a fact of life."[78] Even though these commodity prices lay beyond the initial rationale of attacking cost-push administration, political necessity behooved the CLC to act. On March 6, 1973, the CLC reinstated cost justification and prenotification for oil producers, and on March 29, it imposed ceiling prices on red meat at the processing and distribution levels.[79]

Sensing that Nixon was contemplating taking even more drastic action, CEA chairman Herbert Stein warned him that price controls could do little to resolve an inflation that was no longer generated by economic power and ingrained expectations. Nixon may have enjoyed a political boost from Phase I, Stein cautioned, but "you can't walk on water twice." Stein had unwittingly walked into Nixon's comeback line: "Maybe you can if it's frozen."[80] On June 13, 1973, Nixon announced Freeze II, which now included all food prices beyond the point of first sale. In a sign of how far controls had moved from their initial rationale, wages were allowed to continue under Phase III rules because, as Nixon explained in an address to the nation, "wage settlements reached under the rules of [P]hase III have not been a significant cause of the increase in prices."[81]

Freeze II transformed a program that businesses had once hoped to exploit into their greatest nightmare. By continuing to enforce the margin limit, TLP, and other price controls as costs rose, the administration had absolved labor of any blame while shifting the burden of fighting inflation to large corporations, not the food and raw-material sectors from which cost pressures emanated. With industrial plant operating at a high rate of utilization, it was doubtful that productivity would continue to increase at the same rate it had during the recovery of 1972, leaving less room to absorb rising costs.[82] Pretax profits continued to increase in nominal terms through the third quarter of 1974, but the recovery of after-tax profits had stalled in 1973 and began to fall in 1974, reaching a new postwar low as a share of income that year.[83] As in the lead-up to Phase III, business groups accepted that Freeze II and the subsequent Phase IV were political realities, but they pressed the government to assist firms in adapting to these conditions of excess demand. Once more, they requested the liberalization of price controls, especially TLP, so as to provide for a greater pass-through of costs. They also continued to urge that the government take a firmer line on wages, especially by treating all fringes and the COLA as part of an overall 5.5% guideline so that labor would have to absorb some of these costs.[84]

Instead, Phase IV proved even stricter on prices. Not only did manufacturing and service industries have to notify the CLC of intended price actions, but they could no longer apply a markup to cost increases, generating intense pessimism about squeezed profit margins. Wage controls, in contrast, remained under the self-administered standard of Phase III, with no justification or notifications required.[85] Phase IV did provide for the selective decontrol of entire industries where demand-pull pressures rendered controls entirely ineffective, but such relief came with strings to ensure that management did not capture all of the gains of decontrol for itself. In return for industries having their ceilings lifted, they had to agree to plow the proceeds of this relief into expanding production capacity and to redirect their exports to domestic customers.[86]

Public support for controls evaporated as Freeze II and Phase IV proved unable to contain the cost of living, with the CPI rising at a 9.6% annualized rate in the second half of 1973 and consumer food prices by 18.6%.[87] The final straw for controls arrived in October 1973 with the Arab oil embargo, which reduced oil supplies by an estimated 16% of U.S. petroleum consumption and 8% of energy consumption. The directly purchased energy component of the CPI, measuring gas, electricity, fuel oil, coal, gasoline, and motor oil, surged at a 70.7% annual rate in the first quarter of 1974. High prices of imported oil also transferred real income from the United States to foreigners, leaving a smaller domestic pie over which Americans fought to maintain their aggregate share of income.[88]

Faced with this new challenge, business groups intentionally toned down their warnings about the inflationary effects of labor power and instead emphasized the counterproductive effects of controls on production. Behind the scenes, management believed that this outreach would teach consumers to associate government intervention with shortages and greater inflation. By stressing that only an expansion of supply would counteract these shortages, business could also build public support for greater profits. According to a survey conducted by the National Association of Manufacturers to support this publicity blitz, a fifth of firms had reduced output due to material shortages and another fifth had cut back on production in response to price controls. Seventy percent indicated that controls were leading to shortages, and a third claimed that controls had caused them to cut back on plans for capital expansion.[89]

The business spokespeople who had once viewed controls as at least a partial answer for their wage problems furthermore publicly recanted their attitudes. In October 1973, the leaders of the National Association of Manufacturers and the U.S. Chamber of Commerce jointly submitted a formal request to Nixon to end controls immediately. Admitting that they had supported controls at their outset, they explained that the program had outlived its usefulness, especially as the government had decontrolled and exempted some sectors but not others.[90] Testifying before Congress in February 1974, General Electric chairman and CEO Reginald Jones similarly admitted that his company had supported controls in August 1971 as a way to decrease the inflationary expectations that were pressing wages upward. Since then, it had become clear to his firm that controls had failed to achieve this intended objective. Because controls had exempted the prices of many raw inputs while regulating the prices and margins of the products GE sold, the company faced difficulties in obtaining affordable supplies at present prices. Jones claimed that GE desired to invest in more productive and energy-efficient equipment but had concluded that margin limitations had reduced the potential return on these projects while hampering the company from sourcing these funds internally.[91]

With the Economic Stabilization Act set to expire at the end of April 1974, the White House finally agreed that the state of the economy no longer justified the use of mandatory controls. The CLC had already stepped up the pace of decontrol where shortages and excess demand made controls infeasible. Phase IV had initially covered 42.6% of the CPI and 69.4% of the wholesale price index (WPI). By April 1, 1974, only about a quarter of the CPI and a third of the WPI remained under price controls.[92] Still, given the number of prominent industries that had negotiated decontrol commitments with the CLC, the administration believed that it would be necessary to preserve some authority to monitor their compliance in the future. It would also be useful to maintain oversight of sectors that had long been linked to concerns about administration and cost-push inflation. With neither labor nor management keen on the perpetuation of controls, however, Congress instead presented the administration with a choice: extend the existing authority to implement controls over the entire economy or abandon all formal wage and price interventions. With Nixon unable to achieve a bill on his own terms, he chose to allow his controls to expire for good.[93]

CONCLUSION

Nixon's memoirs, published in 1978, understandably focused much more on foreign policy than on the domestic economy. In the few pages granted to inflation and unemployment, Nixon perhaps surprisingly did not launch into an impassioned defense of his actions. Instead, he all but admitted that controls had been the easy way out and that he had erred in succumbing to this temptation: "The August 15, 1971, decision to impose them was politically necessary and immensely popular in the short run. But in the long run I believe that it was wrong. The piper must always be paid, and there was an unquestionably high price for tampering with the orthodox economic mechanisms."[94]

Yet, at the time when Nixon had abandoned his commitment to macroeconomic restraint, the administration had actually *gained* credibility and public approval by making mandatory controls the center of its anti-inflationary program. That Democratic congresspeople preferred incomes policy to a trade-off between inflation and unemployment is understandable. But the last time that Nixon had been in the White House, macroeconomic restraint had encouraged business groups to hold the line against rising labor costs with a minimum of government interference. In the late 1950s, General Electric and U.S. Steel had used wage-price policy to contain the costs of collective bargaining without having to fight an uphill political battle to curtail the power of organized labor. A decade later, companies such as General Motors attempted to replicate this voluntary restraint, but they found their efforts ineffective. Attributing this failure to an unfavorable shift in the industrial-labor power balance, individual firms turned to the White House to achieve their objectives through less-than-voluntary means. State compulsion would force labor to leave a greater share of the surplus of productivity for management until labor-law reforms could ensure that the strategies of the New Look would again prevail.

It would only take a few years for this business community to realize that it had made a serious mistake in ceding its wage-price autonomy to the government. Despite firms' best efforts to tighten the wage standard and reduce the severity of price controls, they found that they had little ability to manipulate governmental incomes policy even with a Republican in the Oval Office. Rather than shifting income and power from labor to capital as management had intended, Nixon's controls forced profits and prices to shoulder more of the real costs of disinflation than the business community had anticipated. By the time that oil shocks and production shortages provided management with a way out of these controls, there was little reason to believe that voluntary restraint would fare any better than it had at the start of the decade.

CHAPTER SEVEN

Abort, Retry, Fail

STAGFLATION, COMPETITION, AND THE END OF WAGE-PRICE POLICY

ON SEPTEMBER 14, 1974, millions of Americans turned on their televisions to hear a respected authority explain how an inflation entering the double digits could be cured: "The country's got to produce more goods. Then we've got to have a little more unemployment. So when we have more goods to buy, and less people who can afford to buy the goods, then the prices will come down." That speaker was not the president of the United States but someone Americans trusted much more: Carroll O'Connor, in character as Archie Bunker, the lovable if inarticulate patriarch of the groundbreaking sitcom *All in the Family.* Befitting its reputation for exploring pressing social issues, *All in the Family* opened its fifth season with a four-part episode titled "The Bunkers and Inflation," during which the family struggles financially as Archie's union goes on strike for higher wages. Of course, when Archie Bunker spoke, that usually meant that the writers of the show were aiming to lampoon some aspect of white, middle-aged, blue-collar conservatism. Archie's explanation that a crash course of unemployment in the short run would lead to a lower rate of inflation in the long run was met with a laugh track and the befuddled confusion of his liberal son-in-law foil, Mike Stivic, aka "Meathead," played by Rob Reiner: "That is the stupidest damn thing you've ever said."[1]

Even without the laugh track and Meathead's commentary, most viewers would probably have laughed at Archie's cure for inflation. Not since

Dwight Eisenhower and William Martin had policymakers proposed manipulating this trade-off, as Archie seemingly did, by intentionally placing the economy through the wringer. Was unemployment not high enough already, falling under 6% in only one year over the entire decade following Nixon's resignation? Fortunately, Keynesian economists had for decades described a better mechanism to stop this worst-of-both-worlds scenario known as stagflation: incomes policy. By putting an end to the wage-price spiral, inflation would fall with less sacrifice of employment. Expressed otherwise, incomes policy would permit unemployment to fall farther and faster without risking the resumption of the zero-sum game of robbing Peter to pay Paul.[2]

Restraint of any kind would initially prove a much harder sell to the business community than it had before Nixon's controls. Following the oil shocks, management continued to doubt that it could voluntarily resurrect the methods of the New Look in a period of stagflation. At the same time, management had come to expect that incomes policies would shift the burden of restraint onto profits rather than wages. Many business spokespeople now emphasized deficits and regulatory costs as greater threats to investment than unions. Until the government reduced these pressures, businesses newly freed from controls argued that they and their profits would have to take their chances with import competition and recession by raising prices.[3]

This corporate response to stagflation only reinforced the belief of the Keynesian Consensus that private enterprise could not be trusted to set prices and wages in the public interest. As politicians interacted with such familiar wage-price targets as the auto and steel industries, they concluded that management would neither try to contain wages nor show restraint on prices unless compelled to do so by the government. Only months after the collapse of Nixon's controls, the White House Council on Wage and Price Stability (COWPS) resumed efforts to combat inflation without resorting to excessive macroeconomic restraint. Initially designed as a way to monitor private behavior and identify potential areas for structural improvement, COWPS quickly evolved into a more coercive agency, culminating in its reintroduction of quasi-mandatory wage-price guideposts, now known by the suspiciously similar substitute of "guidelines." Once again, however, COWPS turned a blind eye toward the conditions that firms blamed for generating inflation, and management perceived little choice but to throw in its lot with higher prices.

The private sector's behavior over the span of the 1970s said less about its own irresponsibility than that of the government, especially the Federal Reserve. Looking backward onto this period, it is possible to discern a recurring "stop-and-go" pattern in the operation of monetary policy stretching back to the mid-1960s. No sooner had employment deteriorated in response to restraint than the Fed would reverse course by easing interest rates and releasing massive amounts of stimulus into an economy that was already operating at or beyond its full potential. The bad luck of adverse supply shocks certainly did not make the task of policymakers any easier, but this pattern of macroeconomic management, even in its stop phases, lacked anti-inflationary credibility. Instead, the private sector learned to expect that inflation would continue in the future. What COWPS labeled inflationary momentum on the part of management was thus only the most recent example of self-interested actors responding rationally to the economic conditions generated by Washington.[4]

Management would only have cause to modify its thinking at the decade's end, when Federal Reserve chairman Paul Volcker called the bluff of the Keynesian Consensus that macroeconomic disinflation would be too painful for society to tolerate without an incomes policy. Archie Bunker would have the last laugh, as his cure for inflation, more goods with fewer people able to afford them, was put to the test in the double-dip recessions of the early 1980s. As the old titans of domestic industry strained under the costs of labor peace, new challengers at home and abroad injected downward pressure on prices and developed more flexible methods of labor relations. Under these conditions, management learned that it would have to prioritize the needs of the individual firm, not those of erstwhile oligopolies. Firms that survived this shakeout emerged stronger and more productive than before, but wage-price policy, the idealized system of distribution that had shaped managerial thinking for decades, had lost its relevance in this newly competitive marketplace.

THE RETURN OF THE SPIRAL

After several years of operating under price controls designed and operated by federal bureaucrats rather than corporate officials, the business community declared itself cured of what it now deemed its temporary madness. As

Carl Madden of the U.S. Chamber of Commerce explained when testifying to Congress against the use of incomes policies in 1975, his organization was more than willing to recant its previous support for controls. The Chamber had once pragmatically accepted controls when that course of action had appeared inevitable in 1971, but no longer: "As a result of the experience that business has had, it is now opposed to controls."[5] Controls were supposed to have been an alternative means to the end of increasing profitability, but as they had prevented companies from adjusting their prices in response to excess demand and supply shocks, profits had worsened in the final years of the Nixon administration. Though at first glance the after-tax profits of nonfinancial corporations appeared to have risen from the mid-1960s through the end of controls, accounting for the inflated replacement cost of plant and equipment and revaluing inventories at present prices revealed that profits had actually fallen, from about $36 billion in the late 1960s to $32.9 billion in 1973, according to the Department of Commerce.[6]

Still, despite this newfound resistance to federal incomes policy, corporate management remained extremely concerned about what would happen when the end of controls unleashed pent-up cost pressures. Companies with upcoming negotiations were at best uncertain and at worst extremely pessimistic about the prospect for wages given labor's renewed focus on obtaining protection from the cost of living.[7] During Phase II of the controls, businesses had pressed the Pay Board to hold total labor compensation to less than the sum of productivity and inflation, in effect forcing labor to shoulder some of the real costs of disinflation. Now, not only did unions demand that management shield real wages, but they also insisted that their fringe benefits and incentive pay receive protection against the effects of inflation as well. This extension of COLA clauses entailed substantial costs. In the case of the United Steelworkers contract with the can industry, for instance, applying the COLA to fringes could add an additional 30% to the costs of escalation.[8] Some businesses resolved to resist the spread of COLA clauses, and the number of man-days lost to work stoppages doubled in 1974 from the year before to match the trend that had prevailed before the start of controls (see table 3). Yet as GE and GM had discovered prior to the Nixon controls, and as labor-relations experts and veterans of controls now counseled, the spread of the COLA appeared inevitable.[9] After a jump of a quarter from 1974 to 1975, half of all workers in major bargaining contracts of one thousand or more employees enjoyed some form of escalation clause, matching the previous high mark obtained right before the New Look of the late 1950s (see table 1).

Struggling to contain this tide of wage costs, management was beginning to reconsider whether higher wages were the cause of inflation as opposed to its effect. According to the new chronology promoted by corporate spokespeople, when the Great Inflation began in the 1960s and when the Nixon controls had collapsed in 1973–1974, there had been no change in the structure of business or labor, nor had there been an explosion of monopoly power. Unions had also not given rise to worldwide supply shocks and commodity-price spikes. Comparing these two periods of inflation, corporate spokespeople instead recognized that both had transpired alongside a sudden increase in government spending and monetary expansion. Their conclusion was that policymakers lulled into a false sense of security by incomes policies had overheated the economy, unleashing the inflation to which business and labor then responded by adjusting prices and wages. Perhaps the government had then validated this spiral through an increased money supply or greater deficit spending, but in that case, suggested George Hagedorn of the National Association of Manufacturers, it was the government's response that was to blame for perpetuating inflation.[10]

In distinguishing the exercise of union market power from inflation, corporate spokespeople sought to undercut any rationale for a return to incomes policy. Businesspeople who were accustomed to dealing with the government recognized that were they to continue to emphasize a structural explanation of inflation, they would simply be providing fodder for the Keynesians who doubted that the private market and free collective bargaining could set wages and prices in the public interest. Shortly after the end of controls, R. Heath Larry, the U.S. Steel executive who had succeeded R. Conrad Cooper as the industry's lead negotiator, expressed doubts that modifying labor law would resolve all of the potential sources of inflation. As a result, Larry argued that business should focus on seeking voluntary changes to the institution of collective bargaining, lest efforts to involve the government in labor-law reforms lead to undesirable interventionist consequences.[11] Later in the decade, Richard Landry of the U.S. Chamber of Commerce similarly argued before Congress that because there had been no widening of the differential in wages of bargaining groups of one thousand and five thousand workers, large unions were not inherently more inflationary than other labor groups were. As a result, the government would do better to focus its attention only on the special cases where wages and profit margins generated inflationary pressures, not industry as a whole.[12]

While management voiced less concern about the effects of labor costs, it did not abandon the theory of cost-push inflation entirely. Rather, it trained its ammunition on the newest claims of stakeholders on corporate income: regulation imposed by the state on behalf of customers, workers, and society in general. During the 1960s and early 1970s, the consumer, environmental, and quality-of-work movements had pressed the government to intervene in an expanding array of business operations. Businesses faced a host of new regulations designed to shield the health and safety of workers and consumers, oversee pension funds, and safeguard the environment from pollution. Meeting regulatory standards required industries to make heavy investments in technologies that sapped financial resources without contributing to the production process.[13] By the mid-1970s, for instance, the steel industry argued that environmental controls claimed about 20% of its cash flow, equal to the amounts spent on expansion and the development of new sources of energy. While the industry could tap outside capital at a high cost to fund its production needs, it protested that it would not be able to find lenders willing to cover nonproductive regulatory investment.[14] The auto industry similarly argued that the most important anti-inflationary action that the government could take was a moratorium on future regulations. General Motors estimated that of the $817/car increase in costs experienced from 1972 to 1974, the years of the Nixon controls, safety and environmental regulations contributed $218, compared to $599 in payroll and materials. The next year's models would entail an additional $250/car in regulatory costs, and $750 million would be spent on environmental upgrades over the subsequent three years.[15]

Unable to escape the demands not only of labor but also of the public as expressed through regulatory requirements, management concluded that its only viable response was to pass on costs in the form of higher prices. Shortages in the wake of controls had temporarily diminished resistance on the part of purchasers to higher costs, allowing industrial marketers to raise prices, although not always by enough to cover costs. According to one industrial survey, a third of manufacturers also made use of price-escalation clauses in long-term sales contracts, akin to the ability of the COLA to shift the burden of inflation. Many firms had also ceased to quote prices at the time of sales in favor of quoting prices at shipments so as to protect themselves from unanticipated cost changes in the meantime.[16] Management recognized that higher prices could not provide a long-run strategy to expand profits. Buyers would eventually show resistance to higher prices, and in the absence of stronger protectionist policies, they could turn to foreigners for steady streams of supplies at lower prices. Still, even when markets softened into recession by the end of 1974 and the forces of competition reasserted themselves later on in the decade, these industries signaled to both their customers and the government that they still intended to pass some of their costs, especially those of labor and energy.[17]

"HERE WE GO AGAIN!"

As the business community recast inflation as the inevitable result of government actions rather than private-sector decisions, the Keynesian Consensus was also beginning to rethink the role of big business and big labor in causing inflation. Supply shocks in the price of food and oil had clearly originated far from the industrial core of the U.S. economy, and with the war in Vietnam finally coming to a close, even the Keynesian veterans of the Kennedy and Johnson administrations could admit that the spending of the 1960s had been excessive. The economics discipline further agreed with the business community that the costs of regulation could indeed outweigh its overall benefits and so contribute to inflation and slowed productivity growth.[18] Nevertheless, Keynesian economists who doubted that big business and big labor had *caused* stagflation still looked to structural rigidities and private market power to explain the *persistence* of inflation. When supply shocks distributed a large slice of the overall pie to foreigners, firms and unions with power over prices and wages responded by seeking to maintain their own slices at the expense of the remainder of society. As a result, the economy had adjusted to the spike in the overall price level not by reducing other relative prices, as would have been expected in a more competitive economy, but through a wage-price spiral and increased unemployment. Fiscal and monetary restraint might be able to break this momentum by pushing unemployment even higher, but, as always, an incomes policy held out hopes of engineering a less painful disinflation.[19]

The best remembered and most infamous of these approaches to incomes policies in the wake of the Nixon controls was announced by President Gerald Ford on October 8, 1974. Though he laid out a thirty-two-step program to combat inflation, ranging from greater fiscal responsibility through budget cuts and a surtax on high-income households to the supply-side initiatives of an investment tax credit and a "substantial purging process" of government regulation, public perception fixated on a single statement: "There is only one point on which all advisers have agreed: We must whip inflation right now."[20] Ford called for a volunteer mobilization to follow the government's lead in making scarce resources go further. This Whip Inflation Now (WIN) initiative quickly became the public face of the administration's anti-inflation program. WIN became best known for its ubiquitous presence on buttons, decals, and numerous tchotchkes signaling resistance against wage and price increases. Letters poured into the White House pledging to fight inflation and conserve energy, with millions of WIN buttons distributed in return. A Citizens Action Committee was appointed to organize the campaign, establishing local committees to monitor prices and decide the winning entry for the "Design the WIN Flag" contest.[21]

In the interest of writing an objective history, it is safe to say that the WIN program was the most half-baked of all of the anti-inflationary initiatives of the twentieth century. As Ford's CEA chairman, Alan Greenspan, later recalled his thoughts upon hearing of this program for the first time, "This is unbelievable stupidity. What am I doing here?"[22] WIN did not directly impact fiscal and monetary policy, let alone the market imperfections considered to be sources of cost-push inflation. As a completely voluntary program, there was no reason to believe that the informal enforcement of WIN stickers and pledges would override the rational, self-preserving response to a double-digit inflation. Instead, the "Now" component of WIN gave the public a false impression of the daunting task ahead, making it even more difficult to shift expectations of inflation through fiscal and monetary restraint.[23] Within weeks, even the White House had come to grasp that political slogans were no replacement for sound economic policy. Ford neglected to mention the initiative as part of his 1975 State of the Union Address, and within three months, the Citizens Action Committee had turned its focus to energy conservation. Soon, all that remained of WIN was the faint embossing of the few remaining pieces of letterhead and millions of pieces of memorabilia gathering dust.[24]

WIN has gone down in history as the main focus of the Ford administration's anti-inflation efforts, distracting from a much more interventionist approach to curbing cost-push inflation that arose from the ashes of the Nixon controls. Though Nixon had returned to preaching the importance of a steady policy of fiscal and monetary restraint as an alternative to the "shock treatment" of recession and unemployment in the final months of his presidency, he had also requested that Congress establish a new Cost of Living Task Force to monitor wages, prices, and the supply situation. Officially, this task force would rely on public hearings, informal contact with labor and management, and data analysis. As Nixon proposed it to Congress, the task force would expand the existing ability of the White House to collect data on wages and prices and ensure "that Government have [*sic*] the information it needs to persuade labor and management to do their duty in the effort to reduce inflation."[25] In private, however, as the CEA advised Nixon that it had underestimated the need for restraint and the difficulties of balancing the budget, Nixon fully intended for this agency to engage in jawboning, a strong reversal from his first-term policies: "We know what will work and what will not work. We will have no controls and no tax cut, but we will use jawboning to get restraint on wages and prices."[26]

Congress had failed to act on this agency by the time that Nixon resigned, but President Ford took advantage of his brief honeymoon upon taking office to renew this request. Within two weeks, Ford had signed the Council on Wage and Price Stability Act into law. COWPS was tasked primarily with reviewing the effect of "economic concentration and anti-competitive practices," industrial supply and demand factors, and collective bargaining. In a concession to the arguments of business groups, COWPS also received a mandate to investigate the costs of government regulation.[27] Though COWPS initially could only hold public hearings and lacked the powers to subpoena information or require mandatory reporting from its targets, business leaders anticipated that the agency would inevitably grow more interventionist. The very creation of this agency so soon after the collapse of the CLC suggested that the political climate was still favorable to increased interference in wage and price setting. The marginal comment of one Republic Steel executive on a bulletin of the Machinery and Allied Products Institute updating its members on this new agency aptly summed up this collective hesitance: "Here we go again!"[28]

The executive director of COWPS, the Princeton economist Albert Rees, sought to reassure the private sector that his agency would not become a tool for harassment. Rees took care to differentiate his agency from the guideposts of the 1960s, emphasizing that the economists of COWPS were focused less on inflation and more on the performance of individual markets. Rees believed that COWPS should prioritize consumer issues such as the costs of medical care, the repricing of retail shelf inventory, and resolving why rising sugar prices seemed to impact the price of regular and diet sodas equally. Still, he accepted that COWPS would also have to investigate the unionized manufacturing industries that had long been the conventional targets of wage-price policy. In these sectors, Rees felt that COWPS could dampen inflationary expectations by holding back the front-runners in the wage-price spiral until everyone else caught up. An incomes policy could also prevent the nominal gains of macroeconomic stimulus from being dissipated into wages and prices and so make a given amount of stimulus go a longer way.[29]

Given this orientation, conflict between COWPS and corporate pricing strategies remained inevitable, as the steel industry quickly learned. Having agreed to three-year contracts in 1968 that raised costs by 6.9% a year and in 1971 by 10.6% a year, the industry had not taken advantage of the Nixon controls to reverse its cost trend. Instead, the industry and the union had agreed in March 1973 to prioritize the problem of foreign competition through an "Experimental Negotiating Agreement" (ENA). Essentially the same approach as Operation Heresy in 1967, the ENA committed the two parties to binding arbitration in order to assure customers that there would be no strike and hence no need to stock up on imported steel as a hedge. Several long-running concerns of the industry, including the COLA, were not covered by the arbitration guarantee, and the USWA also retained the right to strike over local issues. In return for giving up the right to strike over national issues, the USWA received a "slice of the melon" estimated to result from uninterrupted operations. The industry also agreed in principle to a COLA and AIF on the model of the UAW, dropping its long-held insistence on basing wages on steel's own subaverage productivity trend. The ENA devised in the midst of price controls thus ironically resulted in the single most expensive labor agreement in the post-1945 steel industry: a three-year contract finalized in early April 1974 that, after factoring in the costs of an uncapped COLA, raised employment costs by 11.7% a year (see table 2).[30]

Having made no attempt at voluntary wage restraint, the steel industry harbored no intention of stabilizing prices once controls ended. On December 16, 1974. U.S. Steel announced a 4.7% price increase, prompting President Ford to request that the company provide written justification to COWPS for analysis.[31] U.S. Steel explained to COWPS that its costs would increase by 7.5%, or $20.51/ton, between September 1974 and February 1975, but COWPS noted that actual costs had only increased by $8.69/ton at the time of the price increase, with the remainder representing prospective changes in ore prices. On the basis of this analysis, COWPS requested a rollback of at least 20% of the increase, and U.S. Steel compromised with a 16% reduction. COWPS then convinced several other steelmakers that attempted to raise prices to make similar rollbacks, and the steel industry also provided a promise that it would not raise prices before June 1, 1975, without prior approval.[32]

Following this incident, COWPS undertook a formal study of the industry's costs, profits, and capital needs that presented a highly critical view of the industry's traditional justifications for its pricing policy. The steel industry advanced its familiar thesis that it lacked the capital to expand production at present prices. Republic Steel, for instance, complained that while it had spent over $100 million on capital investment in 1974, this amount was far below what it needed in order to modernize and expand its capacity, especially in light of sums required to meet environmental regulations over the next several years.[33] COWPS's own report, however, unequivocally rejected this argument by labeling the steel industry an oligopoly in which price leaders—namely, U.S. Steel and Bethlehem—set prices at full costs plus some target rate of return. COWPS proved more receptive to the industry's arguments about the costs of regulation, but it rejected the industry's claims that higher prices were needed to increase the rate of return on capital or offset the effects of past inflation. Instead, challenging the industry's estimates that meeting capacity needs would cost $2.4 billion a year for five years, COWPS estimated that the industry required only $900 million a year, an amount that profits and prices could currently provide.[34]

Representatives of the steel industry contested nearly every point raised in the COWPS study, from its estimates of capital investment to its conclusion that allowing greater import competition was the best cure for this textbook model of oligopoly pricing.[35] Rather than the industry relying solely on the familiar claims of its economic experts, however, it also chose to make a show of strength by continuing to raise prices. In its most blatant provocation, U.S. Steel announced in August 1976 that it intended to increase prices on the flat-rolled sheet steel used in cars and appliances, which the COWPS report had noted were suffering from heavy import competition and low demand. The remainder of the industry soon followed and then threatened to request an antidumping investigation and tariffs were these prices unable to stick. Much as Lyndon Johnson had responded to Bethlehem Steel's testing of his nerves a decade before, however, President Ford announced his disturbance at these price movements and asked COWPS to undertake a second investigation of the steel industry. U.S. Steel and the remainder of the industry then rescinded their increases in return for the cancellation of this probably damning study.[36]

As COWPS criticized corporate pricing, it provided little assistance to management in containing the costs of labor and regulation. With 4.5 million union workers set to negotiate new collective bargaining contracts in 1976, COWPS considered that year to be critical to preventing the spread of an inflationary pattern of compensation. COWPS sought permission from the White House to prepare studies on these important negotiations, but the administration insisted for political reasons that COWPS limit itself to providing only background statistics. Under no conditions was COWPS permitted to discuss anticipatory settlement sizes, lest it appear to be formulating a new guidepost.[37] The growth of wages and benefits did deescalate in 1976, with new contracts for bargaining units of five thousand workers or more valued at an average annual increase of 6.6% (exclusive of the COLA), compared to 8.1% the previous year. Still, COWPS issued rear-view evaluations that labeled many high-profile settlements as inflationary. These included the Teamsters contract, which disguised its total costs by pushing major wage gains to the end of the contract, and the Rubber Workers contract, which replaced straight wage increases with a COLA clause.[38]

COWPS also fell short in its treatment of regulatory costs. Rees believed that there was no way for COWPS to challenge New Deal–era "sacred cows," including labor law. Still, he agreed with industry about the need to analyze the social regulations that had developed over the past decade and did not yet possess a vested interest of supporters, such as Environmental Protection Agency (EPA) pesticide regulations; National Highway Traffic Safety Administration safety rulings; or Occupational Safety and Health Administration shelter requirements.[39] To accomplish this goal, Executive Order 11821 of November 27, 1974, required COWPS to issue an "Inflation Impact Statement" for new regulations, but the overburdened and underequipped agency had little capacity to carry out yet another function. Only nine of the twenty-five agencies required to make Inflation Impact Statements had even submitted any paperwork by the time that Ford left office. The forty-one statements evaluated by COWPS, of which the agency commented on twenty-three, and the eight legislative proposals evaluated by the Office of Management and Budget were only a drop in the bucket compared to the estimate of Rees's successor, William Lilley III, that there were thirty-one hundred new federal regulations and amendments produced per year and ten thousand in the pipeline at any given time.[40]

MOMENTUM AND DECELERATION

By the time that Ford left office, further showdowns with steel had not prevented inflation from seemingly taking on a cost-push life of its own. After peeling away energy, food, and other volatile "headline" inflation factors, the remaining core inflation rate had leveled off at 6%–7% a year by 1977. This measure roughly paralleled the difference between the growth of labor compensation and national productivity, bolstering the Keynesian interpretation that the momentum of the wage-price spiral perpetuated inflation. Unemployment meanwhile had risen swiftly from 5.5% in August 1974 to a peak of 9% by May 1975 before falling to a little under 8% by the end of 1976, marking the sharpest recession since the Great Depression (see table 4). As Barry Bosworth, Jimmy Carter's eventual choice to run COWPS, soon asked, if 9% unemployment in 1975 had not been enough to eliminate inflation completely, how many more jobs had to be destroyed before inflation subsided?[41]

In 1978, Arthur Okun, the final chairman of the Johnson CEA and a frequent consultant to the Carter CEA, published a short but influential paper that provided a concrete estimate for how painful a purely macroeconomic disinflation would be. On examination of six different Phillips Curve models, Okun calculated that raising unemployment by one percentage point for a year would result in a permanent reduction of the inflation rate of only 0.16–0.5 percentage points, with an average estimated reduction of 0.3 points. Expressed otherwise, this "sacrifice ratio" meant that a permanent reduction of inflation by one percentage point would require the approximate reduction of a year's GNP by a stunning ten percentage points. Okun concluded that while macroeconomic restraint alone would be effective if maintained for long enough, it was inefficient unless supplemented with "the direct influence of public policy on costs."[42]

Bosworth viewed 1978 as the last chance for the administration to establish a less inflationary wage pattern before the next major round of collective bargaining began in 1979. Identifying inflationary expectations as the force behind the momentum of inflation, Bosworth suggested establishing a numerical "deceleration standard," a rule dictating how much precisely firms and unions would be expected to lessen their rate wage and price increases from the underlying momentum. According to the explanation of this standard offered in the 1978 *Economic Report,* no one individual or group would agree to reduce their own pace of wages out of fear that they would fall behind in the income squabble. A government-sponsored deceleration program attacked this momentum by requiring every market to reduce its rate of wage and price growth at the same time, but not necessarily by the same amount. Achieving a half-percentage-point overall deceleration would require the concentrated, unionized sectors where wages and prices had grown the fastest to decelerate by more than the nonunionized sector.[43]

Bosworth suggested the government could secure compliance with this standard by offering Real Wage Insurance (RWI) to workers who abided by the nominal wage guideline. If inflation ultimately eroded their real earnings, workers would receive a tax refund that would ensure that their real take-home pay did not suffer. Unfortunately for this proposal, the administration could not request these tax refunds at a time in which it was also pursuing general budget restraint as part of a macroeconomic program to combat inflation. The business community also offered heavy resistance to RWI because, as the Chamber of Commerce explained, using the tax system to control inflation represented "one more step towards mandatory controls." Without RWI, the deceleration standards went into effect no more binding than had been WIN, and even Carter described the program as "(inevitably, I guess) very general in nature & mostly wishful thinking."[44]

With COWPS struggling to devise an incomes policy, Secretary of Labor Ray Marshall suggested an alternative approach modeled on the "trigger-price mechanism" (TPM) used in trade policy. The TPM was intended to improve enforcement of the antidumping laws by identifying in advance the price at which import sales would trigger a dumping investigation. Just as in trade policy, Marshall suggested that wages would also be subject to a TPM that would lead to an investigation if broken.[45] Building on this concept, COWPS developed a wage guideline of 7% a year over the life of a contract. Compared to the official forecast of 1.75% labor-productivity growth over the coming year, this guideline implied an increase in unit labor costs of 5.25%. After factoring in a 0.5% increase in Social Security taxes, predicted unit labor costs would rise 5.75%. Because annual unit-cost growth over the previous two years had been 6.25%, adherence to this wage guideline would permit firms to decelerate their rate of price inflation by at least one-half percentage point from the average of 1976–1977. If wages rose less than the guideline permitted, management was expected to slow the pace of prices even more to reflect the full reduction in unit costs. In no case would a firm be allowed to raise prices by more than 9.5%.[46]

Business groups remained skeptical that this newest approach to an incomes policy would prove any more effective than in the past. While they responded favorably to the deregulatory and fiscal initiatives that accompanied Carter's anti-inflation program, the resort to guidelines suggested that Carter would repeat the mistake of Johnson and Nixon: shifting the blame for inflation to the private sector in order to obtain political cover to engage in inflationary stimulus.[47] This skepticism was not mistaken. In terms of regulatory costs, Carter's headline efforts to remove New Deal regulations on air travel and trucking did little to address the concerns about the cost-push effects of the more recent social and environmental regulation, not least as his flagship order requiring economic analysis of new regulations exempted independent agencies such as the EPA.[48] On the fiscal front, Carter proposed a conservative approach, but the expansion of the federal deficit in 1979 and 1980 led financial markets to build even higher expectations of inflation into interest rates.[49]

Most importantly, Federal Reserve policy worked against the intent of the anti-inflation program. Dissatisfaction with Arthur Burns's handling of the economy had led the Democratic Congress to pass the Federal Reserve Reform Act of 1977, which in addition to new disclosure requirements also for the first time explicitly established a mandate for monetary policy: "to promote effectively the goals of maximum employment, stable prices, and moderate long-term interest rates."[50] A similar set of objectives was included in a stagflation-inspired revision of the Employment Act the next year, which enshrined "reasonable price stability" as one goal of federal economic policy.[51] Carter's replacement for Burns as Federal Reserve chairman, the former Textron CEO G. William Miller, did not share these priorities. After his appointment in January 1978, Miller resisted pressures to tighten monetary policy in the event of accelerating inflation. While his preference for anti-inflationary measures other than aggregate demand management won his appointment a warm welcome from organized labor, Miller's support within the White House quickly vanished. Under Miller, the Federal Reserve consistently overshot its monetary target, counteracting any attempt to lessen expectations of inflation through a more restrained monetary policy. When Carter purged his Cabinet in July 1979, he took the opportunity to move his handpicked Fed chairman to the Treasury, where he presumably could do less damage.[52]

As if a bad demand-pull situation could not get any worse, this excessive monetary stimulus helped to accommodate the second oil shock of 1979–1980, which sent costs rising and productivity plummeting. Just as in 1973–1974, a sharp jump in imported oil prices lowered the overall share of real resources available to Americans, prompting a renewed scramble to maintain the aggregate share of a shrinking pie. As a result of this newest supply shock, the underlying assumptions of the guidelines were themselves empirically invalidated. The price-deceleration target of 0.5 percentage points rested on the calculation that the annual growth of unit labor costs would fall from 6.25% to at least 5.75%, the difference between a 7.5% rise in labor compensation and a 1.75% growth of labor productivity. In hindsight, not only had the administration overestimated labor-productivity growth at 1.75%, but it had assigned the wrong sign to this measure. From the fourth quarter of 1978 to the fourth quarter of 1979, real output per man-hour in the nonfarm business sector fell by 1.36%, and while productivity improved after hitting a nadir in the second quarter of 1980, it still remained under the 1978 figure at the end of 1980.[53]

Compounding the effects of this decline in productivity on unit labor costs, COWPS issued guideline policies that tolerated labor costs above the 7% guideline and widened the differential between union and nonunion workers. COWPS initially took the economically correct position that payments made to maintain the real level of fringe benefits were to count against the 7% standard as they increased nominal labor costs. Intense pressure from unions—and firms facing employees disgruntled by this rule—caused COWPS to modify this rule within weeks. In a second fateful decision, COWPS had also declared that COLA clauses would be evaluated on the assumption of 6% inflation; when inflation exceeded this amount, the administration inadvertently sanctioned settlements costing firms more than the 7% labor-compensation guideline.[54] The Carter administration did attempt to enforce its guidelines through Executive Order 12092 of November 1, 1978, which limited government contracts to firms that certified their compliance with the guidelines. Yet even as the White House publicly accused firms of violating its standards and won redress on some wage actions, the procurement sanction remained a paper tiger. In the first year and a half of the program, not a single government contract was rejected for being out of compliance. In that time, COWPS had identified only nine companies out of compliance on prices. Just one, Mobil Oil, met the $5 million threshold for its contract to be refused, but the Department of Defense granted Mobil a special waiver to continue supplying the government.[55]

There were 3.2 million workers with new contracts monitored by COWPS in the first year of the guidelines program, and Fred Kahn, the wizard of airline deregulation whom Carter had then appointed as his inflation czar, estimated that at least half were in compliance—on paper, that was. When evaluating COLA clauses at the actual consumer price index rate, which thanks to the oil shock was close to 12% over the first program year and not the 6% assumption used by COWPS, contracts presented as being in compliance in fact cost something more like 10%–11%. The result was that workers with COLAs, who were more likely union workers, continued to outpace the gains of workers without escalator-clause protection.[56] During the first program year of the guidelines, comprising the four quarters through September 1979, the growth of employment costs did decelerate from 8% to 7.7%, but this aggregate figure masked two separate trends: the growth of nonunion employment costs decelerated from 8% to 7.3%, but union wage gains accelerated from 7.9% to 8.4%. The CEA argued that this differential would probably have been worse in the absence of the guidelines, but the 1980 *Economic Report* implicitly admitted in a table evaluating several major bargaining negotiations that these high-profile settlements violated the 7% wage guideline even before costing the COLA on more realistic assumptions of annual inflation. Overall, the differential between employment costs increases in the union and nonunion sector would expand from a half percentage point in calendar year 1979 to 2.9 percentage points in 1980, with union wages rising by 10.9%.[57]

Negotiations at Chrysler Motors in late 1979 served as a clear indication that as monetary stimulus accommodated supply shocks, labor and management no longer prioritized combating the wage-price spiral, even when the fate of the enterprise held in the balance. Always the weakest of the postwar Big Three automakers, Chrysler had been hit especially hard by recession, spiking oil prices, and import competition during the 1970s. Teetering on the edge of bankruptcy, Chrysler's new CEO, Lee Iacocca, had approached Congress for a three-year, $1.5 billion bailout in order to buy time for the company to turn itself around. Yet as the 124,000 members of the United Auto Workers at Chrysler faced the threat of permanent layoffs in an already weak Detroit job market, they negotiated a labor contract in 1979 that still followed the basis of the Treaty of Detroit. On the assumption of 9% inflation, the contract would cost the company $1.4 billion over the next three years, eating up nearly the entire bailout package. Chrysler workers had taken a small "sacrifice" of about $200 million, or 12%–15%, less than the contracts negotiated at Ford and GM awarded, but the fact that labor compensation would still rise by the same magnitude as the entire bailout suggested to the White House that cost-push inflation had become impervious to unemployment.[58]

The steel industry had also seemingly turned a blind eye to the wage-price spiral. In 1977, the industry had agreed to extend the ENA on the familiar logic that it would be better to pay a high cost now than to risk a strike, import penetration, and government intervention only to end up paying the same amount.[59] The industry's Coordinating Committee acknowledged internally that the government and popular press interpreted the ENA as evidence that the industry was willingly pricing itself out of the market. Nevertheless, the lack of protectionist answers to the import problem, the failure to secure labor-law reforms, and the continuing bite of regulatory costs left the committee with the sense that it had little choice other than to continue this costly approach to labor peace and take its chances with higher prices.[60] Despite concerns on the part of the Coordinating Committee that the industry's customers no longer tolerated having the costs of higher wages passed on as prices and that the AIF far exceeded the industry's own productivity, it chose to renew the ENA again in 1980 while lobbying for protectionist trade policies to mitigate the effects of its inevitable price increases.[61] It would be a pale comfort that COWPS evaluated this settlement as costing 24% over the next three years on the basis of its COLA assumption. In private, both the industry and the administration recognized that the true cost of this contract would be much higher, at anywhere from 30% to 38.5% over three years, depending on the true rate of inflation.[62]

The chief negotiator for the steel industry's Coordinating Committee, R. Heath Larry, was also the leader of the business delegation to the COWPS Pay Advisory Committee (PAC) established to give labor and management say in the formulation of the guideline program. Instead of backing restraint, Larry and the other business representatives to the PAC emphasized that the White House had to grant employers "greater freedom to pay what they have to pay" on both the wage and price side. Testifying before Congress against the extension of COWPS, Larry expressed the widely held concern that Carter had failed to follow through on the fiscal, monetary, and regulatory components of his anti-inflation program, resulting in "voluntary" guidelines that only yielded wage-price restraint through jawboning.[63] The AFL-CIO's representatives to the PAC shared Larry's hostility, chafing at the government's call for wage restraint in the face of accelerating inflation. While unwilling to reject a presidential incomes policy publicly during the middle of an election season, both business and labor made it clear that they did not believe the deceleration program should continue for a third year following the election.[64]

The combined opposition of industry and labor spelled the end of yet another federal effort to impose the public interest into the private scramble for income. COWPS had all but given up on enforcing its guidelines by May 1980, at which point Kahn noted that it had received reports from only thirty companies of labor compensation over the PAC's revised guideline of 8.5%. This was an unbelievably low number considering that three-quarters of manufacturing workers had broken the 7% standard the previous year and that the average hourly earnings index would grow by 9.2% over the second program year.[65] At least labor peace had been preserved, for compared to the spike in strikes that had occurred during the early Nixon years, the percentage of man-days lost to work stoppages in major bargaining units actually declined slightly from 1978 to 1980 (see table 3). As Kahn reflected, Carter could take some credit for convincing the American public that there was no easy solution to this economic malaise. He had also demonstrated to Democrats in particular how strong unions in concentrated industries were able to win higher wages at the expense of the less organized, citing the record in motor vehicles and steel, among others. Still, Kahn could not help but conclude, "we contributed to this salutary recognition as much by our failures as by our successes!"[66]

VICTORY ON INFLATION

If Jimmy Carter deserves any credit for combating inflation, it is only because he ultimately appointed the man who would succeed where the White House had failed. In July 1979, Carter nominated Paul Volcker, then president of the Federal Reserve Bank of New York, to be Federal Reserve chairman. Unlike his immediate predecessors at the Fed, Arthur Burns and G. William Miller, Volcker refused to allow the possibility of recession to sway his commitment to price stability. As Volcker later explained his thinking, stagflation had exposed the intellectual shortcomings of the Keynesian Consensus and its solution for economic stability: "The idea associated with Keynesians of a so-called Phillips Curve trade-off between unemployment and inflation did not seem to be working well. . . . Both unemployment and inflation were rising, and further delay in dealing with inflation would only ultimately make things worse."[67] Everyone knew inflation had something to do with having too much money, and so Volker decided that targeting the money supply directly would be the clearest way to signal the Fed's intention to achieve price stability. At the Federal Open Market Committee (FOMC) meeting of October 6, 1979, Volcker convinced the Fed to set its operating procedures unambiguously in terms of the money supply. A direct monetary target would make it more likely that the Fed would actually hit its target for the monetary growth rate after persistently missing its targets during Burns's and Miller's tenures. Moreover, interest rates would rise if demand for money exceeded the amount the Fed was willing to supply, immediately demonstrating to the market that the Fed was serious about inflation.[68]

The untested nature of monetary targeting initially provoked precisely the opposite effect. A year after implementing the new monetary operating procedures, interest rates and inflation had barely budged. In the meantime, piles of two-by-four wood planks were stacking up in Volcker's office, mailed by representatives of the construction industry in protest of high interest rates.[69] On the campaign trail, Carter attacked the Fed for raising interest rates and generating unemployment, although as a *Washington Post* reporter noted, Carter's criticism reflected poorly on the presidential candidate responsible for appointing five of the seven Fed governors, including

Volcker.[70] Keynesian economists likewise complained about the high costs of Volcker's disinflation program, suggesting once again that monetary policy was failing to combat the underling mechanism of cost-push inflation and that an incomes policy was necessary to shield society from self-interested malfeasance.[71] Carter even briefly activated the Credit Control Act of 1969 for the first and only time in that legislation's history, although as Volcker later recounted, the public interpreted credit controls as a sign of national emergency, precipitating a significant downturn in consumption in the summer of 1980.[72]

Yet rather than give in to these calls to return to the Keynesian status quo on inflation, Volcker and a majority of the FOMC recognized that they would have to work even harder to convince market participants that the Federal Reserve was committed to combating inflationary expectations.[73] Volcker soon obtained a critical partner in his effort to call the Keynesian cost-push bluff: Ronald Reagan, who pledged not to interfere with the Fed's macroeconomic course of action against inflation. As Volcker recalled, Reagan had no inclination to get involved with monetary policy, and his "visceral aversion to inflation" instinctively kept him from tampering with the Fed.[74] Reagan's initial CEA chairman, Murray Weidenbaum, echoed this perspective when commending the president for his economic approach in early 1982: "In the past, when the going got rough, the public was led to expect government actions that increased inflationary pressures and encouraged the Federal Reserve to follow easy money policies. Your program to date provides little basis for maintaining these expectations."[75]

Shielded by Reagan, the Federal Reserve maintained its process of monetary restraint. Unemployment rose from close to 7% on inauguration day to double digits by the end of 1982, setting yet another record for the worst postwar recession. But this persistence soon paid off. In October 1982, the consumer price index fell to a rate of 5% annualized growth, a rate not previously reached since November–December 1976, and by 1984, a decline in long-term interest rates suggested that monetary policy had achieved credibility as a constraint on inflation.[76] For every percentage-point reduction in the inflation rate, Volcker's disinflation had sacrificed only about three percentage points of GNP growth, less than a third of Okun's fearful estimate.[77]

Although economists have since disagreed about why Volcker's sacrifice ratio was so low, nearly all have agreed that his efforts demonstrated that at least one core tenet of midcentury models of inflation had been incorrect: the link between wages and price inflation. Phillips Curve models that incorporated wages explained the distribution of income, but they exhibited next to no explanatory power for price inflation compared to models that incorporated past and future trends in the price level.[78] By the end of the 1990s, Federal Reserve economists had concluded that anchoring expectations of future inflation and keeping aggregate demand under control would suffice to ensure that wages rose in line with productivity. Wage growth above the trend of labor productivity was now taken as an indication that excess demand had led to a tight labor market, not that cost-push inflation was spiraling out of control.[79]

REAGAN, MANAGEMENT, AND COMPETITION

As corporations had learned decades before in the New Look, translating recessionary conditions into wage moderation required more finesse than the Fed's impersonal economic modeling suggested. Pressure for givebacks and concessions had occurred in previous periods of macroeconomic distress, most notably during the New Look of the late 1950s and early 1960s. High unemployment subsequently had exerted less apparent impact on wages and prices during the 1970s, but the corporate community of that decade had despaired that it no longer possessed the tools of the New Look. Instead, the resort to the old strategy of paying for labor peace had perpetuated costly settlements during that decade, especially given the existential fear of the steel industry that even the possibility of a strike would lead to higher imports.[80]

The significant deceleration in the pace of wage gains by the end of the double-dip recessions thus came as a welcome change. In January 1983, the Bureau of Labor Statistics reported that major collective bargaining contracts of one thousand or more workers agreed on in the first nine months of 1982 had registered the lowest gains on record since the agency had started keeping track in 1967. New contracts averaged only 3.5% a year, compared to 6.4% a year over the life of the expiring contract. Bucking Keynesian expectations that market power would sustain a wage-price spiral even in the face of the threat of mass unemployment, settlements that covered five thousand or more workers actually came in at even less than average, at 2.5% per year over the life of the contract.[81]

These trends proved even more surprising at the time, considering that management had secured this moderation without the compulsion of incomes policies. On the campaign trail, Ronald Reagan had attacked Carter for taking the coward's way out in blaming inflation on everyone but himself, echoing the business community in identifying the root of inflation in Washington's own mismanagement. Reagan denounced wage-price policy for attacking symptoms, not causes, and for shackling the free market while giving the government a free pass to spend recklessly and generate massive uncertainties about its intentions. RWI and other forms of tax-based incomes policy also came in for condemnation as chaotic, complex, and unable to address the fiscal and monetary pressures at the source of inflation. Once inaugurated, Reagan wasted little time in doing away with the vestiges of COWPS that had already become unworkable on Carter's watch. Nine days after taking the oath of office, Reagan announced he was disbanding COWPS, labeling the council "a failure" and "totally ineffective in controlling inflation."[82]

Reagan had learned about the relationship between private and public responsibility from a surprising source: none other than General Electric vice president Lemuel Boulware. Back in the 1950s, when B-list actor Reagan hosted television's *GE Theater*, he toured the company's plants for informal appearances and autograph sessions as part of Boulware's Employee and Community Relations Program. Over time, Boulware introduced more structured economic content to these visits, utilizing Reagan as a mouthpiece for management. During the lead-up to the 1960 bargaining round that witnessed the success of the New Look and the collapse of the IUE's strike efforts, Reagan spoke to the rank and file on the dangers of inflation and the threat of big government to personal freedom. GE eventually pulled Reagan out of the plants, concerned that his direct outreach to employees was a step too far even for GE's cavalier attitudes toward bypassing elected union officials, but Reagan continued to stump in the localities where GE plants were located. This was quite an ironic role for an actor who, as president of the Screen Actors Guild, had just overseen a successful five-week strike of the major studios.[83]

As historians have previously noted, Boulware's lessons in economics and policy left an indelible impact on the Gipper.[84] Although Reagan holds the distinction of being the only president of the United States to have also been president of a union, upon reaching the Oval Office, he acted decisively to shift the power dynamics of industrial-labor relations back toward management. Of course, the long decline of unionization in the United States had begun well before Reagan entered office. As a percentage of the workforce, union membership had peaked in 1954, at 34.7% of nonagricultural workers, before falling to 28.8% a decade later and 23.2% in 1974. By the time that Reagan had left office, unionization had declined to 16% of the nonagricultural workforce, in line with its historical trend.[85] Nevertheless, that union numbers failed to replenish as the economy recovered and expanded under Reagan did suggest a fundamental shift away from the power dynamics that had prevailed over previous decades. Most famously, when faced with an illegal strike by the Professional Air Traffic Controllers Organization (PATCO) in August 1981, Reagan fired over eleven thousand strikers and banned them from future federal employment. Compared to Richard Nixon's capitulation to the crippling illegal strike of the postal workers a decade before, Reagan had sent a clear signal to the private sector that the White House would tolerate management taking a much harder line against organized labor.[86]

Less visible but even more important to the industrial-labor fabric than the PATCO strike were Reagan's appointees to the National Labor Relations Board, who agreed that the National Labor Relations Act had previously been interpreted to the detriment of employers. Under Reagan, the NLRB relaxed restrictions on employer communications, holding that discussions of the economic realities and drawbacks of unionization were free speech. Conversely, the NLRB tightened the screws on the rules of union conduct, broadening bans on the secondary boycott and ruling against the reinstatement of sympathy strikers. With plant closures an increasingly pertinent issue, the NLRB emphasized that management was not required to make labor an equal partner in the entrepreneurial process whenever employment was at stake.[87] Overall, from a little shy of half of NLRB rulings classed as pro-labor at the end of the Carter years, over 70% of the NLRB's rulings could be considered on the side of management after Reagan's first term.[88] Reagan's NLRB also notably supported management simply by doing nothing at all. The growing backlog of cases concerning unfair labor practices signaled to management that it could afford to bend or break the law without suffering serious repercussions.[89]

Management certainly looked to take advantage of this permissive climate toward its remaining unionized labor forces, with the steel industry leading the charge in returning to the hard-nosed bargaining strategies developed in the late 1950s under economic conditions that now appeared rather mild by comparison. In 1982, the capacity utilization for the steel industry fell to under 50%, its lowest level since 1938. In the 1950s, the industry's higher prices would have allowed it to break even at this level; but thanks to the rising costs of labor and other charges, the industry's break-even point had risen to close to 80% of capacity, and it fell $3 billion into the red, the first total loss since the Great Depression. Due to the ENA, however, the industry's unionized workforce had continued to thrive. In 1982, the average steelworker received hourly compensation of about $24/hour, 73% more than the average manufacturing worker. In 1964, in contrast, that premium had been only 24%. Indeed, management often found it cheaper to continue to operate obsolescent plants than to liquidate them because it would still have to pay the unfunded pension and health-care costs of union workers even after shuttering the plant.[90]

As the domestic steel industry struggled under its cost burden, the competitors about whom it had long fretted seized their moment. Although Japanese steelmakers paid higher costs for capital, ore, coal, and scrap, they had constructed their production facilities with up-to-date technology that vastly outpaced that of the United States. For instance, the basic oxygen furnace first developed in the 1950s was used in 75% of Japanese production in 1981, compared to only 60% in the United States, and continuous casting was used in 70.7% of Japanese production compared to only 21.1% in the United States. These technologies allowed the Japanese to undercut U.S. steelmaking costs drastically. According to one estimate, the Japanese beat the United States at $286/ton compared to $374/ton in 1980, with Japanese unit labor costs of $64/ton less than half of the U.S. figure of $135/ton.[91]

Given this cost structure, as well as the Japanese reputation for high-quality steel, the costly labor peace of the ENA failed in its objective to prevent an expansion in import penetration. In 1980, 16.2% of domestic steel consumption was imported, only slightly above the 13.8% of a decade before, thanks to trade barriers and voluntary quotas. The appreciation of the dollar under the influence of high interest rates and Reaganomics quickly drove this share even higher, reaching over a quarter of the domestic market in 1984.[92] The steel industry and the United Steelworkers jointly pressed the government to impose trade barriers to block this surge in imports. Reagan was generally supportive of free trade, but he did agree to extend voluntary arrangements with steel-exporting nations in order to appease this powerful midwestern interest group.[93]

Even had these restrictions proven as effective as intended, they could not have shielded the integrated steelmakers from new domestic competitors: nonintegrated facilities known as minimills that used cutting-edge technologies such as electric furnaces to match foreigners' costs. Minimills initially entered the steel market to take advantage of the spread between their lower costs and the high prices set by the domestic oligopoly, but they soon undercut the price umbrella that U.S. Steel had established in order to obtain market share. Located primarily in the South, minimills also avoided unionization and implemented a model of team-oriented labor relations adapted from the Japanese. In the pioneering approach of Nucor Steel, labor compensation was tied to the performance of bonus groups composed of approximately thirty employees apiece. Incentive plans encouraged employees to cooperate with management in solving problems that stood in the way of higher productivity. By instituting an employee stock-ownership plan, Nucor also ensured that employees would hold an interest in the financial viability of their employer.[94]

Deep in the red financially and with price competition growing fiercer, the steel industry's Coordinating Committee finally recognized that its decade-long experiment with securing labor peace through the ENA was no longer worth its costs. The new lead negotiator for the industry's Coordinating Committee, J. Bruce Johnston of U.S. Steel, privately admitted in discussions with his counterpart at Republic Steel that the ENA was no longer sustainable because competition had deprived the industry of its ability to pass on higher labor costs to consumers: "History will confirm (I hope not posthumously), that the greed was not corporate. If public opinion does not get out of the mind set of the 1880–1920 period and come to understand that in basic industries what may have once been short-lived oligopolies have now been replaced by long-lived wage monopolies, those industries will disappear from the marketplace."[95] The Coordinating Committee especially regretted its abandonment of its traditional emphasis on steel's subaverage rate of productivity growth when, as part of the ENA, it had agreed to provide an AIF of 3% tooled to the national long-run average of productivity change.[96] Over the subsequent decade, the industry's own output per man-hour had grown at a pace half that of the national rate, resulting in even-higher unit labor costs that the industry was unable to pass on to its customers. Steel's TFP, moreover, had barely increased at all.[97]

J. Bruce Johnston, like his first-initialed predecessors R. Conrad Cooper and R. Heath Larry, deemed the rebalancing of capital and labor to be the key to the industry's quest to modernize its facilities without raising prices. Writing to USWA president Lloyd McBride, Johnston admitted that labor costs were not the only source of the industry's problems, placing much blame on government policies that had imposed regulatory costs, dismantled trade barriers, and discouraged capital investment. Johnston notably considered incomes policies to have had the same effect as market competition in preventing the industry from achieving the financial targets necessary for its long-run survival: "In strong markets, [incomes policies] have included outright price controls, jawboning, so-called Voluntary Limitations, and Restraints. In soft markets, malign neglect of trade law enforcement and toleration of dumped and subsidized steel restrains price levels otherwise available even in those soft markets." Still, Johnston emphasized that average employment costs in the steel industry, $22.69/hour in February 1982, were $11.08/hour over the average for all manufacturing and eating into the capital resources the industry needed to keep pace with its competitors. With plants closing and plans for additional layoffs in place, Johnston invited the USWA's cooperation in solving the problem of "a burden which the marketplace will no longer support."[98]

Johnston's drive for concessions echoed the hard-nosed approach taken by R. Conrad Cooper in 1959. Later in the bargaining process, Johnston even took it as a point of pride that "the crazies" on the left labeled him an obstacle to a collective bargaining, as the last negotiator to have faced such a vehement opposition was none other than Cooper himself.[99] Yet where Cooper's Plan A in 1959 had been to freeze nominal compensation, Johnston's Coordinating Committee recognized that the new competitive climate required a more severe objective: "To obtain a reduction in employment costs equal to the amount of reduction obtained by the auto industry (expressed as a percentage of employment costs) or a reduction of $5.00 per hour worked in employment costs, whichever is greater." The Coordinating Committee's confidential strategy called for exploring every possible place in which costs could be cut, especially in terms of benefits, COLA, and overtime pay. The industry also considered tying the payment of the COLA and other benefits to certain productivity milestones in order to ensure that the union would have a financial interest to cooperate in raising productivity.[100]

Unlike in 1959, when David McDonald had rejected Cooper's approach and demanded that the industry continue sharing the rents of oligopoly pricing with labor, McBride recognized that the zero-sum struggle over the fruits of productivity could not continue. In July 1982, McBride proposed terms to the Coordinating Committee that made Cooper's 1959 Plan A of a one-year wage freeze look irresponsibly costly in comparison: a three-year wage freeze and eighteen-month deferment of the COLA, estimated to save the industry $2 billion over the life of the contract. The industry countered with a plan totaling $6 billion in givebacks in return for a stock-ownership plan and additional unemployment benefits. After several false starts, the two sides agreed on wage cuts of $1.31/hour in March 1983, of which $1.25/hour would be restored over the three years of the contract in lieu of a net wage change. The contract also included an abeyance of the COLA for five quarters, the elimination of the Savings and Vacation Plan instituted in the early 1960s, and reductions to overtime and paid holidays. Overall, the industry would obtain savings of $2.15/hour. Although management did not provide the union with a total guarantee against shutting down facilities, it accepted that all savings from the wage concessions would be applied to modernizing steelmaking plant, and it also agreed to provide higher unemployment benefits.[101]

THE END OF WAGE-PRICE POLICY

Compared to the resounding support that Cooper had received from the Coordinating Committee after the partial victory of 1959, Johnston's New Look–style bargaining came in for much criticism despite having unquestionably achieved its cost-reduction objectives. Notwithstanding the permissive attitude of the Reagan years, executives at other Coordinating Committee firms questioned whether U.S. Steel's "bad boy" approach to labor relations was still the correct one. In light of the productive Japanese and minimill strategies, Johnston's penchant for picking fights appeared anachronistic. More importantly, from a structural point of view, the members of the Coordinating Committee questioned whether industry-wide bargaining itself made sense anymore. Imports and minimills had fractured the homogeneity of the integrated steel industry, and the USWA was willing to authorize settlements tailored to the condition of individual companies.

Rather than follow U.S. Steel's price leadership and then allow that company to use the Coordinating Committee to standardize the costs of all other integrated producers, these other firms recognized that their own self-interest now lay in competing with their new challengers as well as with each other.[102]

Johnston's refusal to allow any firm other than Bethlehem to have a seat at the negotiating table was thus quickly met by the remaining members of the Coordinating Committee choosing to strike out on their own in search of a better bargain with the USWA. In 1984, National Steel withdrew from the Coordinating Committee in order to prove its commitment to working out a more cooperative approach to the USWA. That same year, the Department of Justice permitted LTV Steel to acquire the assets of the failed Republic Steel so as to create a stronger, rationalized single company. Republic's management described one advantage of this merger as the ability for an enlarged LTV to inject multilateralism into the Coordinating Committee, but when U.S. Steel refused to relinquish its authority, LTV withdrew. After nearly three decades, the Coordinating Committee formally disbanded in May 1985.[103]

The 1986 negotiation round in the steel industry was the first in over three decades to feature individual companies bargaining with the USWA. Most of the industry took advantage of the collapse of the Coordinating Committee to adopt a more cooperative approach, trading wage concessions for profit sharing, stock-purchase plans, and limitations on layoffs and subcontracting. Johnston alone continued to emulate the hard-nosed tactics of Cooper and Boulware by demanding larger concessions without limits on contracting out the workforce. By that point, U.S. Steel was just one division of USX, a conglomerate for which only a quarter of revenues derived from steel. USX chose to weather a strike for 184 days—over two months longer than the 1959 steel strike—using the threat of permanent plant closures as leverage to obtain its desired concessions. For all of this antagonism, Johnston ultimately secured terms that essentially matched the givebacks obtained by Bethlehem Steel with much less conflict. In return for a profit-sharing plan and restrictions on subcontracting, USX received wage concessions and would be allowed to eliminate 1,346 jobs through attrition, although it would have to recall an equal number of workers off layoffs.[104]

No longer bound by the commonly identifiable interests of oligopoly or the group bargaining of the Coordinating Committee, the vertically integrated steel industry learned that competition could no longer mean matching the price of a rival and going no further. As minimills in particular continued to seek out additional market share by plowing productivity gains back into price reductions, the former giants of the industry had no choice but to follow. USX's U.S. Steel division, created at the dawn of the twentieth century to be the price leader of an oligopoly in which it controlled two-thirds of the nation's steelmaking capacity, was now forced to reinvent itself as one player amid a competitive market. From 1982 to 2000, before the great influx of Chinese steel in the early 2000s, the real price of steel dropped by half, even as output rose by 30%, and markups had also been slashed to half of their 1960s level.[105]

In order to keep up with these front-runners, of course, integrated steelmakers had to take drastic measures, and few survived this shakeout in independent form. As production and investment concentrated in only the most viable facilities, employment plummeted. After trickling down slowly from the oil shock, from slightly over 600,000 workers in 1973 to 506,000 in 1980, steel employment fell into a nosedive over the 1980s. Employment declined by half from 1980 to 1985, and it would near 100,000 by the mid-1990s.[106] Compensation costs grew as profit sharing allowed employees to benefit from the industry's recovery, and legacy benefit costs increased with the ranks of retirees; but thanks to these radical rationalizations, unit labor costs fell slightly in the mid-1980s and remained approximately stable into the early 1990s. For the steel industry as a whole, output per man-hour had risen by 2.9% a year on average from 1947 to 1995, but that pace accelerated to 5.6% from 1990 to 1995 among the industry's survivors as output increased and man-hours fell. Total-factor productivity growth averaged 1.8% a year from 1958 to 1994, pulled up by stunning growth of 3.6% a year from 1990 to 1994.[107]

Alongside steel, the forces of competition also rendered anachronistic the most explicit of any wage-price policy ever devised by corporate management: the auto industry's wage formula. Facing high energy prices, double-dip recessions, and a climb in imported vehicles to over a quarter of the domestic market, the U.S. auto industry understood that it needed a cheaper and more productive approach to labor peace than the sharing of national productivity gains that Engine Charlie Wilson had proposed in 1948. The deleterious labor conduct that had precipitated the disastrous GM strike of

1970 had only deteriorated over the course of the 1970s, pushing up labor costs and slowing productivity growth at precisely the same time that Japanese automakers thrived under their own system of labor relations.[108] By the early 1980s, autoworkers in Japan were estimated to be at least 20% more productive than their American counterparts, and many contemporaries attributed a large part of this success to the Japanese ability to avoid adversarial labor relations. Japanese autoworkers were treated as part of the overall workplace family, paid according to their and the firm's performance and receiving a guarantee of lifetime employment. Workers organized into teams whose members could be reassigned to different tasks as needed, and management delegated important responsibilities to shop-floor employees, including the authority to stop the assembly line when they encountered a problem, on the grounds that it would be cheaper to fix problems as they arose than to allow defects to accumulate.[109]

The domestic auto industry's traditional wage-price policy had already suffered a serious blow from the government's intervention in the Chrysler bailout. Chrysler's vice president of industrial relations Thomas Miner suggested that the UAW had been initially unwilling to make concessions in the 1979 bargaining round due to its belief that the government would inevitably force it to renegotiate after the passage of the bailout legislation. The Chrysler Loan Guarantee Act, passed on December 21, 1979, indeed required Chrysler to prove its long-run "viability," including by obtaining another $259 million in union concessions. The UAW agreed to postpone its negotiated agreements in return for an employee stock-ownership plan, but it fully expected the compensation of Chrysler workers to catch up with the rest of the industry when the contract expired in 1982. Before that could happen, Chrysler's finances continued to deteriorate, forcing the company to tap the loan fund again in January 1981. The government mandated another round of givebacks from the UAW, which finally agreed to eliminate the COLA and future AIF increases. Together with other concessions, these givebacks totaled savings of $622 million. In return, Chrysler pledged to create a profit-sharing plan, provide the union with financial data demonstrating the continued need for restraint, and avoid closing certain plants. Amazingly, only 56% of employees voted for a proposal that was necessary to maintain the viability of Chrysler as an independent corporate entity; Miner suggested most of the remainder were employed at plants that probably would have been bought by another company had Chrysler gone bankrupt.[110]

By breaking the AIF's link between national productivity and wages, Chrysler had not only abandoned four decades of bargaining precedent. Just as individualized bargaining was then on its way to the steel industry, so too had Chrysler placed the needs of the individual firm above those of the industry as a whole. As a result of this change in focus, by 1982 Chrysler's wages were 20%–25% less than those of GM and Ford, both of which now eagerly eyed a way to win givebacks of their own in the next round of bargaining.[111] Desperate to obtain lower costs, General Motors initially agreed in principle to the UAW's proposal that any giveback in labor compensation would be passed entirely to the consumer in the form of lower prices. This deal quickly fell apart once the UAW realized that, just as GM had refused to open its books to Walter Reuther in 1945, so too would the union possess no mechanism to enforce this promise.[112]

In a reversal of 1948, it would be Ford Motors that would develop a new approach to labor peace based not on sharing the gains of national productivity but on binding the interests of the employees to those of their employer. Ford's head of labor relations, Peter Pestillo, had cut his teeth in labor relations at General Electric in the 1960s, but despite the permissive thrust of the Reagan Revolution, this veteran of midcentury labor relations now proclaimed an about-face from the antagonistic methods that his previous employer had perfected. Pestillo described the 1982 collective bargaining negotiations between Ford and the UAW as marking an important shift from "guerilla warfare" tactics to a cooperative Japanese model "driven by their personnel system and not their legal system." Pestillo followed through on this vision by giving line workers more say in operations, removing managers who created labor frictions, and treating the number of grievances not as a sign of toughness but as a measure of inefficiency that had to be reduced.[113]

In return for adopting this new approach to labor relations, Ford Motors, which had only reluctantly accepted GM's wage formula for labor peace three decades before, finally won the right to set compensation based on its own economic conditions. In 1982, the UAW agreed to discard the wage formula: a total wage freeze for thirty months, a nine-month deferral of the COLA, and, most importantly, abandonment of the AIF. A consistent and annual AIF would not be restored until the 1999 collective bargaining round. In the meanwhile, the UAW shifted its focus to stemming layoffs, preventing job closures, and replacing lost wages with profit sharing. Ford's management, for its part, agreed to promote greater cooperation with the UAW, including a temporary moratorium on plant closings, better severance pay, and a profit-sharing plan.[114] Following the Ford deal, GM and the UAW agreed to a similar contract that eliminated the AIF, postponed the COLA, and, along with other savings, reduced labor costs by 10%, or $2/hour. In the place of GM's previously proposed price reductions, the company agreed to establish a profit-sharing program, delay plant closings for two years, and increase funding for laid-off workers. Even then, the contract won approval by an even narrower majority than had approved the Chrysler deal, with only 52% of union members in favor.[115]

The auto industry had followed steel in abandoning a wage-price policy based on national averages. The elimination of the AIF's anchor of national productivity signaled that wages, prices, and productivity in the auto industry would henceforth be benchmarked to the competitive lead of Toyota and other Japanese carmakers, not the oligopoly leadership of GM. Automakers had rarely been concerned in the past that their productivity growth would fall short of the national trend embodied in the AIF, but having long paid compensation in advance of this limit, absorption of these costs could not provide a sound basis to compete with Toyota and other productive rivals. The abandonment of the COLA similarly acknowledged that automakers could no longer count on price adjustments whenever nominal labor costs rose.[116]

Steel and autos were far from the only industries to adopt such an individualized perspective in the face of recession and competition. In 1985, the Conference Board, the venerable business research organization then entering its seventh decade as the leading monitor of trends in the corporate world, issued a report on what it deemed "the new look in wage policy and employee relations." Despite the apparently unintentional similarity in terminology, this report described an industrial economy radically different from that discussed in Herbert Northrup's 1961 essay. Rather than attempting to control conflict in order to manipulate the distribution of income, management and labor now cooperated to maintain the viability of their shared enterprise. The Conference Board noted that unionized firms were transitioning away from the traditional pattern-following practices of past decades in favor of basing wages on the productivity, labor costs, and profits of the individual company. Companies were experimenting with innovative practices to share information with shop-floor workers, hoping to solve problems as they arose. By tying compensation to corporate profits rather than productivity and inflation on a nationwide scale, moreover, companies provided their employees with skin in the game that would encourage them to improve their performance.[117]

Even in sectors that did not face the same degree of stress as steel and autos, contemporaries noted that pattern bargaining was seemingly on the decline. The advent of individualized wage deals weakened the rationale for traditional wage-price policies as a means to prevent compensation in highly productive industries from pulling up wages in sectors unable to afford it without higher prices. Instead, labor agreed to decouple real compensation from the standard metrics of the previous decades and focus on the health of the individual firm. Pattern bargaining was not entirely eliminated within all industries, but where it persisted, it now appeared much less concerned with basing wages on the productivity of the front-runner than it was in stabilizing total labor costs between plants and product lines.[118] While COLA clauses remained fairly common in the unionized sector, caps, freezes, and other limitations further weakened the relationship between the national price level and firm-level nominal labor costs. In the span of a few years, the level of protection provided by COLAs fell from 60%–70% of wages to about 50%. Just as management had emphasized in the late 1950s, labor had come to appreciate that one man's purchasing power was another man's costs.[119]

CONCLUSION

In the decade following the collapse of Nixon's controls, wage-price policy died several deaths. First had come the realization of management that inflation was, in fact, not the result of excessive compensation but only its cause. Given the spike in the price of food and oil and Nixon's failure to secure labor-law reforms, voluntary wage restraint seemed impossible during the stagflation of the 1970s, but corporate America had by now recognized that incomes policies were no solution to the long-running challenges of capital investment and international competitiveness. Instead, management called on the government to recognize that public policy, not private market power, forced society to suffer from inflation. If only the government would put its own fiscal and monetary house in order and curb regulatory costs, greater productivity would allow management to put a stop to the wage-price spiral without having to sacrifice the pursuit of labor peace. Unable to wait for the government to undertake these actions, however, management decided that the best way to achieve its financial objectives would be to raise prices now and take its chances with soft markets and import competition.

While the private sector had turned its attention to the macroeconomic and regulatory climate, COWPS remained focused on labor costs and wage-price policy. The somewhat skeptical Rees had attempted to use his post to convince industries such as steel that they could afford a more restrained approach to pricing, but industry largely rejected any conclusions of academics and bureaucrats that cast doubt on the drive for higher prices and profits. Under Carter, COWPS attempted a more activist approach to curbing the wage-price spiral. Yet as the private sector continued to view restraint as far from being in its best interests, the quasi-mandatory guidelines were honored in the breach more than in practice.

The failures of COWPS meant that incomes policy was dead in all but name by the time that Ronald Reagan officially brought an end to two decades of guideposts, guidelines, and controls. In their place, Reagan emphasized that the private sector would show restraint once Washington had itself acted responsibility, and he did so with the credibility and conviction that Richard Nixon's backboning had lacked. Paul Volcker did not embark on his path of monetary stringency because of the arguments of NAM or the Business Roundtable, but implicitly, he provided what they had asked for since the Johnson administration: putting the government's own house in order before demanding restraint on the part of the private sector. Several years of intense monetary pain demonstrated beyond a doubt that the wage-price spiral had persisted due to the irresponsibility of federal, not private, policymakers.

In the industries and unions long at the center of discussions of cost-push inflation, the wage restraint that developed against this recessionary backdrop differed in a major respect from that of the New Look of the late 1950s. The Boulwarist tactics that Reagan restored to management had been intended to contain cost trends and boost capital accumulation before it was too late for the industries in question. By the time Reagan came into office, that day of reckoning was already at hand. The giants of the unionized manufacturing sector discovered that the tactics devised to stabilize unit labor costs in the 1940s and 1950s were no longer sufficient to meet the challenges of the 1980s and beyond. Foreign competition had weakened the market power of business and labor to the extent that the New Deal's political economy of corporate oligopoly and union monopoly was no longer tenable.

As that economic structure collapsed, a wage-price policy designed to mirror the idealized distribution of income could no longer meet the challenges of a competitive climate. For decades, orthodox wage-price policy had overlooked the role of the firm in favor of a focus on the aggregate productivity of the nation as a whole and the price relief permitted to an entire industry. Yet, by the 1980s, as new competitors captured market share through lower costs and prices, the managements of individual firms were forced to recognize that their best interests no longer lay in parallel conduct and industry-wide patterns. Rather than standardize costs as an industry and then rely on the safety valve of prices to shield profits, members of steel and other erstwhile oligopolies now had to learn to act on their own. Gone were the AIF, paeans to national productivity growth on the average, and hand-wringing about the spread of inflationary patterns. Half a century after the National Labor Relations Act had declared that market power rested at the root of the Depression, the search for a national wage-price policy modeled on a textbook economy had given way to an individualized emphasis on competition.

Conclusion

IN THE TECHNICAL SENSE, a corporate manager is nothing more than the employee of the corporation's owners, and hence the manager's economic and legal responsibilities are to act in the best interests of his or her employers, the corporation's shareholders.[1] But in order to fulfill that purpose, the manager has no choice but to interact with the corporation's various stakeholders: not just its investors but also the consumers, workers, suppliers, regulators, and dozens of other groups that contribute to the enterprise and bear the consequences of management's decisions. In a perfectly competitive economy, these transactions would proceed according to the dictates of market forces, but in a modern economy dominated by concentrations of economic power operating under the watchful eye of the government, both management and its stakeholders can choose how they will approach these interactions.

Wage-price policy was never simply about setting targets for wage growth or moderating pricing. Instead, wage-price policy was at its core a means to force those who wielded power in this modern economy to recognize the repercussions of their actions on other stakeholders. Wage-price policy demanded that those who have power take for themselves no more than their fair share of the fruits of progress that the competitive market would otherwise have granted them. Labor compensation should rise at the same pace as labor productivity grew over the long run for the nation as a whole. Industries with above-average productivity could afford to pass on the savings in unit labor costs to consumers in the form of lower prices, while those with below-average productivity could raise prices to preserve returns on capital. On average, prices would remain stable, and investors would receive steady returns.

Yet this emphasis on rewarding stakeholders suffered from a fatal flaw. Even as wage-price policy established a guide for the exercise of managerial power, it did nothing to remove management's fundamental discretion over how prices would be set. In an era in which industrial giants openly admitted that they calculated prices to meet a targeted return on investment, and in which smaller players within an industry could simply follow the leader, management was not about to cede this control of its pricing power to any of its stakeholders. Had the management of a competitor firm possessed a different set of priorities—say, lower prices for consumers and higher market share for the firm—the story would have been very different, as the integrated steel industry ultimately learned in the 1980s. But for the members of an oligopoly industry, price leadership was more than a profitable means to bring order to an industry's prices and margins. Unlike cartelization and express collusion, conscious parallelism was and still is today considered a perfectly legal strategy precisely because it is the rational course of conduct in a situation in which each participant knows how the others will respond to one's own actions.

When price administration had received condemnation for causing the Great Depression by privileging profits over purchasing power, New Deal policymakers had sought to counteract this managerial unilateralism by empowering organized labor to bargain for a share of income at the collective bargaining table. Yet this countervailing power did nothing to eliminate management's ability to divert a larger share of income to profits by raising prices. Instead, the ability to administer wages merely permitted one politically influential group to share in oligopoly profits. Labor's demands frequently exceeded the limitations of productivity that all agreed were noninflationary, especially as multiyear bargaining took hold and fringe benefits became common, and as Lemuel Boulware warned his compatriots, it was ultimately management that chose whether or not to meet these demands. Yet rather than choosing to fight for restraint, for most of the postwar Golden Age, management was willing to pay a premium for labor peace because it knew that it could relieve any excess pressure on profits and returns on capital by releasing the safety valve of pricing. With strong domestic markets, limited competition from foreigners, and federal policymakers less tolerant of unemployment than they were of inflation, the oligopolies at the core of the industrial economy knew that they had little to fear from the consequences of the wage-price spiral. Indeed, as the government imposed additional regulations in the course of the 1960s and 1970s, higher prices became a means through which management could shift the costs of these lofty objectives back onto society without straining profits more than they already were.

Even the General Motors wage formula, which enshrined the central relationship of wage-price policy as a rule for managerial practice, could not establish labor peace without departing from the noninflationary balance between stakeholders that Engine Charlie Wilson had hoped to achieve. On paper, the automatic improvement factor ensured that labor's wages rose at roughly the same rate as labor productivity did for the nation as a whole, and the cost-of-living adjustment meant that these would be real, not nominal, gains. But as quickly became apparent, the GM wage formula had merely set a floor to labor's demands in each bargaining round. As management chose to prioritize labor peace by permitting fringe benefits to escalate over the noninflationary limit of the AIF, Engine Charlie's wage-price policy purchased harmony by slicing the United Auto Workers a larger share of the corporate pie. To be fair, quality-adjusted auto prices remained fairly stable over the course of the 1950s and 1960s, suggesting that the auto industry's productivity growth was indeed fast enough for its management to afford these payments. But in an era of pattern bargaining, the choices of the United States' largest and most influential firm carried immense weight with how others would slice their pies as well. For steel and other industries that were less able to absorb these costs than the auto industry was, the safety valve of higher prices continued to beckon.

How could society ensure that the powerful few would not abuse their discretion and shift the repercussions of their actions to other stakeholders? At the most extreme, direct controls have promised to eliminate the exercise of discretion entirely by forcing management and labor to abide by the government's own terms. Yet historically, controls have not removed discretion as much as they have transposed it to other modes of adjustment: changed product patterns, delayed investment, and increased industrial-labor frictions. As the Office of Price Administration learned during and after World War II, when wage controls prioritized peace and rising costs pushed up against fixed prices, firms curtailed output and shifted production to goods with higher margins so long as demand existed. True, during the Korean War, the Office of Price Stabilization managed to avoid the large-scale dislocation that the Office of Price Administration had generated in apparel and other industries, but that was because fiscal and monetary policy kept overall demand in check, rendering price controls largely a non-issue. Even then, once the Supreme Court had ruled that the president could not simply seize control of the steel industry, the industry's management proved fully capable of exercising its discretion to condition acceptance of government-brokered bargaining and an end to the strike on price relief.

Less statist than direct controls but possessing more substance than the generalized exhortations for restraint issued by Truman and Eisenhower were the Kennedy-Johnson guideposts and Carter guidelines. In theory, guideposts and guidelines promised to restrain labor's demands to what could be afforded out of productivity growth on average, in turn removing any pretext for firms to expand margins and deviate from price stability on the average. By shifting the Phillips Curve, the decline of the wage-price spiral would allow the government to expand the economy to full employment with less inflation than the orthodox Keynesian models of cost-push inflation predicted. These incomes policies still permitted firms and unions to strike their own bargains over the distribution of income as long as the consequences did not adversely impact other stakeholders, but if concentrations of power exercised their authority in ways inconsistent with this overall model, then the extrajudicial sanctions of jawboning would force them to do so for the sake of society.

In practice, the guideposts and guidelines failed to deliver on their promised outcomes because they attempted to shut off the safety valve of prices without addressing the underlying pressures that had precipitated its use. As the cost of living rose, there was no reason for labor to show restraint on wages, and the politicians who had instituted these incomes policies were repeatedly unwilling to force such a key constituency to absorb the rising cost of living into a fixed slice of income. Instead, the White House directed its sanctions against management and investors, expecting profits to bear the costs of price stability for the good of society. Yet with structural reforms such as revamped antitrust law or reduced trade barriers off the table, the ad hoc remedies of jawboning and the procurement sanctions of the guidelines proved little threat. If management's own private calculations recommended the continued exercise of the pricing safety valve, guideposts and guidelines could not convince it to behave otherwise for long. Even after the steel industry repeatedly had its hand slapped for attempting to grab too large a slice of the pie, tacit approval for its subsequent price movements suggested that the White House had also learned its lesson about how much restraint it could reasonably expect.

Ultimately, management could be persuaded to relinquish its pricing power only when it recognized that a strategy of restraint would be in its own best interests. During the New Look of the late 1950s, the managers who had ridden the wage-price merry-go-round of the Age of Escalation finally understood that they would need to find an alternative strategy if they were to remain competitive in increasingly global markets. Management had always acknowledged that higher prices promised benefits today at the risk of competition tomorrow, but in the face of what were at the time recessions of unprecedented severity, raising prices now would prove needlessly counterproductive. Instead, from the work of John Kendrick, management had learned that the conventional wage-price policy based on long-run economic growth ignored shifts in capital investment over the short run. Limiting the expansion of labor costs to the growth rate of productivity, preferably its total-factor variety, would still permit labor to obtain a real share of the growing pie over the long run without starving investors of their returns or forcing consumers to bear the costs of industrial-labor peace.

Still, the New Look could not provide a permanent and durable solution to the challenge of managerial discretion because it arose against a backdrop of pattern bargaining and oligopoly industry. The managers who formed ELRIC accepted the productivity gospel of Lemuel Boulware because they feared that costly settlements in autos and other industries would spread to those that were less able to pay these costs out of present prices, and that pressure continued to exist even after the successes of the New Look. Likewise, while the steel industry's Coordinating Committee emerged as a means to forestall union whipsawing through a unified front, this institution also provided a more formal means for the oligopoly to standardize costs across firms at a time when imports had begun to give management second thoughts about moving in lockstep. Had it not been for the trade barriers such as Lyndon Johnson subsequently approved for steel late in his second term, price shading and secret discounts may have irreparably fractured that industry's consciously parallel behavior much sooner than it ultimately did.

The New Look also failed to provide a permanent solution to the wage-price spiral because the industrial-labor techniques on which it relied had developed in response to a very specific set of economic and legal circumstances. By the late 1960s, management discovered that it could no longer count on the Boulwarist methods of General Electric or the hard-nosed bargaining of steel's Coordinating Committee to force moderation in labor's demands. Instead, as the labor-law pendulum swung back toward unions over the course of the 1960s and increased exposure to foreign competition perversely weakened managerial resistance to a work stoppage, the business community grew so flummoxed that it believed that only direct controls could force labor to recognize the valid claims of capital on corporate income. While these ideas were somewhat influential at Nixon's Pay Board during Phase II, management's preferences were by and large ignored by the Price Commission, which insisted that the gains of productivity must also be shared with consumers. As a result, Nixon's controls suffered the same fate as every other form of incomes policy. Once supply shocks and excessive economic stimulus pressed management to return to its traditional approach toward pricing, support for controls among the business community quickly evaporated for good.

Only in the 1980s was management forced to acknowledge that it no longer possessed the discretion to select any alternative but restraint. Industry could not hide behind tariffs and quotas, as rivals both foreign and domestic established U.S. factories and set about capturing market share through higher productivity and lower margins and prices. At the same time, Ronald Reagan's elimination of incomes policies and Paul Volcker's monetary-induced recessions sent a credible signal to the private sector that those who continued to raise wages and prices even higher would be forced to suffer the consequences. In these conditions, management could no longer base wages or prices on national averages and pattern bargaining across industries. Instead, in a market characterized by competition, the management of individual firms realized that it was every man for himself, and those who failed to secure labor's understandings of the constraints that now bound the individual enterprise would not have an enterprise to manage for long.

This story of competition's triumph holds true for the great industries of the Golden Age United States. After all, the last time anyone expressed concern about steel prices, it was because the price was too low to sustain employment, not too high. But outside of these former oligopolies, the same challenges of corporate market power that beset the midcentury economy continue to exist, regardless of whether management expresses a preference for exercising its discretion to reward shareholders, other stakeholders, or itself. Since the 1970s, corporate concentration has actually intensified due to a relaxation of the hypervigilance on the part of antitrust authorities toward new mergers, but courts have continued to hold that the consciously parallel behavior of modern oligopolies does not by itself violate antitrust law. Financial measures such as the average markup over cost and return on investment have also risen, although most of these gains have been captured by firms in the top 10% of the distribution. And, as has often been remarked, labor's share of income has gradually declined over the past half century.[2]

Where concentration and the exercise of power persist, the competitive transformation in steel, autos, and other former oligopoly industries demonstrates a more viable solution for disciplining corporate power than the quixotic effort to force management to subjugate its own interests to those of society. Wage-price policy ultimately failed to balance the needs of all of the corporation's stakeholders because it confused the consequences of economic power with the underlying structural causes of this discretion. Antitrust law has accepted that requiring oligopolies to desist from consciously parallel behavior would be to impose irrationality on the market, and the Federal Reserve has learned that it bears the ultimate responsibility for permitting the wage-price spiral to continue. Likewise, the exercise of managerial discretion toward corporate stakeholders must also be recognized as a response to market conditions and structures, not a perversion of the market in itself. To resurrect and enforce wage-price policy today would be to repeat the historical mistake of permitting policymakers and society to blame industry for responding to forces outside of managerial control: excessive fiscal and monetary expansion; regulations and trade barriers that limit competition and contribute to sluggish productivity; tolerance of heightened corporate concentration; and a legal framework that permits select groups of organized stakeholders to assert excessive claims not simply on profits but on the remaining share of pie enjoyed by all other

Americans. As long as market structures sustain managerial discretion, society can only expect management to act in the best interests of all of its stakeholders once it is in its own private self-interest to do so, for while management may function as a replacement for the impersonal rules of the marketplace, in the end, it is only human.

TABLES

Table 1

The Prevalence of Cost-of-Living Adjustment (COLA) Clauses, 1947–1975

YEAR	ALL WORKERS UNDER MAJOR CONTRACTS[a] (MILLIONS)	NUMBER COVERED ON JANUARY 1 (MILLIONS)	% COVERED BY ESCALATION	% INCREASE IN CPI[b]
1947	*	*	*	8.9
1948	*	0.25	*	2.7
1949	*	*	*	–1.8
1950	*	0.8[c]	*	5.8
1951	*	3.0[c]	*	5.9
1952	*	3.5	*	0.9
1953	*	*	*	0.6
1954	7.5[d]	*	*	–0.5
1955	7.5[d]	1.7	23	0.4
1956	7.8[d]	*	*	2.9
1957	7.8[d]	3.5	45	3.0
1958	8.0	4.0	50	1.5
1959	8.0	4.0	50	1.5
1960	8.1	4.0	49	1.5
1961	8.1	2.7[e]	33[e]	0.7
1962	8.0	2.5	31	1.2

Table 1 *continued*

YEAR	ALL WORKERS UNDER MAJOR CONTRACTS[a] (MILLIONS)	NUMBER COVERED ON JANUARY 1 (MILLIONS)	% COVERED BY ESCALATION	% INCREASE IN CPI[b]
1963	7.8	1.9	24	1.6
1964	7.8	2.0	26	1.2
1965	7.9	2.0	25	1.9
1966	10.0	2.0	20	3.4
1967	10.6	2.2	21	3.0
1968	10.6	2.5	24	4.7
1969	10.8	2.7	25	6.1
1970	10.8	2.8	26	5.5
1971	10.6	3.0	28	3.4
1972	10.4	4.3	41	3.4
1973	10.5	4.1	39	8.8
1974	10.3	4.0	39	12.1
1975	10.2	5.1	50	—

Source: U.S. Council on Wage and Price Stability, *Cost of Living Escalator Clauses and Inflation* (Washington, DC: Government Printing Office, 1975), 12.

[a] Contracts covering one thousand workers or more in private industry. Prior to 1966, the construction, service, finance, insurance, and real estate industries were excluded.

[b] December to December.

[c] September figures.

[d] Estimates.

[e] Midpoint in range of BLS estimate, rounded to nearest one-tenth of one million.

* = not available

Table 2

Steel Industry Labor Settlements, 1945–1977

YEAR	LENGTH IN YEARS	TOTAL % CHANGE IN EMPLOYMENT COST	AMOUNT OF INCREASE PER HOUR WORKED IN $	AVERAGE ANNUAL COMPOUNDED % INCREASE IN EMPLOYMENT COST
1945	1	7.4	.10	7.4
1946	1	11.3	.16	11.3
1947	1	7.4	.12	7.4
1948	1	4.4	.11	4.4
1949	1	8.8	.16	8.8
1950	2	10.1	.21	4.9
1952	2	8.5	.20	4.2
1953	[a]	3.0[a]	.07	3
1954	1	8.4	.21	8.4
1955	1	8.5	.23	8.5
1956	3	28.6	.84	8.7
1959	2.5	9.4	.36	3.6
1962	1	2.2	.09	2.2
1963	2	5.4	.23	2.7
1965	3[b]	12.4	.56	4.0
1968	3	22.2	1.09	6.9
1971	3	35.2	2.06	10.6
1974[c]	3	39.3	3.34	11.7
1977[c]	3	31.6	4.03	9.6

Source: Memo, R. C. Fisher to W. J. De Lancey, February 7, 1980, re: Information on Steel Industry Labor Settlements, Industry Bargaining, Confidential File, Oct. 1972—Nov. 1983 (Folder 2 of 2), Box 72, Republic Steel Corporation Records, 1895–2001, MS. 4949, Western Reserve Historical Society, Cleveland, OH.

[a] Wage reopener included under previous contract

[b] Includes four-month contract extension

[c] Early settlement under the Experimental Negotiating Agreement (ENA)

Table 3
Work Stoppages Involving One Thousand or More Workers, 1947–1986

YEAR	NUMBER OF WORK STOPPAGES BEGINNING IN PERIOD	NUMBER OF WORKERS INVOLVED (THOUSANDS)[a]	DAYS IDLE[b] NUMBER (THOUSANDS)	% OF WORKING TIME[c]
1947	270	1,629	25,720	n/a
1948	245	1,435	26,127	.22
1949	262	2,537	43,420	.38
1950	424	1,698	30,390	.26
1951	415	1,462	15,070	.12
1952	470	2,746	48,820	.38
1953	437	1,623	18,130	.14
1954	265	1,075	16,630	.13
1955	363	2,055	21,180	.16
1956	287	1,370	26,840	.20
1957	279	887	10,340	.07
1958	332	1,587	17,900	.13
1959	245	1,381	60,850	.43
1960	222	896	13,260	.09
1961	195	1,031	10,140	.07
1962	211	793	11,760	.08
1963	181	512	10,020	.07
1964	246	1,183	16,220	.11
1965	268	999	15,140	.10
1966	321	1,300	16,000	.10
1967	381	2,192	31,320	.18
1968	392	1,855	35,367	.20
1969	412	1,576	39,397	.16
1970	381	2,468	52,761	.29
1971	298	2,516	35,538	.19
1972	250	975	16,764	.09
1973	317	1,400	16,260	.08
1974	424	1,796	31,809	.16
1975	235	965	17,563	.09
1976	231	1,519	23,962	.12
1977	298	1,212	21,258	.10

YEAR	NUMBER OF WORK STOPPAGES BEGINNING IN PERIOD	NUMBER OF WORKERS INVOLVED (THOUSANDS)[a]	DAYS IDLE[b] NUMBER (THOUSANDS)	% OF WORKING TIME[c]
1978	219	1,006	23,774	.11
1979	235	1,021	20,409	.09
1980	187	795	20,844	.09
1981	145	729	16,908	.07
1982	96	656	9,061	.04
1983	81	909	17,461	.08
1984	62	376	8,499	.04
1985	54	324	7,079	.03
1986	69	533	11,861	.05

Source: U.S. Bureau of Labor Statistics, "Work Stoppages Involving 1,000 or More Workers, 1947–2016," last modified February 9, 2018, https://www.bls.gov/news.release/wkstp.t01.htm.

[a] Number of workers involved includes only those workers who participated in work stoppages that began in the calendar year. Workers are counted more than once if they are involved in more than one stoppage during the reference period. Numbers are rounded to the nearest thousand.

[b] Days idle includes all stoppages in effect during the reference period. For work stoppages that are still ongoing at the end of the calendar year, only those days of idleness in the calendar year are counted.

[c] Percentage of estimated working time is calculated using employment estimates from the Current Employment Statistics program and the number of work days in the month and number of days idle from the Work Stoppages program.

Table 4
Unemployment, Inflation, and Unit Labor Costs, 1948–1989

YEAR	UNEMPLOYMENT RATE	INFLATION RATE	CORE INFLATION RATE	UNIT LABOR COSTS, % CHANGE FROM YEAR BEFORE
1948	3.8	7.7	*	6.0
1949	6.1	–1.0	*	–0.3
1950	5.2	1.1	*	–0.7
1951	3.3	7.9	*	6.0
1952	3.0	2.3	*	3.5
1953	2.9	0.8	*	3.1
1954	5.6	0.3	*	1.2
1955	4.4	–0.3	*	–0.6
1956	4.1	1.5	*	6.7
1957	4.3	3.3	*	3.2
1958	6.8	2.7	2.3	1.6
1959	5.5	1.0	2.0	0.3
1960	5.5	1.5	1.5	3.1
1961	6.7	1.1	1.2	0.1
1962	5.6	1.2	1.3	–0.6
1963	5.6	1.2	1.3	0.0
1964	5.2	1.3	1.5	0.2
1965	4.5	1.6	1.3	0.1
1966	3.8	3.0	2.5	2.2
1967	3.8	2.8	3.5	3.9
1968	3.6	4.3	4.7	3.9
1969	3.5	5.5	5.8	6.6
1970	5.0	5.8	6.2	5.4
1971	6.0	4.3	4.7	2.1
1972	5.6	3.3	3.1	2.9
1973	4.9	6.2	3.5	4.4
1974	5.6	11.1	8.3	11.3
1975	8.5	9.1	9.2	7.5
1976	7.7	5.7	6.6	4.1
1977	7.1	6.5	6.3	6.4
1978	6.1	7.6	7.3	7.1
1979	5.9	11.3	9.7	9.8

YEAR	UNEMPLOYMENT RATE	INFLATION RATE	CORE INFLATION RATE	UNIT LABOR COSTS, % CHANGE FROM YEAR BEFORE
1980	7.2	13.5	12.4	10.8
1981	7.6	10.3	10.5	8.0
1982	9.7	6.1	7.4	8.2
1983	9.6	3.2	3.9	0.4
1984	7.5	4.3	5.1	2.0
1985	7.2	3.5	4.4	3.1
1986	7.0	1.9	4.0	2.7
1987	6.2	3.7	3.9	3.2
1988	5.5	4.1	4.4	3.4
1989	5.3	4.8	4.5	2.0

Sources: "Unemployment: Civilian Unemployment Rate (UNRATE), Expressed as the Annual Average," FRED, Federal Reserve Bank of St. Louis, accessed December 21, 2020, https://fred.stlouisfed.org/series/UNRATE/. Inflation: "Consumer Price Index for All Urban Consumers, All Items (CPIAUCNS), Expressed as Annual Average, Percent Change from Year Ago," FRED, Federal Reserve Bank of St. Louis, accessed December 21, 2020, https://fred.stlouisfed.org/series/CPIAUCNS. Core inflation: "Consumer Price Index for All Urban Consumers: All Items Less Food and Energy (CPILFESL), Expressed as Annual Average, Percent Change from Year Ago," FRED, Federal Reserve Bank of St. Louis, accessed December, 2020, https://fred.stlouisfed.org/series/CPILFESL. Unit labor costs: "Nonfarm Business Sector: Unit Labor Costs (ULCNFB), Expressed as Annual Average, Percent Change from Year Ago," FRED, Federal Reserve Bank of St. Louis, accessed December 21, 2020, https://fred.stlouisfed.org/series/ULCNFB.
Note: Core inflation series begins in 1958.

NOTES

INTRODUCTION

1. Report of the Special Committee on "Future Manufacturing Lines of General Motors Corporation," 1921, Folder 825, Box 25, John McDonald Papers, GEN Mss 622, Beinecke Rare Book and Manuscript Library, Yale University, New Haven, CT.
2. Business Roundtable, "Business Roundtable Redefines the Purpose of a Corporation to Promote 'An Economy That Serves All Americans,'" August 19, 2019, accessed September 8, 2019, https://www.businessroundtable.org/business-roundtable-redefines-the-purpose-of-a-corporation-to-promote-an-economy-that-serves-all-americans.
3. Ronald G. Coase, "The Nature of the Firm," *Economica*, n.s., 4, no. 16 (November 1937): 386–405; Alfred D. Chandler Jr., *Strategy and Structure: Chapters in the History of the Industrial Enterprise* (Cambridge, MA: MIT Press, 1962); Louis Galambos, "The Emerging Organizational Synthesis in Modern American History," *Business History Review* 44, no. 3 (Autumn 1970): 279–290; Alfred D. Chandler Jr., *The Visible Hand: The Managerial Revolution in American Business* (Cambridge, MA: Harvard University Press, 1977); Naomi Lamoreaux, *The Great Merger Movement in American Business, 1895–1904* (Cambridge: Cambridge University Press, 1985); Martin J. Sklar, *The Corporate Reconstruction of American Capitalism, 1890–1916: The Market, the Law, and Politics* (Cambridge: Cambridge University Press, 1988); Neil Fligstein, *The Transformation of Corporate Control* (Cambridge, MA: Harvard University Press, 1990); Alfred D. Chandler Jr., *Scale and Scope: The Dynamics of Industrial Capitalism* (Cambridge, MA: Harvard University Press, 1990).
4. See, e.g., the Accountable Capitalism Act proposed by Senator Elizabeth Warren

during her presidential campaign: https://www.warren.senate.gov/imo/media/doc/Accountable%20Capitalism%20Act%20One-Pager.pdf. On internal pressures, see "The 'Stakeholder' CEOs," *Wall Street Journal*, August 19, 2019, https://www.wsj.com/articles/the-stakeholder-ceos-11566248641. On macroeconomic trends, see Michael W. L. Elsby, Bart Hobjin, and Aysegul Sahin, "The Decline of the U.S. Labor Share," *Brookings Papers on Economic Activity*, Fall 2013, 1–63; Simcha Barkai, "Declining Labor and Capital Shares" (Stigler Center New Working Paper Series 2, November 2016); Cyrille Schwellnus, Andreas Kappeler, and Pierre-Alain Pionnier, "Decoupling of Wages from Productivity: Macro-Level Facts" (OECD Economics Department Working Papers, No. 1373, January 24, 2017); David Autor, David Dorn, Lawrence F. Katz, Christina Patterson, and John Van Reenen, "Concentrating on the Fall of the Labor Share," *American Economic Review* 107, no. 5 (2017): 180–185; Anna Stansbury and Lawrence H. Summers, "Productivity and Pay: Is the Link Broken?" (Peterson Institute for International Economics Working Paper, 2018). The advent of contemporary shareholder primacy is often attributed to Milton Friedman, "The Social Responsibility of Business Is to Increase Its Profits," *New York Times Magazine*, September 13, 1970. For recent historical work dating this trend to the 1980s and beyond, see Brian Cheffins, *The Public Company Transformed* (Oxford: Oxford University Press, 2018); Brian Cheffins, "Stop Blaming Milton Friedman!" (University of Cambridge Faculty of Law Research Paper No. 9/2020, European Corporate Governance Institute—Law Working Paper No. 523/2020, March 11, 2020), http://dx.doi.org/10.2139/ssrn.3552950.

5. Claudia Goldin and Robert Margo, "The Great Compression: The Wage Structure in the United States at Mid-Century," *Quarterly Journal of Economics* 107 (1992): 1–34; Thomas Piketty and Emmanuel Saez, "Income Inequality in the United State, 1913–1998," *Quarterly Journal of Economics* 118, no. 1 (February 2003): 1–39; Thomas Piketty, *Capital in the Twenty-First Century*, trans. Arthur Goldhammer (Cambridge, MA: Harvard University Press, 2014); Robert J. Gordon, *The Rise and Fall of American Growth: The U.S. Standard of Living Since the Civil War* (Princeton, NJ: Princeton University Press, 2016); Marc Levinson, *An Extraordinary Time: The End of the Postwar Boom and the Return of the Ordinary Economy* (New York: Basic Books, 2016).
6. Historical formulations of this arrangement can be found in Peter F. Drucker, *Concept of the Corporation* (New York: John Day, 1946); John Kenneth Galbraith, *The Affluent Society* (Boston: Houghton Mifflin, 1958); Adolf A. Berle Jr. and Gardiner C. Means, *The Modern Corporation and Private Property*, rev. ed. (New York: Macmillan, 1967); John Kenneth Galbraith, *The New Industrial State*, 4th ed. (Boston: Houghton Mifflin, 1985). Modern perspectives on the diminished response to shareholders include Mary A. O'Sullivan, *Contests for Corporate Control: Corporate Governance and Economic Performance in the United States and Germany* (New York: Oxford University Press, 2000); William Lazonick and Mary O'Sullivan, "Maximizing Shareholder Value: A New Ideology for Corporate Governance," *Economy and Society* 29, no. 1 (February 2000): 13–35. Mary A.

O'Sullivan, "Living with the U.S. Financial System: The Experiences of General Electric and Westinghouse Electric in the Last Century," *Business History Review* 80 (Winter 2006): 621–655; Brian R. Cheffins, "Corporate Governance since the Managerial Capitalism Era," *Business History Review* 89 (Winter 2015): 717–744. For historical views on the power of the state and organized labor during the postwar era, see Ellis W. Hawley, *The New Deal and the Problem of Monopoly: A Study in Economic Ambivalence* (Princeton, NJ: Princeton University Press, 1966); Howell John Harris, *The Right to Manage: Industrial Relations Policies of American Business in the 1940s* (Madison: University of Wisconsin Press, 1982); David Vogel, *Fluctuating Fortunes: The Political Power of Business in America* (New York: Basic Books, 1989); Steven Fraser and Gary Gerstle, eds., *The Rise and Fall of the New Deal Order, 1930–1980* (Princeton, NJ: Princeton University Press, 1990); Lizabeth Cohen, *A Consumers' Republic: The Politics of Mass Consumption in Postwar America* (New York: Vintage Books, 2003); Meg Jacobs, *Pocketbook Politics: Economic Citizenship in Twentieth-Century America* (Princeton, NJ: Princeton University Press, 2005); Bruce Western and Jake Rosenfeld, "Unions, Norms, and the Rise in U.S. Wage Inequality," *American Sociological Review* 76, no. 4 (2011): 513–526; Carola Frydman and Raven Molloy, "Pay Cuts for the Boss: Executive Compensation in the 1940s," *Journal of Economic History* 72, no. 1 (March 2012): 225–251; Nelson Lichtenstein, *State of the Union: A Century of American Labor*, rev. ed. (Princeton, NJ: Princeton University Press, 2013); Brantly Callaway and William J. Collins, "Unions, Workers, and Wages at the Peak of the American Labor Movement," *Explorations in Economic History* 68 (April 2018): 95–108.

7. Elizabeth A. Fones-Wolf, *Selling Free Enterprise: The Business Assault on Labor and Liberalism* (Urbana: University of Illinois Press, 1994); Kim Phillips-Fein, *Invisible Hands: The Businessmen's Crusade against the New Deal* (New York: Norton, 2009); Darren Dochuk, *From Bible Belt to Sunbelt: Plain-Folk Religion, Grassroots Politics, and the Rise of Evangelical Conservatism* (New York: Norton, 2011); Benjamin C. Waterhouse, *Lobbying America: The Politics of Business from Nixon to NAFTA* (Princeton, NJ: Princeton University Press, 2014); Jason Stahl, *Right Moves: The Conservative Think Tank in American Political Culture since 1945* (Chapel Hill: University of North Carolina Press, 2016).
8. Jefferson Cowie, *Capital Moves: RCA's Seventy-Year Quest for Cheap Labor* (Ithaca, NY: Cornell University Press, 1999); Tami J. Friedman, "Exploiting the North-South Differential: Corporate Power, Southern Politics, and the Decline of Organized Labor after World War II," *Journal of American History* 95, no. 2 (September 2008): 323–348; Elizabeth Tandy Shermer, *Sunbelt Capitalism: Phoenix and the Transformation of American Politics* (Philadelphia: University of Pennsylvania Press, 2013).
9. In 1963, 75% of American steel was produced in Ohio, Pennsylvania, Michigan, Indiana, and Illinois; forty years later, 63% still was. Allan Collard-Wexler and Jan De Loecker, "Reallocation and Technology: Evidence from the US Steel Industry," *American Economic Review* 105, no. 1 (2015): 150.

10. Charles S. Maier, "The Politics of Productivity: Foundations of American International Economic Policy after World War II," *International Organization* 31, no. 4 (Autumn 1977): 607–633.
11. Andrew Shonfield, *Modern Capitalism: The Changing Balance of Public and Private Power* (London: Oxford University Press, 1965); Barry Eichengreen, *The European Economy since 1945: Coordinated Capitalism and Beyond* (Princeton, NJ: Princeton University Press, 2007).
12. Robert Leeson, "The Political Economy of the Inflation-Unemployment Trade-Off," *History of Political Economy* 29, no. 1 (Spring 1997): 117–156; John T. Woolley, "Exorcising Inflation-Mindedness: The Transformation of Economic Management in the 1970s," *Journal of Policy History* 10, no. 1 (January 1998): 131–152; Daniel J. B. Mitchell and Christopher L. Erickson, "The Concept of Wage-Push Inflation: Development and Policy," *Labor History* 49, no. 4 (November 2008): 417–438; James Forder, *Macroeconomics and the Phillips Curve Myth* (Oxford: Oxford University Press, 2014); Norikazu Takami, "The Baffling New Inflation: How Cost-Push Inflation Theories Influenced Policy Debate in the Late-1950s United States," *History of Political Economy* 47, no. 4 (December 2015): 605–629.
13. Carl Kaysen and Donald F. Turner, *Antitrust Policy: An Economic and Legal Analysis* (Cambridge, MA: Harvard University Press, 1959); Rudolph J. R. Peritz, *Competition Policy in America, 1888–1992: History, Rhetoric, Law* (New York: Oxford University Press, 1996); Sam Peltzman, "Industrial Concentration under the Rule of Reason," *Journal of Law and Economics* 57 (August 2014): 101–120; Carl Shapiro, "Protecting Competition in the American Economy: Merger Control, Tech Titans, Labor Markets," *Journal of Economic Perspectives* 33, no. 3 (Summer 2019): 69–93; Naomi R. Lamoreaux, "The Problem of Bigness: From Standard Oil to Google," *Journal of Economic Perspectives* 33, no. 3 (Summer 2019): 94–117.
14. Alan Brinkley, *The End of Reform: New Deal Liberalism in Recession and War* (New York: Vintage Books, 1995); Robert M. Collins, *The Business Response to Keynes, 1929–1964* (New York: Columbia University Press, 1981); Herbert Stein, *The Fiscal Revolution in America: Policy in Pursuit of Reality*, 2nd rev. ed. (Washington, DC: AEI Press, 1996); Michael A. Bernstein, *A Perilous Progress: Economists and Public Purpose in Twentieth-Century America* (Princeton, NJ: Princeton University Press, 2004); Robert L. Hetzel, *The Monetary Policy of the Federal Reserve: A History* (Cambridge: Cambridge University Press, 2008); Alan H. Meltzer, *A History of the Federal Reserve*, 2 vols. (Chicago: University of Chicago Press, 2009).
15. Grant McConnell, *Steel and the Presidency: 1962* (New York: Norton, 1963); George J. McManus, *The Inside Story of Steel Wages and Prices, 1959–1967* (New York: Chilton, 1967); Maeva Marcus, *Truman and the Steel Seizure Case: The Limits of Presidential Power* (New York: Columbia University Press, 1977); Kim McQuaid, *Big Business and Presidential Power: From FDR to Reagan* (New York: William Morrow, 1982), 199–222; Benjamin C. Waterhouse, "Mobilizing for the

Market: Organized Business, Wage-Price Controls, and the Politics of Inflation, 1971–1974," *Journal of American History* 100, no. 2 (September 2013): 454–478.

16. The most important scholarship on wage-price policy was sponsored by the Brookings Institution in the late 1960s and 1970s. Many of these volumes were written by former White House insiders, and the keystone of the series, *Exhortation and Controls,* was produced in collaboration with the National Archives on the basis of presidential library records. The full series includes the following: John Sheahan, *The Wage-Price Guideposts* (Washington, DC: Brookings Institution, 1967); Arnold R. Weber, *In Pursuit of Price Stability: The Wage-Price Freeze of 1971* (Washington, DC: Brookings Institution, 1973); Robert F. Lanzillotti, Mary T. Hamilton, and R. Blaine Roberts, *Phase II in Review: The Price Commission Experience* (Washington, DC: Brookings Institution, 1975); Craufurd D. Goodwin, ed., *Exhortation and Controls: The Search for a Wage-Price Policy, 1945–1971* (Washington, DC: Brookings Institution, 1975); Arnold R. Weber and Daniel J. B. Mitchell, *The Pay Board's Progress: Wage Controls in Phase II* (Washington, DC: Brookings Institution, 1978). See also Allen J. Matusow, *Nixon's Economy: Booms, Busts, Dollars, and Votes* (Lawrence: University Press of Kansas, 1998); W. Carl Biven, *Jimmy Carter's Economy: Policy in an Age of Limit* (Chapel Hill: University of North Carolina Press, 2002).

CHAPTER 1. MONOPOLY AND THE PROBLEM OF THE NEW DEAL

1. Alfred D. Chandler Jr., *The Visible Hand: The Managerial Revolution in American Business* (Cambridge, MA: Harvard University Press, 1977); Naomi R. Lamoreaux, Daniel M. G. Raff, and Peter Temin, "Beyond Markets and Hierarchies: Toward a New Synthesis of American Business History," *American Historical Review* 108, no. 2 (April 2003): 404–433.
2. Ellis W. Hawley, *The New Deal and the Problem of Monopoly: A Study in Economic Ambivalence* (Princeton, NJ: Princeton University Press, 1966); Meg Jacobs, *Pocketbook Politics: Economic Citizenship in Twentieth-Century America* (Princeton, NJ: Princeton University Press, 2005).
3. Andrew H. Bartels, "The Office of Price Administration and the Legacy of the New Deal, 1939–1946," *Public Historian* 5, no. 3 (Summer 1983): 5–29; Meg Jacobs, "'How About Some Meat?': The Office of Price Administration, Consumption Politics, and State Building from the Bottom Up, 1941–1946," *Journal of American History* 84, no. 3 (December 1997): 910–941; Lizabeth Cohen, *A Consumers' Republic: The Politics of Mass Consumption in Postwar America* (New York: Vintage Books, 2003); Jacobs, *Pocketbook Politics,* 221–261.
4. Robert M. Collins, *The Business Response to Keynes, 1929–1964* (New York: Columbia University Press, 1981); Alan Brinkley, *The End of Reform: New Deal Liberalism in Recession and War* (New York: Vintage Books, 1995); Herbert Stein, *The Fiscal Revolution in America: Policy in Pursuit of Reality,* 2nd rev. ed. (Washington, DC: AEI Press, 1996).
5. If capital (K) and labor (L) are the only inputs in the economy, with capital receiving rents (R) and labor wages (W), to produce a total output (Y) at some price

level (P), then WL + RK = PY. This can be rewritten as W = P(Y/L) (1–1[RK/PY]). At the assumption of a constant distribution of income, RK/PY will be constant. Therefore, at a constant price level P, W varies directly with labor productivity (Y/L). This derivation is adapted from Arthur F. Burns and Paul A. Samuelson, *Full Employment, Guideposts, and Economic Stability* (Washington, DC: American Enterprise Institute, 1967), 51.

6. George Soule, "The Productivity Factor in Wage Determinations," *American Economic Review* 13, no. 1 (March 1923): 139. See also Walton H. Hamilton, "A Theory of the Rate of Wages," *Quarterly Journal of Economics* 36, no. 4 (August 1922): 605; Edward A. Filene, "The Minimum Wage and Efficiency," *American Economic Review* 13, no. 3 (September 1923): 411–415; Sam A. Lewisohn, "Wage Policies and National Productivity," *Political Science Quarterly* 39, no. 1 (March 1924): 97–105; Herbert Feis, John P. Frey, Waddill Catchings, and W. A. Berridge, "The Consuming Power of Labor and Business Fluctuations," *American Economic Review* 16, no. 1 (March 1926): 78–88; Paul H. Douglas, "The Modern Technique of Mass Production and Its Relation to Wages," *Proceedings of the Academy of Political Science in the City of New York* 12, no. 3 (July 1927): 17–41; Jacobs, *Pocketbook Politics*, 72–81; Thomas Stapleford, "Defining a 'Living Wage' in America: Transformations in Union Wage Theories, 1870–1930," *Labor History* 39, no. 1 (January 2008) 1–22.
7. I. M. Rubinow, "The Recent Trend of Real Wages," *American Economic Review* 4, no. 4 (December 1914): 793–817; Paul Douglas and Frances Lamberson, "The Movement of Real Wages, 1890–1918," *American Economic Review* 11, no. 3 (September 1921): 409–426; Soule, "Productivity Factor," 129–140.
8. Alvin H. Hansen, "Factors Affecting the Trend of Real Wages," *American Economic Review* 15, no. 1 (March 1925): 27–42.
9. The classic statement of these "stylized facts" is given by Nicholas Kaldor, "A Model of Economic Growth," *Economic Journal* 67, no. 268 (December 1957): 591–624; Nicholas Kaldor, "Capital Accumulation and Economic Growth," in *The Theory of Capital*, ed. D. C. Hague (London: Macmillan, 1963), 177–222. See also Roc Armenter, "A Bit of a Miracle No More: The Decline of the Labor Share," *Federal Reserve Bank of Philadelphia Business Review*, Third Quarter 2015, 4.
10. J. M. Keynes, "Relative Movements of Real Wages and Output," *Economic Journal* 49, no. 193 (March 1939): 49.
11. Paul H. Douglas, "The Movement of Real Wages and its Economic Significance," *American Economic Review* 16, no. 1 (March 1926): 17–53; Charles W. Cobb and Paul H. Douglas, "A Theory of Production," *American Economic Review* 18, no. 1 (March 1928): 139–165; Paul H. Douglas, *Real Wages in the Untied States, 1890–1926* (New York: Houghton Mifflin, 1930); Alvin H. Hansen, review of *Real Wages in the United States, 1890–1926*, by Paul H. Douglas, *American Economic Review* 20, no. 4 (December 1930): 747–752. On income trends in the 1920s, see Jeremy Atack and Peter Passell, *A New Economic View of American History: From Colonial Times to 1940*, 2nd ed. (New York: Norton, 1994), 594.
12. Edward Chamberlin, *The Theory of Monopolistic Competition* (Cambridge, MA:

Harvard University Press, 1933), esp. 8–10, 30–55. On Chamberlin's role in introducing "oligopoly" as a distinct term, see also Edward H. Chamberlin, "On the Origin of 'Oligopoly,'" *Economic Journal* 67, no. 266 (June 1957): 211–218.

13. Joan Robinson, *The Economics of Imperfect Competition* (London: Macmillan, 1933).
14. Alfred S. Eichner, "Portrait: Gardiner C. Means," *Challenge* 22, no. 6 (January–February 1980): 56–59.
15. Adolf A. Berle Jr. and Gardiner C. Means, *The Modern Corporation and Private Property*, rev. ed. (New York: Macmillan, 1967), 18–116, 293–313.
16. Hawley, *New Deal*, 37–49, 130–146, 187–204; Steven Fraser, *Labor Will Rule: Sidney Hillman and the Rise of American Labor* (Ithaca, NY: Cornell University Press, 1991), 259–323; Jacobs, *Pocketbook Politics*, 95–135; Bernard C. Beaudreau, "Why Did the National Industrial Recovery Act Fail?," *European Review of Economic History* 20, no. 1 (2016): 79–101; Jason E. Taylor, *Deconstructing the Monolith: The Microeconomics of the National Industrial Recovery Act* (Chicago: University of Chicago Press, 2019). For the traditional view that the NRA did not create additional collusion, see Barbara Alexander and Gary D. Libecap, "The Effect of Cost Heterogeneity in the Success and Failure of the New Deal's Agricultural and Industrial Programs," *Explorations in Economic History* 37, no. 4 (October 2000): 370–400. For evidence that the NRA did encourage collusion, see Chris Vickers and Nicholas L. Ziebarth, "Did the National Industrial Recovery Act Foster Collusion? Evidence from the Macaroni Industry," *Journal of Economic History* 74, no. 3 (September 2014): 831–862.
17. U.S. Senate, *Industrial Prices and Their Relative Inflexibility: Letter from the Secretary of Agriculture, Transmitting in Response to Senate Resolution no. 17, a Report Relating to the Subject of Industrial Prices and Their Relative Inflexibility*, 74th Cong., 1st Sess., Senate Document No. 13 (Washington, DC: Government Printing Office, 1935), 1–8.
18. U.S. Senate, 10–12.
19. U.S. Senate, 14–16, 27–36. See also Gardiner C. Means, "The Distribution of Control and Responsibility in a Modern Economy," *Political Science Quarterly* 50, no. 1 (March 1935): 59–69; Gardiner Means, "Price Inflexibility and the Requirements of a Stabilizing Monetary Policy," *Journal of the American Statistical Association* 30, no. 190 (1935): 401–413.
20. U.S. Senate, *Industrial Prices and Their Relative Inflexibility*, iii–iv. On Means's influence, see Frederic S. Lee, "A New Dealer in Agriculture: G. C. Means and the Writing of Industrial Prices," *Review of Social Economy* 46, no. 2 (1988): 197–199; Rudolph J. R. Peritz, *Competition Policy in America, 1888–1992: History, Rhetoric, Law* (New York: Oxford University Press, 1996), 145–147. On ideas of underconsumption, see also Jacobs, *Pocketbook Politics*, 72–75; Michael Bleaney, *Underconsumption Theories: A History and Critical Analysis* (New York: International, 1976).
21. Atack and Passell, *New Economic View*, 592–597.
22. National Labor Relations Act, P.L. 74-198, 49 Stat. 449 (1935), codified at 29 U.S.C. § 151 et seq. See also Jacobs, *Pocketbook Politics*, 107–108, 136–148.

23. Hawley, *New Deal*, 169–204. Statistics on union membership taken from Gerald Mayer, *Union Membership Trends in the United States* (Washington, DC: Congressional Research Service, 2004), 23.
24. Harry A. Mills, "The Union in Industry: Some Observations on the Theory of Collective Bargaining," *American Economic Review* 25, no. 1 (March 1935): 7.
25. Alvin H. Hansen, "Economic Progress and Declining Economic Growth," *American Economic Review* 29, no. 1 (March 1939): 13.
26. Edwin G. Nourse and Horace B. Drury, *Industrial Price Policies and Economic Progress* (Washington, DC: Brookings Institution, 1938); Edwin G. Nourse, *Price Making in a Democracy* (Washington, DC: Brookings Institution, 1944).
27. Larry C. Peppers, "Full-Employment Surplus Analysis and Structural Change: The 1930s," *Explorations in Economic History* 10 (1973): 197–210; Christina D. Romer, "What Ended the Great Depression?," *Journal of Economic History* 52, no. 4 (December 1992): 757–784.
28. Franklin D. Roosevelt, "Message to Congress on Curbing Monopolies," April 29, 1938, in *The American Presidency Project*, ed. Gerhard Peters and John T. Woolley, https://www.presidency.ucsb.edu/node/209657. See also David Lynch, *The Concentration of Economic Power* (New York: Columbia University Press, 1946), 23–28.
29. Alfred S. Eichner, "Portrait: Gardiner C. Means," *Challenge* 22, no. 6 (January–February 1980): 58.
30. Lynch, *Concentration of Economic Power*, 17–22; Hawley, *New Deal*, 383–386; Jacobs, *Pocketbook Politics*, 126, 139–140.
31. Lynch, *Concentration of Economic Power*, 70; Charles C. Cox, "Monopoly Explanations of the Great Depression and Public Policies toward Business," in *The Great Depression Revisited*, ed. Karl Brunner (Boston: Kluwer Nijhoff, 1981), 179.
32. Willard L. Thorp and Walter F. Crowder, "Concentration and Product Characteristics as Factors in Price-Quantity Behavior," *American Economic Review* 30, no. 5 (February 1941): 47–48; Lynch, *Concentration of Economic Power*, 364–368; Hawley, *New Deal*, 461–469.
33. U.S. Senate, *Final Report and Recommendations of the Temporary National Economic* Committee, 77th Cong., 1st Sess., Document No. 35 (Washington, DC: Government Printing Office, 1941), 22–40.
34. United States v. International Harvester Co., 274 U.S. 693, 708–709 (1927).
35. Interstate Circuit, Inc. v. United States, 306 U.S. 208, 221–222, 226–227 (1939).
36. Corwin D. Edwards, "Can the Antitrust Laws Preserve Competition?," *American Economic Review* 30, no. 1 (March 1940): 164–179.
37. Hawley, *New Deal*, 420–438; Alan Brinkley, "The Antimonopoly Ideal and the Liberal State: The Case of Thurman Arnold," *Journal of American History* 80, no. 2 (September 1993): 557–579.
38. United States v. Hutcheson, 312 U.S. 219 (1941). See also Archibald Cox, "Labor and the Antitrust Laws: A Preliminary Analysis," *University of Pennsylvania Law Review* 104, no. 2 (November 1955): 261–265.

39. Brinkley, "Antimonopoly Ideal," 573–578.
40. Hugh Rockoff, "The United States: From Ploughshares to Swords," in *The Economics of World War II: Six Great Powers in International Comparison*, ed. Mark Harrison (Cambridge: Cambridge University Press, 1998), 81–121.
41. Allan H. Meltzer, *A History of the Federal Reserve*, vol. 1, *1913–1951* (Chicago: University of Chicago Press, 2003), 579–724.
42. Leon Henderson and Donald M. Nelson, "Prices, Profits, and Government," *Harvard Business Review* 19, no. 4 (July 1941): 389–404.
43. Virgil B. Zimmermann, *Problems in Price Control: National Office Organization and Management* (Washington, DC: Government Printing Office, 1947); Harvey C. Mansfield, *A Short History of the OPA* (Washington, DC: Office of Temporary Controls, 1948).
44. J. K. Galbraith, "Price Control: Some Lessons from the First Phase," *American Economic Review* 33, no. 1 (March 1943): 253–259; J. K. Galbraith, "Reflections on Price Control," *Quarterly Journal of Economics* 60, no. 4 (August 1946): 475–489; John Kenneth Galbraith, *A Theory of Price Control* (1952; repr., Cambridge, MA: Harvard University Press, 1980).
45. Nelson Lichtenstein, *Labor's War at Home: The CIO in World War II* (Cambridge: Cambridge University Press, 1982), 68–82.
46. George W. Taylor, "Wage Regulation in Postwar America," *American Economic Review* 34, no. 1, part 2 (March 1944): 185; Thomas A. Stapleford, *The Cost of Living in America: A Political History of Economic Statistics, 1880–2000* (Cambridge: Cambridge University Press, 2009), 184–218. On overall earnings, see Robert A. Margo, "Hourly and Weekly Earnings of Production Workers in Manufacturing: 1909–1995," table Ba4361-4366 in *Historical Statistics of the United States: Earliest Times to the Present: Millennial Edition*, ed. Susan B. Carter, Scott Sigmund Gartner, Michael R. Haines, Alan L. Olmstead, Richard Sutch, and Gavin Wright (New York: Cambridge University Press, 2006); Peter H. Lindert and Richard Sutch, "Consumer Price Indexes, for All Items: 1774–2003," table Cc1-2 in Carter et al., *Historical Statistics.*
47. Galbraith, "Price Control," 253–259; Galbraith, "Reflections on Price Control," 475–489; Galbraith, *Theory of Price Control*, 1–27.
48. Memo, Donald Nelson, Chester Bowles, and A. D. Whiteside to Fred Vinson, October 23, 1943, McDonald's Proposals re: Low End Problem, Box 7; Vinson to Bowles and Nelson, November 16, 1943, Vinson Letter of November 16, 1943, Box 10, Office Files of Gardner Ackley, Records of the Office of Price Administration (RG 188), National Archives, College Park, MD; "The War Production Board: Is It?," *Fortune*, March 1943, 96; Wilfred Carsel, *Wartime Apparel Price Control* (Washington, DC: Office of Price Administration, 1947), 64–71, 87–88; Frank Walton, *Thread of Victory: The Conversion and Conservation of Textiles, Clothing, and Leather for the World's Biggest War Program* (New York: Fairchild, 1945), 160–168, 254–258.
49. Memo, David Ginsburg to Leon Henderson, May 9, 1942; Memo, Henry M. Hart Jr. to Galbraith, July 22, 1942; Galbraith to Henderson, November 21,

1942, Low-End Regulation, Box 4, Office Files of Benjamin Caplan, compiled 1942–1946, RG 188, National Archives.

50. "MPR 287," in *Pike and Fischer OPA Price Service,* ed. James A. Pike and Henry G. Fischer, vol. 2, *Consumer Goods Desk Book* (Rochester, NY: Federal Regulations, 1944–1946), 28106, 28123, 28152–28155.
51. "Majority Report and Recommendation of the Panel, NWLB Case No. 111-286-c," March 15, 1943, Folder 3c, Box 178, David Dubinsky, President's Records, 1932–1966 (5780/002), Kheel Center for Labor-Management Documentation and Archives, M. P. Catherwood Library, Cornell University, Ithaca, NY.
52. "Prospectus on Collection of Financial Data from Dress Manufacturers," Survey of Dress Manufacturers, Box 1, Women's Outwear Section, Records Containing Economic Data, 1943–1946; Memo, Abraham Boykoff and Roy Cave to Elmer Schaller, September 22, 1943, RMPR 287—Price Action, Box 13, Women's Outwear Section, Price Action Files, RG 188, National Archives.
53. Memo, Joseph Forer to Cornelius J. Moynihan, November 25, 1944, BLS—Wage Analysis Data Affecting MPR 287, Box 7, Women's Outwear Section, Price Action Files, RG 188, National Archives.
54. Memo, Louis Schneider to Florence Walsh, ca. 1944, re: Revisions of RMPR 287, RMPR 287 Revision, Box 1, Women's Outwear Section, Records Containing Economic Data, RG 188, National Archives.
55. Zimmerman, *Problems in Price Control,* 121–127.
56. Minutes of the Meeting of the Joint Board Dress & Waistmakers Union, March 22, 1944, Volume 6, Box 1, ILGWU New York Dress Joint Board Minutes, 1922–1976 (5780/0033), Kheel Center.
57. "Hearing with Dress Manufacturers Associations," May 18, 1944; Memo, Forer to Harry E. Witherell, August 1,1944; Memo, Forer to Moynihan, November 25, 1944, BLS—Wage Analysis Data Affecting MPR 287, Box 7, Women's Outwear Section, Price Action File, RG 188, National Archives.
58. Joint Board Report, 1947, Folder 9, Box 2, ILGWU Joint Board Dress & Waistmakers' Union of Greater New York, Managers' Correspondence, 1909–1978 (5780/047), Kheel Center.
59. Chester Bowles, "Crisis in Clothes," *Collier's,* January 19, 1946, 14–15, 63–64.
60. Laura Brown Webb, "Recent Changes in the Character of Civilian Textiles and Apparel," *Monthly Labor Review* 57, no. 3 (September 1943): 421–434.
61. Webb, "Recent Changes"; Memo, Schneider to Walsh, ca. 1944, re: Revisions of RMPR 287, RMPR 287 Revision, Box 1, Women's Outwear Section, Records Containing Economic Data, RG 188, National Archives.
62. United States, War Production Board, *The Textile Shortage in the First Quarter of 1945* (Washington, DC: Government Printing Office, 1945), 19; United States, War Production Board, *Consumer Demand and Purchases of 75 Clothing and Textile Items* (Washington, DC: Government Printing Office, 1945), 36–37.
63. Margo, "Hourly and Weekly Earnings"; Lindert and Sutch, "Consumer Price Indexes"; National Bureau of Economic Research, "Real Average Hourly Earnings, Production Workers, Manufacturing for United States (M08343USM232SNBR),"

FRED, Federal Reserve Bank of St. Louis, accessed June 18, 2020, https://fred.stlouisfed.org/series/M08343USM232SNBR.

64. Memo, Walter Salant to Thomas Emerson, September 28, 1945, re: Background for Determination of Wage Policy, Memoranda 1945, Box 39; Report, "Factors Relating to Wage-Price Policy," Wage Policy Decisions of Autumn 1945, Box 66, Walter S. Salant Papers, Harry S. Truman Library, Independence, MO.
65. Verbatim Report National Labor-Management Conference, November 30, 1945, Volume 1, Box 1377, Harry S. Truman Papers, White House Central Files: Official File, 1945–1953, Truman Library.
66. Harry S. Truman, "Executive Order 9599—Providing for . . . the Orderly Modification of Wartime Controls over Prices, Wages, Materials and Facilities," August 18, 1945, in Peters and Woolley, *American Presidency Project*, https://www.presidency.ucsb.edu/node/278117.
67. United Auto Workers, *Purchasing Power for Prosperity: The Case of the General Motors Workers for Maintaining Take-Home Pay* (Detroit: United Auto Workers, 1945); Nelson Lichtenstein, *Walter Reuther: The Most Dangerous Man in Detroit* (Urbana: University of Illinois Press, 1995), 175–193, 219–229.
68. Sumner H. Slichter, "Problems of Wage Policy after the War," *Proceedings of the Academy of Political Science* 21, no. 1 (May 1944): 64–88; Emerson P. Schmidt, "Inflation and the Postwar," *Social Science* 19, no. 4 (October 1944): 200–205; National Industrial Conference Board, *Wages during the Transition Period* (New York: NICB, 1945).
69. U.S. Bureau of Labor Statistics, *Productivity and Unit Labor Cost in Selected Manufacturing Industries, 1939–1945* (Washington, DC: Government Printing Office, 1946). Business groups cited these statistics as evidence that Truman's wage-price policy would push costs up against a fixed price level: National Industrial Conference Board, *Wages during the Transition Period,* 56–62.
70. Gavin Wright, "Indexes of National Productivity, by Sector and Type of Input: 1889–1957," table Cg265-272 in Carter et al., *Historical Statistics;* U.S. Bureau of Economic Analysis, "Costs per Unit of Real Gross Value Added of Nonfinancial Corporate Business: Compensation of Employees (Unit Labor Cost) (A460R-D3A052NBEA)," FRED, Federal Reserve Bank of St. Louis, accessed June 18, 2020, https://fred.stlouisfed.org/series/A460RD3A052NBEA.
71. Letter, Buck Harrington to Walter Carpenter, November 9, 1945; Letter, Alfred Sloan to Carpenter, November 16, 1945, re: General Motors P.R.—Labor Situation, Box 837, General Motors Corp. (1/3/45–12/28/45), Walter Carpenter Papers, Acc. 542, Hagley Museum and Library, Wilmington, DE.
72. Peter Drucker, "Who Should Get a Raise, and When?," *Harper's,* March 1946, 215–223; Sumner H. Slichter, "Wage-Price Policy and Employment," *American Economic Review* 36, no. 2 (May 1946): 304–318; Alfred P. Sloan Jr, "Business Trend for 1947," *Vital Speeches of the Day,* 1947, 237–241.
73. Harry S. Truman, "Executive Order 9651—Amending Executive Order 9599," October 30, 1945, in Peters and Woolley, *American Presidency Project,* https://www.presidency.ucsb.edu/node/230929.

74. Wilhelm Röpke, "Offene und Zuruckgestaute Inflation," *Kyklos* 1, no. 1 (February 1947): 57–71; Abba P. Lerner, "The Inflationary Process: Some Theoretical Aspects," *Review of Economics and Statistics* 31, no. 3 (August 1949): 193–200.
75. "Work Stoppages Caused by Labor-Management Disputes in 1945," *Monthly Labor Review* 62, no. 5 (May 1946): 718–735; U.S. Department of Labor, *Work Stoppages Caused by Labor-Management Disputes in 1946,* Bulletin No. 918 (Washington, DC: Government Printing Office, 1947).
76. U.S. Bureau of Economic Analysis, "Real Personal Consumption Expenditures (DPCERL1A225NBEA)," FRED, Federal Reserve Bank of St. Louis, accessed June 18, 2020, https://fred.stlouisfed.org/series/DPCERL1A225NBEA. For an overview of tax changes following World War II, see Carl Shoup, "The Revenue Act of 1945," *Political Science Quarterly* 60, no. 4 (December 1945): 481–491.
77. Margo, "Hourly and Weekly Earnings"; Christopher Hanes, "Wholesale and Producer Price Indexes, by Commodity Group: 1890–1997," table Cc66-83 in Carter et al., *Historical Statistics;* National Bureau of Economic Research, "Real Average Hourly Earnings (M08343USM232SNBR)," FRED, Federal Reserve Bank of St. Louis, accessed June 18, 2020, https://fred.stlouisfed.org/series/M08343USM232SNBR.
78. U.S. Bureau of Labor Statistics, "All Employees: Total Nonfarm Payrolls (PAYEMS)," FRED, Federal Reserve Bank of St. Louis, accessed June 18, 2020, https://fred.stlouisfed.org/series/PAYEMS; National Bureau of Economic Research, "Unemployment Rate for United States (M0892BUSM156SNBR)," FRED, Federal Reserve Bank of St. Louis, accessed June 18, 2020, https://fred.stlouisfed.org/series/M0892BUSM156SNBR.
79. Memo, Bowles to the President, January 18, 1946; Memo, Bowles to the President, January 24, 1946, Bowles, Chester, Box 97, President's Secretary's File, Truman Library. Memo, Bowles to the President, February 6, 1946, Folder 230—Truman, Harry S., Box 11, Chester Bowles Papers, 1942–1982, MS 628, Manuscripts and Archives, Yale University Library, New Haven, CT.
80. Oral history interview with John W. Snyder, January 10, 1968, by Jerry N. Hess, pp. 235–237, Truman Library, http://www.trumanlibrary.org/oralhist/snyder5.htm; Barton J. Bernstein, "The Truman Administration and the Steel Strike of 1946," *Journal of American History* 52, no. 4 (March 1966): 798–800.
81. For $2.50, see Memo, Bowles to John Collet, January 5, 1946; Memo, Bowles to Collet, January 10, 1946, Folder 52—Collet, J. Caskie, Box 4, Bowles Papers, Yale University Library. On the justification of $5.30, see Memo, John Collet to Charles Ross, February 20, 1946, OF 342 Steel Iron (1945–February 1947), Box 1162, White House Central Files: Official File, Truman Library.
82. Lichtenstein, *Walter Reuther,* 242–243.
83. Interview with the President, June 10, 1946, F 231—Truman, Harry S., Box 11, Bowles Papers, Yale University Library.
84. James Boylan, *The New Deal Coalition and the Election of 1946* (New York: Garland, 1981), 32–70; Jacobs, *Pocketbook Politics,* 225–227; Cohen, *Consumers' Republic,* 102–105.

85. Memo, Collett to the President, October 12, 1946; Letter, President to Emil Schram, October 18, 1946, Meat, Box 112, President's Secretary Files, Truman Library.
86. Boylan, *New Deal Coalition*, 121–177.
87. Lindert and Sutch, "Consumer Price Indexes"; Hanes, "Wholesale and Producer Price Indexes."
88. G. L. Bach and Albert Ando, "The Redistributional Effects of Inflation," *Review of Economics and Statistics* 39, no. 1 (February 1957): 1–13; U.S. Bureau of Economic Analysis, "Costs per Unit of Real Gross Value Added of Nonfinancial Corporate Business: Compensation of Employees (Unit Labor Cost) (A460RD3A052N-BEA)," FRED, Federal Reserve Bank of St. Louis, accessed June 18, 2020, https://fred.stlouisfed.org/series/A460RD3A052NBEA; U.S. Bureau of Economic Analysis, "Shares of Gross Domestic Income: Compensation of Employees, Paid: Wage and Salary Accruals: Disbursements (W269RE1A156NBEA)," FRED, Federal Reserve Bank of St. Louis, accessed June 18, 2020, https://fred.stlouis fed.org/series/W269RE1A156NBEA.
89. L. D. Howell, *Marketing and Manufacturing Services for Textiles* (Washington, DC: Government Printing Office, 1952), 107; A. H. Raskin, "Strike Is Averted in Dress Industry," *New York Times*, March 5, 1947, 27.
90. "Approximate Garments by Price Range," February 16, 1949, Folder 11, Box 3, ILGWU Managers' Correspondence; "Conditions in the Women's Garment Industry," December 20, 1948, Folder 2, Box 1, ILGWU Research Department Reports 1938–1985 (5780/078), Kheel Center.
91. Stephen K. Bailey, *Congress Makes a Law: The Story behind the Employment Act of 1946* (New York: Columbia University Press, 1950). See also Collins, *Business Response*, 96–111; Stein, *Fiscal Revolution*, 197–205.
92. Martin Bronfenbrenner and Franklyn D. Holzman, "Survey of Inflation Theory," *American Economic Review* 53, no. 4 (September 1963): 623; Craufurd D. Goodwin and R. Stanley Herren, "The Truman Administration: Problems and Policies Unfold," in *Exhortation and Controls: The Search for a Wage-Price Policy, 1945–1971*, ed. Craufurd D. Goodwin (Washington, DC: Brooking Institution, 1975), 16–19.
93. The original paper is M. W. Reder, "The Theoretical Problems of a National Wage-Price Policy," *Canadian Journal of Economics and Political Science* 14, no. 1 (February 1948): 46–61. The quote is taken from M. W. Reder, "The Significance of the 1948 General Motors Agreement," *Review of Economics and Statistics* 31, no. 1 (February 1949): 10. See also Abba P. Lerner, "Money as a Creature of the State," *American Economic Review* 37, no. 2 (May 1947): 312–317.
94. Albert Hart, *Defense without Inflation* (New York: Twentieth Century Fund, 1951); Albert G. Hart, "General Strategy of Economic Policy for Less-than-Total War," *American Economic Review* 41, no. 1 (March 1951): 51–59.
95. "The Uneasy Triangle," *Economist*, August 9, 1952, 322–323; "The Uneasy Triangle—II: The Limits of Free Bargaining," *Economist*, August 16, 1952, 376–378; "The Uneasy Triangle—III: How Full Employment?," *Economist*, August 23,

1952, 434–435. Paul Samuelson attributed the articles to Wiles in Burns and Samuelson, *Full Employment*, 46.

96. Harry S. Truman, "Special Message to the Congress on the First Day of the Special Session," November 17, 1947, in Peters and Woolley, *American Presidency Project*, https://www.presidency.ucsb.edu/node/232540; Jacobs, *Pocketbook Politics*, 237–242.
97. H. W. Singer, "Wage Policy in Full Employment," *Economic Journal* 57, no. 228 (December 1947): 438–455; Lerner, "Inflationary Process," 198–200.
98. Paul H. Douglas, "The Economic Theory of Wage Regulation," *University of Chicago Law Review* 5, no. 2 (February 1938): 193–194; Paul H. Douglas, "The Effect of Wage Increases upon Employment," *American Economic Review* 29, no. 1 (March 1939): 138–157; John T. Dunlop and Benjamin Higgins, "'Bargaining Power' and Market Structures," *Journal of Political Economy* 50, no. 1 (February 1942): 1–26; Nourse, *Price Making*, 270–274; Richard A. Lester, "Reflections on the 'Labor Monopoly' Issue," *Journal of Political Economy* 55, no. 6 (December 1947): 513–536.
99. John T. Dunlop, "Wage Policies of Trade Unions," *American Economic Review* 32, no. 1 (March 1942): 290–301; J. Shister, "The Theory of Union Wage Rigidity," *Quarterly Journal of Economics* 57, no 4 (August 1943): 522–542; Philip Taft, "Democracy in Trades Unions," *American Economic Review* 36, no. 2 (May 1946) 359–369; John T. Dunlop, "The Economics of Wage-Dispute Settlement," *Law and Contemporary Problems* 12, no. 2 (Spring 1947): 281–296; Arthur M. Ross, "The Trade Union as a Wage-Fixing Institution," *American Economic Review* 37, no. 4 (September 1947): 566–588; Arthur M. Ross, *Trade Union Wage Policy* (Berkeley: University of California Press, 1948), 99–111.
100. U.S. Council of Economic Advisers, *The Economic Report of the President: Transmitted to the Congress, January 8, 1947* (Washington, DC: Government Printing Office, 1947), 20–21.
101. U.S. Council of Economic Advisers, *Midyear Economic Report of the President: Transmitted to the Congress, July 21, 1947* (Washington, DC: Government Printing Office, 1947), 32–37.
102. Paul A. Samuelson, *Economics: An Introductory Analysis* (New York: McGraw-Hill, 1948), 409–443, 529–531 (quote on 435–436).
103. Abba P. Lerner, *Economics of Employment* (New York: McGraw-Hill, 1951), 191–241.
104. For a contemporary review of this literature, see Clark Kerr, "The Short-Run Behavior of Physical Productivity and Average Hourly Earnings," *Review of Economics and Statistics* 31, no. 4 (November 1949): 299–309.

CHAPTER 2. THE PRICE OF PEACE

1. Howell John Harris, *The Right to Manage: Industrial Relations Policies of American Business in the 1940s* (Madison: University of Wisconsin Press, 1982); Nelson Lichtenstein, *Walter Reuther: The Most Dangerous Man in Detroit* (Urbana: University of Illinois Press, 1995), 271–298; David Stebenne, *Arthur J. Goldberg:*

New Deal Liberal (New York: Oxford University Press, 1996), 45–153; Jennifer Klein, *For All These Rights: Business, Labor, and the Shaping of America's Public-Private Welfare State* (Princeton, NJ: Princeton University Press, 2003), 205–254.

2. Alfred P. Sloan Jr., "Business Trend for 1947," *Vital Speeches of the Day,* 1947, 237–241; C. E. Wilson, "Problems Industry Faces," *Vital Speeches of the Day,* 1947, 181–184; Chamber of Commerce of the United States, *Wage Determinism and the Economics of Liberalism* (Washington, DC: Chamber of Commerce of the United States, 1947), 49–100.
3. Chamber of Commerce of the United States, *Wage Determinism,* 80–81.
4. United States v. Hutcheson, 312 U.S. 219, 232 (1941).
5. Allen Bradley Co. v. Local Union No. 3, IBEW, 325 U.S. 797, 810–811 (1945). See also Archibald Cox, "Labor and the Antitrust Laws: A Preliminary Analysis," *University of Pennsylvania Law Review* 104, no. 2 (November 1955): 252–284; Bernard D. Meltzer, "Labor Unions, Collective Bargaining, and the Antitrust Laws," *Journal of Law & Economics* 6 (October 1963): 162–164.
6. James Boylan, *The New Deal Coalition and the Election of 1946* (New York: Garland, 1981).
7. 80 H.R. 3020, Pub. L. 80-101, 61 Stat. 136 (June 23, 1947); James A. Gross, *Broken Promise: The Subversion of U.S. Labor Relations Policy, 1947–1994* (Philadelphia: Temple University Press, 1995), 1–14.
8. Gross, *Broken Promise,* 32–36.
9. Herbert R. Northrup, *Boulwarism: The Labor Relations Policies of the General Electric Company: Their Implications for Public Policy and Management Action* (Ann Arbor: University of Michigan Press, 1964), 17–38.
10. Memo from Boulware, ca. late 1947, re: The next round of wage increases and what General Electric is doing about it now, F155, Box 8, Lemuel R. Boulware Papers, Ms. 52, Kislack Center, University of Pennsylvania, Philadelphia, PA. See also A. H. Raskin, "GE Making Drive to Win Employees," *New York Times,* January 18, 1948, 53; "GE Rebuffs Union on Pay Increases," *New York Times,* March 3, 1948, 15.
11. Charles E. Wilson, *The Price-Wage Spiral Can Be Stopped: A Message to General Electric Stockholders by Charles E. Wilson, President* ([New York: General Electric], 1948).
12. A. H. Raskin, "General Electric's Cut-Back in Prices Held Too Little to Affect Living Cost," *New York Times,* January 7, 1948, 1, 22.
13. "Truman Praises G.E. Price Cuts," *Baltimore Sun,* January 1, 1948, 2. Nourse is quoted in "Price Cut," *Washington Post,* January 4, 1948, B4. See also "General Electric's Price Reductions," *Los Angeles Times,* January 1, 1948, A4.
14. "No Third Round Pattern Set in Postwar Wages," *Boston Globe,* April 11, 1948, C26; "Wage Rises Pose Policy Problems," *New York Times,* February 2, 1948, 25, 27; J. A. Livingstone, "Climate's Different for Third Round," *Washington Post,* March 7, 1948, M23.
15. Benjamin Fairless, *Statement on Steel Price Reductions, April 22, 1948* (New York: U.S. Steel Corp., 1948); *U.S. Steel Annual Report—1948,* ProQuest Historical

Annual Reports, ID 88187813; see also Statement of Ben Morell, April 27, 1948, Daily Diary 1948—14, Box 5, Edwin G. Nourse Papers, 1908–1963, Harry S. Truman Library, Independence, MO. For Nourse's interpretation, see Memo, Nourse to the President, May 3, 1948, Daily Diary 1948—13, Box 5, Nourse Papers, Truman Library.

16. Report of Management Meeting, no. 4, September 1947, Management Meetings—1947, Box 1, Reports of Management Meetings 1947–1954, Acc. 422, Benson Ford Research Center, The Henry Ford, Dearborn, MI; Allan Nevins and Frank Ernest Hill, *Ford: Decline and Rebirth, 1933–1962* (New York: Charles Scribner's Sons, 1963), esp. 331–339.
17. Minutes of Industrial Relations Committee Meeting, March 26, 1948, M. L. Denise Records, Acc. 1933, Benson Ford Research Center; "Ford Union Rejects Pay Cut," *New York Times*, May 17, 1948, 1, 12.
18. Alfred P. Sloan Jr., *My Years with General Motors*, ed. John McDonald and Catharine Stevens (Garden City, NY: Doubleday, 1963), 393–394.
19. Notes of interview with Harry W. Anderson, January 18, 1955, Folder 850, Box 25, John McDonald Papers, 1890–1999, GEN Mss. 622, Beinecke Rare Book and Manuscript Library, Yale University, New Haven, CT.
20. Letter, Donaldson Brown to Charles E. Wilson, January 6, 1948, Correspondence: General Motors Corp. (10/22/46–1/20/48), Box 838, Walter S. Carpenter Jr. Business Papers, 1926–1975, Acc. 542, Hagley Museum and Library, Wilmington, DE.
21. Letter, Wilson to Sloan, January 17, 1955, Folder 878, Box 26, McDonald Papers, Beinecke Library. The hospital story and 1935 efforts can be found in Sloan, *My Years with General Motors*, 395–397.
22. Memo, S. M. Du Brul to B. D. Kunkle, April 9, 1941, re: Wage Rate Adjustments; Letter, Virgil Jordan to Sloan, April 15, 1941; Memo, Sloan to Kunkle, April 22, 1941, pp. 1–7, Folder 10 Industrial Economics Section—Cola, AIF; Report, Wage Level Adjustment, Folder 11 Industrial Economics Section 8-29, Box 6, Andrew T. Court Collection, Acc. 1299, Walter P. Reuther Library, Wayne State University, Detroit, MI.
23. Letter, Walter S. Carpenter to Albert Bradley, January 22, 1948, Correspondence General Motors 1948, Box 847, Carpenter Papers, Hagley Library.
24. Verbatim Transcript, Volume 29, May 21, 1948, United Auto Workers General Motors Department Collection, Part 2, Acc. 113, Reuther Library; Bureau of National Affairs, "GM Statement of Wage Policy: 1948," in *Collective Bargaining Negotiations and Contracts*, vol. 2, *Techniques and Trends in Bargaining* (Washington, DC: Bureau of National Affairs, 1948), 16:51–54.
25. U.S. Council on Wage and Price Stability, *Cost of Living Escalator Clauses and Inflation* (Washington, DC: Government Printing Office, 1975), 12.
26. Kathy Groehn El-Messidi, *The Bargain: The Story behind the 30-Year Honeymoon of GM and the UAW* (New York: Nellen, 1980), 59–62; Herbert S. Briggs, "1.14—Its Meaning in the GM Contract," *Conference Board Management Record* 12, no. 10 (October 1950): 375.

27. Memo, Thomas Hitch to John Davis, June 10, 1948, re: The General Motors Contract, Daily Diary 1948—28, Box 5, Nourse Papers, Truman Library.
28. Sloan, *My Years with General Motors*, 399.
29. Solomon Fabricant, *Employment in Manufacturing, 1899–1939: An Analysis of Its Relation to the Volume of Production* (New York: National Bureau of Economic Research, 1942). For instance, American Airlines would later cite Fabricant as a key reason that it adopted a 2% or 3¢ AIF in 1950 in its contract with the Transport Workers Union (CIO). Harold Stieglitz, "Annual Improvement Increases," *Conference Board Management Record* 13, no. 7 (July 1951): 238–240.
30. Notes of interview with Harry W. Anderson, January 18, 1955, Folder 850, Box 25, McDonald Papers, Beinecke Library.
31. Kathyanne Groehn El-Messidi, "Sure Principles Midst Uncertainties: The Story of the 1948 GM-UAW Contract" (PhD diss., University of Oklahoma, 1976), 88–92.
32. Proceedings of Special Session of International Executive Board, May 27–28, 1948, pp. 16–17, Box 5, United Auto Workers International Executive Board Meeting Collection, Acc. 257, Reuther Library.
33. Letter, Wilson to Carpenter, May 25, 1948, Correspondence General Motors 1948, Box 847, Carpenter Papers, Hagley Library. On Seaton's offer, see El-Messidi, "Sure Principles," 93–94.
34. UAW Press Release, May 25, 1948, Correspondence General Motors 1948, Box 847, Carpenter Papers, Hagley Library.
35. Letter, Carpenter to Wilson, May 27, 1948, Correspondence General Motors 1948, Box 847, Carpenter Papers, Hagley Library.
36. "Can GM Afford to Budget $100,000,000 a Year for Political Relations?," ca. March 1948, Folder 11 GM—Political Relations Budget, Box 8, Court Collection, Reuther Library.
37. Letter, Brown to Sloan, September 16, 1947, Correspondence: General Motors Corp. (10/22/46–1/20/48), Box 838; Letter, Brown to Bradley, July 14, 1948, Correspondence General Motors 1948, Box 847, Carpenter Papers, Hagley Library. See also *General Motors Corporation Annual Report—1948*, pp. 23–24, ProQuest Historical Annual Reports, ProQuest ID 88186391.
38. J. A. Livingston, "Wilson Denies GM-UAW Pact Means Built-In Inflation," *Washington Post*, November 22, 1950, 14.
39. U.S. Bureau of Labor Statistics, *Wage Chronology: General Motors Corp, 1939–66* (Washington, DC: Government Printing Office, 1966), 9–10; National Industrial Conference Board, *Cost of Living Provisions in Union Contracts*, Studies in Personnel Policy 113 (New York: National Industrial Conference Board, 1951), 4–10; Walter W. Ruch, "Pay and Prices Cut by General Motors," *New York Times*, February 25, 1950, 1, 8; "General Motors Cuts Passenger Car Prices $10–40," *Wall Street Journal*, February 25, 1949, 2; "General Motors Autos Get a 2d $10 to $40 Cut," *New York Herald Tribune*, May 24, 1949, 1, 26.
40. Lichtenstein, *Walter Reuther*, 279–280; Louis G. Seaton, "The Thinking behind the 1950 General Motors Agreement," in *Wage Policy and Problems in a Prepared-*

ness Economy, by American Management Association, Personnel Series 136 (New York: American Management Association, 1950), 3–10.

41. "Steel, Electrical Industry Officials Show Surprise, Disappointment over New General Motors Wage Contract," *Wall Street Journal*, May 26, 1948, 2; Charles E. Wilson, *Wages and Prices: A Message to General Electric Stockholders by Charles E. Wilson, President, July 26, 1948* (New York: General Electric, 1948).
42. M. W. Reder, "The Significance of the 1948 General Motors Agreement," *Review of Economics and Statistics* 31, no. 1 (February 1949): 7–14; Peter O. Steiner, "The Productivity Ratio: Some Analytical Limitations on Its Use," *Review of Economics and Statistics* 32, no. 4 (November 1950): 321–328; Solomon Fabricant, "Of Productivity Statistics: An Admonition," *Review of Economics and Statistics* 31, no. 4 (November 1949): 309–311; Jules Backman and A. L. Gitlow, "Automatic Annual Improvement Provisions," *Review of Economics and Statistics* 32, no. 1 (February 1950): 103–105.
43. Letter, Bradley to Sloan, January 19, 1959, re: Chapter 23 Personnel and Labor Relations, Folder 881, Box 26, McDonald Papers, Beinecke Library.
44. Negotiation Minutes, September 9, 1958, Folder 3 General Motors Department, 1958–9, Box 102, United Auto Workers (UAW) President's Office: Walter P. Reuther Collection, Acc. 261, Reuther Library. On the outcome of that year's bargaining, see Damon Stetson, "General Motors and U.A.W. Agree after a Walkout," *New York Times*, October 3, 1958, 1, 13; Lichtenstein, *Walter Reuther*, 295–298.
45. U.S. Bureau of Labor Statistics, *Wage Chronology*, 9–10. Data on earnings are taken from "Wage and Fringe Benefits per Hour Worked, General Motors Corporation," attachment to Memo, George Weaver to Nat Weinberg, September 2, 1965, re: Attached GM Wage and Fringe Cost Increase Table, UAW Fringe Benefits 1955–1968 1 of 2, Box 62, United Auto Workers (UAW) Research Department Collection, Part I, Acc. 350, Reuther Library. Straight-time and total figures are in turn reproduced from General Motors, *Sixteen Years of Progress through Collective Bargaining* (Detroit: General Motors, 1964).
46. Robert J. Gordon, *The Measurement of Durable Goods Prices* (Chicago: University of Chicago Press, 1990), 345, reproduced in Robert A. Margo, "Quality-Adjusted Price Indexes for New and Used Automobiles: 1906–1983," table Cc63-65 in *Historical Statistics of the United States: Earliest Times to the Present: Millennial Edition*, ed. Susan B. Carter, Scott Sigmund Gartner, Michael R. Haines, Alan L. Olmstead, Richard Sutch, and Gavin Wright (New York: Cambridge University Press, 2006).
47. Gavin Wright, "Indexes of National Productivity, by Sector and Type of Good: 1947–2000," table Cg281-291 in Carter et al., *Historical Statistics*; Christopher Hanes, "Wholesale and Producer Price Indexes, by Commodity Group: 1890–1997," table Cc66-83 in Carter et al., *Historical Statistics*; Margo, "Quality-Adjusted Price Indexes."
48. Memo, Maurice Tobin to the President, May 25, 1950, re: Comments on the

General Motors–United Automobile Workers Five-Year Contract, Labor General, Box 138, President's Secretary's File, Truman Library.

49. U.S. Council on Wage and Price Stability, *Cost of Living Escalator Clauses and Inflation*, 12; Sanford M. Jacoby, "The Development of Cost-of-Living Escalators in the United States," *Labor History* 28, no. 4 (1987): 526–529.

50. Nevins and Hill, *Ford*, 317–345.

51. John Loftus, "General Motors' Pay Pledge Linked to 4th Round View," *New York Times*, November 19, 1948, 24.

52. Minutes of Industrial Relations Subcommittee Meeting, September 12, 1949; Minutes of Industrial Relations Committee Meeting, September 13, 1949; Minutes of Industrial Relations Committee Meeting, September 14, 1949, Box 1, Denise Records, Benson Ford Research Center.

53. Hugh Rockoff, *Drastic Measures: A History of Wage and Price Controls in the United States* (Cambridge: Cambridge University Press, 1984), 177–199; Paul G. Pierpaoli Jr., *Truman and Korea: The Political Culture of the Early Cold War* (Colombia: University of Missouri Press, 1999).

54. Proceedings of Regular Session of Internal Executive Board, September 11–15, 1950, pp. 11–21, Box 7, United Auto Workers International Executive Board Meeting Collection, Reuther Library.

55. Minutes of Industrial Relations Subcommittee Meeting, August 25, 1950; Minutes of Industrial Relations Subcommittee Meeting, August 30, 1950, Box 1, Denise Records, Benson Ford Research Center. See also James Bambrick, "Trends in Labor Relations," *Conference Board Management Record* 12, no. 9 (September 1950): 339–341.

56. U.S. Office of Price Stabilization, "Ceiling Price Regulation 1—New Passenger Automobiles," December 18, 1950, 1–12, in *Ceiling Price Regulation*, vol. 1 (Washington, DC: Government Printing Office, 1950–1953); U.S. Office of Price Stabilization, "Wage Stabilization Regulation 1—New Passenger Automobiles," December 22, 1950, in *Miscellaneous Orders and Regulations* (Washington, DC: Government Printing Office, 1951–1952), Harvard Law School Library, Cambridge, MA. On Reuther's intervention, see Proceedings of Regular Session of International Executive Board, January 30–February 2, 1951, pp. 16–24, Box 8, United Auto Workers International Executive Board Meeting Collection, Reuther Library.

57. Letter, Carpenter to Sloan, January 18, 1951, Correspondence—General Motors, 1951; "Plan for Industrial Mobilization," January 1951, Correspondence—General Motors 1952, Box 847, Carpenter Papers, Hagley Library. See also the dissent of GM and Ford to a statement by the Committee for Economic Development rejecting the AIF on grounds that productivity should be passed entirely to consumers: Committee for Economic Development, *Price and Wage Controls* (New York: CED, 1951), 33.

58. Natalie Friedman, "Wage Picture—Second Half of 1950," *Conference Board Management Record* 13, no. 2 (February 1951): 57–60; U.S. Council on Wage and Price Stability, *Cost of Living Escalator Clauses and Inflation*, 12.

59. Meeting of the International Executive Board, CIO, August 29, 1950, in *Minutes of the Executive Board of the Congress of Industrial Organizations, 1935–1955*, ed. Robert H. Zieger (Bethesda, MD: University Publications of America, 1991), 183–190, microfilm edition, reel 14.
60. "Contract Settlement Announcements—Nov. 15 to Dec. 15," *Conference Board Management Report* 13, no. 1 (January 1951): 44–45. On competition within the CIO, see Robert H. Zieger, *The CIO: 1935–1955* (Chapel Hill: University of North Carolina Press, 1995), 300–301.
61. American Management Association, "Long-Range Implications of Present-Day Labor Issues: A Panel Session," in *Spotlighting the Labor-Management Scene*, Personnel Series 147 (New York: American Management Association, 1952), 41.
62. Conference with Wage Stabilization Board, January 10, 1951, Wage Stabilization Board—2, Box 146, Series VII, National Association of Manufacturers Records, 1895–2013, Acc. 1411, Hagley Library.
63. U.S. Office of Price Stabilization, "General Wage Regulation 6," February 27, 1951, 1–2, in *Miscellaneous Orders and Regulations;* Jack Stieber, "Labor's Walkout from the Korean War Wage Stabilization Board," *Labor History* 21, no. 2 (Spring 1980): 239–260.
64. Bureau of National Affairs, "General Regulation No. 6—Administrative Interpretations," in *Wage and Salary Stabilization Handbook . . . in Effect December 6, 1951* (Washington, DC: Bureau of National Affairs, [1951]), 135–136; on fringe benefits, see U.S. Wage Stabilization Board, *Health, Welfare and Pension Programs under Wage Stabilization: Report to the Wage Stabilization Board* (Washington, DC: Government Printing Office, 1951), 2; U.S. Wage Stabilization Board, *A Report on Wage Stabilization* (Washington, DC: Government Printing Office, 1951), 10; Bureau of National Affairs, "General Regulation No. 8: Cost-of-Living Escalator Clauses," in *Wage and Salary Stabilization Handbook*, 134–137; Stieber, "Labor's Walkout," 259.
65. Herbert Northrup, "From Special Case to General Policy," *Conference Board Management Report* 13, no. 11 (November 1951): 382–384. See also Arthur M. Ross, "Productivity and Wage Control," *Industrial and Labor Relations Review* 7, no. 2 (January 1954): 177–191.
66. Harold Stieglitz, "Annual Improvement Increases," *Conference Board Management Record* 13, no. 7 (July 1951): 266–268.
67. Memo, Boulware to Ralph Cordiner, July 3, 1951, Folder 164, Box 8; Letter, Boulware to James Carey, March 6, 1952; Letter, Boulware to Malcolm Denise, March 10, 1952, Box 57, Boulware Papers, Kislack Center.
68. United Steelworkers of America, Presented in the Matter of United Steelworkers of America and Various Steel and Iron Ore Companies, Case No. D-18-c (1952), 54–58; U.S. Wage Stabilization Board, *Report and Recommendations of the Wage Stabilization Board, in the Matter of United Steelworkers of America–CIO and Various Steel and Iron Ore Companies, Case no. D-18-C*, p. 3, Wage Stabilization Board Steel Dispute—1952, Box 2038, Lukens Steel Company Records, Acc. 50, Hagley Library; *Statement by Benjamin F. Fairless, President, United States Steel*

Corporation, before the Wage Stabilization Board, New York, N.Y., February 4, 1952 (New York: U.S. Steel, 1952), 16.

69. U.S. Wage Stabilization Board, *Report and Recommendations,* pp. 28–31.
70. Memo, Arthur J. Goldberg to Charles Murphy, March 25, 1952, re: Recommendations of the Wage Stabilization Board in the Steel Dispute, Steel Strike—March 1952, Box 32, Charles S. Murphy Files, Truman Library.
71. Memo, Harold Enarson to John Steelman, February 15, 1952, re: Shape of Things to Come in the Steel Wage Dispute, Steel Negotiations Memos, 1951–52, Box 5, Harold L. Enarson Papers, 1940–1945, Truman Library.
72. Memorandum of Discussions between Messrs. Fairless, Murray and Steelman, May 3, 1952, Steel Strike, 1952, Box 10, David H. Stowe Papers, Truman Library.
73. U.S. Office of Price Stabilization, "Ceiling Price Regulation 22—Manufacturers' General Ceiling Price Regulation," April 25, 1951, 1–16, in *Ceiling Price Regulation,* vol. 2 (Washington, DC: Government Printing Office, 1950–1953), Harvard Law School Library. A second regulation, CPR 30, applied essentially the same formula for machinery producers but made provision for a wider range of production costs: U.S. Office of Price Stabilization, "CPR 30—Machinery and Related Manufactured Goods," May 4, 1951, in *Ceiling Price Regulation,* vol. 3 (Washington, DC: Government Printing Office, 1950–1953), Harvard Law School Library. Automakers remained under CPR 1 but in September 1951 received the ability to adjust up to new cutoffs: U.S. Office of Price Stabilization, "GPR 673," July 10, 1951; "GPR 857," September 14, 1951; "GPR 864," September 19, 1951, in *OPS Press Releases—GPR,* vol. 2 (Washington, DC: Government Printing Office, 1951–1953), Harvard Law School Library; U.S. Office of Price Stabilization, "Ceiling Price Regulation 1, Revision 1—New Passenger Automobiles," September 7, 1951, 1, in *Ceiling Price Regulation,* vol. 1.
74. U.S. Office of Price Stabilization, "GPR 1343," March 31, 1952, in *OPS Press Releases—GPR,* vol. 3 (Washington, DC: Government Printing Office, 1951–1953), Harvard Law School Library.
75. U.S. Office of Price Stabilization, "GPR 1380," April 16, 1952, 18–20, in *OPS Press Releases—GPR,* vol. 3; U.S. Office of Price Stabilization, *The People's Stake: Stabilization and Steel Prices* (Washington, DC: Government Printing Office, 1952), 3–8.
76. *Youngstown Sheet & Tube v.* Sawyer, 343 U.S. 579 (1952); Maeva Marcus, *Truman and the Steel Seizure Case: The Limits of Presidential Power* (New York: Columbia University Press, 1977), 73–74, 79–80. On the price adjustment, see U.S. Office of Price Stabilization, "GPR 1547," July 28, 1952, in *OPS Press Releases—GPR,* vol. 3; U.S. Office of Price Stabilization, "Steel Special Order 1—Adjustable Pricing Order for Steel Mill Products," July 30, 1952, in *Miscellaneous Orders and Regulations;* U.S. Office of Price Stabilization, "Supplemental Regulation 100, GCPR Rev. 1," August 19, 1952, in *General Ceiling Price Regulation* (Washington, DC: Government Printing Office, 1951–1953), Harvard Law School Library.
77. U.S. Office of Price Stabilization, "GPR 1218," February 11, 1952; "GPR 1219," February 10, 1952, in *OPS Press Releases—GPR,* vol. 3; U.S. Office of Price

Stabilization, *Price Stabilization, October 1951 to September 1952, Summary of Operations* (Washington, DC: Government Printing Office, 1952), 10.

78. Herbert Stein, *The Fiscal Revolution in America: Policy in Pursuit of Reality,* 2nd rev. ed (Washington, DC: AEI Press, 1996), 286–289; Alan H. Meltzer, *A History of the Federal Reserve,* vol. 2, bk. 1, *1951–1969* (Chicago: University of Chicago Press, 2009), 102–105; U.S. Office of Price Stabilization, *Price Stabilization to April 1953* (Washington, DC: Government Printing Office, 1953), 7–9.
79. Joseph W. Garbarino, *Wage Policy and Long-Term Contracts* (Washington, DC: Brookings Institution, 1962), 73–111; Joseph W. Garbarino, "Bargaining Strategy and the Form of Contracts," *Industrial Relations* 1, no. 2 (February 1962): 79–80.
80. Bureau of National Affairs, *Basic Patterns in Union Contracts,* vol. 15 (Washington, DC: Bureau of National Affairs, 1954), 75–76; Bureau of National Affairs, *Basic Patterns in Union Contracts,* vol. 36 (Washington, DC: Bureau of National Affairs, 1961), 1–2.
81. Lily Mary David and Donald L. Helm, "Deferred Wage Increases in 1957 and Wage Escalator Clauses," *Monthly Labor Review* 80 (January 1957): 50–52.
82. National Industrial Conference Board, *Preparing for Collective Bargaining* (New York: National Industrial Conference Board, 1959), 74–81.
83. H. M. Douty, "Post-War Bargaining in the United States," *Economica,* n.s., 23, no. 92 (November 1956): 326; Yung-Ping Chen, "Fringe Benefits Growth and Social Security," *Monthly Labor Review,* November 1981, 3–10.
84. U.S. Chamber of Commerce, *Fringe Benefits: 1957* (Washington, DC: Chamber of Commerce, 1958); U.S. Chamber of Commerce, *Employee Benefits Historical Data: 1951–1979* (Washington, DC: Chamber of Commerce, 1981).
85. For a review of this literature, see W. R. McIntyre, *Fringe Benefits,* vol. 2 of *Editorial Research Reports 1959* (Washington, DC: CQ Press, 1959), http://library.cqpress.com/cqresearcher/cqresrre1959081900.
86. Bureau of National Affairs, "Steel Board Wage Dispute Recommendations: 1949," in *Collective Bargaining Negotiations and Contracts,* vol. 2, *Techniques and Trends in Bargaining* (Washington, DC: Bureau of National Affairs, 1949), 15:521–577.
87. M. A. Themer, "General Wage Issues for 1955, Presentation to Industrial Relations Committee," January 17, 1955, Industrial Relations Committee Meeting Minutes, January 17, 1955, Box 1, Denise Records, Benson Ford Research Center (quotes on pp. 7, 10). For more on this critique, see Jules Backman, "Wage-Productivity Comparisons," *Industrial and Labor Relations Review* 8, no. 1 (October 1954): 59–67. On Ford's logic, see Memo, Andrew Court to S. M. DuBrul, January 6, 1955, re: The Automobile Outlook for 1955, Folder 5-7 Curtice Letters Forecasts, Box 5, Court Collection, Reuther Library; Nevins and Hill, *Ford,* 406–426.
88. Northrup, *Boulwarism,* 51–69; Division Managers Meeting Report, November 17, 1954; Directors' Meeting Notes, December 17, 1954; Opening Remarks by Mr. Boulware, Folder 170, Box 8, Boulware Papers, Kislack Center. For the later evaluation, see "What about Pay Increases Which Starve Recovery and Feed

Inflation," *Public and Employee Relations News,* May 19, 1958, Folder 198, Box 10, Boulware Papers, Kislack Center.

89. Hill and Knowlton Release: Background Information: The Steel-Labor Negotiations of 1956, July 1956, Folder 18, Box 72, United Steelworkers of America (USWA) Research Department Records, 1921–1981, HCLA 1965, Historical Collections and Labor Archives, Special Collections Library, Pennsylvania State University, State College, PA.
90. NLRB v. Truck Drivers Local Union No. 449, 353 U.S. 87, 94–96 (1957).
91. R. Conrad Cooper, "Productivity in the Steel Producing Subsidiaries of United States Steel," in *Company Testimony before Presidential Factfinding Board Steel Industry Case, August 1949,* by Steel Wage Case Steering Committee, vol. 3 ([Washington, DC], 1950), 1499–1542.
92. "Progress Report Regarding Development of a Measure and Index of Productivity," May 8, 1956, Box 3, R. Conrad Cooper Papers, AIS 91.1, Archives Service Center, University of Pittsburgh, Pittsburgh, PA; R. Conrad Cooper, "Productivity in United States Steel," in *Administered Prices: Part 3, Steel (and Appendix A),* by U.S. Senate, Committee on the Judiciary, Subcommittee on Antitrust and Monopoly, 85th Cong., 1st Sess. (Washington, DC: Government Printing Office, 1958), 1131–1138.
93. Coordinating Committee Progress Report to the General Administration Committee, August 23, 1956; Memo, Cooper to Clifford Hood, September 10, 1956; Memorandum, July 17, 1956; Memorandum, October 12, 1956, Unmarked Folder (Remarks, comments, statements, statistics), Box 3, Cooper Papers, Archives Service Center, University of Pittsburgh.
94. Facts on Steel: Profits, Productivity, Prices, and Wages, esp. pp. 28–31; Economic Facts and the Steelworkers' Proposals, 1956, pp. 8–10, Folder 15, Box 105; Memo, Research Department to McDonald, May 23, 1956, re: Survey of Certain "Fringe" Benefits, Folder 2, Box 214, USWA President's Office Records, 1916–1980, HCLA 1961, Historical Collections and Labor Archives, Special Collections Library, Pennsylvania State University.
95. Statement by David McDonald, June 24, 1956, Folder 4; Meeting with Company Representatives, June 6, 1956, June 13, 1956, June 15, 1956, Folder 9, Box 214, USWA President's Office Records, Pennsylvania State University; Circular from David McDonald, June 14, 1957, re: Policy Concerning Inclusion of Cost-of-Living Escalator Clauses in New Contracts, Folder 18, Box 72, USWA Research Department Records, Pennsylvania State University.
96. Memo, Clarence D. Long to the Council of Economic Advisers, Labor-Steel Strike of 1956 (1), Box 111, Arthur F. Burns Papers, 1928–1969, Dwight D. Eisenhower Presidential Library, Abilene, KS; Paul A. Tiffany, *The Decline of American Steel: How Management, Labor, and Government Went Wrong* (New York: Oxford University Press, 1988), 147–152.
97. U.S. Bureau of Labor Statistics, "Nonfarm Business Sector: Unit Labor Cost (ULCNFB)," FRED, Federal Reserve Bank of St. Louis, accessed June 18, 2020, https://fred.stlouisfed.org/series/ULCNFB; U.S. Bureau of Labor Statistics,

"Nonfarm Business Sector: Real Compensation per Hour (COMPRNFB)," FRED, Federal Reserve Bank of St. Louis, accessed June 18, 2020, https://fred.stlouisfed.org/series/COMPRNFB; U.S. Bureau of Labor Statistics, "Nonfarm Business Sector: Compensation per Hour (COMPNFB)," FRED, Federal Reserve Bank of St. Louis, accessed June 18, 2020, https://fred.stlouisfed.org/series/COMPNFB.

98. Charles L. Schultze, *Recent Inflation in the United States,* 86th Cong., 1st Sess., Joint Committee Print, Study Paper no. 1 (Washington, DC: Government Printing Office, 1959); Sumner Slichter, "Argument for 'Creeping' Inflation, *New York Times Magazine,* March 8, 1959, 87–90.

CHAPTER 3. CORPORATE PRICING AND THE PUBLIC INTEREST

1. Christina D. Romer and David H. Romer, "A Rehabilitation of Monetary Policy in the 1950's," *American Economic Review* 92, no. 2 (May 2002): 121–127.
2. Robert Leeson, "The Political Economy of the Inflation-Unemployment Trade-Off," *History of Political Economy* 29, no. 1 (1997): 117–156; Daniel J. B. Mitchell and Christopher L. Erickson, "The Concept of Wage-Push Inflation: Development and Policy," *Labor History* 49, no. 4 (November 2008): 417–438; Norikazu Takami, "The Baffling New Inflation: How Cost-Push Inflation Theories Influenced Policy Debate in the Late-1950s United States," *History of Political Economy* 47, no. 4 (December 2015): 605–629.
3. Kim McQuaid, *Big Business and Presidential Power: From FDR to Reagan* (New York: William Morrow, 1982), 169–198; Raymond J. Saulnier, *Constructive Years: The U.S. Economy under Eisenhower* (Lanham, MD: University Press of America, 1991); William M. McClenahan Jr. and William H. Becker, *Eisenhower and the Cold War Economy* (Baltimore: Johns Hopkins University Press, 2011).
4. U.S. Senate, Committee on the Judiciary, Subcommittee on Antitrust and Monopoly, *Administered Prices: Part 1: Opening Phase: Economists' Views,* 85th Cong., 1st Sess. (Washington, DC: Government Printing Office, 1958), 87–90, 124–125.
5. George J. Stigler, "Administered Prices and Oligopolistic Inflation," *Journal of Business* 35, no. 1 (January 1962): 2–5, 11–12; Richard T. Selden, "Cost-Push versus Demand-Pull Inflation, 1955–57," *Journal of Political Economy* 67, no. 1 (February 1959): 1–20.
6. Charles L. Schultze, *Recent Inflation in the United States,* 86th Cong., 1st Sess., Joint Committee Print, Study Paper no. 1 (Washington, DC: Government Printing Office, 1959), 102–103, 120.
7. Schultze, *Recent Inflation,* 69–70, 132–134; Arthur F. Burns, *Prosperity without Inflation* (New York: Fordham University Press, 1957); Sumner Slichter, "Thinking Ahead," *Harvard Business Review,* September–October 1957, 15–16, 21–22, 26–36, 162–170; Sumner H. Slichter, "We Have Little to Fear," *Rotarian,* November 1957, 9, 50–53; Alfred Kuhn, "Market Structures and Wage-Push Inflation," *ILR Review* 12, no. 2 (January 1959): 243–251.
8. U.S. Council on Wage and Price Stability, *A Study of Steel Prices* (Washington, DC: Government Printing Office, 1975), 6–9.

9. U.S. Senate, Committee on the Judiciary, Subcommittee on Antitrust and Monopoly, *Administered Prices: Part 2*, 85th Cong., 1st Sess. (Washington, DC: Government Printing Office, 1958), 204.
10. U.S. Senate, *Administered Prices, Part 2*, 242–252.
11. U.S. Senate, *Steel Imports: Staff Study of the Committee on Finance, United States Senate*, 90th Cong., 2nd Sess., Document 107 (Washington, DC: U.S. Government Printing Office, 1968), 166.
12. Gardiner C. Means, *Pricing Power and the Public Interest: A Study Based on Steel* (New York: Harper and Brothers, 1962), 65–150. For the overall statistics, see "Labor Department Background Statistics on Steel Strike," *Washington Post*, August 20, 1959, A8.
13. U.S. Senate, *Administered Prices: Part 2*, 250–252; Thomas Diamond, "This New Round of Steel Expansion," *Harvard Business Review* 34, no. 3 (1956): 85–93; Paul A. Tiffany, *The Decline of American Steel: How Management, Labor, and Government Went Wrong* (New York: Oxford University Press, 1988), 83–102, 128–152.
14. Benjamin F. Fairless, "Steel's Depreciation Problem," in *Year Book of the American Iron and Steel Institute: 1956* (New York: American Iron and Steel Institute, 1956), 44–45.
15. U.S. Senate, *Steel Imports: Staff Study*, 420; U.S. Senate, *Administered Prices: Part 2*, 248–252, 259–260.
16. M. A. Adelman, "Steel, Administered Prices and Inflation," *Quarterly Journal of Economics* 75, no. 1 (February 1961): 16–40.
17. U.S. Senate, *Steel Imports: Staff Study*, 138–139. See also "Labor Department Background Statistics," A8.
18. U.S. Senate, *Administered Prices: Part 2*, 312–315.
19. U.S. Senate, *Administered Prices, Part* 2, 601–602, 621–623, 631–632.
20. A. D. H. Kaplan, Joel B. Dirlam, and Robert F. Lanzillotti, *Pricing in Big Business: A Case Approach* (Washington, DC: Brookings Institution, 1958).
21. Robert F. Lanzillotti, "Pricing Objectives in Large Companies," *American Economic Review* 48, no. 5 (December 1958): 924–927.
22. Lanzillotti, 929, 933; Donaldson Brown, "Pricing Policy in Relation to Financial Control," *Management and Administration* 7, no. 3 (1924): 283–286.
23. Lanzillotti, "Pricing Objectives," 937–938; Kaplan, Dirlam, and Lanzillotti, *Pricing in Big Business*, 127–130, 269–272; John M. Blair, "Administered Prices and Oligopolistic Inflation: A Reply," *Journal of Business* 37, no. 1 (January 1964): 81; John Kenneth Galbraith, *The New Industrial State*, 4th ed. (Boston: Houghton Mifflin, 1985).
24. Kaplan, Dirlam, and Lanzillotti, *Pricing in Big Business*, 49–54.
25. Kaplan, Dirlam, and Lanzillotti, 14–18; Lanzillotti, "Pricing Objectives," 932.
26. Kaplan, Dirlam, and Lanzillotti, *Pricing in Big Business*, 204–205; Lanzillotti, "Pricing Objectives," 939–940.
27. Lanzillotti, "Pricing Objectives," 923n4; Alfred E. Kahn, "Pricing Objectives in Large Companies: Comment," *American Economic Review* 49, no. 4 (September 1959): 670–678.

28. George J. Stigler, "Administered Prices and Oligopolistic Inflation," *Journal of Business* 35, no. 1 (January 1962): 5–8.
29. Price Statistics Review Committee, *The Price Statistics of the Federal Government* (New York: National Bureau of Economic Research, 1961); Stigler, "Administered Prices," 8–9; George J. Stigler and James K. Kindahl, *The Behavior of Industrial Prices* (New York: National Bureau of Economic Research, 1970), 8–9, 71–74. For an explanation of the steel industry's behavior based on more conventional means of collusion, see George J. Stigler, "A Theory of Oligopoly," *Journal of Political Economy* 72, no. 1 (February 1964):44–61; George J. Stigler, "The Economic Effects of the Antitrust Laws," *Journal of Law and Economics* 9 (October 1966): 225–258; Richard A. Posner, "Oligopoly and the Antitrust Laws: A Suggested Approach," *Stanford Law Review* 21 (June 1969): 1587n66.
30. Daniel Scroop, "A Faded Passion? Estes Kefauver and the Senate Subcommittee on Antitrust and Monopoly," *Business and Economic History On-Line* 5 (2007): 5–9; Robert Bud, "Antibiotics, Big Business, and Consumers: The Context of Government Investigations into the Postwar American Drug Industry," *Technology and Culture* 46, no. 2 (April 2005): 334–338.
31. U.S. Senate, *Administered Prices: Part 1*, 2–3.
32. U.S. Senate, *Administered Prices, Part 1*, 3.
33. Neil Fligstein, *The Transformation of Corporate Control* (Cambridge, MA: Harvard University Press, 1990), 160–225; Rudolph J. R. Peritz, *Competition Policy in America, 1888–1992: History, Rhetoric, Law* (New York: Oxford University Press, 1996), 197–199.
34. United States v. Bethlehem Steel Corporation, 168 F. Supp. 576, 585–587, 616 (S.D.N.Y. 1958).
35. Bethlehem Steel, 168 F. Supp. at 604–607.
36. John Herling, *The Great Price Conspiracy: The Story of the Antitrust Violations in the Electrical Industry* (Washington, DC: Robert B. Luce, 1962); U.S. Senate, Committee on the Judiciary, Subcommittee on Antitrust and Monopoly, *Administered Prices: Part 13: Identical Bidding (TVA)*, 86th Cong., 1st Sess. (Washington, DC: Government Printing Office, 1960); U.S. Senate, Committee on the Judiciary, Subcommittee on Antitrust and Monopoly, *Administered Prices: Part 27: Price Fixing and Bid Rigging in the Electrical Manufacturing Industry*, 87th Cong., 1st Sess. (Washington, DC: Government Printing Office, 1961); U.S. Senate, Committee on the Judiciary, Subcommittee on Antitrust and Monopoly, *Administered Prices: Part 28: Price Fixing and Bid Rigging in the Electrical Manufacturing Industry*, 87th Cong., 1st Sess. (Washington, DC: Government Printing Office, 1961).
37. For contemporary overviews of this challenge, see Eugene V. Rostow, "The New Sherman Act: A Positive Instrument of Progress," *University of Chicago Law Review* 14, no. 4 (June 1947): 568–573; Edward S. Mason, *Economic Concentration and the Monopoly Problem* (Cambridge, MA: Harvard University Press, 1957), 1–53, 371–388.
38. United States v. Aluminum Co. of America (Alcoa), 148 F.2d 416, 429–432 (2d Cir. 1945). See also Rostow, "New Sherman Act," 576–579.

39. George David Smith, *From Monopoly to Competition: The Transformation of Alcoa, 1888–1986* (Cambridge: Cambridge University Press, 1988), 189–250, 274–285, 316–320.
40. Alcoa, 148 F.2d at 424.
41. American Tobacco Co. v. United States, 328 U.S. 781, 789–790, 798–804 (1946).
42. American Tobacco, 328 U.S. at 804–806.
43. See Posner, "Oligopoly and the Antitrust Laws," 1584–1587. More conventional views of the tobacco industry's behavior can be found in Rostow, "New Sherman Act," 580–583; William H. Nicholls, "The Tobacco Case of 1946," *American Economic Review* 39, no. 3 (May 1949): 284–296; Carl Kaysen, "Collusion under the Sherman Act," *Quarterly Journal of Economics* 65, no. 2 (May 1951): 263–270; Jesse W. Markham, "The Nature and Significance of Price Leadership," *American Economic Review* 41, no. 5 (December 1951): 891–905; Donald F. Turner, "The Definition of Agreement under the Sherman Act: Conscious Parallelism and Refusals to Deal," *Harvard Law Review* 75, no. 4 (February 1962): 660–662.
44. American Tobacco, 328 U.S. at 809–15.
45. American Tobacco, 328 U.S. at 783.
46. FTC v. Cement Institute, 333 U.S. 683, 715–716, 715 n.17 (1948).
47. U.S. Senate, Committee on the Judiciary, Subcommittee on Antitrust and Monopoly, *Administered Prices: Part 8: 1958 Steel Price Increase,* 85th Cong., 2nd Sess. (Washington, DC: Government Printing Office, 1959), 4374–4375.
48. U.S. Senate, Committee on the Judiciary, Subcommittee on Antitrust and Monopoly, *Administered Prices: Steel,* Report no. 1387, 85th Cong., 2nd Sess. (Washington, DC: Government Printing Office, 1958), 119–120.
49. U.S. Senate, Committee on the Judiciary, Subcommittee on Antitrust and Monopoly, *Administered Prices: Automobiles,* 85th Cong., 2nd Sess. (Washington, DC: Government Printing Office, 1958), 168–182.
50. Milgram v. Loew's, Inc., 192 F.2d 579 (3rd Cir. 1951); *cert. denied,* 343 U.S. 929 (1952).
51. Pevely Dairy Co. v. United States, 178 F.2d 363, 367–369 (8th Cir. 1949); *cert. denied,* 339 U.S. 942 (1950).
52. Theatre Enterprises v. Paramount Distributing, 346 U.S. 537, 541–542 (1954).
53. Turner, "Definition of Agreement," 657–678. See also Louis B. Schwartz, "Administered Prices, Oligopoly and the Sherman Act," *A.B.A. Antitrust Section* 7 (1958): 24–25; Michael J. Doyle, "Conspiracy: Evidentiary Value of Conscious Parallelism," *Marquette Law Review* 45, no. 4 (Spring 1962): 633–636; U.S. Senate, Committee on the Judiciary, Subcommittee on Antitrust and Monopoly, *Administered Prices: A Compendium on Public Policy,* 88th Cong., 1st Sess. (Washington, DC: Government Printing Office, 1963), 178–180; Michael D. Blechman, "Conscious Parallelism, Signaling and Facilitating Devices: The Problem of Tacit Collusion under the Antitrust Laws," *New York Law School Law Review* 24 (1979): 885–887.
54. Carl Kaysen and Donald F. Turner, *Antitrust Policy: An Economic and Legal Analysis* (Cambridge, MA: Harvard University Press, 1959).

55. U.S. Attorney General's National Committee to Study the Antitrust Laws, "Report of the Attorney General's National Committee to Study the Antitrust Laws," *Journal of Reprints for Antitrust Law and Economics*, 1980, 51–54.
56. U.S. Senate, *Administered Prices: Part 8*, 4377–4379, 4387–4388, 4391. The Department of Justice would test the theory that public price announcements served as communications in the 1970s but failed to establish this principle in cases involving the auto and electrical-equipment industries: Blechman, "Conscious Parallelism," 889–809.
57. U.S. Senate, *Administered Prices: Part 1*, 119.
58. U.S. Senate, *Administered Prices: Part 1*, 38.
59. U.S. Congress, Joint Economic Committee, *Economic Policy Questionnaire: Tabulation of Replies Submitted to the Subcommittee on Economic Stabilization*, 85th Cong., 2nd Sess. (Washington, DC: Government Printing Office, 1959).
60. For Kefauver's bill, see U.S. Senate, Committee on Government Operations, *Establish a Department of Consumers*, 86th Cong., 2nd Sess. (Washington, DC: Government Printing Office, 1960).
61. U.S. Senate, Committee on the Judiciary, Subcommittee on Antitrust and Monopoly, *Administered Prices: Part 11: Price Notification Legislation*, 86th Cong., 1st Sess. (Washington, DC: Government Printing Office, 1959), 5183–5185.
62. U.S. Senate, *Administered Prices: Part 11*, 5708–5710.
63. U.S. Senate, *Administered Prices: Part 11*, 5612–5614.
64. Telegram, Estes Kefauver to the President, May 22, 1958, Box 480, OF 114 Economics 1958 (11), White House Central Files, Dwight D. Eisenhower Presidential Library, Abilene, KS.
65. Telegram, Kefauver to the President, August 2, 1958; Letter, President to Kefauver, August 14, 1958, Box 480, OF 114 Economics 1958 (11), White House Central Files, Eisenhower Library.
66. Diary Entry, January 16, 1956, Jan 56 Diary, Box 12, DDE Diary Series, Eisenhower Library.
67. Diary Entry, February 13, 1956, Diary—Copies of DDE Personal [1955–1956] (1), Box 9, DDE Diary Series, Eisenhower Library.
68. Letter, President to Bernard Baruch, March 10, 1953, Box 3, DDE Diary Dec. 52–July 53 (3), DDE Diary Series, Eisenhower Library.
69. Dwight D. Eisenhower, "Annual Message to the Congress on the State of the Union," January 10, 1957, in *The American Presidency Project*, ed. Gerhard Peters and John T. Woolley, https://www.presidency.ucsb.edu/node/233260.
70. U.S. Council of Economic Advisers, *Economic Report of the President, Transmitted to the Congress: January 1957* (Washington, DC: Government Printing Office, 1957), iv, 3, 40–44.
71. RJS Notes re: FRB Luncheon April 30, 1957, May 3,1957, Federal Reserve Board, Chairman, Conference with, 1957–1960, Box 7, Raymond J. Saulnier Papers, 1938–1986, Eisenhower Library.
72. Robert P. Bremner, *Chairman of the Fed: William McChesney Martin Jr. and the*

Creation of the Modern American Financial System (New Haven, CT: Yale University Press, 2004), 120–148.

73. For defenses of Eisenhower's position, see Neil H. Jacoby, "Thinking Ahead," *Harvard Business Review*, May–June 1957, 15–16, 20–24, 28–30, 32, 160–162; Peter L. Bernstein, "Is Long-Term Inflation Inevitable?," *Harvard Business Review* 35, no. 4 (1957): 51–57; George L. Bach, "Inflation in Perspective," *Harvard Business Review* 36, no. 1 (1958): 99–110; Henry Hazlitt, *What You Should Know about Inflation*, 2nd ed. (Princeton, NJ: D. Van Nostrand, 1960); Gottfried Haberler, *Inflation: Its Causes and Cures* (Washington, DC: American Enterprise Association, 1960).

CHAPTER 4. MANAGEMENT'S NEW LOOK

1. Herbert R. Northrup, "Management's 'New Look' in Labor Relations," *Industrial Relations* 1, no. 1 (October 1961): 9–24.
2. David Stebenne, *Arthur J. Goldberg: New Deal Liberal* (New York: Oxford University Press, 1996), 120–232; Jack Metzgar, *Striking Steel: Solidarity Remembered* (Philadelphia: Temple University Press, 2000).
3. Paul A. Tiffany, *The Decline of American Steel: How Management, Labor, and Government Went Wrong* (New York: Oxford University Press, 1988), 153–166; James D. Rose, "The Struggle over Management Rights at US Steel, 1946–1960: A Reassessment of Section 2-B of the Collective Bargaining Contract," *Business History Review* 72, no. 3 (Autumn 1998): 446–477.
4. Memo, Lemuel Boulware to George L. Beaver, February 21, 1958, Box 66, Lemuel R. Boulware Papers, 1917–1990, Ms. Coll. 52, Kislack Center, University of Pennsylvania, Philadelphia, PA.
5. Memo, Boulware to Ralph Cordiner, September 2, 1955, Box 62, Boulware Papers, Kislack Center.
6. Letter, Boulware to Allan B. Kline, October 8, 1956, Box 64, Boulware Papers, Kislack Center.
7. For a text of the speech, see "Wages' Role in Inflation Discussed," *New York Herald Tribune*, December 9, 1956, K3, 18.
8. Letter, Boulware to Lewis H. Haney, January 11, 1957; Letter, Boulware to Paul McCracken, January 31, 1957; Letter, Boulware to Frank Rising, February 20, 1957; Letter, Boulware to F. L. Headley, March 22, 1957, Box 65, Boulware Papers, Kislack Center.
9. Memo, Boulware to Hoyt Steele, April 2, 1959; Letter, Boulware to J. M. Larkin, April 29, 1959; Letter, Boulware to Guy Waterman, September 25, 1959, Box 68, Boulware Papers, Kislack Center.
10. Letter, Boulware to Eugene Rossides, February 24, 1959, Box 67, Boulware Papers, Kislack Center.
11. Notes on talk by Reuben Robertson, May 10, 1952, Business Advisory Council, Box 4, John W. Snyder Papers, 1918–1980, Harry S. Truman Library, Independence, MO; Telegram, Reuben Robertson to Crawford Greenewalt, June 14,

1952, Industrial Relations, 1952–1954, Box 10, Crawford H. Greenewalt Papers, 1928–1968, Acc. 1814, Hagley Museum and Library, Wilmington, DE.

12. Letter, Robertson to Greenewalt, November 30, 1953; Letter, Greenewalt to H. W. Ward, December 8, 1953, Employee Relations—Employers' Labor Relations Information Committee, 1953–7, Box 9, Greenewalt Papers, Hagley Library.
13. Memo, Boulware to Cordiner, June 8, 1954, re: ELRIC Meeting (and Steel); Letter, Boulware to Robertson, February 26, 1954, Box 60; Memo, Boulware to Cordiner, April 20, 1956, Box 63, Boulware Papers, Kislack Center.
14. Employers' Labor Relations Information Committee, Fifth Annual Report of the President, 1958, Employee Relations—Employers' Labor Relations Information Committee, 1958, Box 9; Letter, L. F. McCollum to Greenewalt, June 5, 1959, Employee Relations—Employers' Labor Relations Information Committee, 1959, Box 9, Greenewalt Papers, Hagley Library.
15. American Management Association, "Meeting the Cost/Quality Challenge: A Top Management Symposium," in *Ends and Means of Modern Management,* AMA Management Report no. 30 (New York: American Management Association, 1959), 72–122; Richard A. Beaumont, *Productivity and Policy Decisions* (New York: Industrial Relations Counselors, 1959); American Management Association, Personnel Division, "Productivity Forum," in *Meeting the Productivity Challenge,* AMA Management Report no. 40 (New York: American Management Association, 1960), 45–53.
16. Memo, Boulware to C. E. St. Thomas, March 7, 1957, Box 65; Letter, Boulware to Ray Vicker, August 24, 1959, Box 68; "What about Pay Increases Which Starve Recovery and Feed Inflation," *Public and Employee Relations News,* May 19, 1958, Folder 198, Box 10, Boulware Papers, Kislack Center; "Wages' Role in Inflation Discussed," *New York Herald Tribune,* December 9, 1956, K3, 18.
17. Letter, G. G. Mitchell to E. F. du Pont, February 27, 1959, Employee Relations—Employers' Labor Relations Information Committee, 1959, Box 9, Greenewalt Papers, Hagley Library.
18. U.S. Bureau of Economic Analysis, "Shares of Gross Domestic Product: Imports of Goods and Services (B021RE1Q156NBEA)," FRED, Federal Reserve Bank of St. Louis, accessed June 18, 2020, https://fred.stlouisfed.org/series/B021RE1Q156NBEA.
19. "Year-End Review of Freedom's Old but New Problem of Better Defense or Better Living or Both!," *Public and Employee Relations News,* December 31, 1957, Folder 188, Box 9, Boulware Papers, Kislack Center; Walter H. Wiewel, "What's Behind the Rise in Foreign Competition," in *The Business Man in Politics,* by American Management Association, AMA Management Report no. 37 (New York: American Management Association, 1959), 84–92; William M. Allen, "Business, Politics and Survival," in *Ends and Means of Modern Management,* by American Management Association, AMA Management Report no. 30 (New York: American Management Association, 1959), 19–25; Lloyd Ulman, "Collective Bargaining and Inflation," *California Management Review,* Spring 1960, 51–58.

20. Simon Kuznets, *National Product since 1869* (New York: National Bureau of Economic Research, 1946); Warren Nutter, *Growth of Industrial Production in the Soviet Union* (Princeton, NJ: Princeton University Press, 1962); Alexander Gerschenkron, *Economic Backwardness in Historical Perspective: A Book of Essays* (Cambridge, MA: Harvard University Press, 1962); W. W. Rostow, *The Stages of Economic Growth: A Non-Communist Manifesto,* 2nd ed. (Cambridge: Cambridge University Press, 1971); Solomon Fabricant, "Perspective on Productivity Research," *Review of Income and Wealth* 20, no. 3 (September 1974): 235–249.
21. Andrew Shonfield, *Modern Capitalism: The Changing Balance of Public and Private Power* (London: Oxford University Press, 1965). For a more recent interpretation of the institutional underpinnings of western and eastern European growth, see Barry Eichengreen, *The European Economy since 1945: Coordinated Capitalism and Beyond* (Princeton, NJ: Princeton University Press, 2007), 15–51.
22. See, for instance, the early familiarity of the United Auto Workers with Kendrick: Memo, Dennis Purnell to Nat Weinberg March 18, 1952, re: National Productivity, Productivity 1956–60 2 of 2, Box 58, United Auto Workers (UAW) Research Department Collection, Part I, Acc. 350, Walter P. Reuther Library, Wayne State University, Detroit, MI.
23. John W. Kendrick, "National Productivity and Its Long-Term Projection," in *Long-Range Economic Projection* (Princeton, NJ: Princeton University Press, 1954), 67–104, http://www.nber.org/chapters/c2931. The original paper from May 1951 is available at http://digitalassets.lib.berkeley.edu/irle/ucb/text/lb001933.pdf.
24. National Association of Manufacturers, *Productivity: Gauge of Economic Performance* (New York: NAM, 1952); National Association of Manufacturers, *Labor's Share in the Proceeds of Production* (New York: NAM, 1953); M. A. Themer, "General Wage Issues for 1955, Presentation to Industrial Relations Committee," January 17, 1955, Industrial Relations Committee Meeting Minutes, January 17, 1955, Box 1, M. L. Denise Records, 1946–1955, Acc. 1933, Benson Ford Research Center, The Henry Ford, Dearborn, MI.
25. According to Sloan's stream-of-consciousness dictation from 1954, "To have a broader understanding of these economic factors of the labor contract a grant was made to the bureau of economics or something like that, an economic research organization in New York to study the thing from a research point of view. That's been going on for about a year and we should try in this story to get what we can and some months from now ought to be a good deal available data that they have developed on this very subject. In order to see what background and what validity there is in the contract as it now stands with General Motors particularly the impact of that contract on the American economy as a whole." Dictation on Labor Relations, 115-b and 116-b, Folder 898, Box 27, John McDonald Papers, 1890–1999, GEN Mss. 622, Beinecke Rare Book and Manuscript Library, Yale University, New Haven, CT. Kendrick was identified as the recipient of this funding in a letter by GM chairman Emeritus Albert Bradley for use in Sloan's memoirs: "Professor John Kendrick arrives at a long-term productivity

factor of 1.9%. This is based on a tremendous amount of work done by the National Director of Economic Research, under a grant from the Sloan Foundation, bringing up to date figures on wages and productivity." Letter, Albert Bradley to Alfred Sloan, January 19, 1959, re: Chapter 23 Personnel and Labor Relations, F 881, Box 26, McDonald Papers, Beinecke Library.

26. John W. Kendrick, "Productivity, Costs and Prices: Concepts and Measures," in *Wages Prices Profits and Productivity*, by American Assembly (New York: Columbia University Press, 1959), 37–59; John W. Kendrick, "How Good Is the Productivity Record?," in *Year Book of the American Iron and Steel Institute: 1959*, by American Iron and Steel Institute (New York: American Iron and Steel Institute, 1959) 189–212.
27. John W. Kendrick and Daniel Creamer, *Measuring Company Productivity: Handbook with Case Studies* (New York: Conference Board, 1965).
28. John W. Kendrick, *Productivity Trends in the United States* (Princeton, NJ: Princeton University Press, 1961), esp. 60, 70–72, 118–126, available at http://www.nber.org/chapters/c2239.pdf, http://www.nber.org/chapters/c2241.pdf.
29. John W. Kendrick, "The Wage-Productivity-Price Issue," *California Management Review* 2, no. 3 (Spring 1960): 42–50.
30. Memo, Stanley Ruttenberg to all AFL-CIO Research Directors, July 6, 1960, Productivity Measures—BLS Seminar, October 4, 1960, Box 58, UAW Research Department Collection, Part I, Reuther Library.
31. Memo, Nat Goldfinger to Woodrow Ginsburg, June 27, 1958, Productivity Unit of Total Factor Input, Box 73; Memo, Harry Chester to Nat Weinberg, November 19, 1959, re: Notes on Kendrick's Total Factor Productivity Index; Memo, Harry Chester to W. L. Ginsburg, April 27, 1960, re: Total Factor Productivity; Memo, Harry Chester to W. L. Ginsburg, April 29, 1960, re: How Our Economy Is Working; Harry Chester, Wages and Productivity—The Customary Approach, October 26, 1960, Productivity 1956–60 1 of 2; Minutes of the Seminar on Productivity for the Labor Research Advisory Council, October 6, 1960, Productivity Measures—BLS Seminar, October 4, 1960, Box 58, UAW Research Department Collection, Part I, Reuther Library.
32. Northrup, "New Look," 10; Comments on IUE's Statements Relating to Wages and Productivity, September 16, 1960, Memos, 1960–61, Box 27, Francis E. Highton Papers, 1948–1976, AIS 1991.02, Archives Service Center, University of Pittsburgh, Pittsburgh, PA.
33. Kendrick, "Wage-Productivity-Price Issue," 45–46.
34. Kendrick and Creamer, *Measuring Company Productivity*, 59–101.
35. Letter, C. F. Hood to Greenewalt, April 18, 1958; Letter, Hood to Greenewalt, March 18, 1958; Letter, Henry Ford II to Greenewalt, March 28, 1960, Employee Relations, General 1953–1966, Box 6, Greenewalt Papers, Hagley Library. On the spread of this presentation, see Memo, Employee Relations Department to Executive Committee, February 13, 1959, re: Employee Relations Department Annual Report—1958; Memo, Employee Relations Department to Executive Committee, February 12, 1960, re: Employee Relations Department Annual

Report—1959; Memo, Employee Relations Department to Executive Committee, February 10, 1961, re: Employee Relations Department Annual Report—1960, Annual Reports to Executive Committee (1958–1959), Box 1, DuPont Human Resources Records, Acc. 1615, Hagley Library.

36. Bernard Rogers and Roger Fulton, "The Measure of Productivity—A Challenge to Management," in *The 32nd NAM Institute on Industrial Relations, March 14–18, 1960*, pp. 73–76, Hagley Library.

37. Ralph J. Cordiner, "For Members of the ELRIC Board: Observations on the Usefulness of Productivity in Establishing Compensation Levels," Employee Relations—Employers' Labor Relations Information Committee, 1960–1961, Box 9, Greenewalt Papers, Hagley Library.

38. Letter, Highton to Arthur S. Thornbury, December 19, 1960; Highton Memo, re: Letter on Wage Policy from Arthur S. Thornbury, December 23, 1960, Memos, 1960–61, Box 27, Highton Papers, Archives Service Center, University of Pittsburgh.

39. Highton's statements can be found in the files marked "A Competitive Wage Guidepost, 1964" and "1966 Guideposts: Reference Materials" in Box 24 of his papers, as well as "The Guideposts for Noninflationary Wage Increases," 1963 Negotiations, Presentation to IUE on Productivity, Profits & Wages, Box 11, Highton Papers, Archives Service Center, University of Pittsburgh. Among his final publications on this issue is Frank E. Highton, "The Pay Board and Productivity Bargaining," *Personnel* 50, no. 1 (January–February 1973): 8–20.

40. Boulware Memorandum, December 1958, Folder 196, Box 10; Letter, Boulware to Guy Waterman, April 9, 1956, Box 63; Letter, Boulware to Leslie Gould, February 5, 1959, Box 67, Boulware Papers, Kislack Center.

41. Gilbert J. Gall, *The Politics of Right to Work* (Westport, CT: Greenwood, 1988); Glenn W. Miller and Stephen B. Ware, "Organization Labor in the Political Process: A Case Study of the Right-to-Work Campaign in Ohio," *Labor History* 4, no. 1 (1963): 51–67.

42. James A. Gross, *Broken Promise: The Subversion of U.S. Labor Relations Policy, 1947–1994* (Philadelphia: Temple University Press, 1995), 92–144.

43. Letter, Boulware to Harrison M. Terrell, February 20, 1954, Box 60, Boulware Papers, Kislack Center.

44. Herbert R. Northrup, *Boulwarism: The Labor Relations Policies of the General Electric Company: Their Implications for Public Policy and Management Action* (Ann Arbor: University of Michigan Press, 1964); Lemuel R. Boulware, *The Truth about Boulwarism: Trying to Do Right Voluntarily* (Washington, DC: Bureau of National Affairs, 1969).

45. Memo, Highton to J. S. Parker, October 12, 1960, Memos, 1960–61, Box 27; Report, "Pricing the Proposal"; J. S. Parker, "Opening Comments," June 20, 1960, Exec Office Presentation, 1960 Proposal, Box 28, Highton Papers, Archives Service Center, University of Pittsburgh.

46. General Electric Co., 150 NLRB 192, 215–218, 216 n.14, 224–226 (1964).

47. General Electric Co., 150 NLRB at 225 & n.27.

48. General Electric Co., 150 NLRB at 193–196, 226–228, 232.
49. General Electric Co., 150 NLRB at 228–229.
50. Archibald Cox, "The Duty to Bargain in Good Faith," *Harvard Law Review* 71, no. 8 (June 1958): 1401–1442; "'Boulwareism': Legality and Effect," *Harvard Law Review* 76, no. 4 (February 1963): 816–817; Andrew F. Shea, "Labor Law—Labor Management Relations Act—Section 8(a)(5)—Refusal of Employer to Bargain in Good Faith—General Elec. Co & International Union of Elec. Workers, AFL-CIO," *Boston College Law Review* 6, no. 4 (1965): 949–957.
51. General Electric Co., 150 NLRB at 193–196, 232. GE's legal philosophy is also discussed in Herbert R. Northrup, "The Case for Boulwarism," *Harvard Business Review* 41 (September–October 1963): 86–97; Northrup, *Boulwarism*, 107–120; "Boulwareism," 812; Richard C. Cooper, "Boulwarism and the Duty to Bargain in Good Faith," *Rutgers Law Review* 20, no. 4 (Summer 1966): 659–666.
52. Northrup, "Case for Boulwarism," 91–92.
53. General Electric Co., 150 NLRB at 250–253; Northrup, *Boulwarism*, 71–90.
54. Memo, Boulware to Cordiner, November 16, 1960, Box 69, Boulware Papers, Kislack Center.
55. U.S. Council of Economic Advisers, *Economic Report of the President: Transmitted to the Congress, January 1962* (Washington, DC: Government Printing Office, 1962), 177–178.
56. M. A. Adelman, "Steel, Administered Prices and Inflation," *Quarterly Journal of Economics* 75, no. 1 (February 1961): 23; American Iron and Steel Institute, *Steel's Competitive Challenge* (New York: American Iron and Steel Institute, 1961), 14, 34.
57. American Iron and Steel Institute, Committee on Foreign Relations, *Foreign Trade Trends Iron and Steel, 1960 Edition* (New York: American Iron and Steel Institute, 1960), 40.
58. Adelman, "Steel, Administered Prices and Inflation," 16–40; Lawrence B. Krause, "Import Discipline: The Case of the United States Steel Industry," *Journal of Industrial Economics* 11, no. 1 (November 1962): 33–47; Walter Adams and Joel B. Dirlam, "Steel Imports and Vertical Oligopoly Power," *American Economic Review* 54, no. 5 (September 1964): 626–655.
59. R. L. Gray, "Bid for Survival," in *Year Book of American Iron and Steel Institute: 1958*, by American Iron and Steel Institute (New York: American Iron and Steel Institute, 1958), 69–79; Benjamin F. Fairless, "Facing Up to Competition," in American Iron and Steel Institute, *Year Book of American Iron and Steel Institute: 1959*, 146–147.
60. American Iron and Steel Institute, *Steel's Competitive Challenge*, 15.
61. Memo, James A. Stephens, "1956 and Future Steel Negotiations," February 4, 1957, Industry Bargaining, Confidential File, August 1956–September 1958, Folder 1 of 2; Memo, Thomas Patton to John H. Morse, January 4, 1957, Confidential File, August 1956–September 1958, Folder 2 of 2, Box 72, Republic Steel Corporation Records, 1895–2001, MS. 4949, Western Reserve Historical Society (WRHS), Cleveland, OH.

62. Memo, R. C. Hoquist to Virgil Day, February 5, 1957, Folder 184, Box 9, Boulware Papers, Kislack Center.
63. Minutes, June 26, 1959, Industry Bargaining, Confidential File, Oct. 1958–June 1960, 4 of 4, Box 72, Republic Steel Records, WRHS.
64. Letter, Boulware to Phelps H. Adams, July 15, 1959, Box 68, Boulware Papers, Kislack Center.
65. Coordinating Committee Progress Report to the General Administration Committee, August 23, 1956; Memo, R. Conrad Cooper to Hood, September 10, 1956; Memorandum, July 18, 1956; Memorandum, October 16, 1956, Unmarked Folder, Box 3, R. Conrad Cooper Papers, AIS 91.1, Archives Service Center, University of Pittsburgh.
66. Memo, R. H. Larry to the Coordinating Committee, July 30, 1958, Industry Bargaining, Confidential File, August 1956–September 1958, Folder 2 of 2, Box 72, Republic Steel Records, WRHS.
67. Memo, E. J. Magee to Thomas Patton and H. C. Lumb, September 8, 1958, Industry Bargaining, Confidential File, August 1956–September 1958, Folder 2 of 2, Box 72, Republic Steel Records, WRHS.
68. American Iron and Steel Institute, *Economic Trends in the Iron and Steel Industry* (New York: American Iron and Steel Institute, 1959).
69. Report of the 1959 Negotiating Team to the Chief Executives, June 24, 1960, Folder, Industry Bargaining, Confidential File, Oct. 1958–June 1960, Folder 1 of 4, Box 72, Republic Steel Records, WRHS.
70. Memo, Coordinating Committee Negotiating Team to David McDonald, April 10, 1959, Basic Agreement, Republic Steel Corp. and USWA, Correspondence file, 1959 (Folder 2 of 2), Box 52, Republic Steel Records, WRHS. See also A. H. Raskin, "Steel Union Asks Freeze on Prices," *New York Times*, April 14, 1959, 1, 28; A. H. Raskin, "Steel Men Favor Pay-Price Freeze," *New York Times*, April 15, 1959, 1, 22; "Steel Union Continues to Reject Proposals It Forego Wage Hike," *Wall Street Journal*, April 28, 1959, 26.
71. Minutes, May 14, 1959; Minutes, May 15, 1959; Industry Bargaining, Confidential File, Oct. 1958–June 1960, Folder 4 of 4, Box 72, Republic Steel Records, WRHS.
72. 1959 Proposals of the United Steelworkers of America, Folder 3; Long-Term Employment Trends in the Basic Steel Industry, May 6, 1956; Opening Remarks of David J. McDonald, May 5, 1959; McDonald Memo, May 8, 1959, Folder 4, Box 94, United Steelworkers of America (USWA) President's Office Records, 1916–1980, HCLA 1961, Historical Collections and Labor Archives, Special Collections Library, Pennsylvania State University, State College, PA.
73. Economic Summary in Support of 1959 Wage Policy, Folder 19 Economic Summary, Box 105, USWA President's Office Records, Pennsylvania State University. A detailed discussion of the union's distinction between real and nominal variables is in Memo, Otis Brubaker, etc., to David McDonald, etc., May 19, 1959, re: Rebuttal Comments to "Economic Trends in the Iron and Steel Industry," Folder 18, Box 22, United Steelworkers of America (USWA) Research Department

Records, 1921–1981, HCLA 1965, Historical Collections and Labor Archives, Special Collections Library, Pennsylvania State University. The 1958–1959 comparison is found in Statement of International Wage Policy Committee, June 25, 1959, Folder 5, Box 94, USWA President's Office Records, Pennsylvania State University.

74. Minutes, May 15, 1959, Industry Bargaining, Confidential File, Oct. 1958–June 1960, Folder 4 of 4, Box 72, Republic Steel Records, WRHS. The first dedicated BLS report on postwar output per man-hour, which made heavy use of Kendrick's man-hour data, was released in December 1959 and showed a 3.1% annual increase in total private real product per man-hour for 1947–1958 and a 2.4% rate in the nonagricultural sector and 2.3% and 2.0% increases, respectively, for 1909–1958. U.S. Bureau of Labor Statistics, *Trends in Output per Man-Hour in the Private Economy, 1909–1958* (Washington, DC: Government Printing Office, 1959).
75. Minutes, May 14, 1959; Progress Report Regarding 1959 Collective Bargaining, June 15, 1959, Industry Bargaining, Confidential File, Oct. 1958–June 1960, Folder 4 of 4, Box 72, Republic Steel Records, WRHS.
76. Memo, Proposed Position, May 27, 1959, Industry Bargaining, Confidential File, Oct. 1958–June 1960, Folder 4 of 4; Memorandum, September 26, 1959, Industry Bargaining, Confidential File, Oct. 1958–June 1960, Folder 3 of 4, Box 72, Republic Steel Records, WRHS.
77. Statement by David McDonald, June 10, 1959; Letter, McDonald to Coordinating Committee, June 11, 1959; "Statement of International Wage Policy Committee, June 12, 1959; Letter, McDonald to Coordinating Committee, June 23, 1959, Folder 5, Box 94, USWA President's Office Records, Pennsylvania State University.
78. Minutes, Monday, July 20, 1959, Industry Bargaining, Confidential File, Oct. 1958–June 1960, Folder 3 of 4, Box 72, Republic Steel Records, WRHS.
79. Memorandum of Joint Meeting, July 13, 1959, Industry Bargaining, Confidential File, Oct. 1958–June 1960, Folder 3 of 4; Minutes, June 26, 1959; Cooper Statement in the Negotiating Meeting of July 2, 1959, Industry Bargaining, Confidential File, Oct. 1958–June 1960, Folder 4 of 4, Box 72, Republic Steel Records, WRHS.
80. Northrup, "New Look," 9.
81. Minutes, June 26, 1959, Industry Bargaining, Confidential File, Oct. 1958–June 1960, Folder 2 of 4, Box 72, Republic Steel Records, WRHS.
82. Union Proposals to Companies, June 24, 1959, Industry Bargaining, Confidential File, Oct. 1958–June 1960, Folder 2 of 4, Box 72, Republic Steel Records, WRHS. For costs, see Memo, J. Louis Irwin to Members of Management Committee, July 14, 1959, Industrial Relations 1958–1960, Box 2021, Lukens Steel Company Records, Acc. 50, Hagley Library.
83. U.S. Department of Labor, Bureau of Labor Statistics, *Background Statistics on the Steel Dispute* (Washington, DC: Government Printing Office, 1959), items 9–14.
84. Steel Industry Review of Background Statistics Bearing on the Steel Dispute,

U.S. Department of Labor Exhibit 9, Folder, 10, Box 73, USWA Research Department Records, Pennsylvania State University.

85. U.S. Board of Inquiry to Report on a Labor Dispute Affecting the Steel Industry, *Report to the President in the 1959 Labor Dispute in the Steel Industry, Submitted by the Board of Inquiry under Executive Orders 10843 and 10848, October 19, 1959* (Washington, DC: Government Printing Office, 1959).

86. An Economic Documentation of the Steelworkers' Position in the 1959 Steel Strike, October 1959, Folder 12, Box 73; United Steelworkers of America, Fact-Finding in the Steel Dispute: The Meaning of the Mitchell Report, September 1959, Folder 5, Box 74, USWA Research Department Records, Pennsylvania State University; Memo, McDonald to Coordinating Committee, October 4 1959, Folder 8, Box 96, USWA President's Office Records, Pennsylvania State University.

87. Call Log, January 2, 1960, Telephone Calls January 1960; Minutes of Cabinet Meeting, January 6, 1960, Staff Notes—January 1960 (2), Box 47, DDE Diary Series; Letter, Richard Nixon to Alexander Jones, January 21, 1960, OF 124—D Strikes, Steel Strikes (7), Box 540, White House Central Files, Official File, 1953–1961, Dwight D. Eisenhower Presidential Library, Abilene, KS.

88. Metzgar, *Striking Steel,* 81.

89. Report of the 1959 Negotiating Team to the Chief Executives, June 24, 1960, Folder, Industry Bargaining, Confidential File, Oct. 1958–June 1960, Folder 1 of 4, Box 72; Letter, Cooper to Mitchell, January 6, 1960; Press Release, January 9, 1960, Basic Agreement, Republic Steel Corp. and USWA, Correspondence file, 1960–1961, Box 52, Republic Steel Records, WRHS; R Conrad Cooper, "The Problem," in *Year Book of American Iron and Steel Institute: 1960,* by American Iron and Steel Institute (New York: American Iron and Steel Institute, 1960), 217–222; Roger Blough, "Aftermath in Steel," January 18, 1960, OF 124—D Strikes, Steel Strikes (7), Box 540, White House Central Files, Eisenhower Library.

90. Summary Report of Activities of the Human Relations Research Committee, February 17, 1962, Folder 13, Box 79, USWA Research Department Records, Pennsylvania State University. See also John A. Orr, "The Rise and Fall of Steel's Human Relations Committee," *Labor History* 14, no. 1 (1973): 69–82.

91. Memo, Otis Brubaker to David McDonald, etc., August 4, 1960, re: First Progress Report; Memo, Otis Brubaker to David McDonald, etc., November 15, 1960, re: Third Progress (?) Report; Memo, Otis Brubaker to David McDonald, etc., February 3, 1961, re: Fourth Progress Report; Memo, Otis Brubaker to David McDonald, etc., June 5, 1961, re: Fifth Progress Report; Memo, Frank Pollara to Members of the Economic Guides Subcommittee, November 17, 1961, re: Meeting with Don Pease; Memo, Otis Brubaker to David McDonald, etc., January 29, 1962, re: Ninth Progress Report; Joint Interim Report, January 22, 1962, Folder 13, Box 79; Notes on Status of "Economic Guides" Research, January 17, 1962, Folder 16, Box 79, USWA Research Department Records, Pennsylvania State University.

92. Memo, Otis Brubaker to David McDonald, etc., August 4, 1960, re: First Progress Report, Folder 13, Box 79, USWA Research Department Records, Pennsylvania State University.
93. National Industrial Conference Board, *The Kaiser–Steel Union Sharing Plan* (New York: National Industrial Conference Board, 1963); U.S. Department of Labor, Bureau of Labor Statistics, *Improving Productivity: Labor and Management Approaches* (Washington, DC: Government Printing Office, 1971), 20–21.
94. U.S. Department of Labor, Bureau of Labor Statistics, *Improving Productivity,* 20–21.
95. By the early 1980s, the plan had ultimately ended up becoming a cost burden to the company: Donna K. Walters, "How the Former Kaiser Companies Have Fared: Steel," *Los Angeles Times,* August 4, 1985.
96. U.S. Council of Economic Advisers. *Economic Report of the President; Transmitted to the Congress, January 1961* (Washington, DC: Government Printing Office, 1961), 58–59.

CHAPTER 5. ASSUMING DIRECT CONTROL

1. Robert M. Collins, *The Business Response to Keynes, 1929–1964* (New York: Columbia University Press, 1981); Cathie J. Martin, *Shifting the Burden: The Struggle over Growth and Corporate Taxation* (Chicago: University of Chicago Press, 1991); Herbert Stein, *The Fiscal Revolution in America: Policy in Pursuit of Reality,* 2nd rev. ed. (Washington, DC: AEI Press, 1996); Robert M. Collins, *More: The Politics of Growth in Postwar America* (Oxford: Oxford University Press, 2000); Michael A. Bernstein, *A Perilous Progress: Economists and Public Purpose in Twentieth-Century America* (Princeton, NJ: Princeton University Press, 2004).
2. Grant McConnell, *Steel and the Presidency: 1962* (New York: Norton, 1963); George J. McManus, *The Inside Story of Steel Wages and Prices, 1959–1967* (New York: Chilton, 1967). The steel showdown sometimes receives credit for encouraging Kennedy to embark on the Fiscal Revolution, but the developments of the wage-price guideposts are generally reduced to a misguided side project: Kim McQuaid, *Big Business and Presidential Power: From FDR to Reagan* (New York: William Morrow, 1982), 199–222; Irving Bernstein, *Promises Kept: John F. Kennedy's New Frontier* (Oxford: Oxford University Press, 1991), 140–146, 372–453; Herb Stein, *Presidential Economics: The Making of Economic Policy from Roosevelt to Clinton,* 3rd rev. ed. (Washington, DC: American Enterprise Institute, 1994), 104–106; Arthur M. Schlesinger Jr., *A Thousand Days: John F. Kennedy in the White House* (New York: Houghton Mifflin, 2002), 630–636.
3. Joseph A. Califano Jr., *The Triumph and Tragedy of Lyndon Johnson: The White House Years* (New York: Simon and Schuster, 1990).
4. John Sheahan, *The Wage-Price Guideposts* (Washington, DC: Brookings Institution, 1967); William J. Barber, "The Kennedy Years: Purposeful Pedagogy," in *Exhortation and Controls: The Search for a Wage-Price Policy, 1945–1971,* ed. Craufurd D. Goodwin (Washington, DC: Brookings Institution, 1975), 159–191; and

James L. Cochrane, "The Johnson Administration: Moral Suasion Goes to War," in Goodwin, *Exhortation and Controls,* 193–292.

5. The classic argument in favor of a causal role is George L. Perry, "Wages and the Guideposts," *American Economic Review* 57, no. 4 (September 1967): 897–904. A significant but minuscule effect on prices is described in Arthur J. Alexander, "Prices and the Guideposts: The Effects of Government Persuasion on Individual Prices," *Review of Economics and Statistics* 53, no. 1 (February 1971): 67–75. Later studies have criticized these approaches for failing to account for changes in structural unemployment and inflationary expectations: Robert J. Gordon, "Wage-Price Controls and the Shifting Phillips Curve," *Brookings Papers on Economic Activity* 2 (1972): 385–421. Sidney Weintraub notes that Perry had overlooked another potential causal factor that could explain why wages grew slower in the early 1960s than in the 1950s: Jimmy Hoffa was still in jail. Sidney Weintraub, "Incomes Policy: Completing the Stabilization Triangle," *Journal of Economic Issues* 6, no. 4 (December 1972): 105–122.
6. Robert P. Bremner, *Chairman of the Fed: William McChesney Martin Jr. and the Creation of the Modern American Financial System* (New Haven, CT: Yale University Press, 2004), 186–259; Allan H. Meltzer, *A History of the Federal Reserve,* vol. 2, book 1, *1959–1969* (Chicago: University of Chicago Press, 2009), 480–557.
7. A. W. Phillips, "The Relation between Unemployment and the Rate of Change of Money Wage Rates in the United Kingdom, 1861–1957," *Economica,* n.s., 25, no. 100 (November 1958): 283–299; Alan Bollard, *A Few Hares to Chase: The Economic Life and Times of Bill Phillips* (Oxford: Oxford University Press, 2016), 159–182.
8. Abba P. Lerner, "Employment Theory and Employment Policy," *American Economic Review* 57, no. 2 (May 1967): 1–18.
9. Paul A. Samuelson and Robert M. Solow, "Analytical Aspects of Anti-inflation Policy," *American Economic Review* 50, no. 2 (May 1960): 177–194. Solow describes the drafting of the article and his intellectual debt to Phillips in Robert M. Solow, John B. Taylor, and N. Gregory Mankiw, "Fifty Years of the Phillips Curve: A Dialog on What We Have Learned," in *Understanding Inflation and the Implications for Monetary Policy: A Phillips Curve Retrospective,* ed. Jeff Fuhrer, Yoland K. Kodrzycki, Jane Sneddon Little, and Giovanni P. Olivei (Cambridge, MA: MIT Press, 2009), 71–96.
10. Samuelson and Solow, "Analytical Aspects," 189–193.
11. Samuelson and Solow, 194.
12. Arthur F. Burns and Paul A. Samuelson, *Full Employment, Guideposts, and Economic Stability* (Washington, DC: American Enterprise Institute, 1967), 53–56.
13. Paul Samuelson, Prospects and Policies for the 1961 American Economy: A Report to President-Elect Kennedy, January 6, 1961, p. 23, Recovery Program 12/60–1/61, Box 20, Walter W. Heller Personal Papers, #103, John F. Kennedy Presidential Library, Boston, MA.

14. Memo, Walter Heller to Solow, February 20, 1961, The Heller Council 2/61–3/61, Box 3, Heller Papers, Kennedy Library.
15. David Stebenne, *Arthur J. Goldberg: New Deal Liberal* (New York: Oxford Unimittee on Labor-Management Policy," *Review of Social Economy* 19, no. 2 (September 1961): 114–132.
16. Notes on Meeting of Advisory Committee on Labor-Management Policy, 10/16–17/61 and Its Subcommittee No. 5, Sound Wages and Price Policies, Labor Management Advisory Committee 4 of 5, Box 36, Kermit Gordon Personal Papers, #86, Kennedy Library. On Goldberg's selection process, see Stebenne, *Arthur J. Goldberg*, 256–257.
17. Free and Responsible Collective Bargaining and Industrial Peace, August 4, 1961; Report by Consultants to Subcommittee No. 4, Policies Designed to Ensure That American Products Are Competitive in World Markets, Labor-Management Advisory Committee 3 of 5, Box 36, Gordon Papers, Kennedy Library; Lloyd Ulman, Notes on Meeting of Advisory Committee on Labor-Management Policy, 10/16–17/61, Subcommittee No. 5, Sound Wage and Price Policies, Wage-Price Guideposts 2/61–12/61, Box 24, Heller Papers, Kennedy Library.
18. Jack Stieber, "The President's Committee on Labor-Management Policy," *Industrial Relations* 5, no. 2 (February 1966): 15.
19. Membership List of Subcommittees, Labor Management Advisory Committee 5 of 5, Box 36, Gordon Papers, Kennedy Library.
20. Memo to the Subcommittee on Sound Wage and Price Policies, August 4, 1961, Labor Management Advisory Committee 4 of 5, Box 36, Gordon Papers, Kennedy Library.
21. For other labor and management squabbles, see Additional Comments of Labor Consultants in re August 4 Draft of Consultants Memo to Subcommittee, August 11, 1961, Labor Management Advisory Committee, 3 of 5; Memo, Joseph L. Block to George Taylor, ca. August 1961; David McDonald, Economic Guides for Responsible Collective Bargaining, July 10, 1961, Labor Management Advisory Committee 4 of 5, Box 36, Gordon Papers, Kennedy Library; Comments by Henry Ford II on Report of Subcommittee No. 5, Sound Wage and Price Policies, November 20, 1961, Wage-Price Guideposts 1/62–9/62, Box 24, Heller Papers, Kennedy Library.
22. Statement on Sound Wage and Price Policies, November 3, 1961, Labor Management Advisory Committee 4 of 5, Box 36, Gordon Papers, Kennedy Library.
23. Memo, Heller to the President, July 10, 1961, re: Meeting of the President's Labor-Management Advisory Committee, Wage-Price Guideposts 2/61–12/61, Box 24, Heller Papers, Kennedy Library.
24. Minutes, Economic Advisers Meeting, June 13, 1961, The Heller Council 5/61–6/61, Box 3, Heller Papers, Kennedy Library. For Kennedy's charge to the CEA and the Federal Reserve's attitudes toward wage-price policy, see Memo, Kermit Gordon to the Files, June 12, 1961, re: Notes on Meeting with the President on Monetary Policy; Memo, Tobin to the Files, August 28, 1961, re: Meeting with

Chairman Martin and the President on August 25th, Meetings with JFK 1961, Box 6, Heller Papers, Kennedy Library. At a luncheon meeting in late May 1961, Martin had informed Heller that he doubted that economic expansion was possible without generating demand-pull inflation, but he also expressed his concerns that the downturn of the late 1950s had resulted from "distortion of the cost and price structure owing to continuing cost push." Memo, James Tobin for the Record, May 30, 1961, re: Luncheon Conversation with Chairman William McC. Martin, Monetary Policy 3/61–5/61, Box 19, Heller Papers, Kennedy Library.

25. Memo, Heller to the President, August 2, 1961, re: The Price Situation in General (and Steel in Particular), Steel 5/61–12/61, Box 21, Heller Papers, Kennedy Library.
26. American Iron and Steel Institute, *Steel's Competitive Challenge* (New York: American Iron and Steel Institute, 1961), 23; American Iron and Steel Institute, *Foreign Trade Trends Iron and Steel, 1962 Edition* (New York: American Iron and Steel Institute, 1962), 42. On the cash-flow deficit, see U.S. Senate, Committee on Finance, *Steel Imports: Staff Study,* 90th Cong., 2d Sess., Document 107 (Washington, DC: Government Printing Office, 1968), 420–422.
27. Notes of Meeting, June 21, 1961, Meetings with JFK 1961, Box 6, Heller Papers, Kennedy Library.
28. Circular, President to Steel Executives, September 7, 1961, Council of Economic Advisers (CEA), September 1961, Box 73, President's Office Files, Kennedy Library.
29. Roger M. Blough, *The Washington Embrace of Business* (New York: Columbia University Press, 1975), 77–78.
30. Memo, Heller to the President, October 13, 1961, Memos to JFK 10/4/61–10/16/61, Box 5, Heller Papers, Kennedy Library; Walter Heller, "The Economic Future and Government Policy," Remarks before the American Life Convention, Chicago, IL, October 13, 1961; Walter Heller, "Prices, Wages, and the Public Interest," Remarks before the Business Council, Hot Springs, VA, October 20, 1961, Council of Economic Advisers (CEA), October 1961, Box 73, President's Office Files, Kennedy Library.
31. Lloyd Ulman, "Unions, Economists, Politicians, and Incomes Policy," in *Economics in the Public Service: Papers in Honor of Walter W. Heller,* ed. Joseph A. Pechman and Walter W. Heller (New York: Norton, 1982), 112.
32. U.S. Council of Economic Advisers, *Economic Report of the President, Transmitted to the Congress, January 1962* (Washington, DC: Government Printing Office, 1962), 167–169, 185–190.
33. David Cole, R. Conrad Cooper, George P. Hitchings, Raymond Saulnier, Robert Solow, and Leonard Woodcock, "The Wage-Price Guideposts," *Conference Board Business Management Record* 25, no. 5 (May 1963): 22–31.
34. "1960 Union Negotiations," Box 26; Memo from Francis Highton, February 6, 1962, re: "Economic Advisers Adopt Boulware's Wage Theory," *UE News,* January 29, 1962, Memos 1962–1963, Box 12, Francis E. Highton Papers, 1948–

1976, AIS 1991.02, Archives Service Center, University of Pittsburgh, Pittsburgh, PA.

35. U.S. Council of Economic Advisers, *Economic Report 1962,* 16–17, 185; Memo, Heller to the President, February 14, 1962, re: The British White Paper on Wage Policy, Memos to JFK 2/62, Box 5, Heller Papers, Kennedy Library.
36. Memo, Heller to Goldberg, December 29, 1961, Council of Economic Advisers (CEA), December 1961, Box 73, President's Office Files, Kennedy Library.
37. Memo, Heller to the President, January 4, 1962, Council of Economic Advisers (CEA), 1962: January–February, Box 74, President's Office Files, Kennedy Library. For the meeting, see David McDonald Oral History Interview—JFK #1, 02/15/1966, interviewed by Charles T. Morrissey, pp. 13–14, Kennedy Library; Blough, *Washington Embrace,* 78–80; Arthur Goldberg's History of the Steel Crisis, ca. 1963, Steel 4/31/62–6/28/62, Box 39, Theodore Sorensen Papers, #222, Kennedy Library.
38. Blough, *Washington Embrace,* 78–79.
39. Memo, Heller to the President, May 5, 1962, re: What the Steel Tables Show, Council of Economic Advisers (CEA), May 1962: 1–5, Box 74, President's Office Files, Kennedy Library.
40. Memo, Heller to the President, May 8, 1962, re: Your Request for Comparative Costs of Steel Settlement, Council of Economic Advisers (CEA), May 1962: 6–15, Box 74, President's Office Files, Kennedy Library.
41. Notes of Telephone Conversation, April 3, 1962, with Roger Blough, Telephone Conversations, Memoranda April–June 1962 [1 of 3], Box 38, C. Douglas Dillon Papers, #60, Kennedy Library. See also Press Release, March 31, 1962, Basic Agreement, Republic Steel Corp and USWA: Correspondence file, 1959 (Folder 1 of 2), Box 52, Republic Steel Corporation Records, 1895–2001, MS. 4949, Western Reserve Historical Society (WRHS), Cleveland, OH.
42. "Exhibit H: Questions and Answers, Roger M. Blough, News Conference, April 12, 1962," in Blough, *Washington Embrace,* 153, 156.
43. It is unclear if Blough or other steel executives explicitly recognized this escape clause in 1962, but he cited this exception in writing his recollections of that year's incident a decade later: Blough, 91.
44. Memo, Heller to the President, May 5, 1962, re: What the Steel Tables Show, Council of Economic Advisers (CEA), May 1962: 1–5, Box 74, President's Office Files, Kennedy Library.
45. Memo, Heller to the President, April 10, 1962, 10:00 PM, Council of Economic Advisers (CEA), April 1962, Box 74, President's Office Files, Kennedy Library.
46. "Exhibit D, Press Release, United States Steel Corporation, April 11, 1962," in Blough, *Washington Embrace,* 128–129; Arthur Goldberg's History of the Steel Crisis, ca. 1963, Steel 4/31/62–6/28/62, Box 39, Sorensen Papers, Kennedy Library.
47. Background Material on Steel, April 13, 1962, Steel (1 of 2), Box 42, Gordon Papers, Kennedy Library.

48. Blough, *Washington Embrace,* 84.
49. W. W. Rostow, *Concept and Controversy: Sixty Years of Taking Ideas to Market* (Austin: University of Texas Press, 2003), 415n11.
50. McDonald Oral History Interview, p. 15.
51. Arthur Goldberg's History of the Steel Crisis, ca. 1963; Draft Steel Price Emergency Act of 1962, Steel 4/31/62–6/28/62, Box 39, Sorensen Papers, Kennedy Library. On internal concerns, see Kermit Gordon and Walter W. Heller Oral History Interview, conducted by Larry J. Hackman and Joseph Pechman, September 14, 1972, p. 33, Kennedy Library.
52. Memo, Nicholas Katzenbach to Robert Kennedy, September 5, 1961, re: Government Actions to Prevent Impending Increases in Steel Prices, Justice, 1961, Box 80, President's Office Files, Kennedy Library.
53. United States v. United States Steel Corporation, 233 F. Supp. 148 (S.D.N.Y. 1964). The government filed these charges after the April 1962 price dispute; the companies ultimately pled nolo contendere. See also "New Theories of Price Conspiracy," *ABA Section of Antitrust Law,* 1964, 99–101; James R. Williamson, *Federal Antitrust Policy during the Kennedy-Johnson Years* (Westport, CT: Greenwood, 1995), 57.
54. Memo, Robert F. Kennedy to the President, "Increase in the Price of Steel," April 12, 1962; Memo, J. Edgar Hoover to Robert F. Kennedy, April 12, 1962; Memo, Lee Loevinger to Robert F. Kennedy, May 31, 1962, Justice, 1962: April–June, Box 80, President's Office Files, Kennedy Library.
55. "Relationship of Net Income after Taxes," Council of Economic Advisers (CEA), May 1962: 1–5, Box 74, President's Office Files, Kennedy Library.
56. Edward Gudeman, recorded interview by Dan B. Jacobs, September 22, 1964, pp. 9–13, John F. Kennedy Library Oral History Program, Kennedy Library. See also Blough, *Washington Embrace,* 100–108.
57. W. Bernard Thulin, "Productivity Guideposts Won't Work," *Harvard Business Review* 40, no. 6 (1962): 70–78; Jules Backman, "Productivity—No Guidepost for Wage Settlements," *Challenge* 10, no. 9 (June 1962): 24–27; Robert A. Bedolis, "A New Frontier for Collective Bargaining," *Management Record* 24, no. 7–8 (July–August 1962): 33–38; David B. Johnson, "The New Frontier Collective Bargaining Policy," *Labor Law Journal,* July 1, 1962, 591–598.
58. Memo, May 29, 1962, re: The Present Decline in Perspective, Council of Economic Advisers (CEA), May 1962: 16–31, Box 74, President's Office Files, Kennedy Library. See also E. Ray Canterbery, "Has Kennedy Stopped Inflation?," *Challenge* 11, no. 3 (December 1962): 11–14.
59. Council of Economic Advisers Oral History Interview—JFK #1, August 1, 1964, by Joseph Pechman, note 5a, John F. Kennedy Library Oral History Program.
60. "Strike Policy and Compulsory Arbitration," *Conference Board Business Management Record* 25, no. 5 (May 1963): 3–12; Charles Bartlett, recorded interview by Fred Holborn, January 6, 1965, pp. 113–114, John F. Kennedy Library Oral History Program.
61. U.S. Council of Economic Advisers, *Economic Report of the President, Transmitted*

to the Congress, January 1963 (Washington, DC: Government Printing Office, 1963), 85–88.

62. Handwritten Notes, April 10, 1963, KP-33, 1963:L KP29-KP36a, Box 43; Handwritten Notes, April 10, 1963, Box 106, Steel; Tape 80.2 (esp. at 44:00) and Tape 80.3, Presidential Recordings: Meetings, President's Office Files, Kennedy Library.
63. James A. Rahl, "Price Competition and the Price Fixing Rule—Preface and Perspective," *Northwestern University Law Review,* no. 2 (May–June 1962): 137–139; Richard B. Heflebower, "Do Administered Prices Involve an Antitrust Problem?," *Northwestern University Law Review,* no. 2 (May–June 1962): 204–205; Carl A. Auerbach, "Administered Prices and the Concentration of Economic Power," *University of Minnesota Law Review* 47 (1962): 139–153; "New Theories of Price Conspiracy," 82.
64. Memo, Kermit Gordon to the President, April 21, 1962, re: Steel: The Longer-Range Problem, Council of Economic Advisers (CEA), April 1962, Box 74, President's Office Files, Kennedy Library.
65. Auerbach, "Administered Prices," 183–186; Theodore P. Kovaleff, "The Two Sides of the Kennedy Antitrust Policy," *Antitrust Bulletin* 37 (Spring 1992): 46–49; Memo, Lee Loevinger to Robert F. Kennedy, May 31, 1962, Justice, 1962: April–June, Box 80, President's Office Files, Kennedy Library.
66. Memo, John Lewis to Charles Schultze, August 31, 1963, Price Wage 1 of 2, Box 41, Gordon Papers, Kennedy Library; "The Guideposts for Noninflationary Wage Increases," 1963 Negotiations, Presentation to IUE on Productivity, Profits & Wages, Box 11, Highton Papers, Archives Service Center, University of Pittsburgh.
67. Memo, John Lewis to the Cost-Push Group, August 23, 1963; Kenneth Arrow, Wage Price Guideposts and Economic Growth; Charles Schultze, Comments on Arrow, September 4, 1963; Arrow, Comments on Schultze, September 13, 1963; Memo, Lewis to Heller, April 14, 1964, Price Wage 1 of 2, Box 41, Gordon Papers, Kennedy Library.
68. Confidential Notes of CEA Meeting, September 21, 1963; Memo, Heller to Professional Staff, October 10, 1963, re: Initial Assignments for the 1964 Annual Report, The Heller Council 7/63–12/63, Box 4, Heller Papers, Kennedy Library.
69. Memo, Heller to the President, October 2, 1963, re: Administration Posture on Steel, Council of Economic Advisers (CEA), October 1963: 1–7, Box 76, President's Office Files, Kennedy Library.
70. Gardner Ackley Oral History Interview I, interviewed by Joe Frantz, April 13, 1973, p. 1, Lyndon B. Johnson Presidential Library, Austin, TX.
71. Memo, Lewis to Heller, December 10, 1963, Documentary Supplement Part II [1 of 2], Box 2, Administrative History of the Council of Economic Advisors, Johnson Library.
72. U.S. Council of Economic Advisers, *Economic Report of the President, Transmitted to the Congress, January 1964* (Washington, DC: Government Printing Office,

1964), 10–11, 97, 112–115. On public acceptance of 3.2%, see "Johnson Sees Strong Economy in '64," *Wall Street Journal*, January 21, 1964, 3; Edwin L. Dale Jr, "Economic Report Marks Milestone," *New York Times*, January 26, 1964, F1; Ackley Oral History Interview I, pp. 29–30.

73. Memo, Heller to the President, December 6, 1963, re: Prices and Wages in 1964, Wage-Price Guideposts, 10/62–12/63, Box 24, Heller Papers, Kennedy Library.

74. Annual Improvement Factor and Cost-of-Living Wage Adjustments, July 1, 1964, Folder 9—Negotiations, 1964, GM, Annual Improvement Factor, Box 131, United Auto Workers (UAW) President's Office: Walter P. Reuther Collection, Acc. 261, Walter P. Reuther Library, Wayne State University, Detroit, MI; W. G. Ginsburg, Notes on Productivity, November 4, 1964, Productivity 1960–64, Box 58, United Auto Workers (UAW) Research Department Collection, Part I, Acc. 350, Reuther Library.

75. Memo, Cliff Carter to the President, April 1, 1964; Memo, Heller to the President, re: Meeting with Walter Reuther, April 9, 1964, EX BE 4/Automobile 11/22/63–5/29/64, Box 9, White House Central Files, Johnson Library.

76. Memo, Ackley to the President, September 10, 1964, re: The Auto Settlement, EX BE 4/Automobile 5/30/64–7/21/65, Box 9; Memo, Willard Wirtz to the President, September 24, 1964, re: General Motors and UAW; Memo, Ackley to the President, re: The Cost of the Ford Settlement, October 23, 1967, EX LA 6/ Automobile, Box 23, White House Central Files, Johnson Library.

77. U.S. Council of Economic Advisers, *Economic Report of the President, Transmitted to the Congress, January 1965* (Washington, DC: Government Printing Office, 1965), 55–59, 90. On 1965, see Memo, Heller to the President, October 8, 1964, re: The Outlook for Price Stability in 1964—A Second Look, C.F. BE 5-4 National Income-Product Data (1964–1965), Box 3, White House Central Files, Johnson Library.

78. Memo, Ackley to the President, June 14, 1965, re: The Steel Labor Negotiations; Memo, Ackley to the President, June 15, 1965, re: Steel Negotiations, Memos to the President, May–June 1965, Box 13, Gardner Ackley Papers, 1936–1999, Bentley Historical Library, University of Michigan, Ann Arbor, MI; Memo, Ackley to the President, August 6 1965, re: Background for your conversation with Abel, EX LA 6/ Steel 11/22/63–8/27/65, Box 29, White House Central Files, Johnson Library. Ackley's memo to Johnson in 1965 was eerily reminiscent of a memo that he had sent to Office of Price Stabilization director Michael DiSalle in 1951 in light of the steel wage-price dispute that would ultimately be the nail in the coffin for Korean price controls: "[It is] the most severe crisis which wage and price stabilization have yet found. . . . Both parties to these negotiations have now declared open warfare upon the standards presumed to apply to the increases they seek. . . . I contend that the government must again declare its policies—as forceful, and in as much detail, as possible." Memo, Ackley to Michael DiSalle, November 13, 1951, The Steel Story, Box 3, Ackley Papers, Bentley Library.

79. Memo, Otis Brubaker to Officers and Executive Board, August 16, 1965, re: Cost-of-Living Loss, Folder 4, Box 41, United Steelworkers of America (USWA) President's Office Records, 1916–1980, HCLA 1961, Historical Collections and Labor Archives, Special Collections Library, Pennsylvania State University, State College, PA.
80. Robert Bedolis, "Steel Union Demands for 1965," *Conference Board Record* 2, no. 2 (February 1965): 25–28; comments made by R. Conrad Cooper to the Joint Negotiating Committee, March 30, 1965, Industry Bargaining, Confidential File, July 1962–Sept. 1972, Folder 2 of 2, Box 72, Republic Steel Records, WRHS; Jack Metzgar, *Striking Steel: Solidarity Remembered* (Philadelphia: Temple University Press, 2000), 158–201.
81. Memo, Jim O'Brien to Hubert Humphrey, July 29, 1965, re: Steel Negotiations, Folder 2; Circular, August 20, 1965; Circular, August 27, 1965, Folder 4, Box 41; Analysis of Mr. Marvin Miller of the August 24, 1965 Offer of the Basic Steel Industry, Folder 5, Box 42; Statement of International Wage Committee, April 22, 1965; Statement of William Simkin, April 24, 1965, File 4 Documents (March–August 1965), Box 104; Statement of International Wage Policy Committee, April 22, 1965, 8 Wage Policy Committee (1965), Box 215 (162), USWA President's Office Records, Pennsylvania State University.
82. U.S. Council of Economic Advisers, *Report to the President on Steel Prices* (Washington, DC: Government Printing Office, 1965), 4.
83. Memo, Joseph Califano to Bill Moyers, September 3, 1965; Memo, Ackley to the President, September 8, 1965, re: The Steel Settlement and the Guideposts, EX LA 6/ Steel 8/27/65–9/8/65, Box 29, White House Central Files, Johnson Library.
84. Memo, Califano to the President, August 27, 1965, EX LA 6/ Steel 11/22/63–8/27/65; Memo, Califano to the President, August 30, 1965, EX LA 6/ Steel 8/27/65–9/8/65, Box 29; Memo, Ackley to the President, August 25, 1965, re: Do We Need to Approve Steel Price Increase in Order to Get a Settlement; Memo, Robert McNamara to the Record, August 25, 1965, BE 4/Steel 2/4/65–8/26/65, Box 13, White House Central Files, Johnson Library.
85. Memo, Jack Valenti to the President, November 5, 1965; Statement by Ackley, December 31, 1965; Memo, Ackley to the President, December 31, 1965, re: A New Year's President from Bethlehem, BE 4/Steel 8/27/65 1/2/66, Box 13, White House Central Files, Johnson Library.
86. Telegram, Johnson to 7 Steel Executives, January 2, 1966; "Agenda," January 1966, EX BE 4/Steel 8/27/65–1/2/66; "Government Policies of Special Interest to the Steel Industry," January 4, 1966, EX BE 4/Steel 1/4/66–3/23/66, Box 13, White House Central Files, Johnson Library.
87. Roger M. Blough Oral History Interview, by Joe Frantz, July 29, 1971, pp. 19–21, Johnson Library. For McNamara's offer, see Telephone Conversation with Robert McNamara, January 4, 1966, Citation Nos. 9407 and 9410, Tape WH6601.02, Johnson Library; U.S. Council of Economic Advisers, *Economic Report of the*

President: Transmitted to the Congress, January, 1966 (Washington, DC: Government Printing Office, 1966), 89.

88. U.S. Bureau of Economic Analysis, "National Income: Corporate Profits before Tax (without IVA and CCAdj) (A053RC1Q027SBEA)," FRED, Federal Reserve Bank of St. Louis, accessed June 18, 2020, https://fred.stlouisfed.org/series/A053RC1Q027SBEA; U.S. Bureau of Economic Analysis, "Corporate Profits after Tax with Inventory Valuation Adjustment (IVA) and Capital Consumption Adjustment (CCAdj) (CPATAX)," FRED, Federal Reserve Bank of St. Louis, accessed June 18, 2020, https://fred.stlouisfed.org/series/CPATAX; U.S. Bureau of Economic Analysis, "Shares of Gross Domestic Income: Corporate Profits with Inventory Valuation and Capital Consumption Adjustments, Domestic Industries: Profits after Tax with Inventory Valuation and Capital Consumption Adjustments (W273RE1A156NBEA)," FRED, Federal Reserve Bank of St. Louis, accessed June 18, 2020, https://fred.stlouisfed.org/series/W273RE1A156NBEA. For more background statistics, see William D. Nordhaus, "The Falling Share of Profits," *Brookings Papers on Economic Activity* 1 (1974): 178–180.
89. U.S. Congress, Joint Economic Committee, *January 1966 Economic Report of the President: Hearings before the Joint Economic Committee Congress of the United States, Part 3 (and Appendix)*, 89th Cong., 2nd Sess. (Washington, DC: Government Printing Office, 1966), 411–413, 431–432; U.S. Council of Economic Advisers, *Economic Report 1966*, 64–67, 261–262.
90. U.S. Council of Economic Advisers, *Economic Report 1966*, 87–93; Memo, Bob Russell to CEA, October 1, 1965, re: Some simple-minded guidepost calculations, Guideposts, Box 5, Ackley Papers, Bentley Library.
91. Memo, Ackley to Califano, re: Wage Restraint in 1967, February 28, 1967, Pricing Files: Labor Management Advisory Committee, Office Files of John E. Robson and Stanford G. Ross, Box 10, Johnson Library. See also Gardner Ackley Oral History II, interviewed by Joe Frantz, March 7, 1974, p. 26, Johnson Library.
92. Memo, Carrol L. Coburn to Walter P. Reuther November 29, 1965, re: Proposed Change in Productivity "Guideposts," Productivity 1965–9, Box 58, UAW Research Department Collection, Part I, Reuther Library.
93. Memo, Ackley to the President, re: The Wage Guidepost, July 11, 1966, EX LA 8 Wages-Hours 4/5/66–12/31/66, Box 33, White House Central Files, Johnson Library.
94. "The Need for Competitive Guideposts Rather than Noninflationary Guideposts," October 18, 1965, 1966 Guideposts: Reference Materials, Box 24, Highton Papers, Archives Service Center, University of Pittsburgh.
95. Negotiations Binder #13—Union Objectives and Demands, Box 15, Highton Papers, Archives Service Center, University of Pittsburgh.
96. Slide Presentation to the IUE Negotiation Committee, September 15, 1966, 1966 Chart Presentation Workbook, Box 9, Highton Papers, Archives Service Center, University of Pittsburgh. For the costs, see Memo, Califano to the Presi-

dent, September 30, 1966; Memo, Califano to the President, October 11, 1966, EX LA 6/Electric, Box 25, White House Central Files, Johnson Library.

97. Robert A. Bedolis, "Union Profile: The IUE'S New President," *Conference Board Record* 2, no. 10 (October 1965), 29–37; Guy Farmer, *Collective Bargaining in Transition*, vol. 1, *Coalition Bargaining and Union Power* (New York: Industrial Relations Counselors, 1967).

98. Memo, Califano to President, September 30, 1966; Memo, Califano to the President, October 11, 1966, EX LA 6/Electric, Box 25, White House Central Files, Johnson Library; Lyndon B. Johnson, "Statement by the President on the Strike Threat at General Electric," October 2, 1966, in *The American Presidency Project*, ed. Gerhard Peters and John T. Woolley, https://www.presidency.ucsb.edu/node/238390; David R. Jones, "G.E. and 11 Unions Agree on a Pact," *New York Times*, October 15, 1966, 1, 34; "Settlement Cost Implications to Date," ca. December 1967, Wages, Prod'y U.L.C. Belleair Jan. 1968, Box 7, Highton Papers, Archives Service Center, University of Pittsburgh.

99. Memo, Ackley to the President, May 15, 1967, re: Report from Business Council Meeting, EX FG 11-3 4/1/67–5/15/67, Box 59, White House Central Files, Johnson Library.

100. Memo, Ackley to the President, June 4, 1966, re: Labor-Management Advisory Committee Meeting, June 3, EX FG 730 President's Advisory Committee on Labor Management Policy (1/1/66–) [2 of 2], Box 280, White House Central Files, Johnson Library.

101. Jeremy Bacon and G. Clark Thompson, "Businessmen Look to Government to Curb Inflation," *Conference Board Record* 3, no. 6 (June 1966): 11–17; Albert T. Sommers, "Business Sentiment and the Business Outlook," *Conference Board Record* 3, no. 11 (November 1966): 3–7; Califano, *Triumph and Tragedy*, 106–121; Letter, William McChesney Martin to the President, April 8, 1966, EX BE Business-Economics 7/28/65–5/28/66, Box 1, White House Central Files, Johnson Library.

102. Califano, *Triumph and Tragedy*, 139–148.

103. Memo, John Robson to Ackley, November 2, 1966, Pricing Files: Clothing, Box 2, Office Files of John E. Robson and Stanford G. Ross, Johnson Library.

104. Memo, Total Factor Productivity, June 27, 1967, Book 2: Coordinate Committee Steel Companies, 1966 thru May 1968, Box 1, R. Conrad Cooper Papers, AIS 91.1, Archives Service Center, University of Pittsburgh.

105. R. Conrad Cooper Memorandum, September 19, 1967; R. Conrad Cooper, Report to the Chief Executives, American Iron & Steel Institute, September 12, 1968, Industry Bargaining, Confidential File, July 1962–Sept. 1972, Folder 2 of 2, Box 72, Republic Steel Records, WRHS.

106. Unsigned Agreement, Experimental Negotiation Agreement, October 10, 1967, Industry Bargaining, Confidential File, July 1962–Sept. 1972, Folder 2 of 2, Box 72, Republic Steel Records, WRHS; Meeting of the Coordinating Committee, November 15, 1967, Book 1, Box 1, Cooper Papers, Archives Service Center, University of Pittsburgh.

107. R. Conrad Cooper, Presentation to the Board of Directors, August 29, 1967, Book 1, Box 1, Cooper Papers, Archives Service Center, University of Pittsburgh; Untitled Note, October 13, 1967; R. Conrad Cooper, Report to the Chief Executives, American Iron & Steel Institute, September 12, 1968, Industry Bargaining, Confidential File, July 1962–Sept. 1972, Folder 2 of 2, Box 72, Republic Steel Records, WRHS.

108. Notes for Negotiations for Union's Opening Presentation, June 3, 1968, Folder 24; Memo, Otis Brubaker to Officers, May 29, 1968, re: Cost-of-Living Increase Protection, Folder 25; Memo, Otis Brubaker, May 22, 1968, re: Productivity . . . vs. Real Hourly Earnings in Steel, Folder 26, Box 43, USWA President's Office Records, Pennsylvania State University.

109. Memo, Cooper to Coordinating Committee, February 7, 1968, Book 2, Box 1, Cooper Papers, Archives Service Center, University of Pittsburgh.

110. Minutes of Meeting, July 24, 1968, Coordinating Committee Meetings and Union Meetings, June 1968–69, Box 1, Cooper Papers, Archives Service Center, University of Pittsburgh; Cooper, Report to the Chief Executives, American Iron & Steel Institute, September 12, 1968, Industry Bargaining, Confidential File, July 1962–Sept. 1972, Folder 2 of 2, Box 72, Republic Steel Records, WRHS.

111. U.S. Senate, *Steel Imports: Staff Study of the Committee on Finance, United States Senate,* 90th Cong., 2nd Sess., Document 107 (Washington, DC: Government Printing Office, 1968), 420, 471, 482; Richard M. Duke, Richard L. Johnson, Hans Mueller, P. David Qualls, Calvin T. Roush Jr., and David G. Tarr, *The United States Steel Industry and Its International Rivals: Trends and Factors Determining International Competitiveness* (Washington, DC: Federal Trade Commission, 1977), 68, 119.

112. Lyndon B. Johnson, "Statement by the President upon Signing the Tax Bill," June 28, 1968, in Peters and Woolley, *American Presidency Project,* https://www.presidency.ucsb.edu/node/236911; Memo, Arthur Okun to the President, July 18 1968, re: Proposed Statement by Your Cabinet Committee on Price Stability, EX LA 8 1/1/68–, Box 33; Press Release, July 22, 1968, EX FG 631 Cabinet Committee on Price Stability, Box 375, White House Central Files, Johnson Library.

113. Edward Knight, *Steel Price Increases and Government Policy: A Survey of the Period 1962–1968* (Washington, DC: Library of Congress Legislative Reference Service, December 1968), 24–31; Press Release, August 6, 1968, EX BE 4/Steel 8/1/68–8/31/68, Box 14, White House Central Files, Johnson Library; Lyndon B. Johnson, "Letter to the Speaker of the House and to the Majority Leader of the Senate on the Steel Price Increases," August 1, 1968, in Peters and Woolley, *American Presidency Project,* https://www.presidency.ucsb.edu/node/237749.

114. Memo, Okun to the President, re: Bethlehem Steel's Big Price Cut, EX BE/4 Steel 9/1/68–, Box 14, White House Central Files, Johnson Library; U.S. Federal Trade Commission, *Staff Report on the United States Steel Industry,* 163–164, 172–178.

115. For a review of these concerns, see Ferdinand L. Molz, "The Political Economy

of Steel Import Quotas," *Journal of Economic Issues* 4, nos. 2–3 (June–September 1970): 60–76.

116. Memo, Jim Gaither to Johnson, August 2, 1968, C.F. BE 5-2 Cost of Living (1968), Box 3, White House Central Files, Johnson Library.
117. Memo, Dean Rusk to the President, re: Voluntary Limitations on Steel Exports to the United States, December 30, 1968; Memo, DeVier Pierson to the President, January 3, 1969, EX TA 6/ST-STZ, Box 23, White House Central Files, Johnson Library; U.S. Federal Trade Commission, *Staff Report on the United States Steel Industry*, 68, 163–164, 172–178.
118. Memo, Nicholas Katzenbach to Califano, November 9, 1965, re: Government Action with Respect to Aluminum, EX BE 4/Aluminum, Box 8, White House Central Files, Johnson Library.
119. Donald F. Turner, "The Scope of Antitrust and Other Economic Regulatory Policies," *Harvard Law Review* 82, no. 6 (April 1969): 1207–1244.
120. Neil Fligstein, *The Transformation of Corporate Control* (Cambridge, MA: Harvard University Press, 1990), 204–223; Williamson, *Federal Antitrust Policy*, 63–68.
121. Phil C. Neal, William F. Baxter, Robert H. Bork, et al., "Report of the White House Task Force on Antitrust Policy," *Antitrust Law and Economics Review* 2 (1968): 11–76.
122. Report of the President's Advisory Committee on Labor-Management Policy, December 6, 1968, EX FG 730 President's Advisory Committee on Labor Management Policy (1/1/66–) [2 of 2], Box 402, White House Central Files, Johnson Library.
123. Memo, Arthur Okun to the President, re: Backsliding in the Business Council, October 21, 1968, EX FG 11-3 8/1/68–, Box 61, White House Central Files, Johnson Library.

CHAPTER 6. IF AT FIRST YOU DON'T SUCCEED

1. Harry B. Yolshpe, John F. Allums, Joseph E. Russell, and Barbara A. Atkin, *Stemming Inflation: The Office of Emergency Preparedness and the 90-Day Freeze* (Washington, DC: Government Printing Office, 1972); Arnold R. Weber, *In Pursuit of Price Stability: The Wage-Price Freeze of 1971* (Washington, DC: Brookings Institution, 1973); C. Jackson Grayson Jr., with Louis Neeb, *Confessions of a Price Controller* (Homewood, IL: Dow Jones-Irwin, 1974); Office of Economic Stabilization, *Historical Working Papers on the Economic Stabilization Program, August 15, 1971 to April 30, 1974* (Washington, DC: Government Printing Office, 1974); Neil de Marchi, "The First Nixon Administration: Prelude to Controls," in *Exhortation and Controls: The Search for a Wage-Price Policy, 1945–1971*, ed. Craufurd D. Goodwin (Washington, DC: Brookings Institution, 1975), 295–352; Robert F. Lanzillotti, Mary T. Hamilton, and R. Blaine Roberts, *Phase II in Review: The Price Commission Experience*, Studies in Wage-Price Policy (Washington, DC: Brookings Institution, 1975); George P. Shultz and Kenneth W. Dam, *Economic Policy beyond the Headlines* (New York: Norton, 1977), 65–85;

Arnold R. Weber and Daniel J. B. Mitchell, *The Pay Board's Progress: Wage Controls in Phase II* (Washington, DC: Brookings Institution, 1978); Hugh Rockoff, *Drastic Measures: A History of Wage and Price Controls in the United States* (Cambridge: Cambridge University Press, 1984), 200–232; Allen J. Matusow, *Nixon's Economy: Booms, Busts, Dollars, and Votes* (Lawrence: University Press of Kansas, 1998).

2. E.g., Jefferson Cowie, *Stayin' Alive: The 1970s and the Last Days of the Working Class* (New York: New Press, 2010); Judith Stein, *Pivotal Decade: How the United States Traded Factories for Finance in the Seventies* (New Haven, CT: Yale University Press, 2010), 22–73.
3. Benjamin C. Waterhouse, "Mobilizing for the Market: Organized Business, Wage-Price Controls, and the Politics of Inflation, 1971–1974," *Journal of American History* 100, no. 2 (September 2013): 454–478; Kim Phillips-Fein, *Invisible Hands: The Businessmen's Crusade against the New Deal* (New York: Norton, 2009), 150–212; Benjamin C. Waterhouse, *Lobbying America: The Politics of Business from Nixon to NAFTA* (Princeton, NJ: Princeton University Press, 2014), 76–139.
4. Waterhouse, "Mobilizing for the Market," 470.
5. For background on these trends, see William D. Nordhaus, "The Falling Share of Profits," *Brookings Papers on Economic Activity* 1 (1974): 169–217.
6. George Perry, "Wages, Productivity, and Profits," *Conference Board Record* 8, no. 3 (March 1971): 41–43.
7. Remarks by W. B. Murphy before the Business Council, Hot Springs VA, May 13, 1972, The Business Council—1972, Box 4, C. B. McCoy Papers, Acc. 1815, Hagley Museum and Library, Wilmington, DE.
8. Richard Nixon, *RN: The Memoirs of Richard Nixon,* vol. 1 (New York: Warner Books, 1978), 31–32. For contemporaries, see Willard Clopton and Mike Causey, "Former OPA Lawyer Makes Good," *Washington Post,* March 3, 1969, B5; Edwin L. Dale Jr., "Nixon Said to Be Miffed by Hint of Price Control," *Atlanta Constitution,* July 10, 1969, 10.
9. William Safire, *Before the Fall: An Inside View of the Pre-Watergate White House* (Garden City, NY: Doubleday, 1975), 509.
10. Memo, William Safire to Objectives Group, October 16, 1969, re: Jawboning vs Backboning, EX BE Business-Economics [1 of 13] 1969, Box 1, White House Central Files, Richard M. Nixon Presidential Library, Yorba Linda, CA.
11. Robert P. Bremner, *Chairman of the Fed: William McChesney Martin Jr. and the Creation of the Modern American Financial System* (New Haven, CT: Yale University Press, 2004), 260–278.
12. U.S. Bureau of Labor Statistics, "Nonfarm Business Sector: Compensation per Hour (COMPNFB)," FRED, Federal Reserve Bank of St. Louis, accessed June 18, 2020, https://fred.stlouisfed.org/series/COMPNFB. For details of compensation, see U.S. Council of Economic Advisers, *Economic Report of the President, Transmitted to the Congress February 1971* (Washington, DC: Government Printing Office, 1971), 58; U.S. Council of Economic Advisers, *Economic Report of the*

President, Transmitted to the Congress January 1972 (Washington, DC: Government Printing Office, 1972), 49.

13. Memo, W. J. Flaherty, July 30, 1969, re: Wages, Issue Catch-Up, Wages, 1969 Company Position Papers, Box 23, Francis E. Highton Papers, 1948–1976, AIS 1991.02, Archives Service Center, University of Pittsburgh, Pittsburgh, PA.
14. Letter, Fred Borch to the President, November 24, 1969, EX BE 5/69 National Economy [40 of 42] December 11–15, 1969, Box 58, White House Central Files, Nixon Library.
15. Francis Highton, Wage Criteria Used in Collective Bargaining, with Particular Reference to Cost of Living, August 6, 1969, Unmarked Folder, Box 23, Highton Papers, Archives Service Center, University of Pittsburgh. See also GE News, Special Edition, October 1969, F135, Box 7, Lemuel Boulware R. Papers, 1917–1990, Ms. 52, Kislack Center, University of Pennsylvania, Philadelphia, PA.
16. James A. Gross, *Broken Promise: The Subversion of U.S. Labor Relations Policy, 1947–1994* (Philadelphia: Temple University Press, 1995), 163–191.
17. General Electric Co., 150 NLRB 192, 192–198, 286–288 (1964). For contemporary legal perspectives on this case, see "'Boulwareism': Legality and Effect," *Harvard Law Review* 76, no. 4 (February 1963): 807–818; Herbert R. Northrup, "The Case for Boulwarism," *Harvard Business Review* 41 (September–October 1963): 86–97; Andrew F. Shea, "Labor Law—Labor Management Relations Act—Section 8(a)(5)—Refusal of Employer to Bargain in Good Faith—General Elec. Co. & International Union of Elec. Workers, AFL-CIO," *Boston College Law Review* 6, no. 4 (1965): 949–957; Richard C. Cooper, "Boulwarism and the Duty to Bargain in Good Faith," *Rutgers Law Review* 20, no. 4 (Summer 1966): 653–695; T.C.C., "Labor Law: General Electric's 'Overall Approach' to Bargaining Held a Violation of Good Faith," *Duke Law Journal*, no. 3 (Summer 1965): 661–667; Morris D. Forkosch, "Boulwareism: Will Labor-Management Relations Take It or Leave It?," *Catholic University Law Review* 19, no. 3 (1970): 311–350.
18. NLRB v. General Electric Co., 418 F.2d 736, 758–763 (2d Cir. 1969). See also Forkosch, "Boulwareism," 335–345; Kenneth B. Hipp, "Labor Law—Duty to Bargain in Good Faith—Boulwarism within the Totality-of-Circumstances Rule," *North Carolina Law Review* 48, no. 4 (1970): 998–1000.
19. Damon Stetson, "G.E. Ruled Unfair by Appeals Court in '60 Bargaining," *New York Times*, October 29, 1969, 1. On the coincidence of timing, see James W. Kuhn, "A New View of Boulwarism: The Significance of the GE Strike," *Labor Law Journal* 21, no. 9 (September 1970): 584.
20. "GE Pact with Inflation Clause Could Boost Hourly Wage Up to 74 Cents over 40 Months," *Wall Street Journal*, February 2, 1970, 6; Memo, Peter Flanigan to the President, January 30, 1970, EX LA 6-10 Electrical [1969–70], Box 16, White House Central Files, Nixon Library.
21. Gerd Wilcke, "Appliance Prices Increased by G.E.," *New York Times*, February 6, 1970, 67. See also "GE Increases Appliance Prices 3%," *Washington Post*, February 7, 1970, A6.
22. William Serrin, *The Company and the Union: The "Civilized Relationship" of the*

General Motors Corporation and the United Automobile Workers (New York: Knopf, 1973), 8–17.

23. Memo, Paul McCracken to the President, September 14, 1970, EX LA 6-6 Automobiles [1969–1970], Box 16, White House Central Files, Nixon Library. On imports, see Serrin, *Company and the Union,* 8–9. On prices, see Robert J. Gordon, *The Measurement of Durable Goods Prices* (Chicago: University of Chicago Press, 1990), 345, reproduced in Robert A. Margo, "Quality-Adjusted Price Indexes for New and Used Automobiles: 1906–1983," table Cc63-65 in *Historical Statistics of the United States: Earliest Times to the Present: Millennial Edition,* ed. Susan B. Carter, Scott Sigmund Gartner, Michael R. Haines, Alan L. Olmstead, Richard Sutch, and Gavin Wright (New York: Cambridge University Press, 2006).
24. Nelson Lichtenstein, *Walter Reuther: The Most Dangerous Man in Detroit* (Urbana: University of Illinois Press, 1995), 419; Memo, George Weaver to Carrol Coburn, July 11, 1969, re: Inadequate Escalator Clause at GM, UAW Wage Rates and Earnings 1958–70; Memo, Harry Chester to Walter Reuther, October 1, 1969, re: Buying Power of Workers, UAW Wage Rates and Earnings 1964–70 1 of 2, Box 63, United Auto Workers (UAW) Research Department Collection, Part I, Acc. 350, Walter P. Reuther Library, Wayne State University, Detroit, MI.
25. Lichtenstein, *Walter Reuther,* 433–438; Serrin, *Company and the Union,* 20–37; Memo, Brendan Sexton to Carrol Coburn and Dick Wilson, August 13, 1970, re: Local Union President's Institute, UAW Wage Rates and Earnings 1964–70 1 of 2, Box 63, UAW Research Department Collection, Part I, Reuther Library.
26. Serrin, *Company and the Union,* 45–58.
27. Serrin, 259–285.
28. Memo, George Shultz to the President, November 11, 1970, EX LA 6-6 Automobiles [1969–1970], Box 16, White House Central Files, Nixon Library.
29. Serrin, *Company and the Union,* 286–287. On auto prices, see Robert J. Gordon, *The Measurement of Durable Goods Prices* (Chicago: University of Chicago Press, 1990), 345, reproduced in Margo, "Quality-Adjusted Price Indexes."
30. Minutes, Four-Man Bargaining Team Meeting—U.S. Steel Suite, Sheraton-Carlton Hotel—December 16, 1970, December 17, 1970, Industry Bargaining, Confidential File, July 1962–Sept. 1972, Folder 2 of 2, Box 72, Republic Steel Corporation Records, 1895–2001, MS. 4949, Western Reserve Historical Society (WRHS), Cleveland, OH.
31. De Marchi, "First Nixon Administration," 329–330, 343.
32. Philip Shabecoff, "President Calls Steel and Labor to White House," *New York Times,* July 1, 1971, 1; Don Oberdorfer, "Nixon Asks for Restraint in Steel Talks," *Washington Post,* July 7, 1971, A1.
33. Richard M. Duke, Richard L. Johnson, Hans Mueller, P. David Qualls, Calvin T. Roush Jr., and David G. Tarr, *The United States Steel Industry and Its International Rivals: Trends and Factors Determining International Competitiveness* (Washington, DC: Federal Trade Commission, 1977), 70.
34. Philip Shabecoff, "3-Year Agreement Averts Strike," *New York Times,* August 2,

1971, 1; Press Release, August 1, 1971, Industry Bargaining, 4-Man Team, General, 1971–July 1981, Box 73, Republic Steel Records, WRHS.

35. Robert Walker, "Steel Price of 8% Announced," *New York Times,* August 3, 1971, 1; de Marchi, "First Nixon Administration," 343.
36. Memo, William De Lancey to Willis Boyer and J. R. Wall, November 13, 1972, re: Labor Relations—The Next Steelworkers' Contract, Industry Bargaining, Confidential File, Oct. 1972–Nov. 1983 (Folder 2 of 2), Box 72, Republic Steel Records, WRHS.
37. See, for instance, Letter, J. M. Roche to the President, October 31, 1969, EX BE 5/69 National Economy [35 of 42] December 4, 1969; Letter, Clyde Skeen to the President, November 8, 1969; Letter, Rupert Thompson Jr. to the President, November 10, 1969, EX BE 5/69 National Economy [36 of 42] December 4, 1969; Letter, J. Ward Keener to the President, November 12, 1969; Letter, Henry Ford II to the President, December 31, 1969, EX BE 5/69 National Economy [37 of 42] December 4, 1969; Letter, H. E. Gray to the President, October 28, 1969, EX BE 5/69 National Economy [39 of 42] December 9–11, 1969, Box 58, White House Central Files, Nixon Library.
38. Memo, Maurice Stans to the President, October 23, 1969, EX BE 5-3 Inflation—Money Scarcity [2 of 8] September–December 1969, Box 62, White House Central Files, Nixon Library.
39. Board Reports, 371st Meeting, June 19, 1970, Box 4, Chamber of Commerce of the United States Records, Acc. 1960, Hagley Library; Memo, E. A. Sprague to A. W. Elliot, April 27 1971, re: Incomes Policy, "Incomes" Policies & Wage-Price Controls—1971–1973, Box 50, Series IV, National Association of Manufacturers (NAM) Records, Acc. 1411, Hagley Library.
40. Memo, Charles Colson to the President, re: Business Community/Economy, August 4, 1971, EX BE 5 National Economy [15 of 23] August 1971, Box 48, White House Central Files, Nixon Library; Committee for Economic Development, *Further Weapons against Inflation: Measures to Supplement General Fiscal and Monetary Policies* (New York: CED, 1970), 52–66.
41. Minutes of Meeting of April 4, 1970, attached to Memo, George Hibbert to Burns, April 14, 1970, FRB Atlanta (1), D1, Arthur Burns Papers, 1969–1987, Gerald R. Ford Presidential Library, Ann Arbor, MI.
42. Stephen C. Shannon, "Work Stoppage in Government: The Postal Strike of 1970," *Monthly Labor Review,* July 1978, 14–22.
43. Memorandum of Discussion, April 7, 1970, in *FOMC Meeting Minutes,* pp. 48–53, FRASER, Federal Reserve Bank of St. Louis, accessed June 19, 2020, https://fraser.stlouisfed.org/title/677/item/22963/content/pdf/fomcmod19700407.pdf.
44. "Text of Burns Speech on Steps to Fight Inflation and to Extend U.S. Prosperity," *New York Times,* December 8, 1970, 34.
45. H. R. Haldeman, *The Haldeman Diaries: Inside the Nixon White House: The Complete Multimedia Edition* (San Francisco: Star Press Multimedia, 1996), CD-ROM, June 27, 1971; Nixon, *RN,* 641.
46. U.S. House of Representatives, Committee on Banking and Currency, *Defense*

Production Act Extension and Economic Stabilization Act, Report Together with Minority Views and Additional Views, 91st Cong., 2nd Sess. (Washington, DC: Government Printing Office, 1970), 9; Richard Nixon, "Statement on Signing Bill Extending the Defense Production Act," August 17, 1970, in *The American Presidency Project*, ed. Gerhard Peters and John T. Woolley, https://www.presidency.ucsb.edu/node/240339.

47. Andrew F. Brimmer, "Multi-national Banks and the Management of Monetary Policy in the United States," *Journal of Finance* 28, no. 2 (May 1973): 445.
48. Matusow, *Nixon's Economy*, 144–148; Douglas Brinkley and Luke A. Nichter, eds., *The Nixon Tapes, 1971–1972* (Boston: Houghton Mifflin, 2014), 231–361. On the previous decision, see Haldeman, *Haldeman Diaries*, August 2, 1971.
49. Haldeman, *Haldeman Diaries*, August 13, 1971; Richard Nixon, "Address to the Nation Outlining a New Economic Policy: 'The Challenge of Peace,'" August 15, 1971, in Peters and Woolley, *American Presidency Project*, https://www.presidency.ucsb.edu/node/240602.
50. Brinkley and Nichter, *Nixon Tapes*, 234.
51. Haldeman, *Haldeman Diaries*, August 13, 1971.
52. Memo, Ray Waldmann to John Ehrlichman, September 22, 1971, re: Consumer Reaction to the New Economic Policy, EX BE 3 Economic Controls [14 of 65] September 21–22, 1971, Box 9, White House Central Files, Nixon Library.
53. Statement by the AFL-CIO Executive Council, August 19, 1971, Wage and Price Freeze, Folder 3, Box 17, United Steelworkers of America (USWA) Research Department Records, 1921–1981, HCLA 1965, Historical Collections and Labor Archives, Special Collections Library, Pennsylvania State University, State College, PA. On violations, see Weber and Mitchell, *Pay Board's Progress*, 2–8.
54. Memo, Charles Colson to the President, re: Business Community/Economy, August 4, 1971, EX BE 5 National Economy [15 of 23] August 1971, Box 48; Memo, Harold Passer to Stans, September 3, 1971, re: Abstract of "Instant Reading," EX BE 5 National Economy [16 of 23] September–November 1971, Box 49, White House Central Files, Nixon Library.
55. Report of the Executive Committee, November 8, 1971, Board Reports, 376th Meeting, November 18–19, 1971, 2/2, Box 4, Chamber of Commerce Records, Hagley Library; Waterhouse, "Mobilizing for the Market," 467–68.
56. Weber, *In Pursuit of Price Stability*, 21n22.
57. Weber, 62–82. On the Broncos, see "National Football League," OEP 282, September 22, 1971, CLC—Executive Policy Committee Meeting—Minutes and Memorandums, Sept. 16–Sept. 22 1971, Box 2, Records of the Cost of Living Council, Records of the Office of the Executive Director, General Correspondence, 1971, NN3-432-81-1, RG 432, Records of the Economic Stabilization Programs, Nixon Library.
58. Weber and Mitchell, *Pay Board's Progress*, 23, 35–36, 257–264.
59. Report of the Executive Committee, November 8, 1971, Board Reports, 376th Meeting, November 18–19, 1971, 2/2, Box 4, Chamber of Commerce Records, Hagley Library; Weber and Mitchell, *Pay Board's Progress*, 28–54.

60. Safire, *Before the Fall*, 592–596; Weber and Mitchell, *Pay Board's Progress*, 275–282.
61. U.S. Council of Economic Advisers, *Economic Report of the President: Transmitted to the Congress, January 1973* (Washington, DC: Government Printing Office, 1973), 60.
62. Weber and Mitchell, *Pay Board's Progress*, 302–303.
63. Lanzillotti, Hamilton, and Roberts, *Phase II in Review*, 9–39. For business complaints, see Memo, Peter Peterson to the President, March 28, 1972, re: Summary of "Instant Reading," EX BE 5 National Economy [17 of 23] December 1971–April 1972, Box 49, White House Central Files, Nixon Library.
64. Memo to Record, November 23, 1971, re: Meeting between . . . BF Goodrich and Miss Nona Slutsky of the Price Commission, Nona Slutsky_Chron, Box 1, Records of the Price Commission and Pay Board Executive Secretariat, PC-EXS-1 NN-375-120, RG 432, Nixon Library.
65. C. Jackson Grayson, "Prices, Productivity—and Demand," *Conference Board Record* 9, no. 4 (April 1972): 13–16; John W. Kendrick, "The Productivity Factor in Phase 2," *Conference Board Record* 9, no. 3 (March 1972): 28–35; Hendrik S. Houthakker, "Are Controls the Answer?," *Review of Economics and Statistics* 54, no. 3 (August 1972): 231–234; "Probing the Problems of Productivity," *Conference Board Record* 9, no. 9 (September 1972): 38–42.
66. Memo, Grayson to Curt Jones, June 7, 1972, Memoranda to Chairman, Box 3; Memo, Neeb to Commissioners, April 17, 1972, re: Enforcement of Profit Margin Limitations, Chron—Louis P. Neeb (4-1-72 thru); Memo, Slutzky to the Record, November 9, 1971, re: Meeting between the Price Commission and Labor Representatives, Correspondence File—Kennedy, Box 1, Records of the Price Commission and Pay Board Executive Secretariat, Nixon Library. See also Grayson with Neeb, *Confessions of a Price Controller*, 122–123, 187–190, 232.
67. Memo, D. T. Kennedy to the Record, December 3, 1971, re: Meeting between officials of the Dow Chemical Company and Mr. L. P. Neeb and D. T. Kennedy of the Office of Price Commission, Chron—Louis P. Neeb (thru 3-31-72), Box 1, Records of the Price Commission and Pay Board Executive Secretariat, Nixon Library; Grayson with Neeb, *Confessions of a Price Controller*, 107.
68. Lanzillotti, Hamilton, and Roberts, *Phase II in Review*, 40–50; On the February figure, see W. H. Pavony to R. L. Lowry and W. N. Daly, February 10, 1972, re: Minutes of Our Meeting Today Concerning TLP Forms, Forms, Box 5, Records of the Price Commission and Pay Board Executive Secretariat, Nixon Library.
69. Alan Greenspan, "The Future of Controls," April 18, 1972, EX BE 3 Economic Controls [42 of 65] May 1972, Box 14; Memo, Passer to Peterson, re: Abstract of Instant Reading November 1972, EX BE 5 National Economy [19 of 23] August–December 1972, Box 49, White House Central Files, Nixon Library; Grayson with Neeb, *Confessions of a Price Controller*, 108.
70. Lanzillotti, Hamilton, and Roberts, *Phase II in Review*, 40–45; Memo, Ahmad Al-Samarrie to Albert Small, January 18, 1972, re: Tentative Reply to Sylvia Porter's Questions to Chairman C. Jackson Grayson Jr. on January 10, 1972,

Economic Indicators, Box 4; Records of the Price Commission and Pay Board Executive Secretariat, Nixon Library.

71. Nordhaus, "Falling Share of Profits"; U.S. Bureau of Economic Analysis, "Shares of Gross Domestic Income: Corporate Profits with Inventory Valuation and Capital Consumption Adjustments, Domestic Industries: Profits after Tax with Inventory Valuation and Capital Consumption Adjustments (W273RE1A156NBEA)," FRED, Federal Reserve Bank of St. Louis, accessed June 18, 2020, https://fred.stlouisfed.org/series/W273RE1A156NBEA.
72. Weber and Mitchell, *Pay Board's Progress*, 92–99; General Electric, "Wages, Price, Profits—and Controls," December 12, 1972, [Cost of Living Council November–December 1972] [2 of 2], Box 142, Staff Member and Office Files, Herbert Stein Papers, White House Central Files, Nixon Library.
73. Memo, Neeb to the Record, December 7, 1972, re: Further Observations on December 6 Industry Meeting, Chron—Louis P. Neeb (4-1-72 thru), Box 1, Records of the Price Commission and Pay Board Executive Secretariat, Nixon Library; Report of Ad Hoc Committee on Wage-Price Controls, February 12, 1973, Board Reports, 381st Meeting, Feb. 22, 23, 1972 (3/3), Box 5, Chamber of Commerce Records, Hagley Library.
74. Memo, W. B. Murphy to Members of the Executive Committee of the Business Roundtable, November 14, 1972, Business Roundtable 1972, Box 5; Minutes of the Executive Committee, March 5, 1973, Business Roundtable Executive Committee, Box 6, McCoy Papers; Draft, Recommendations Regarding Any Extension of Wage-Price Controls, December 18, 1972, Ad Hoc Committee on Phase II, Box 171, Series IX, NAM Records, Hagley Library; Committee for Economic Development, *High Employment without Inflation: A Positive Program for Economic Stabilization* (New York: CED, 1972), 39–61.
75. Press Release, Phase III, January 12, 1973, Phase III Press Releases, Box 145, Stein Papers, Nixon Library.
76. Memo, Edward T. York to James McLane, March 27, 1973, re: 1.5% Weighted Average Price Increase Option, Unmarked Folder, Box 2, Records of the Cost of Living Council, Records of the Office of the Director, RAB-PC-PO-1 (Tom Garvey) NN-275-120, RG 432, Nixon Library.
77. U.S. Council of Economic Advisers, *Economic Report of the President, Transmitted to the Congress February 1974* (Washington, DC: Government Printing Office, 1974), 89; Matusow, *Nixon's Economy*, 223–227.
78. U.S. House of Representatives, Committee on Banking and Currency, *Economic Stabilization—1973*, 93rd Cong., 1st Sess. (Washington, DC: Government Printing Office, 1973), 219–228.
79. U.S. Council of Economic Advisers, *Economic Report 1974*, 94–96.
80. Shultz and Dam, *Economic Policy beyond the Headlines*, 73–74.
81. Richard Nixon, "Address to the Nation Announcing Price Control Measures," June 13, 1973, in Peters and Woolley, *American Presidency Project*, https://www.presidency.ucsb.edu/node/255542.
82. Memo, Joseph R. Wright to Frederick Dent, re: Abstract of Instant Reading

March 1973; Memo, Joseph R. Wright to Dent, re: Abstract of Instant Reading May 1973; Memo, Benjamin Kaplan to Dent, re: Abstract of Instant Reading June 1973, EX BE 5 National Economy [20 of 23] January–June 1973; Memo, Sidney Jones to Dent, September 18, 1973, re: Abstract of Instant Reading September 1973; Memo, Jones to Dent, October 19, 1973, re: Abstract of Instant Reading October 1973, EX BE 5 National Economy [21 of 23] July–October 1973, Box 49, White House Central Files, Nixon Library.

83. U.S. Bureau of Economic Analysis, "National Income: Corporate Profits before Tax (without IVA and CCAdj) (A053RC1Q027SBEA)," FRED, Federal Reserve Bank of St. Louis, accessed June 18, 2020, https://fred.stlouisfed.org/series/A053RC1Q027SBEA; U.S. Bureau of Economic Analysis, "Corporate Profits after Tax with Inventory Valuation Adjustment (IVA) and Capital Consumption Adjustment (CCAdj) (CPATAX)," FRED, Federal Reserve Bank of St. Louis, accessed June 18, 2020, https://fred.stlouisfed.org/series/CPATAX; U.S. Bureau of Economic Analysis, "Shares of Gross Domestic Income."
84. Minutes of the Executive Committee, June 23, 1973, Business Roundtable Executive Committee, 1973–1974, Box 6; Letter, Blough to John Dunlop, July 2, 1973, Business Roundtable, July–Dec. 1973, Box 5, McCoy Papers, Hagley Library; Memo, July 2, 1973, re: Blough's Roundtable on Phase IV, [Cost of Living Council June–July 1973], Box 143; Memo, Henry H. Perritt to the Record, June 29, 1973, re: Summary of Phase IV Consultation with the National Association of Manufacturers, Phase IV Consultations [2 of 2], Box 146, Stein Papers, Nixon Library.
85. U.S. Council of Economic Advisers, *Economic Report 1974*, 97–99.
86. Jonathan Brock and Roger Wilsby, "Removing Controls: The Policy of Selective Decontrol," in *Historical Working Papers on the Economic Stabilization Program, August 15, 1951 to April 30, 1974*, by U.S. Office of Economic Stabilization (Washington, DC: Government Printing Office, 1974), 891–916.
87. U.S. Council of Economic Advisers, *Economic Report 1974*, 89.
88. U.S. Council of Economic Advisers, 23; U.S. Council of Economic Advisers, *Economic Report of the President, Transmitted to the Congress February 1975* (Washington, DC: Government Printing Office, 1975), 48–50; Matusow, *Nixon's Economy*, 241–275.
89. Memo, Jeffrey Eves to E. W. Haskins, November 16, 1973, re: Importance of NAM Ad Campaign on Price Controls, Reading File October 10, 1973; Briefing on the Effects of Wage and Price Controls, April 10, 1974, House Republican Conference, Box 51, Series IV, NAM Records, Hagley Library.
90. Letter, Ed Kenna and Arch Booth to Nixon, October 5, 1973, EX BE 3 Economic Controls [59 of 65] October 1–26, 1973, Box 16, White House Central Files, Nixon Library.
91. Letter, Oscar L. Dunn to Kenna, March 25, 1974, Anti-Control Letters, Box 51, Series IV, NAM Records, Hagley Library.
92. Brock and Wilsby, "Removing Controls," 859–948; U.S. Council of Economic Advisers, *Economic Report 1975*, 224–226; Executive Office of the President, Cost

of Living Council, *Economic Stabilization Program Quarterly Report: Covering the Period January 1, 1974 through May 1, 1974* (Washington, DC: Government Printing Office, 1974), 17–36.

93. Memo, Shultz to the President, January 17, 1974, re: Next Steps for Wage-Price Controls, [Cost of Living Council January 1974]; Memo, Shultz to the President, re: Position on the Economic Stabilization Bill, [Cost of Living Council February–March 1974], Box 144, Stein Papers, Nixon Library; Memo, Herbert Stein, April 4, 1974, re: The Problem of the Economic Stabilization Act, EX BE 3 Economic Controls [63 of 65] February–April, 1973, Box 17, White House Central Files, Nixon Library.
94. Nixon, *RN*, 645–646.

CHAPTER 7. ABORT, RETRY, FAIL

1. "The Bunkers and Inflation (Part 1)," *All in the Family*, directed by H. Wesley Kenney, written by Don Nicholl, Michael Ross, and Bernie West, September 14, 1974.
2. John T. Woolley, "Exorcising Inflation-Mindedness: The Transformation of Economic Management in the 1970s," *Journal of Policy History* 10, no. 1 (January 1998): 131–152; W. Carl Biven, *Jimmy Carter's Economy: Policy in an Age of Limits* (Chapel Hill: University of North Carolina Press, 2002); Samuel Milner, "Assuming Direct Control: The Beguiling Allure of Incomes Policies in Postwar America," *Journal of Policy History* 31, no. 1 (Winter 2019): 42–71.
3. Cathie J. Martin, *Shifting the Burden: The Struggle over Growth and Corporate Taxation* (Chicago: University of Chicago Press, 1991), 107–134; Herbert Stein, *The Fiscal Revolution in America: Policy in Pursuit of Reality*, 2nd rev. ed. (Washington, DC: AEI Press, 1996), 577–596; Kim Phillips-Fein, *Invisible Hands: The Businessmen's Crusade against the New Deal* (New York: Norton, 2009), 150–262; Benjamin C. Waterhouse, *Lobbying America: The Politics of Business from Nixon to NAFTA* (Princeton, NJ: Princeton University Press, 2014), 106–139.
4. Robert E. Lucas Jr., "Econometric Policy Evaluation: A Critique," *Carnegie-Rochester Conference Series on Public Policy* 1 (1976): 19–46; Robert E. Lucas Jr. and Thomas J. Sargent, "After Keynesian Macroeconomics," in *Rational Expectations and Econometric Practice*, vol. 1, ed. Robert E. Lucas Jr. and Thomas J. Sargent (Minneapolis: University of Minnesota Press, 1981), 295–320; Christina D. Romer and David H. Romer, "The Evolution of Economic Understanding and Postwar Stabilization Policy," *Proceedings—Economic Policy Symposium, Jackson Hole, Federal Reserve Bank of Kansas City* (NBER Working Paper No. 9274, 2002), 11–78; Robert L. Hetzel, *The Monetary Policy of the Federal Reserve: A History* (Cambridge: Cambridge University Press, 2008), 108–171; Allan H. Meltzer, *A History of the Federal Reserve*, vol. 2, book 2, *1970–1986* (Chicago: University of Chicago Press, 2009), 843–1131; Marvin Goodfriend and Robert G. King, "The Incredible Volcker Disinflation," *Journal of Monetary Economics* 52 (2005): 981–1015; Iwan Morgan, "Monetary Metamorphosis: The Volcker Fed and Inflation," *Journal of Policy History* 24, no. 4 (2012): 545–571. On political

pressure, see Sarah Binder and Mark Spindel, *The Myth of Independence: How Congress Governs the Federal Reserve* (Princeton, NJ: Princeton University Press, 2017), 124–200.

5. U.S. Senate, Committee on Banking, Housing and Urban Affairs, *Council on Wage and Price Stability Act Amendments of 1975*, 94th Cong., 1st Sess. (Washington, DC: Government Printing Office, 1975), 44–45.
6. U.S. Council of Economic Advisers, *Economic Report of the President, Transmitted to the Congress: February 1975* (Washington, DC: Government Printing Office, 1975), 141–146.
7. Memo, Sidney Jones to Frederick Dent, re: Abstract of Instant Reading March 1974, EX BE 5 National Economy [22 of 23] November 1973–May 21, 1974, Box 50, White House Central Files, Richard M. Nixon Presidential Library, Yorba Linda, CA; Eileen B. Hoffman, "Adjusting Wages to Inflation via the Escalator Clause," *Conference Board Record* 11, no. 8 (August 1974): 54–60.
8. Minutes of the Policy Committee, May 2, 1974, Business Roundtable Policy Committee, 1973–1974, Box 4, C. B. McCoy Papers, Acc. 1815, Hagley Museum and Library, Wilmington, DE.
9. George H. Brown, "New Insights on Inflation," *Conference Board Record* 11, no. 7 (July 1974): 7–10; U.S. Council on Wage and Price Stability, *Cost of Living Escalator Clauses and Inflation* (Washington, DC: Government Printing Office, 1975), 12.
10. U.S. House of Representatives, Committee on Banking, Finance, and Urban Affairs, Subcommittee on Economic Stabilization, *Amendments to the Council on Wage and Price Stability Act*, 95th Cong., 1st Sess. (Washington, DC: Government Printing Office, 1977), 40–84; U.S. House of Representatives, Committee on Banking, Currency, and Housing, Subcommittee on Economic Stabilization, *Incomes Policy Legislation—1975*, 94th Cong., 1st Sess. (Washington, DC: Government Printing Office, 1975), 245–312; U.S. Senate, Committee on Banking, Housing, and Urban Affairs, *Extension of the Council on Wage and Price Stability*, 96th Cong., 1st Sess. (Washington, DC: Government Printing Office, 1979), 325.
11. R. Heath Larry, "Inflation, Labor and the Law," *Duquesne Law Review* 13, no. 2 (Winter 1974): 203–226.
12. U.S. Senate, Committee on Banking, Housing, and Urban Affairs, *Extension of the Council on Wage and Price Stability*, 96th Cong., 1st Sess. (Washington, DC: Government Printing Office, 1979), 75–88. See also Committee for Economic Development, *Fighting Inflation and Promoting Growth* (New York: CED 1976), 51–55.
13. Thomas K. McCraw, *Prophets of Regulation* (Cambridge, MA: Harvard University Press, 1984), 237–239; David Vogel, *Fluctuating Fortunes: The Political Power of Business in America* (New York: Basic Books, 1989), 113–147.
14. Letter, W. J. De Lancey to Michael H. Moskow, October 31, 1975, Folder 20, Box 208, Republic Steel Corporation Records, 1895–2001, MS. 4949, Western Reserve Historical Society (WRHS), Cleveland, OH.
15. Letter, Oscar Lundin to Kenneth Rush, August 13, 1974; Letter, Henry Ford II to

Gerald Ford, October 18, 1974, BE 4-37 8/9/74–12/31/74, Box 15; Letter, R. C. Gerstenberg to Gerald Ford, August 20, 1974, BE 5-3 9/1/74–9/15/74, Box 31, White House Central Files, Gerald R. Ford Presidential Library, Ann Arbor, MI.

16. Judith Bauer, "Coping with Inflationary Costs—by Hiking Product Prices," *Conference Board Record* 11, no. 9 (September 1974): 52–57.
17. Abstract of the Instant Reading on the Economy, May 1975, June 1975, BE 5 6/1/76–7/31/75; Abstract of the Instant Reading on the Economy, September 1975, BE 5 11/1/75–12/31/75, Box 19, White House Central Files, Ford Library.
18. The Economists Conference on Inflation, Summary, September 5, 1974, and September 23, 1974, Summit Conference on Inflation—September 1974—General, Box 52, Council of Economic Advisers Records (1969) 1974–1977 (RG 459), Ford Library.
19. Robert J. Gordon, "The Theory of Domestic Inflation," *American Economic Review* 67, no. 1 (February 1977): 128–134.
20. For the count, see Memo, William Baroody to the President, October 23, 1974, Jones, Jerry (2), Box 4, RG 459, Ford Library.
21. Memo, Paul Theis to William Seidman, September 26, 1974, re: Inflation Fighter Program, BE 5–3 9/26/74–10/2/74; Memo, Russ Freeburg to the President, October 18, 1974, BE 5–2 10/17/74–10/23/74, Box 32, White House Central Files, Ford Library; Memo, Paul Theis to Greenspan, October 2, 1974, re: Inflation Fighter Program Revision, Economic Policy Board (1), Box 7, RG 459, Ford Library.
22. Alan Greenspan, *The Age of Turbulence: Adventures in a New World* (New York: Penguin, 2007), 66.
23. Memo, Herbert Stein to the President, August 12, 1974, re: Recommendations for Current Economic Policy, BE 5 National Economy 8/9/74–8/31/74, Box 16, White House Central Files, Ford Library.
24. Memo, Baroody to the President, January 17, 1975, re: Meeting with Citizens' Action Committee, BE 5-3 1/8/75–1/17/75; Letter, Dick Krolik to Ron Nessen, March 22, 1975, BE 5-3 3/1/75–4/30/75, Box 35, White House Central Files, Ford Library.
25. U.S. House of Representatives, *Message from the President of the United States Transmitting a Draft of Proposed Legislation to Establish the Cost of Living Task Force,* House Document No. 93-329, 93rd Cong., 2nd Sess. (Washington, DC: Government Printing Office, 1974); Richard Nixon, "Special Message to the Congress Proposing Establishment of a Cost of Living Task Force," August 2, 1974, in *The American Presidency Project,* ed. Gerhard Peters and John T. Woolley, https://www.presidency.ucsb.edu/node/256182.
26. Memo, Herbert Stein to the President, August 10, 1974, re: Meeting of President with Economic Officials, San Clemente, July 19, 1974, Memos for the President Aug. 1974, Box 47, Staff Member and Office Files, Herbert Stein Papers, White House Central Files, Nixon Library.
27. Public Law 93-287, 93rd Cong. S. 3919, August 24, 1974, Council on Wage and Price Stability Act, 12 U.S.C. § 1904.

28. Machinery and Allied Products Institute Bulletin, August 16, 1974, Folder 19, Box 208, Republic Steel Records, WRHS. The note was probably written by William J. De Lancey, Republic's president and CEO.
29. Speech, Albert Rees, "Do We Need a Permanent Incomes Policy," October 8, 1975, Council on Wage and Price Stability (2), Box 2, Michael H. Moskow Papers, 1969–1992, Ford Library; Memo, Rees to Economic Policy Board, October 3, 1974, re: Role of Council on Wage and Price Stability; Memo, Rees to Seidman, October 21, 1974, re: Priority List for Council on Wage and Price Stability, Rees, Albert (1), Box 20, William Seidman Files, Office of Economic Affairs, Ford Library.
30. Memo, R. C. Fisher to John Wall, October 10, 1972, re: Labor Negotiations, Industry Bargaining, Confidential File, Oct. 1972–Nov. 1983 (Folder 2 of 2), Box 72; Memo, John Wall to W. B. Boyer and W. J. De Lancey, March 6, 1973, re: Summary of Progress in the Matter of the Experimental Negotiating Agreement, Industry Bargaining, 4-Man Team, Experimental Negotiating Agreement (ENA), 1970–1974, Box 73, Republic Steel Records, WRHS.
31. Richard Madden, "'Concerned' Ford Tells U.S. Steel to Justify Rises," *New York Times*, December 18, 1974, 93.
32. Report, US Steel Price Increase, December 21, 1974, Rees, Albert (3), Box 201, Seidman Files, Ford Library; Memo, Albert Rees to Economic Policy Board, January 2, 1975, re: Agreements Reached with U.S. Steel, Bethlehem Steel, and Colorado Fuel & Iron, BE 4-34 8/9/74–1/20/77, Box 15, White House Central Files, Ford Library.
33. Letter, De Lancey to Harold J. Barnett, February 14, 1975, Folder 19, Box 208, Republic Steel Records, WRHS.
34. U.S. Council on Wage and Price Stability, *A Study of Steel Prices* (Washington, DC: Government Printing Office, 1975).
35. Memo, De Lancey to E. B. Jones et al., October 2, 1975; Letter, De Lancey to Michael H. Moskow, October 31, 1975, Folder 20, Box 208, Republic Steel Records, WRHS.
36. Note from William Lilley to Roger Porter, August 30, 1976, COWPS: Steel Price Increases, Box 55, Seidman Files, Ford Library; "Big Steelmakers Cancel Oct. 1 Price Boosts," *Barron's National Business and Financial Weekly*, September 6, 1976, 26.
37. Annotation on Memo, Lilley to Members of COWPS, June 24, 1976, re: Council on Wage and Price Stability Reports on Remaining 1976 Collective Bargaining Settlements, COWPS March–June 1976, Box 54, Seidman Files, Ford Library.
38. U.S. Council on Wage and Price Stability, *Collective Bargaining Review of 1976 and Outlook for 1977* (Washington, DC: Government Printing Office, 1977), 6.
39. Memo, Rees to Executive Committee of the Economic Policy Board, December 18, 1974, re: Possible Candidates for Hearings in the Public Sector, COWPS: December 1974, Box 54, Seidman Files, Ford Library. See also Memo, Rees to John Dunlop, James Lynn, Seidman, April 14, 1975, re: Inflationary Effects of

the Davis-Bacon Act, COWPS: March–April 1975, Box 54, Seidman Files, Ford Library.

40. Gerald R. Ford, "Executive Order 11821—Inflation Impact Statements," November 27, 1974, in Peters and Woolley, *American Presidency Project*, https://www.presidency.ucsb.edu/node/268735; Executive Summary, attached to Memo, Seidman to Ford, ca. December 1976, re: Inflation Impact Statement Program, Inflation Impact Statements, Box 71; Memo, Lilley to Seidman, July 9, 1976, re: 3100 New Federal Regulations per Year, Lilley, William, 7/1–12/76, Box 192, Seidman Files, Ford Library.
41. Address by Barry P. Bosworth, Director, Council on Wage and Price Stability, Before Associated Press Annual Meeting, Atlanta, GA, May 1, 1978, FG 6-17 1/1/78–6/30/78, Box FG-94, White House Central Files, Jimmy Carter Presidential Library, Atlanta, GA.
42. Arthur M. Okun, "Efficient Disinflationary Policies," *American Economic Review* 68, no. 2 (May 1978): 350.
43. Memo, Bosworth to Charles Schultze, October 7, 1977, re: Inflation Deceleration Proposal; Memo, Bosworth to Schultze, November 1, 1977, re: Anti-Inflation Program Proposals—Follow Up, COWPS 3; Memo, Bosworth to Schultze, December 3, 1977, re: Some Perspectives on the Inflation Issue, COWPS 4, Box 100, Records of the Council of Economic Advisers (CEA Records), Carter Library; U.S. Council of Economic Advisers, *Economic Report of the President: Transmitted to the Congress, January 1978* (Washington, DC: Government Printing Office, 1978), 152–156.
44. Memo, Bosworth to Schultze, December 3, 1977, re: Some Perspectives on the Inflation Issue, COWPS 4, Box 100, CEA Records, Carter Library. On business reaction, see Report of Banking, Monetary and Fiscal Affairs Committee, January 30, 1979, re: Administration's Real Wage Insurance Proposal, Board Reports, 405th Meeting, Feb. 14, 1979, Box 6, Chamber of Commerce of the United States Records, 1912–2011, Acc. 1960, Hagley Library. Carter's comments are from Cover sheet to Memo, Schultze to the President, January 7, 1978, re: An Approach to Reducing Inflation, BE 4-2 Executive 1/1/78–4/30/78, Box BE-16, White House Central Files, Carter Library.
45. Unsigned Memo, August 6, 1978, re: The Inflationary Cost of Recession: Are Inflation and Unemployment Always Tradeoffs; Memo, Ray Marshall to Economic Policy Group, August 20, 1978, re: Inflation Options; Memo from Ray Marshall, August 23, 1978, re: Anti-Inflation Policy, BE 4-2 Executive 8/11/78–8/31/78, Box BE-17, White House Central Files, Carter Library.
46. U.S. Council on Wage and Price Stability, *Fact Book: Wage and Price Standards* (Washington, DC: Government Printing Office, 1978).
47. Remarks by Thomas Murphy at the New York Chamber of Commerce and Industry, November 21, 1978, BE 4-2 Executive 12/2/78–12/10/78, Box BE-18; "How to Slow the Rate of Inflation," BE 4-2 Executive 4/4/79–4/30/79, Box BE-19; Letter, Donald Siebert to the President, October 19, 1978; Statement of

E. M. de Windt, November 3, 1978, BE 4-2 Executive 10/11/78–10/23/78, Box BE-17, White House Central Files, Carter Library.

48. Jimmy Carter, "Executive Order 12044—Improving Government Regulations," March 23, 1978, in Peters and Woolley, *American Presidency Project,* https://www.presidency.ucsb.edu/node/244548.
49. Biven, *Jimmy Carter's Economy,* 202–204.
50. U.S. House of Representatives, Committee on Banking, Finance, and Urban Affairs, *Federal Reserve Reform Act of 1977,* 95th Cong., 1st Sess. (Washington, DC: Government Printing Office, 1977), 1–8; Federal Reserve Reform Act of 1977, 12 U.S.C. § 225a.
51. Full Employment and Balanced Growth Act of 1978, 15 U.S.C. § 3101(b)(2), (c)–(d).
52. Memo, Schultze to the President, April 4, 1978, re: Background for Quadriad Meeting on April 5, Memos to President, 3/78–4/78, Box 53, CEA Records, Carter Library; Biven, *Jimmy Carter's Economy,* 140–144.
53. U.S. Bureau of Labor Statistics, "Nonfarm Business Sector: Real Output per Hour of All Persons (OPHNFB)," FRED, Federal Reserve Bank of St. Louis, accessed June 18, 2020, https://fred.stlouisfed.org/series/OPHNFB/.
54. Memo, Bosworth to EPG Inflation Group, November 24, 1978, re: Wage/Price Standards COWPS 7/6/78–2/22/79, Box 103, CEA Records, Carter Library; U.S. Council on Wage and Price Stability, *Fact Book: Wage and Price Standards,* rev. ed. of December 13, 1978 (Washington, DC: Government Printing Office, 1978).
55. Jimmy Carter, "Executive Order 12092—Federal Anti-Inflationary Procurement Practices," November 1, 1978, in Peters and Woolley, *American Presidency Project,* https://www.presidency.ucsb.edu/node/243766; Memo, Fred Kahn to President, April 1, 1980, re: Use of Sanctions Against Violators of the Price Standards, Memos, 3/20/80–4/23/80, Box 29, Records of the Office of the Special Adviser to the President on Inflation, Carter Library.
56. Memo, Kahn to the President, October 24, 1979, re: The Wage and Price Standards, First and Second Years, Presidential File, 10/79–1/2/80, Box 34, Records of the Office of the Special Adviser to the President on Inflation, Carter Library. On the actual costs, see Memo, Sally Katzen to Pay Advisory Committee, October 23, 1979, Pay Advisory Committee, 10/17–11/5/79, Box 32, Records of the Office of the Special Adviser to the President on Inflation, Carter Library.
57. U.S. Council of Economic Advisers, *Economic Report of the President: Transmitted to the Congress, January 1980* (Washington, DC: Government Printing Office, 1980), 37–38; Daniel J. B. Mitchell, "Recent Union Contract Concessions," *Brookings Papers on Economic Activity* 1 (1982): 167.
58. Memo, Dave Harrison to Schultze, Eads and Gramley, November 20, 1979, re: Total Cost of UAW-Chrysler Pact; Memo, Harrison to Schultze, December 3, 1979, re: Chrysler Labor Force, Chrysler [1]; Memo, Schultze to the President, October 26, 1979, re: Inflation and Chrysler, Chrysler [2], Box 10, CEA Records, Carter Library.
59. Memo, J. C. Meyer to John R. Wall, September 28, 1979, re: Whether or not the

Experimental Negotiating Agreement Should be Renewed; "Experimental Negotiating Agreement (ENA) (1980)," April 11, 1980, Industry Bargaining, 4-Man Team, Experimental Negotiating Agreement (ENA-83), 1979–1982, Box 73, Republic Steel Records, WRHS.

60. "1980 Negotiations, Renewal of the ENA," March 31, 1980, Industry Bargaining, 4-Man Team, Experimental Negotiating Agreement (ENA-83), 1979–1982, Box 72; Letter, W. Lawrence Weeks to J. C. Wilson, October 17, 1977, Folder 24; Speech, "Government and the Steelmakers," July 14, 1978, Folder 27, Box 342, Republic Steel Records, WRHS.

61. Proposed Changes to ENA, April 11, 1980; Memo, John R. Wall to De Lancey, April 22, 1980, Industry Bargaining, 4-Man Team, Experimental Negotiating Agreement (ENA-83), 1979–1982, Box 73, Republic Steel Records, WRHS.

62. Comments by Mr. J. Bruce Johnston at the Board of Directors Meeting, April 29, 1980, Industry Bargaining, Confidential File, Oct. 1972–Nov. 1983 (Folder 1 of 2), Box 72, Republic Steel Records, WRHS; Memo, Kahn to William Miller, April 4, 1980, re: Your Telephone Call to the Steel Companies, Labor—General 2/79–4/79, Box 27, Records of the Special Adviser to the President on Inflation, Carter Library.

63. Testimony of R. H. Larry . . . before the Subcommittee on Economic Stabilization, Committee on Banking, Finance and Urban Affairs, House of Representatives, on Reauthorization of the Council on Wage and Price Stability, March 20, 1980, Pay Advisory Committee, 1/24/80–3/80, Box 32, Records of the Office of the Special Adviser to the President on Inflation, Carter Library.

64. Memo, Kahn to the President, June 4, 1980, re: The Pay Standard—Outstanding Issues and Longer-Term Prospects, Pay Advisory Committee, 4/80–6/16/80, Box 32, Records of the Office of the Special Adviser to the President on Inflation, Carter Library.

65. Memo, Kahn to the President, June 4, 1980, re: The Pay Standard—Outstanding Issues and Longer-Term Prospects, Pay Advisory Committee, 4/80–6/16/80, Box 32, Records of the Office of the Special Adviser to the President on Inflation, Carter Library; U.S. Council of Economic Advisers, *Economic Report of the President: Transmitted to the Congress, January 1981* (Washington, DC: Government Printing Office, 1981), 86, 153.

66. Memo, Kahn to the President, December 15, 1980, re: Major Accomplishments of My Office During Your Administration, Memos 6/16/80–12/15/80, Box 29, Records of the Office of the Special Adviser to the President on Inflation, Carter Library.

67. Paul Volcker and Toyoo Gyohten, *The World's Money and the Threat to American Leadership* (New York: Times Books, 1992), 167.

68. Transcript, October 6, 1979, Federal Open Market Committee Meeting Minutes, Transcripts, and Other Documents, FRASER, Federal Reserve Bank of St. Louis, accessed June 19, 2020, https://fraser.stlouisfed.org/title/677/item/23038/content/pdf/FOMC19791006meeting; Record of Policy Actions of the Federal Open Market Committee, October 6, 1979, Federal Open Market Committee

Meeting Minutes, Transcripts, and Other Documents, FRASER, Federal Reserve Bank of St. Louis, accessed June 19, 2020, https://fraser.stlouisfed.org/title/677/item/23038/content/pdf/19791006RoPA19791123, accessed December 16, 2020; Volcker and Gyohten, *World's Money*, 164–173.

69. Goodfriend and Kind, "Incredible Volcker Disinflation," 999–1000; Morgan, "Monetary Metamorphosis," 556. For an example of Volcker's incoming mail, see Home Builders Association of Mississippi, "Wood 2x4 Mailed to Mr. Paul Volcker, Chairman, Board of Governors," ca. 1980, FRASER, Federal Reserve Bank of St. Louis, accessed June 19, 2020, https://fraser.stlouisfed.org/title/860.
70. Art Pine, "Carter Again Blames Fed on Interest," *Washington Post*, October 10, 1980, D1. See also Kenneth H. Bacon, "Reducing the Heat: Better Economic News Helps Smother Flames of Fed-Carter Dispute," *Wall Street Journal*, October 6, 1980, 1, 32; Robert Magnuson, "Miller Assails Fed Shift to Control of Money Supply," *Los Angeles Times*, October 14, 1980, E1.
71. Walter W. Heller, "Shadow and Substance in Inflation Policy," *Challenge* 23, no. 6 (January–February 1981): 5–13; Alan S. Blinder, "Monetarism Is Obsolete," *Challenge* 24, no. 4 (September–October 1981): 35–41; James Tobin, "Keynes' Policies in Theory and Practice," *Challenge* 26, no. 5 (November–December 1983): 5–11.
72. Meltzer, *History of the Federal Reserve*, 1053–1057; Volcker and Gyohten, *World's Money*, 173.
73. Goodfriend and Kind, "Incredible Volcker Disinflation," 1000–1003; Meltzer, *History of the Federal Reserve*, 1061–1066.
74. Volcker and Gyohten, *World's Money*, 175–176.
75. Memo, Murray Weidenbaum to the President, March 29, 1982, re: The Economy in Late March, March 1982—Weidenbaum Chron File (03/17/1982–03/31/1982), Box 12, Murray Weidenbaum Files, 1981–1982, Ronald Reagan Presidential Library, Simi Valley, CA.
76. Hetzel, *Monetary Policy*, 150–195; Goodfriend and King, "Incredible Volcker Disinflation," 1002–1003; Meltzer, *History of the Federal Reserve*, 1086–1170.
77. N. Gregory Mankiw, *Macroeconomics*, 7th ed. (New York: Worth, 2010), 398–399. Somewhat-higher estimates of the Volcker disinflation sacrifice ratio are given in Robert J. Gordon, "The History of the Phillips Curve: Consensus and Bifurcation," *Economica* 78 (2011): 25.
78. Robert J. Gordon, "The Role of Wages in the Inflation Process," *American Economic Review* 78, no. 2 (May 1988): 276–283; Ben S. Bernanke, "Outstanding Issues in the Analysis of Inflation," in *Understanding Inflation and the Implications for Monetary Policy: A Phillips Curve Retrospective*, ed. Jeff Fuhrer, Yolanda K. Kodrzycki, Jane Sneddon Little, and Giovanni P. Olivei (Cambridge, MA: MIT Press, 2009), 450; Rhys Bidder, "Are Wages Useful in Forecasting Price Inflation?," *FRBSF Economic Letter* 2015, no. 33 (November 2, 2015): 1–5, http://www.frbsf.org/economic-research/files/el2015-33.pdf.
79. Mark E. Schweitzer, "Wage Inflation and Worker Uncertainty," *Federal Reserve*

Bank of Cleveland Economic Commentary, August 15, 1997, 1–4; Thomas M. Humphrey, "Historical Origins of the Cost-Push Fallacy," *Federal Reserve Bank of Richmond Economic Quarterly* 84 no. 3 (Summer 1998): 53–74; Yash Mehra, "Wage-Price Dynamics: Are They Consistent with Cost Push?," *Federal Reserve Bank of Richmond Economic Quarterly* 86, no. 3 (Summer 2000): 27–43.

80. Mitchell, "Recent Union Contract Concessions"; Thomas Miner, "Concession Bargaining," *Chicago-Kent Law Review* 59, no. 4 (October 1983): 981–996; Robert J. Flanagan, "Wage Concessions and Long-Term Union Wage Flexibility," *Brookings Papers on Economic Activity* 1 (1984): 183–221; John T. Dunlop, "Have the 1980's Changed U.S. Industrial Relations?," *Monthly Labor Review*, May 1988, 29–34.
81. George Ruben, "Collective Bargaining in 1982: Results Dictated by Economy," *Monthly Labor Review*, January 1983, 28–37.
82. Draft, "Economic Issues, Wage and Price Controls"; Draft Position Statement, "Wage and Price Controls," December 11, 1979, Wage and Price Controls, Box 5, Doug L. Bandow Files, 1981–1982, Reagan Library; Issues—4c. Inflation Guidelines, COWPS. Vol. Pay Adv. Com., Box 240, Reagan, Ronald: 1980 Campaign Papers, 1965–1980, Reagan Library; Ronald Reagan, "The President's News Conference," January 29, 1981, in Peters and Woolley, *American Presidency Project*, https://www.presidency.ucsb.edu/node/246569.
83. Thomas W. Evans, *The Education of Ronald Reagan: The General Electric Years and the Untold Story of his Conversion to Conservatism* (New York: Columbia University Press, 2006), 3–23, 57–153.
84. Evans, 157–198.
85. Gerald Mayer, *Union Membership Trends in the United States* (Washington, DC: Congressional Research Service, 2004), 22–23.
86. Joseph A. McCartin, *Collision Course: Ronald Reagan, the Air Traffic Controllers, and the Strike That Changed America* (New York: Oxford University Press, 2011); Timothy J. Minchin, *Labor under Fire: A History of the AFL-CIO since 1979* (Chapel Hill: University of North Carolina Press, 2017), 58–70.
87. James A. Gross, *Broken Promise: The Subversion of U.S. Labor Relations Policy, 1947–1994* (Philadelphia: Temple University Press, 1995), 254–264.
88. Vogel, *Fluctuating Fortunes*, 269–271.
89. Gross, *Broken Promise*, 247–254; Minchin, *Labor under Fire*, 113.
90. Harry DeAngelo and Linda DeAngelo, "Union Negotiations and Corporate Policy: A Study of Labor Concessions in the Domestic Steel Industry during the 1980s," *Journal of Financial Economics* 30 (1991): 4–8; William M. Davis, "Collective Bargaining in 1983: A Crowded Agenda," *Monthly Labor Review*, January 1983, 4.
91. Donald F. Barnett and Louis Schorsch, *Steel: Upheaval in a Basic Industry* (Cambridge, MA: Ballinger, 1983), 55–76, esp. table 2-6 on page 64.
92. Garth L. Mangum and R. Scott McNabb, *The Rise, Fall, and Replacement of Industrywide Bargaining in the Basic Steel Industry* (Armonk, NY: M. E. Sharpe, 1997), 63.

93. Douglas A. Irwin, *Clashing over Commerce: A History of US Trade Policy* (Chicago: University of Chicago Press, 2017), 577–578, 598–602.
94. Barnett and Schorsch, *Steel,* 77–103; Mangum and McNabb, *Rise, Fall, and Replacement,* 178–180.
95. Letter, J. Bruce Johnston to John Wall, July 15, 1982, Industry Bargaining, 4-Man Team, General, 1981–1983, Box 73, Republic Steel Records, WRHS.
96. Memo, W. C. Stoner to W. J. De Lancey and J. J. Loftus, February 24, 1981, re: Possible Negotiating Objectives for Renewal of the ENA, Industry Bargaining, 4-Man Team, Experimental Negotiating Agreement (ENA-83), 1979–1982, Box 73, Republic Steel Records, WRHS.
97. U.S. Bureau of Labor Statistics, *Productivity Measures for Selected Industries,* Bulletin 2491 (Washington, DC: Government Printing Office, 1997), 55, 109.
98. Letter, Johnston to Lloyd McBride, May 28, 1982, Industry Bargaining, 4-Man Team, General, 1981–1983, Box 73, Republic Steel Records, WRHS.
99. Letter, Johnston to John Wall, October 8, 1982, 4-Man Team, General, 1981–1983, Box 73, Republic Steel Records, WRHS.
100. "Strategy for Negotiations with United Steelworkers of America," January 21, 1982, Industry Bargaining, 4-Man Team, General, 1981–1983, Box 73, Republic Steel Records, WRHS.
101. Davis, "Collective Bargaining in 1983," 4–6; George Ruben, "Economy Improves; Bargaining Problems Persist in 1983," *Monthly Labor Review,* January 1984, 34–35. On net savings, see Mangum and McNabb, *Rise, Fall, and Replacement,* 87–88; DeAngelo and DeAngelo, "Union Negotiations and Corporate Policy," 11–13.
102. Memo, Wall to J. J. Loftus, January 8, 1982; Memo, Wall to E. B. Jones, September 30, 1982, Industry Bargaining, Confidential File, Oct. 1972–Nov. 1983 (Folder 1 of 2), Box 72, Republic Steel Records, WRHS.
103. Mangum and McNabb, *Rise, Fall, and Replacement,* 89–91; Memo, W. Lawrence Weeks to J. J. Loftus, September 22, 1982, re: Coordinating Committee Steel Bargaining; Memo, Weeks to Loftus, October 4, 1983, re: Collective Bargaining—United Steelworkers of America, Industry Bargaining, Confidential File, Oct. 1972–Nov. 1983 (Folder 1 of 2), Box 72, Republic Steel Records, WRHS.
104. Kenneth Warren, *Big Steel: The First Century of the United States Steel Corporation, 1901–2001* (Pittsburgh: University of Pittsburgh Press, 2001), 341–346; Mangum and McNabb, *Rise, Fall, and Replacement,* 101–125.
105. Allan Collard-Wexler and Jan De Loecker, "Reallocation and Technology: Evidence from the US Steel Industry," *American Economic Review* 105, no. 1 (2015): 131–171.
106. Mangum and McNabb, *Rise, Fall, and Replacement,* 85, 106–107, 174–175.
107. Bureau of Labor Statistics, *Productivity Measures,* 55, 109.
108. J. R. Norsworthy and Craig A. Zabala, "Worker Attitudes, Worker Behavior, and Productivity in the U.S. Automobile Industry, 1959–1976," *ILR Review* 38, no. 4 (July 1985): 556–557.

109. William J. Abernathy, Kim B. Clark, and Alan M. Kantrow, *Industrial Renaissance: Producing a Competitive Future for America* (New York: Basic Books, 1983), 61; Clifford Winston, *Blind Intersection? Policy and the Automobile Industry* (Washington, DC: Brookings Institution, 1987), 16: Harry C. Katz, Thomas A. Kochan, and Jeffrey H. Keefe, "Industrial Relations and Productivity in the U.S. Automobile Industry," *Brookings Papers on Economic Activity* 3 (1987): 685–687, 705–706; Martin Kenney and Richard Florida, *Beyond Mass Production: The Japanese System and Its Transfer to the U.S.* (New York: Oxford University Press, 1993), 23–124; Etsuo Abe and Robert Fitzgerald. "Japanese Economic Success: Timing, Culture, and Organizational Capability," *Business History* 37, no. 2 (1995): 1–31.
110. Miner, "Concession Bargaining."
111. Mitchell, "Recent Union Contract Concessions," 171.
112. John Holusha, "G.M. and Auto Workers to Link Cut in Wages to Lower Car Prices," *New York Times*, January 13, 1982, 1; Ruben, "Collective Bargaining in 1982," 29.
113. Donald Woutat, "Widespread Gains Seen from Ford-UAW Pact," *Los Angeles Times*, February 21, 1982, E1; Peter Behr, "GM Calls Ford Pact a Start," *Washington Post*, March 4, 1982, D10; Donald Woutat, "GM Offers Labor Pact Similar to Agreement Signed by Ford, UAW," *Los Angeles Times*, March 16, 1982, E1; Keith Bradsher, "Behind the Labor Peace at Ford," *New York Times*, March 21, 1999.
114. "Big 3's '83 Car Sales Up 16.7%," *New York Times*, October 5, 1982, D1; James Risen and Deborah Reifman, "UAW Faces Dilemma as Talks Begin," *Los Angeles Times*, July 22, 1984, 1; Harry C. Katz, "The GM-UAW Settlement: Breakthrough or More of the Same?," *Personnel* 61, no. 1 (January 1985): 16–24. On the cancellation and restoration of the formula, see Sean P. McAlinden, *The Meaning of the 2003 UAW-Automotive Pattern Agreement* (Ann Arbor, MI: Center for Automotive Research, June 2004), 8–14, http://www.cargroup.org/wp-content/uploads/2017/02/The-Meaning-of-the-2003-UAW_Automotive-Pattern-Agreement.pdf.
115. Ruben, "Collective Bargaining in 1982," 29; Bruce Kaufman and Jorge Martinez-Vazquez, "Voting for Wage Concessions: The Case of the 1982 GM-UAW Negotiations," *Industrial and Labor Relations Review* 41, no. 2 (January 1988): 185–186.
116. McAlinden, "Meaning of the 2003 UAW-Automotive Pattern Agreement," 8–14.
117. Audrey Freeman, *The New Look in Wage Policy and Employee Relations* (New York: Conference Board, 1985).
118. Jeffrey B. Arthur and Suzanne Konzelmann Smith, "The Transformation of Industrial Relations in the American Steel Industry," in *Contemporary Collective Bargaining in the Private Sector*, ed. Paula B. Voos (Madison, WI: Industrial Relations Research Association, 1994), 135–180; Robert C. Marshall and Antonio Merlo, "Pattern Bargaining," *International Economic Review* 45, no. 1 (February 2004): 239–242.

119. Daniel J. B. Mitchell, "Shifting Norms in Wage Determination," *Brookings Papers on Economic Activity* 2 (1985): 584–586, 595–596; Thomas A. Kochan, Harry C. Katz, and Robert B. McKersie, *The Transformation of American Industrial Relations* (Ithaca, NY: Cornell University Press, 1994).

CONCLUSION

1. The classic statement of management's fundamental responsibility to shareholders can be found in Milton Friedman, "The Social Responsibility of Business Is to Increase its Profits," *New York Times Magazine*, September 13, 1970.
2. On profits and concentration, see Jan De Loecker, Jan Eeckhout, and Gabriel Unger, "The Rise of Market Power and the Macroeconomic Implications" (NBER Working Paper 23687, August 2017), http://www.nber.org/papers/w23687; David Autor, David Dorn, Lawrence F. Katz, Christina Patterson, and John Van Reenen, "Concentrating on the Fall of the Labor Share," *American Economic Review* 107, no. 5 (2017): 180–185; Carl Shapiro, "Antitrust in a Time of Populism," *International Journal of Industrial Organization* 61 (2018): 714–748; Sam Pelzman, "Industrial Concentration under the Rule of Reason," *Journal of Law and Economics* 57 (August 2014): 101–120; U.S. Council of Economic Advisers, "Benefits of Competition and Indicators of Market Power" (CEA Issue Brief, April 2016), https://obamawhitehouse.archives.gov/sites/default/files/page/files/20160414_cea_competition_issue_brief.pdf. For recent legal perspectives on the challenges of applying antitrust law to parallel conduct, see also Bell Atlantic Corp. v. Twombly, 550 U.S. 544, 552–554, 560–563 (2007); Kleen Products LLC v. Georgia-Pacific LLC, 910 F.3d 927, 931–942 (7th Cir. 2018); In re Text Messaging Antitrust Litigation, 782 F.3d 867, 873–875 (7th Cir. 2015). On the labor share of income, see Michael W. L. Elsby, Bart Hobjin, and Aysegul Sahin, "The Decline of the U.S. Labor Share," *Brookings Papers on Economic Activity*, Fall 2013, 1–63; Loukas Karabarbounis and Brent Neiman, "The Global Decline of the Labor Share," *Quarterly Journal of Economics* 129, no. 1 (2014): 61–103; Michael D. Giandrea and Shawn A. Sprague, "Estimating the U.S. Labor Share," *Monthly Labor Review*, February 2017.

INDEX